The Modern History of Japan

The Modern History of Japan

W. G. Beasley

*Professor of the History of the Far East,
University of London*

Charles E. Tuttle Company
Suido 1-chome, 2–6, Bunkyo-ku
Tokyo

Published by the Charles E. Tuttle Company, Inc.
of Rutland, Vermont and Tokyo, Japan
with editorial offices at
Suido 1-chome, 2-6, Bunkyo-ku, Tokyo, Japan
by special arrangement with
Weidenfeld and Nicolson Ltd., London
through Kern Associates

First Tuttle edition, 1982
Fifth printing, 1991

ISBN 4-8053-0480-4
PRINTED IN JAPAN

CONTENTS

ACKNOWLEDGMENTS

I am grateful to the following publishers for permission to reprint short passages from the works stated: Columbia University Press for *Sources of the Japanese Tradition* by W. T. de Bary, Allen and Unwin for *Anthology of Japanese Literature from the Earliest Era to the Nineteenth Century* edited by Donald Keene, for *Japan under Taisho Tenno 1912–1926* by A. M. Young, for *Imperial Japan 1926–1938* also by A. M. Young; also Oxford University Press for *Select Documents on Japanese Foreign Policy 1853–1868* edited by W. G. Beasley, the Japan Society, New York, for the *Complete Journal of Townsend Harris* edited by M. E. Cosenza, the Asiatic Society of Japan, Tokyo, for *Japanese Government Documents*, edited by W. W. McLaren, John Murray for *A Handbook for Travellers in Japan* edited by B. H. Chamberlain and W. B. Mason, Princeton University Press for *The Economic Development of Japan, Growth and Structural Change 1868–1938* by W. W. Lockwood, Chatto and Windus for *The Double Patriots: a Study of Japanese Nationalism*, and Harvard University Press for *Kokutai no Hongi. Cardinal Principles of the National Entity of Japan*, edited by R. K. Hall.

I should also like to express my thanks to my wife, without whose assistance in such matters as typing and the preparation of maps this book would still be far from being finished.

W. G. Beasley

London, 1962

JAPANESE NAMES

Japanese personal names are given in this book in the order in which they are used by the Japanese themselves: family name first, followed by given name.

PREFACE TO THE THIRD EDITION

In the study of Japanese history a decade provides ample time for the publication of new books and the working out of new perspectives. In preparing this edition I have tried to take account of them, though without drastically changing the structure and approach of what I wrote earlier. The principal changes have been made in chapters XIII, XIV, and XVI. Partly this is because the narrative needed to be extended into the 1970s and some parts of the emphasis reconsidered, and partly it is because much has been published in recent years, both in Japan and in the West, about the origins of the Pacific War. I have also taken the opportunity of revising the bibliography, in order to make it a more up-to-date tool of reference.

London, 1980   W.G.B.

CHAPTER I

JAPAN IN THE EARLY
NINETEENTH CENTURY

*Decay of feudalism—changing role of the samurai—growth of
merchant guilds—rural society*

WHEN EUROPEAN explorers of the sixteenth century rounded
the Malay peninsula and moved into Far Eastern waters they
confronted a civilization quite different from those which they
had found in India and western Asia. Over an area extending
from Tongking in the south to Korea in the north they met with
a culture which was in origin Chinese, its members looking to
China as the heart of their international structure and the
source of their dominant beliefs. It was not an entirely uniform
culture, for the degree and nature of Chinese influence had
varied with both time and place. Nevertheless the differences
between one part of the region and another were no greater
than those to be found within the boundaries of Europe, certainly not great enough to make invalid the application of a
common label to the whole.

Japan was part of this civilization. From earliest times she
had been affected by Chinese ideas, deriving from China many
important elements of her culture: her written language, most
of the literary forms which it employed, her concepts of king-
ship and family, the Buddhist religion, the tenets of Confucian
philosophy. Even Japanese art, however original in detail or
in treatment, remained recognizably Chinese in derivation. On
the other hand, political relationships between the two countries had rarely been as close as this might seem to imply.
Sometimes Japan had shown herself willing to accept an inferior status because of the economic benefits it could bring.
Sometimes she had rejected it with scorn, even at the risk of

war. Nor had China ever been able to assert control by force. Morever, political institutions in the two countries had developed on very different lines. Where China had evolved an imperial bureaucracy, dependent largely on the services of a class of scholar gentry, Japan in the twelfth century had turned away from Chinese models towards something much more akin to European feudalism. The phase persisted, despite important changes in both leadership and structure, into the nineteenth century.

Meanwhile, during the decade 1630–40, Japan's rulers had decided to shut out the outside world. Seeking to control all factors that might threaten political stability, they prohibited Japanese from leaving the country and banned foreign priests and traders from coming in, making exceptions only of a handful of Dutch and Chinese merchants who were allowed to visit Nagasaki. The latter, and the books they were sometimes allowed to bring, were thereafter Japan's only source of knowledge about conditions overseas. Nor were Japanese encouraged to extend that knowledge. Until 1800, or even later, their view of international relations was determined largely by what they had learnt in the seventeenth century. In addition, the technology they had then begun to acquire, such as that which had enabled them to start the manufacture of firearms and cannon of a Western type, was checked in its development, so that their country's defences at the beginning of the nineteenth century were still those of a seventeenth-century European state; while the network of trade and settlements they had established after about 1590 in the countries bordering China was allowed entirely to disappear.

For two hundred years this system of *sakoku*, 'the closed country', was maintained. In the nineteenth century, however, it began to weaken in the face of increasing encroachment from an industrialized and expanding West, until treaties were signed and trade resumed. This was in the period 1853–8. Ten years later, under a combination of domestic and foreign pressures, Tokugawa rule was overthrown and the way was cleared for new leaders to seize power, men by whose decision Japan was exposed fully to Western influence. As a result, by the end of the century the derivatives of Western civilization had come to determine, if not the fact of change, at least its direction in Japan, so that in politics, economic organization, literature, philosophy, law, social custom and personal behaviour, in almost every aspect of life, in fact, Europe replaced China as the country's source of models and ideas. It is with this process, and with the events that followed from it, that much of this book will be concerned.

In 1800 Japan was still in many respects a feudal state. Feudalism, it is true, was in decay. A money economy, dominant in the towns and already penetrating the villages, had begun to weaken the bonds of feudal loyalty. Financial chaos threatened the stability of feudal government. Yet the samurai—the knights and men-at-arms of Japanese chivalry—still dominated political society. As a military caste they comprised the country's only army, holding rank, office and land by virtue of this function. One of them, indeed, exercised supreme administrative authority: as Shogun, an office which had been hereditary in the Tokugawa family since 1603, each succeeding head of the Tokugawa house became the emperor's military deputy and therefore *de facto* ruler of Japan. He exercised a power which extended to all men and all places, even to the Imperial Court itself. In Kyoto, the emperor's capital, he was represented by a governor, chosen from among his own relatives or vassals. Court nobles appointed to act in his interests had to swear a special oath of allegiance to him and through them he controlled the appointment of all senior officials at the Court. These, though their titles recalled the days when emperors had both reigned and ruled, were now required to perform duties which were no more than a time-consuming and complex ceremonial. For recompense they depended on the Shogun's favour, which was rarely generous. The wealthiest Court nobles had a rice income smaller than that of many of the Shogun's household officers, while most, though outranking the majority of feudal lords, were forced by poverty to live at a standard much like that of a minor lord's retainers. Their life was regulated in its every detail by the Shogun's laws: their dress, marriages and behaviour, even their literary pursuits and pastimes. The emperor himself was a Tokugawa pensioner and virtually a prisoner in the palace.

In sharp contrast to the Court nobility were the men at

the Shogun's capital of Edo (later to become modern Tokyo). These were the real rulers of Japan, the Shogun being the greatest of them, not only by virtue of his office but also because as a feudal lord he held lands whose estimated yield was some 15 per cent of that of Japan at large.[1] His retainers, excluding those who counted as vassals-in-chief, held as much again. The administration of these vast estates involved thousands of officials, great and small, whose labours brought together the revenue from which were paid the Shogun's household expenses, official salaries, stipends for those of his followers who had no land, and grants in aid to the loyal but impoverished. From the same source came the funds for governing Japan. In Tokugawa Japan, as in medieval Europe, the monarch was expected to live of his own.

The central administration served the Shogun in both his capacities, as imperial deputy and as feudal lord. In theory he was an autocrat, but after 1650 the Tokugawa line rarely produced a man capable of exercising personal authority. Some fell under the influence of favourites from their palace entourage, though in the nineteenth century this was exceptional; for the most part, decisions were taken by officials appointed from the ranks of the Shogun's vassals. Most powerful were the Councillors of State (*Roju*), usually four or five in number, who were responsible for general policy and for supervision of the great lords. Next came the members of the Junior Council, controlling the samurai of lesser rank, and other officials who supervised shrines and temples. All these, as well as the governors of Kyoto and Osaka, were *daimyo*, vassals-in-chief whose lands were valued at or above 10,000 *koku* (50,000 bushels) of rice a year. They were assisted by a number of officials of lower rank. The most important were the Edo magistrates (*machi-bugyo*), who administered the capital with its huge samurai population; the finance commissioners (*kanjo-bugyo*), whose duties included the handling of revenue and the government of the Shogun's own domains; and the censors (*metsuke*), whose task it was to watch for disaffection or maladministration among officials and feudal lords. Of about the same rank, or near it, were the governors of a handful of key cities like Nagasaki, which were under direct Tokugawa rule, and the stewards of the larger Tokugawa estates.

The administrative machine was slow and cumbersome, involving a system of checks and balances which seemed more designed to protect the regime from the ambitions of its own officials than to make any positive contribution to governing the country. Offices were often held by more than one man at a time, the incumbents taking it in turns to carry out the duties appropriate to them. Rarely was it possible to say precisely where the functions of one official ended and those of another began. Nor was it always clear who had the power to take decisions, though the detailed regulation of rank and seniority at least ensured that there would be no doubt about questions of formal precedence. One result of all this was to make it very difficult for an individual or clique to acquire lasting power by monopolizing a few great offices. Another, achieved by restricting all office to direct retainers of the Shogun or those lords bound traditionally to support him, was to give certain groups a vested interest in maintaining Tokugawa power.

Feudal lords were classified in terms of their relationship to the Tokugawa. First came those who were of Tokugawa blood: the *Sanke* (Three Houses) of Kii, Owari and Mito, descended from the founder of the line, Tokugawa Ieyasu; the *Sankyo* (Three Lords) of Tayasu, Hitotsubashi and Shimizu, descended from two eighteenth-century rulers, Yoshimune and Ieshige; and the *Kamon* (Related Houses), more numerous, who usually bore the family's original name of Matsudaira. The first two might provide an heir if the direct line failed. The *Kamon* might fill important office in times of emergency. It was the next group, however, who usually furnished the Shogun's senior advisers: the *fudai* ('dependent') lords, about 150 in all, the descendants of men who had become vassals of Ieyasu during his rise to power. They alone had the right to be appointed to the two councils of state and similar offices. Their leading families were always consulted on decisions of major importance and were qualified to provide a regent should need arise. In all this they differed sharply from the hundred or so *tozama* ('outside') lords, whose families had only submitted to Tokugawa control after the battle of Sekigahara in 1600, for the *tozama* were permanently excluded from office in the central government on the grounds that they were potentially subversive.

All feudal lords were in some degree free from government interference. Within the boundaries of a domain—and for the most powerful this might encompass a whole province, sometimes more—the lord was absolute master. His administration was usually patterned on that of the Tokugawa, senior councillors being chosen from collateral branches of his house or from a few families of leading retainers, while other posts were filled by samurai of middle or lower rank, who served in the specialist bureaucracy of the castle-town or as intendants governing rural districts. In none of this were they directly accountable to the Shogun and his officers. Nor did the domain owe taxes to the central government. On the other hand, the lord as a person had no such freedom: the Shogun had the power to transfer him from one fief to another, reduce the size of his holding, or even confiscate it altogether if he failed in his loyalty or duties. Although military service had become largely nominal in the long years of peace after 1650, once in a generation or so a *daimyo* was likely to find himself called upon to carry out expensive public works, like flood control, road building, or structural repairs to buildings, such as were often made necessary by fire or earthquake. Marriage alliances were subject to the Shogun's approval. So was the building or repair of castles. Most important of all, each lord was required to spend six months of the year in Edo, leaving members of his family there as hostages when he returned to his own province. This system, known as *sankin-kotai* ('alternate attendance'), was fundamental to the whole mechanism of control.

In the last resort, it was the distribution of land which enabled the Tokugawa to enforce these measures, for in a feudal society land was the basis of military strength and force was the ultimate sanction. The early Tokugawa rulers—Ieyasu, his son and grandson—had carried out a major redistribution of fiefs, by which they and their supporters had acquired not only the lion's share of the whole, but also control of all strategic areas. The Shogun and his retainers held between them land estimated as yielding some 30 per cent of Japan's annual agricultural production. In addition, Tokugawa branch families contributed another 10 per cent and the *fudai* lords twice as much again. Most of these holdings were concentrated in central Japan, thus ensuring that the regime could dominate

6

the two capitals, Edo and Kyoto, and the whole length of the great road which connected them, the Tokaido. By contrast, the *tozama* lords, aggregating only 40 per cent of the whole by land value, were situated largely in the south and west or in the north-east, the most powerful of them being subject to the watchful attentions of a *fudai* established on their borders.

It must not be thought, however, that the *fudai* lords were individually the stronger, for it had always been the policy of the Tokugawa to avoid giving their followers domains large enough to make them a threat to the house they served. Indeed, while the *fudai* together controlled some six million *koku* out of a national total of just under thirty million, only one had a personal holding of over 200,000 *koku*. This was Ii of Hikone, whose lands straddled the eastern approaches to Kyoto. Of the Tokugawa branch houses, Aizu, Fukui and Mito were about the same size as Hikone, whereas Wakayama (Kii) and Nagoya (Owari) both exceeded half a million *koku*.[2] Yet some of the *tozama* were wealthier still. Kanazawa, north of Kyoto on the Japan Sea coast, was rated at over a million *koku*. Four others were more than half that size: Sendai in the north-east and the three Kyushu domains of Kagoshima (Satsuma), Kumamoto and Fukuoka. This still left eleven *tozama* domains of 200,000 *koku* and over. Several of them played an important part in the history of the period and are worth mentioning by name: Saga (Hizen) in Kyushu; Yamaguchi (Choshu), on the straits between Kyushu and Honshu; Hiroshima and Okayama, farther east on the shores of the Inland Sea; and Kochi (Tosa) in the southern part of the island of Shikoku.

The domain values cited above are those which were officially recorded by the Shogun's government. In the seventeenth century they had been fairly realistic estimates of the crop. In the two hundred years that followed, however, peace and technical improvements had brought great increases in agricultural production in some areas, without any corresponding adjustment in rated values, so that by 1800 some domains were notoriously 'rich', yielding far more than the official figure, while others were just as notoriously 'poor'. What is particularly significant about this is that the change had been to the relative disadvantage of the Shogun and his vassals. This was chiefly because increases had been greater at the periphery than in the centre. In the provinces round Edo and Kyoto, where most Tokugawa and *fudai* domains were found, the land had been longer settled and harder worked. It therefore offered less margin for development. By contrast, in the north-east and south-west it was easier to find new land to bring under cultivation, a fact which was soon reflected in the tax yields of the local lords, most of whom were *tozama*. Moreover, some of these lords benefited from a growing diversity in crops and economic activity in general, which eventually made it possible for villages to bear a higher rate of tax, especially along the shores of the Inland Sea and in parts of Kyushu and Shikoku. In such areas, tax yields of the nineteenth century were sometimes more than double those of the seventeenth. One result was that the domains in question were better able to cope with the financial problems brought by economic change than were the majority of those on which the stability of the regime depended—a by-product of the Tokugawa pattern of land distribution which was both unforeseen and most unwelcome to officials.

One might also argue that Tokugawa policies were responsible for a good deal of the social change which took place in the period, though this was directly contrary to their purpose. Official doctrine propounded a view of society which was one of fixed stratification: a hierarchy of samurai, farmer, artisan, and merchant, each segment subdivided and the distinctions between them rigidly maintained. The samurai was soldier and ruler. The farmer produced rice—and taxes—and was therefore honoured as the foundation of the state. The artisan's role was useful but subordinate. Merchants came last, because they engaged chiefly in the pursuit of profit, and opinions differed about whether they were merely a necessary evil, or more positively something parasitic and corrupting. Yet the debates on this subject, which were many, proved little to the purpose. Long before the nineteenth century the merchant had assumed a place in Japanese society bearing little relation to that which the traditionally-minded thought it proper to accord him, while the processes of change had done much to destroy the satisfying simplicity that was supposed to characterize the life of samurai and farmer.

In earlier periods the samurai had been a farmer-warrior, tilling the land in times of peace and following his lord into battle in times of war; but with the increasing scale and complexity of warfare in the fifteenth and sixteenth centuries fighting had tended to become a specialist activity, so that the functions of the samurai and the farmer became distinct. In the end the farmer was forbidden to carry arms, the samurai was incorporated into something very like the garrison of an occupied territory, living in a strongly-defended castle from which the surrounding countryside was governed. It was in this way that the typical domain of the Tokugawa period took shape. It was large and geographically compact. Within its frontiers the lord brooked no rival to his authority over men and land, whether from the once-powerful shrines and temples or from his followers, only a few of whom were allowed to retain fiefs of their own. These were subject to a system of control which was a replica in miniature of that which the Shogun imposed on Japan at large. Ordinary samurai for the most part lost their land entirely. Required to be in attendance on their lord and live in or around his castle, they were no longer able to supervise in person either cultivation or the collection of dues, these rights being assumed by the feudal lord acting through officials. In return, the samurai was granted a stipend from the domain treasury, its value determined by the estimated annual yield of the piece of land from which it was nominally derived. Many lost even this final link with the village: their stipends were fixed arbitrarily, in extreme cases at a sum payable in cash.

The transformation of the samurai was carried a stage further by the Tokugawa success in restoring and then maintaining law and order after centuries of civil war. Peace made the samurai less needed as a soldier. On the other hand, the nature of the new domains made him all the more important as an administrator. In every castle-town there was a multitude of posts to be filled, their duties ranging from the formulation of policy to the government of a rural district, from control of finance or archives to service as attendants, guards and messengers. All were filled by samurai, usually samurai of a specified rank. So great was the preoccupation with civil office that a famous scholar, Yamaga Soko, writing towards the end of the

9

seventeenth century, was able to describe the life of a samurai as follows:

'In minor matters, such as dress, food, dwelling, and all implements and their uses, he must live up to the best samurai traditions of good form . . . Among major matters there are the maintenance of peace and order in the world; rites and festivals; the control of feudal states and districts; mountains and forests, seas and rivers, farms and rice fields, temples and shrines; and the disposition of suits and appeals among the four classes of people.'[3]

Yamaga, as his writings showed elsewhere, did not by any means despise the samurai's place in warfare. None the less, his outlook takes us a long way from the concept of the samurai as a rough and uncouth soldier.

Once it had been deprived of battle as a lubricant of social mobility, Japanese society quickly became preoccupied with questions of personal and family status. The samurai found himself the possessor by virtue of birth or adoption of a position which it was a great deal easier to lose by failure to fulfil ceremonial duties than it was to improve by meritorious service. Ranks tended to proliferate, as did the regulations concerning them. For all this it is possible to identify three broad divisions of the feudal class. First came those who were linked with the lord's own house by blood or long service: the upper samurai, few in number, much wealthier than the rest and often holding land of their own. Second were the middle samurai, full members of their class by rank and privilege, but usually excluded from the very highest posts. Last were those who are often called the lesser samurai, a group rather more numerous in most domains than the other two together. They were men whose military duty as foot-soldiers and the like gave them some claim to samurai status and access to the minor offices of government, but whose economic and social position was vastly inferior to that of the samurai proper. Indeed, it is not easy to recognize some of them as members of a ruling class at all.

It was extremely difficult to move upward from one of these divisions to another. An able man might sometimes achieve promotion for himself, while two or three generations of able men might do so for a whole family, but for the majority rank was hereditary and fixed. All manner of things were determined by it: access to office, type of education, even habits of speech. If they belonged to the same domain, men of the same rank were likely to know each other well, since the regulations about place of residence made it almost certain that their families were neighbours. Their houses and dress would be similar, though they might differ considerably in wealth. They had almost certainly gone to the same school. This made the groups within the castle-town community exceedingly close-knit—even in the largest domain there was not likely to be more than 5,000 families of middle and upper samurai, in the smaller ones only a few hundred—but this very fact helped to accentuate the barriers which cut groups off from one another.

In a society where every man knew his place, it is not surprising that the ruling philosophy was of a kind calculated to keep him in it. The Confucian ideas associated with the name of the Sung philosopher, Chu Hsi, were admirably suited to this purpose, for they emphasized the subordination of wife to husband, of son to father, of subject to ruler, in a manner which in Tokugawa Japan brought about a natural alliance between feudal authority and Confucian scholarship. The duties of loyalty and service were expounded in official schools maintained by the Shogun's government and feudal lords. To them went almost all samurai of middle and upper rank to learn the duties of their station, to learn above all that a man's own welfare counted for less than that of the group, whether family or domain, to which he belonged. The attitude was reinforced by the pervading social and religious concept of obligation (*ho-on*). This brought together strands from Buddhist as well as Confucian thought, emphasizing that man's primary task was to live in such a way as would constitute a return for favours received: to the deity for his blessings, to the universe which supported life, to parents for their love, to political superiors for their protection. Thus loyalty and filial piety came together and were given religious sanction.

These ideas, in association with elements from an older tradition, became part of *bushido*, the code of the warrior class. In its Tokugawa form this was as much a code of the bureaucrat as of the soldier. Death in the service of one's lord remained the ultimate expression of loyalty, bringing something not far short of salvation in a religious sense; but if this could not be, then dutiful service and honest advice were not to be despised. Learning and scholarship were also to be valued for the training they gave, though it was a training more appropriate to administration than the battlefield. Even the time-honoured military virtues of austerity and frugality were given a new gloss. Diligence and economy were the form in which they were now enjoined, the one to ensure the maximum contribution in service, the other the minimum consumption by way of recompense. This, too, was a kind of loyalty.

Ideals of behaviour which the ruling class prescribed for itself were readily adopted by the rest of society. In this sense, *bushido* influenced all groups, at least all those which sought social recognition. On the other hand, this did not make its rules any easier to observe, especially where they ran counter to economic change. Frugality was one of them. Peace and the growth in agricultural production had contributed to a rapid development of commerce in the seventeenth century, making possible a rise in standards of living which was enjoyed in most parts of the country. Even in remote castle-towns one could now obtain products from as far afield as Kyushu and Hokkaido. In the great cities of Edo, Kyoto and Osaka luxuries abounded. Edo, especially, played a major part in samurai life, since feudal lords, accompanied always by a large retinue of followers, were required to live there for half the year. Here were many temptations by way of goods and entertainment, temptations which most found it impossible to resist. Unfortunately, they had to be paid for, usually in cash. For samurai—of whatever rank—who received their incomes in rice, the provision of money to be spent in Edo became a serious problem, one which could be solved only with the help of the merchant and financier. The improvident soon found that their new habits had left no margin to meet the sort of unexpected expenditure or loss of income which might be occasioned by fire or flood. For them the merchant became moneylender, making advances against future income. Others, who were more careful, were eventually caught in the same web despite themselves, for city prices rose faster than crops increased and it was easier to acquire expensive tastes than to lose them. By 1700 the whole samurai class was in a state of chronic debt.

In the eighteenth century samurai indebtedness continued

to grow, despite efforts which feudal rulers made to check it. Moreover, since the Tokugawa and domain governments faced the same difficulties as did individuals, they were rendered unable to help their retainers to any great extent and were often forced to levy new imposts on them. These levies, euphemistically described as loans, might amount to half a samurai's stipend. They caused great discontent, the tenets of *bushido* notwithstanding. In many domains this led the middle samurai, blaming their troubles on the incapacity of their superiors, to agitate for, and sometimes obtain, a larger share in administration. Lesser samurai, whose case was far worse, also tended to become supporters of reform movements of various kinds, while many sought personal solutions outside the existing feudal framework altogether, relinquishing their samurai status to become farmers or merchants, or using the devices of marriage and adoption to bring wealth into the family in return for social standing. This process, familiar enough among impoverished aristocracies at any time or place, helped to induce a greater degree of social mobility at the lower levels of the ruling class, to which officialdom contributed by engaging in what was virtually a sale of rank. It was the merchants and a new class of rural landlords who largely benefited.

Indeed, the corollary of samurai debt was merchant wealth. As domestic commerce grew in scale so it had become more complex, with townsmen (*chonin*) emerging as specialists in a wide range of different occupations: wholesaling, warehousing, transport, rice-broking, money exchange, credit transactions, speculative dealing of every kind. Typical is this description of a Kyoto merchant, taken from one of the stories of the novelist, Ihara Saikaku, written in 1688:

'As the clerks from the money exchanges passed by he noted down the market ratio of copper and gold; he inquired about the current quotations of the rice brokers; he sought information from druggists' and haberdashers' assistants on the state of the market in Nagasaki; for the latest news on the prices of ginned cotton, salt, and saké, he noted the various days on which the Kyoto dealers received dispatches from the Edo branch shops. Every day a thousand things were entered in his book. . . .'[4]

With specialized knowledge so important, it is not surprising that the samurai left the handling of his finances to the merchant, or that in the process he became indebted to him. All the same, merchants did not easily gain the upper hand. The feudal lord and his retainers still possessed authority, as well as prestige, and did not hesitate to use it. Repayment of loans was difficult to enforce against members of a ruling class, particularly when their refusal to honour debts was likely to be upheld by a central government which officially despised trade and was not above confiscating a merchant's goods in their entirety if its own interests were at stake. Faced with this situation, merchants in towns organized themselves into monopoly guilds, seeking security through collective action. In part they were successful. The guilds, membership of which was a valuable commodity, capable of being bought and sold, became characteristic of the eighteenth century. They helped to keep prices and profits high. Moreover, they came frequently into alliance with the Tokugawa and domain governments, acting as bankers, official purveyors or agents in the marketing of rice and other products, their members receiving in return social privileges and protection. The effects of this on the feudal structure we must consider in the next chapter. Here it is enough to emphasize that one result was to give the privileged merchants of the towns a status more in keeping with their wealth than hitherto. Many of them became city elders, firmly subordinated to feudal control but exercising a good deal of authority in local matters.

Not all town-dwellers were rich, of course. There was a host of small traders, struggling to make ends meet, as well as apprentices, journeymen, pedlars and day labourers, their ranks constantly swollen by new recruits. Most of the latter came from the countryside, where harsh taxes and bad harvests combined to drive a succession of impoverished farmers to seek their fortune in the town; and although the majority found only a different kind of poverty, their total numbers helped to change the nature of society by making the urban element of significant size for the first time in Japanese history. Kyoto, a political and commercial centre, famous also for its craftsmen, had long been a great city. In size and importance, however, it now had to take second place to Edo, which grew from being a mere fishing village in 1590 to a huge conglomeration with a population, excluding samurai, of over 500,000 in 1721.[5] Samurai accounted for at least half as much again and made this by far the country's largest consumer market. Osaka, by contrast, was a city of merchants. It was rather smaller than Kyoto—under 300,000 to Kyoto's 400,000 in the seventeenth century—but it was the focus of large-scale commerce and finance for all central and western Japan. A few castle-towns, like Nagoya, were also large, reflecting the size of the domains for which they were political and economic centres. If one adds the many smaller castle-towns, perhaps one-sixth of all Japanese were town-dwellers by 1850.

Town life in the Tokugawa period, especially that of Edo and Osaka, contributed a new element to Japanese culture. It was an element of noise and turbulence and colour, quite unlike the restraint proper to a long-established aristocracy, and it derived from that part of the population which might be described as *nouveaux riches*, the great merchants and their households. To cater to their whims and those of their feudal overlords, there developed what contemporaries called *ukiyo*, the floating world: a world, in the words of a modern historian, 'of fugitive pleasures, of theatres and restaurants, wrestling-booths and houses of assignation, with their permanent popu-lation of actors, dancers, singers, story-tellers, jesters, courte-sans, bath-girls and itinerant purveyors, among whom mingled the profligate sons of rich merchants, dissolute samurai and naughty apprentices'.[6] It was with this world that much of the period's art and literature were concerned. Colour prints depicted actors and famous courtesans, as well as street scenes in busy commercial quarters. The theatre, especially the puppet drama, found its themes in subjects which the townsmen loved: the clash between feudal loyalty and personal inclination —typical of Tokugawa Japan and popular because it took its audience into high society—or the fortunes, good and bad, of rich merchants and poor journeymen, of their mistresses and wives. Novels and short stories followed the same course. It was not a literature for the prudish, but it was bursting with life. By comparison, the verse and landscapes of the Chinese tradition seemed anaemic and artificial.

For those who could afford it life in the city was one of extravagant costume, exotic foods and elaborate pastimes.

Samurai, without doubt, were attracted by it. However, the more serious-minded were distrustful, thinking it something calculated to rob a man of his substance and to weaken his moral fibre, something that would make him a worse soldier and retainer. Hence reformers fulminated against the city's luxury and corruption. So, too, did spokesmen of the merchant class, for the greater respectability which the privileged towns-men had achieved led them to affirm, not to reject, the dominant values of society. They, as much as the samurai, aspired to a code of loyalty, filial piety and frugality in service. They were as much to be blamed if they abandoned themselves to a life of pleasure.

Still more shocking by the canons of the age was the spec-tacle of farmers enjoying some of the same luxuries. It was bad enough that many should be forced by poverty to abandon their land and flock to the city, to the obvious detriment of agricultural production. It became worse when a few, though remaining in the village, acquired wealth enough to ape their betters. That they had the facilities to do so was a reflection of commercial growth, making available in rural areas what had at first been limited to the towns. That they had the money was a reflection of economic development in a wider sense. This, by the nineteenth century, had brought about far-reaching changes in landholding and the structure of village wealth.

The classic pattern of the Tokugawa village was that of the early seventeenth century: a community consisting of peasant farmers bound to the soil, each cultivating a plot large enough to support his family and paying the whole of any surplus to his lord as feudal dues. This was the ideal—a sort of equality in misery—which feudal officials sought to maintain. Yet inequalities had in fact existed from the beginning. Farmers of substance usually had dependants of one kind or another to help them on their land, men who were bound to them either by ties of blood and marriage or by traditional bonds not far short of slavery. Some villagers were distinguished also by hereditary rights to local office, often backed by claims that they were the 'old' families, descended from original settlers of the area. It was from such groups that the village headmen and councillors were drawn. They played an influential part in village life, it being their duty to apportion individual shares of taxation, which the domain imposed simply on the village as a unit, as well as to settle local disputes, arrange details of irrigation, organize festivals and so on. Above them were a number of district officials, who were also local residents, though they often ranked as minor members of the feudal class. To most Japanese these were the most familiar representatives of authority. The samurai official proper, from the Shogun's capital or the lord's castle, was an exalted and rather terrifying figure, appeal to whom was very much a last resort.

The increase in the area of land under cultivation and in yield per acre, which went on throughout the seventeenth century and well into the eighteenth century in many places, tended to enlarge the existing disparities of wealth within the village, since it was mostly those who already held plots larger than the average who had the resources to open up new land or pay for improvements in technique. However, it was the development of a commercial economy, especially in central, south and west Japan, that finally proved disruptive of the traditional village structure. It not only brought to the farmer new implements, fertilizers and strains of seed, but also made possible a decrease in local self-sufficiency. Once trade became widespread, it was no longer necessary for every man to grow his own grain. Instead, where conditions favoured it, he could turn to one of the cash crops for which the growth of city culture and the rise in standards of living had created a demand: silk, cotton, paper, wax, rape seed, indigo and others. These became ancillary crops for many, main crops for some. The result, in areas where this occurred, was to involve the village deeply in the commercial sector of the economy, making the farmer's prosperity subject to market fluctuations which were completely outside his own control.

The change did not make life any easier for the majority. Speculation, natural disasters and occasional ill-advised interference by feudal governments helped to make selling prices vary widely. Costs for such things as fertilizers were kept high by the monopoly rings of city merchants. Moreover, there was always the danger that domain governments might take a proprietary interest in any really profitable commodity, declaring it an official monopoly and buying in the crop at forced prices. With all this, as well as high taxation, the farmer's life and income were precarious. More and more had recourse to the moneylender, often losing their land because of it, at least in part, so that many independent cultivators of the earlier period became tenants or even landless labourers. Some made their way to the towns. Others remained to form a pool of workers for the local industries which began to spring up in rural areas, such as cotton spinning and weaving, dyeing, the brewing of saké (rice wine), or the manufacture of paper.

These developments were at their height during the last quarter of the eighteenth century and the first quarter of the nineteenth, a period which saw also the emergence of a class of rural entrepreneurs whose wealth was not based exclusively on land. For the most part they, too, originated in the ranks of peasant cultivators. Unlike their fellows, however, they were the sort of men who seized the opportunities which the new economy presented and were able by thrift, hard work and good judgment to extend their operations into retailing, moneylending, manufacture and similar non-agricultural pursuits, retaining an interest in the soil as landlords but devoting relatively little of their time to its management. Among them were some who handled the marketing of commercial crops, others who organized a putting-out system which harnessed the surplus labour capacity of farming households to the manufacture of textiles, even a few who established small-scale factories. Such men were to be found in almost every village in the provinces round Kyoto and along the Inland Sea.

In food, dress, education and entertainment they lived like samurai of middle rank or better. Yet no matter how great their wealth it was not easy for them to win formal recognition. In some areas they engaged in a bitter and eventually successful struggle to secure appointment to village office, important to them not only for the prestige it conferred, but also because it provided a means of manipulating tax assessments and other matters vital to their interests. Elsewhere they acquired status by marrying into the families of minor domain officials. In many domains they were even able to gain it in their own right, for, as financial pressure on governments increased, so did the temptation to raise money by the sale of rank. The newly rich of the countryside were invited to subscribe to so-called loans, their reward for doing so being a grant of rank which was in strict proportion to the size of contribution. In this way many a farmer, turned moneylender, acquired the right to bear a family name and wear the two swords of the samurai.

Tokugawa Ieyasu, it is said, expected most of his descendants to be mediocrities, or worse, and set out to create an administrative machine which would protect them from their own folly. Certainly the regime he founded gave every sign of being dedicated to the task of self-preservation. The country's rulers, both Shogun and feudal lords, tried to freeze society in the pattern it had assumed at the end of the sixteenth-century civil wars, a pattern in which they shared between them a more effective authority than had ever before been achieved in Japanese history. The result was an age of political conservatism and rigid class structure, of rule and precedent, place and privilege.

The attempt to outlaw change was remarkably successful. Nevertheless, as we have seen, by the beginning of the nineteenth century it had failed in a number of important ways. This was partly because new forms of wealth fell into the hands of groups which did not already have prestige and power, making them potentially subversive of the existing order: the merchants of the towns and the entrepreneurs of rural areas. The former proved less of a threat to samurai dominance than one might have supposed, for during the eighteenth century they entered into a kind of symbiotic relationship with feudal government, putting their commercial and financial skills to the service of the ruling class in return for rank, security and profit. On the other hand, rich villagers were likely to be more dangerous. They invested their profits heavily in land and thereby touched the regime at a sensitive point. The castle-town system, while leaving the samurai dependent on the land for his income, had removed him from direct participation in its use and management, thus making it possible for the new landlords to interpose themselves, as it were, between feudalism and the farm. It was a situation that had occurred several times in Japanese history and had always been the prelude to the replacement of one regime by another.

This is not to imply that there was any immediate danger of a concerted attempt by the landlords to overthrow feudalism or the Tokugawa. Indeed, most of them seemed satisfied with the semi-samurai status which their wealth had gained them, while in many parts of the country the village economy—and hence its social structure—had as yet been hardly touched by change at all. More immediate difficulties arose from the financial chaos which had overtaken both central and domain governments and from the disorder to which it led in the countryside. Attempts by the domain to improve its finances by increasing taxation, their effects accentuated in some areas by the stresses in village life which accompanied the enrichment of the few and the impoverishment of the many, brought a rising level of peasant revolt. After 1800, outbreaks averaged five or six a year, the most frequent objects of violence being the residences of moneylenders, landlords or unpopular village and domain officials.

The middle and upper samurai were quick to recognize that these developments might eventually break their own hold on Japanese society. Many of them called for reform, though they could not agree upon its nature. Some urged in effect a return to the past, a policy which was to be carried out by means of sumptuary laws, limitations on the growth of towns, even a redistribution of the land, all aimed at reducing trade and forcing the population back to its old habits. Others planned to ride the tiger, that is, to come to terms with the new trends and use them to bolster traditional authority. Both groups, not only by what they did, but also by the struggles into which they entered to secure the power to do it, played an important part in shaping Japan's political future.

CHAPTER II

ECONOMIC PROBLEMS
AND REFORMS

Mizuno Tadakuni—Zusho Hiromichi—Murata Seifu

IN THE eighteenth century money became of prime concern
to Japan's feudal rulers. From the Shogun to the humblest
samurai, from the central government to that of the smallest
domain, failure to adjust to the needs of a changing economy
brought growing financial stress. It was a stress, moreover, due
in large measure to factors outside their own control. The
concentration of the ruling class in castle-towns, especially the
huge agglomeration that was Edo, had acted as a stimulus to
trade. Commercial efficiency, in turn, had put temptations in
the way of buyers. Since most samurai had been reduced to
idleness by the years of peace, encouraged to engage in scholarship and martial exercises or to perform administrative tasks
which rarely took up all their time, it is not surprising that
their tastes and habits grew expensive. Income, despite the rise
in agricultural production, failed to keep pace with costs. This
was often as much a result of laxity among tax-collectors, the
almost inevitable concomitant of hereditary office-holding, as
it was of higher standards of living; but it meant, whatever the
cause, that a misfortune like fire or flood, bringing an increase
in expenses or a drop in revenue, put a domain almost invariably in debt to the city rice-brokers who handled its finances.
Individual samurai suffered by a similar process, though on a
smaller scale. At the opposite extreme, the Tokugawa government succumbed slowly but inexorably to the same pressures.
And once in debt, neither the samurai nor his lord found it
easy to recover.

Intermittent attempts at reform in the eighteenth century proved to have only a local and temporary effect, so that by the time Tokugawa Ieyoshi succeeded his father as Shogun on October 1, 1837, the situation had reached a stage of crisis. Ieyoshi was not the man to take much interest in questions of government finance. Nor were his ministers concerned with the economic problems of Japan at large. Nevertheless, it was during the period of his rule, which lasted till 1853, that officials in Edo and several of the great domains initiated economic policies that were to have a considerable bearing on the fate of the regime. It is therefore at this point that a discussion of late Tokugawa history can conveniently begin.

The finances of the Tokugawa government—the Bakufu, or 'tent government', as it was called, because of its origins as the Shogun's military headquarters—depended in the first place on rice. Most dues from rural areas were paid in it. Most normal expenditure was calculated in it: household expenses, official salaries, samurai stipends. The actual amounts involved were capable of considerable variation, depending both on the harvest and on the efficiency to be expected from officials—in 1742–51, for example, after a period of administrative reform, the annual average rice revenue rose to 800,000 *koku* (1 *koku* = 5 bushels approximately), whereas in 1782–91, which were years of atrocious weather, it was only just over 600,000 *koku*—but in general it was a great deal more likely that revenue would drop, because of bad luck or bad management, and that expenditure would rise, because of luxurious living, than the reverse. A minister of character and determination, having the Shogun's confidence, could do much to improve administration and cut expenses. Such a circumstance, however, was fortuitous and rare. More often appeals for economy fell on deaf ears and officials were left with no other recourse than to seek ways of increasing government income.

An essential difficulty was that there was a limit to the amount which farmers could be made to pay. Where dues were comparatively low, or farm output was increasing, it was possible to tap the surplus by a variety of devices. They ranged from the imposition of supplementary taxes to the use of false instruments in conducting surveys. It was even possible in some respects to reduce the annual variations. Thus in the eighteenth century tax-collectors began to levy dues on the basis of periodic averages, instead of fixing the amount after inspection of the crop, a change that transferred to the farmer the responsibility for providing against future fluctuations in the harvest. All the same, there was a point beyond which tax could be made neither heavier nor more predictable, namely, that at which demands provoked the cultivator to revolt or to abandon his land. Samurai officials frequently misjudged it, but it put an effective ceiling on the revenue they raised.

Faced with this problem the Bakufu turned to sources of revenue in cash. Some of these it had possessed from the beginning: profits from gold and silver mines, most of which were under Tokugawa control; certain small amounts paid by the villages as taxation on minor crops; a tax on house property in the towns; and several miscellaneous dues, such as transit charges on the movement of goods. Profits from mining, the only item on this list which was of any consequence, declined sharply towards the end of the seventeenth century because the most easily worked deposits of the precious metals had been exhausted, but a substitute was soon found in debasement of the coinage. Beginning in 1695, this rapidly became one of the most regular and profitable ways of raising funds. To it after 1721 was added a levy on merchant associations, usually taking the form of annual cash payments made in return for a grant of monopoly rights.

These innovations enabled the Bakufu in the first half of the eighteenth century to supplement its rice revenue by cash receipts which varied between about 1·5 and 2 million gold *ryo* a year.[7] To set against this were expenditures of something like 1·2 million *ryo* in a good year, 1·6 million in a bad one, so that it was possible, given sound administration, to make ends meet. On the other hand, administration was not always sound and these resources were not invariably sufficient to maintain a balance. Officials, therefore, continued their search for something new to tax. Opening up fresh land was one possibility, but most of what was suitable had already been exploited earlier in the Tokugawa period and further efforts at reclamation were handicapped by technical difficulties beyond the power of the age to solve. Another possibility, direct taxation

23

of the feudal lords, was politically dangerous, as the Shogun Yoshimune had discovered when he attempted it in 1722–31. This left only commerce. Most of the country's wealth, or so it seemed to contemporary observers, was now finding its way into the hands of city merchants. It appeared reasonable that they should contribute part of it to ease the burdens of the state. Means of effecting this were eventually found by levying forced loans, known as *goyo-kin*; and although these were hardly taxation in the strict sense, since they were irregular in timing and arbitrary in amount, they were usefully high in yield. The first to be recorded, that of 1761–2, raised 700,000 *ryo* from Osaka merchants, out of a total of 1·7 million *ryo* which had been demanded. Later ones were smaller, but after 1800 they became frequent enough to rival recoinage as a source of government funds. Thus in the years 1853–60 about 1·4 million *ryo* was received from loans of this kind, some 900,000 *ryo* coming from Edo and Osaka, the rest from rich residents of the countryside.

One trouble with these policies, especially debasement of the coinage, was that they pushed up prices. By so doing they introduced an element of contradiction into feudal rule. It was obviously necessary, if political stability were to be preserved, that ministers should retain the loyalty of the feudal class. This involved among other things ensuring its members a degree of economic privilege. Yet the very actions of government in its search for solvency were of a kind to increase the upward spiral of commodity prices, making it more and more difficult for retainers to live on a fixed stipend payable in rice. Officials sought constantly for a way out of this dilemma, or rather, one might say, tried solutions first for one part of it, then the other, without always recognizing the connection between the two. A common response was to blame human behaviour: merchants for taking excessive profit, samurai for abandoning their traditional frugality. Hence exhortation became a conspicuous feature of reform. It was reinforced by a number of more practical measures, designed to encourage samurai virtue by a system of rewards and punishments or to discourage luxury by sumptuary laws. In addition, Bakufu statesmen tried to control the interest payable on samurai debts, though in this they were more often than not defeated by the men they meant to aid, since the latter, finding themselves unable to live without credit and equally unable to get it at the official rates, simply evaded the regulations. None the less, the authorities usually found ways in a crisis of robbing the moneylender of part of his profits and protecting the samurai from the worst results of his improvidence. Certainly a merchant who wished to recover money from a defaulting samurai could expect scant help or sympathy from those in power.

There were, then, two main elements in economic reform as the later Tokugawa rulers saw it: on the one hand, an attempt to restore government finances; on the other, an attack on the problem of samurai impoverishment. Both emerged clearly in the work of Tokugawa Yoshimune, Shogun from 1716 to 1745, though he was more successful in bequeathing to his son a full treasury, the fruits of long and careful administration, than in overcoming the difficulties that faced his vassals. Even what he did achieve depended so greatly on his personal supervision and example that it barely survived his death. In fact, forty years later all was to be done again. This time the reformer was Matsudaira Sadanobu, Yoshimune's grandson and Bakufu chief minister from 1786 to 1793. His measures included a cancellation of samurai debts, encouragement of military training and an insistence on Confucian orthodoxy in the official schools, together with a whole quiverful of rules about dress, food, hairstyles, gifts and similar matters. Once again, however, the effects were short-lived, Sadanobu's edicts being ignored and his reserves dissipated well before his own life ended.

The first three decades of the nineteenth century saw a considerable increase in the level of commercial activity in Japan and as a consequence a worsening economic situation for the Bakufu and its retainers. In the period 1834–41 expenditure exceeded normal cash revenue by over half a million *ryo* a year, with the result that only a series of desperate expedients prevented total financial chaos. In the same years, moreover, there was increasing evidence of unrest in the form of peasant revolts. Rioting, accompanying demands for tax relief, had begun in the previous century, but the number of outbreaks had increased sharply since 1800 and their scale had grown. In January 1823, for example, a mob said to be 70,000 strong stormed the town of Miyazu, a little north-west of Kyoto, in protest against a special tax designed to repay money which the feudal lord had borrowed. Six months later a still more serious rising occurred in the Tokugawa domain of Kii. In 1836 the whole of Kai, a province under Bakufu control, broke into revolt, this being the largest of some twenty-six incidents recorded for that year, while in 1837 a minor Bakufu official, Oshio Heihachiro, planned a rising in Osaka because of his indignation at local maladministration and maintenance of high rice prices in a time of great distress. His plot was betrayed and Oshio committed suicide after achieving no more than a minor disturbance, but news of the affair provoked outbreaks as far afield as Hiroshima in one direction and Niigata in the other.

It is against this background that one must set the reforms undertaken by the *fudai* lord, Mizuno Tadakuni, in the first few years of Ieyoshi's rule. As an ambitious young man, Mizuno had accepted a transfer from the fief of Karatsu in Kyushu to the rather less valuable but more central one of Hamamatsu, not far from Nagoya, in order to improve his chances of a political career. This was in 1817, when he was twenty-three. He then served in turn as governor of Osaka and governor of Kyoto, until in 1828 he was made senior adviser to Ieyoshi, the Shogun's heir. Promotion to the Council of State followed in 1834. The accession of Ieyoshi increased his influence, but it was not until 1841, with the death of Ieyoshi's father, that he achieved complete control of policy and announced his intention of carrying out reforms on the lines laid down by Yoshimune and Matsudaira Sadanobu. For the next two years decrees flowed from his office in a steady stream.

Mizuno's methods of raising revenue were not strikingly original and cannot really be described as reforms. His main recourse was to recoinage and forced loans, the yields from which were considerable: 1·6 million *ryo* from recoinage in 1841–2, equal to a whole year's revenue, and an estimated one million *ryo* in loans collected from Edo and Osaka merchants in 1843. Attempts were also made to increase the returns from land tax. In 1842 these provoked a brief revolt in Omi province, just east of Kyoto, when local inhabitants discovered that a Bakufu survey party was accepting bribes as well as using false instruments; but financially they achieved little more than those of Mizuno's immediate predecessors. Of more interest was his long-term plan for reversing the drift of rural population to the towns. Orders were issued in the spring of 1843 which forbade new emigration into Edo, directed those residents of the city who had no family and no permanent job to return to their former homes, and put limits on the period for which farmers were allowed to engage in casual urban employment. All these were measures designed to increase the available sources of agricultural labour.

In his attitude towards samurai debt, Mizuno did not go as far as Matsudaira Sadanobu, who had cancelled old debts and tried to limit interest on new ones, but he nevertheless ordered a reduction of interest rates to 10 per cent in September 1842. He also instituted a system of debt redemption, though it was not generous enough to the samurai to win him much popularity. It was the attempt to reduce commodity prices, however, which was the outstanding feature of his reforms. An attack on luxury and immorality, which involved restrictions on theatres, brothels and other temptations to extravagance, in addition to the customary injunctions about simplicity in food and dress, was supplemented by a series of moves against the city merchants. One of the first was the dissolution of privileged merchant associations, on the grounds that their monopoly practices were keeping prices high. In 1842 the government also prohibited attempts to corner the market in particular commodities and issued a warning against holding back goods in the hope of greater profits. Meanwhile, attention was turned to the retail trade. After several months of investigation by Bakufu agents, Edo drapers were ordered to cut prices on some items by as much as half, a general price reduction of 20 per cent being decreed shortly after. Some tradesmen tried to evade the laws by giving short measure and poor quality, or chose to ignore them altogether; but this was dangerous, since the customer might prove to be a spy from the magistrate's office sent to test conformity with the regulations, as many merchants soon discovered to their cost.

For all this, the controls on commerce were self-defeating. Many businesses closed their doors to wait for better times and it was soon made clear that nothing could force goods on to the market when prices were artificially low. Even the abolition of merchant monopolies was not an unmixed blessing, since it destroyed the credit system on which the whole structure of trade depended. The resulting dislocation, far from reducing prices by enlivening competition, raised them higher still.

From this point of view, Mizuno's experiment was an unmistakable failure. And failure was something a man in his position could ill afford. Able himself, he made use of able subordinates; but he never created a personal following bound to him by special bonds of loyalty, partly because he never identified himself fully with any particular group, partly because of an unsympathetic quality in his character which made him isolated, a Puritan in an age which was far from puritanical. By contrast, he made enemies freely: the city merchants; rivals for power; those who suffered by his policy of retrenchment (like the ladies of the Shogun's household). Previous reformers had been able to sustain themselves in such a situation by their own high rank—Yoshimune a Shogun, Sadanobu a Shogun's grandson—but Mizuno was a mere *fudai* lord of 60,000 *koku* and as such depended heavily on the support of members of the Tokugawa family. With one of them, Tokugawa Nariaki of Mito, he quarrelled over foreign policy in 1842, when the question arose of modifying the seclusion laws. Others were alienated by his plan, announced in the late summer of 1843, to take over in the Shogun's name all land in the immediate vicinity of Edo and Osaka, offering annual stipends to the existing holders by way of compensation. A storm of protest forced him to drop the scheme, but it was already too late to save his power. On November 4, 1843, he was dismissed from office; and though he was recalled briefly to handle a foreign crisis in the following year, this was the end of Mizuno's active career as a reformer. It was also the end for the time being of attempts-at Bakufu reform.

The great domains were influenced indirectly by Bakufu economic policies, since these modified the general situation with which they had to deal, but they were not immediately subject to the Shogun's officers and did not have to enforce within their own boundaries any of the reform edicts issued in his name. They sometimes followed a similar course because they faced similar problems. Sometimes, however, their leaders found different solutions and achieved more lasting success.

Many domains were in financial straits long before the end of the seventeenth century, especially those, like Satsuma and Choshu, which had been reduced in size after suffering defeat at the hands of the Tokugawa. Nor were the others far behind. By 1750 it was a commonplace among contemporary writers that all *daimyo* were indebted to the great Osaka merchants. Fundamentally the reasons for this were the same as those which impoverished the Bakufu—a cash expenditure rising faster than a rice revenue—but there were certain respects in which the domains had less responsibility for their own misfortunes and less means of avoiding them. For example, the *sankin-kotai* system required a lord to spend six months of every year in Edo. While there he was expected to live in state, for part of the object was to weaken him financially, with the result that anything up to half his revenue had to be spent on the upkeep of a permanent establishment in the capital and his own expenses while living in it. From time to time, moreover, he would face Bakufu demands for the carrying out of public works or for troops to take part in the manning of coast defences. These were costly items. Since they could rarely be anticipated and few domain governments held a reserve from which to pay them, each such demand, like the damage caused by earthquake or typhoon, threatened to push the level of expenditure above that of income. Once it did so, recourse was had to loans from city merchants and payment of interest was thereafter added to existing burdens.

For these reasons most domains ended by incurring debts which were proportionately far greater than those of the Bakufu. For example, Kanazawa, the largest of the *tozama* holdings, had gold and silver debts in 1785 of over 2 million *ryo*, equivalent to something like three or four years' revenue. Satsuma was in much the same position, or worse, being in debt to the extent of 1·3 million *ryo* in 1807 and about 5 million in 1829, by which time officials were finding it difficult to raise funds even for day-to-day administration, while Choshu owed a little over 1·3 million *ryo* in 1840. In each case most of the creditors were the financiers of Osaka and Edo.

Very little of a feudal lord's rice revenue was available for interest payments on, or redemption of, these debts. The assessed value of his domain—a million *koku* for Kanazawa and almost 800,000 *koku* for Satsuma, to take these as examples—was a statement not of revenue but of estimated total crop, between 30 and 50 per cent of which was likely to be collected in dues. Some of this went to those members of his family, senior retainers, shrines and temples who still held land direct. Some was earmarked for the payment of samurai stipends. From the rest the fief treasury had to provide for all the lord's private and public expenditure within his own territories, before converting what was left into cash for use elsewhere. The balance available for this purpose was very small: about 100,000 *koku* in Kanazawa, only 20,000 *koku* in Satsuma, though there were some domains which specialized in rice production for the market, like Sendai, and were able to spare a great deal more. In addition there were the dues received in cash, which were of a similar kind to those levied by the Bakufu. Almost all these were spent outside the domain, but their yield was low, providing only a small proportion of total revenue.

Like the Tokugawa, domain governments were forced by this situation to try new ways of raising money. The prospects of their taxing merchants were much less, of course, since the commercial wealth of a single castle-town was not at all comparable with that of the great cities under Tokugawa rule. Furthermore, they were not permitted to issue coinage and hence had no opportunity to debase it. Their efforts therefore took a different form. The forced loans to which they had recourse were often required of samurai, for example, as well as merchants, a departure from tradition that for the samurai marked a growing divergence between his own interests and those of his lord. Nor were the amounts negligible in themselves. In Kanazawa they were 10 to 15 per cent of samurai stipends in 1794, the higher rate operating for those with larger incomes. This was cut to between 5 and 10 per cent in 1810, but a higher level was restored in 1830, as financial difficulties grew, while in 1837 special Bakufu demands on the fief caused a levy of 50 per cent for the next three years. After this, samurai distress again led to a general reduction, until in 1852 the rate was down to as little as 5 per cent for the majority.

By comparison, the figures for the Shikoku domain of Tosa seem to have been much higher. Beginning in 1728 with a complex system of levies graded from nil to 50 per cent in accordance with rank and income, they fluctuated throughout the rest of the century, with the maximum occasionally forced down to 25 per cent by samurai opposition. Indeed, samurai poverty was so great by 1800 that the practice was abandoned altogether. It was re-established a few years later, however, when the maximum was again set at 50 per cent, this being the level at which Tosa officials seem always to have aimed, though they did not always achieve it.

Another device by which funds were raised was that of monopoly trading. For the most part this was undertaken in co-operation with the privileged merchants of the castle-town —who stood in much the same relationship to the domain as did those of Edo and Osaka to the Bakufu, though their activities were on a provincial rather than a national scale—and was directed not only at increasing revenue, but also at acquiring profit from markets outside the domain boundaries. For this reason the monopolies were in 'export' goods, that is, those for which there was a steady demand in other parts of the country. Organization usually took one of two forms. Under the first, a group of merchants would be granted exclusive rights to purchase a given local product, on condition that they subsequently turned it over to officials for shipment to Edo and Osaka, where it was sold on the wholesale market. In this way, the merchants took their profits from the producer, the domain from the buyer. Alternatively, the domain might control the whole process by establishing its own offices to buy the goods, as well as to ship and sell them. In this case the feudal lord was able to employ his political authority to fix prices and increase the profits, while appointing merchants to minor official posts to handle the detailed running of the system.

From the official viewpoint, one important advantage of the monopolies was that they produced an income in gold and silver. This not only represented 'real' wealth in the mercantilist terms common to Tokugawa Japan, but was also immediately available to meet the heavy expenses which were incurred in Edo. Moreover, the farmer-producer was often paid in the domain's own paper money, which he was required to accept at face value, or in some form of credit note which could be used only in certain permitted ways. In other words, he was forced to take a low price in a dubious form of payment. It is not surprising, therefore, that the introduction of mono-polies brought more unrest in the countryside and that the merchant-officials who acted as the domain's agents were among the most frequent targets of peasant violence.

Monopoly arrangements of various kinds increased greatly in number between 1800 and 1830, affording evidence of the growing financial pressure on domains. They were not, how-ever, universally successful as a solution to financial ills. In many cases there is no doubt that the lion's share of the profit found its way into the pockets of the merchants who adminis-tered the system, not into the treasury for whose benefit it was ostensibly run, and this, together with mounting signs of rural unrest, provoked many samurai to demand reform. In some fiefs, usually where the *daimyo* was himself a man of some ability, they were able to carry it out.

Economies in expenditure and improvements in adminis-tration were the most familiar features of a reformer's policy, just as they were in Edo; but, these apart, one can still identify two main differences of emphasis in what was done. The first constituted an attempt in the manner of Mizuno Tadakuni to strengthen the traditional sources of feudal revenue and protect these elements in society that did most to produce it, this in-volving an attack on the commercialization of agriculture, on luxury in the towns, on the decline in samurai standards of behaviour. The second aimed at achieving solvency by ex-ploiting commercial wealth, subordinating the interests of the merchant to those of the domain, but co-operating with him to some extent in monopoly arrangements made at the expense of the farmer and the artisan. Both policies had their advocates, often within a single domain's officialdom. All the same one can readily cite examples of domains that chose to follow sub-stantially one course or the other. Notable among them were Satsuma and Choshu.

Zusho Hiromichi's career as a reformer in Satsuma stands as one of the most successful of the period. Zusho was born in 1776 into a samurai family of low rank, but he entered his lord's household and rose steadily to high office in it by 1825. A few years later he was made responsible for financial reform, an event which marked his emergence into the domain government proper and was followed by new appointments and grants of rank. From 1833 until his death in 1848 he was senior minister with an annual stipend of a thousand *koku*, devoting his attention largely to the task of increasing Satsuma revenue and redeeming the domain's enormous debts.

One of his early cares was to reduce waste in the collection of dues and in the shipment of rice to Osaka. He also took steps to improve the yield and quality of the fief's main crops. In more original vein, trade with the Ryukyu islands was encouraged, this being an indirect means of trade with China, with which country the islands still maintained a tributary relationship; and, most important of all, control over the sugar production of Oshima and neighbouring areas was greatly tightened. The latter had been a source of income to Satsuma ever since sugar had first formed part of the Ryukyu tax payments in 1647, becoming more so in the eighteenth century, when the domain had begun to buy up the rest of the Oshima crop as well, making dealing in it an official monopoly. It was left to Zusho, however, to make the controls really effective. This he did by regulations issued in 1830, which provided that all sugar had to be sold to the domain for subsequent disposal in the Osaka market. The purchase price was fixed, crops were regularly inspected and the death penalty was imposed for any attempt at private trading, while profits were further increased by paying the producer in credit notes which he could only use to buy goods from official dealers at prices which were kept artificially high. The result was a sharp improvement in domain finances. Annual proceeds from sugar sales almost doubled in the decade after 1830, providing profits which made possible a costly programme of military reform.

One factor that made such arrangements workable in Satsuma was the exceptionally high proportion of samurai in the population, many of them resident in the countryside, not the castle town. Their numbers made peasant revolt wellnigh impossible and their adherence to traditional values greatly eased the task of subjecting merchants to feudal control. In Choshu the position was different, though there, too, samurai numbers were large. Choshu lacked any single crop or product that could compare with Satsuma's sugar as a source of profit. Moreover, its economic patterns were more complex. In its wealthier areas, chiefly along the shores of the Inland Sea, development had been closely linked with the commercial market, which made it more difficult for officials to regulate than that of more backward regions. Monopolies had been created at various times in salt, wax, paper, indigo, saké and cotton, but none had provided a reliable, continuing revenue, partly because they had provoked political opposition. The reactions of Choshu farmers ranged from evasion of the domain's commercial regulations to outright revolt. In the summer of 1831, for example, anti-monopoly demonstrations near the town of Mitajiri touched off major riots, which then spread into mountainous districts, where they took the form of protests against tax levels and usury. They were followed by further outbreaks in 1832, 1833 and 1837.

In 1838 the *daimyo*, Mori Yoshichika, decided to initiate financial reforms, entrusting their execution to Murata Seifu, a samurai of modest rank now raised to high office for the first time. Murata began in traditional manner with exhortations to retrenchment and frugality. Three years later he evolved a more far-reaching plan to encourage agricultural production (and hence tax revenue). It had two corollaries: first, that official participation in monopolies should end—except for a profitable shipping and warehousing organization in Shimonoseki—on the grounds that they aroused rural hostility without affording significant benefit to the treasury; second, that men of ability be promoted to office, regardless of inherited rank, to ensure effective supervision.

Murata was able by these measures to reduce the burdens on samurai income in Choshu and to build up an emergency reserve which was of importance to the domain's subsequent political activities. He did so, however, at the cost of incurring the hostility of the castle-town merchants, especially by a plan for redeeming the debts of domain and samurai at rates that were little short of outright cancellation. The opposition, manifested through samurai, many of whom found it impossible to live without merchant loans, brought about his fall in 1844. Yet this did not resolve the underlying issues. For the rest of the Tokugawa period there was to be a political struggle in Choshu between representatives of a variety of interests: samurai traditionalism; domain monopoly; an incipient anti-monopoly capitalism in the countryside; even a form of radicalism that questioned the continuing relevance of the feudal structure as a whole.

This brief examination of the reform movements in Edo, Satsuma and Choshu during the Tempo era (1830–43) serves to emphasize some developments that were to be of major importance for Japanese history in the second half of the nineteenth century. The first derives from the nature of Japanese economic change itself. In the country's more advanced areas, the alliance established in the eighteenth century between feudal rulers and urban merchants, manifested in the political protection afforded to merchant guilds and in co-operation in the running of official monopolies, had provoked resentment on the part of rural producers and entrepreneurs, who sought either to evade or to challenge monopoly controls. One consequence was the emergence of new economic networks outside the towns, concerned with the production and sale of commercial crops or the manufacture of goods for the market. These found a labour force in the farms, principally through by-employment, thereby cutting down emigration to the towns. The entrepreneurs, too, were mostly drawn from the village, men who turned away from farming as their primary activity towards trade, manufacture and finance. They subscribed to economic beliefs, focused on profit and productivity, which were in significant respects alien to those of feudal society. It is even arguable, though still a matter of controversy, that these changes, combined with nil or negligible population growth, brought about a rise in *per capita* income, hence in purchasing power, which was to be crucial to economic modernization. Certainly they helped to give shape and impetus to modernization when the treaties of the 1850s, bringing Japan forcibly into closer relations with the capitalist West, provided it with an external stimulus.

Equally important was the fact that economic policy and economic interests were established as major elements in the country's political life. Involvement in Bakufu and domain monopolies gave samurai the habit of intervening in commercial and industrial matters, which carried over into the Meiji period's policies of mercantilism and state paternalism. The concept of economic growth remained alien to Tokugawa officialdom, it is true, but not the idea that the state had an economic function. At a different level, economic change, by redistributing wealth, threatened the dominance of traditional groups in both the village and the castle-town and thus gave new direction to political disputes. Those who looked to agriculture as the basis of respectability and authority came readily into conflict with those who enjoyed the comforts commerce could provide, or who saw the exploitation of new forms of wealth as the only solution to the problems of feudal impoverishment. Newly rich peasant entrepreneurs sought political influence in the village, not only for the status it could bring, but also for the sake of tax advantages. Samurai, reduced to poverty by misfortune or improvidence, sought political solutions to financial ills, whether as reactionaries, putting pressure on domain administrators, or as 'men of ability', to whom office was the obvious outlet for ambition. In other words, the social upheaval caused by commercialization introduced 'politics' into 'administration'. By so doing it gave crucial experience to the samurai who were to be the future rulers of Japan.

In the shorter term economic change brought a shift in the balance of power between Bakufu and domains. A number of domains, facing more manageable problems than the Bakufu, because their economies were less advanced, had better success in overcoming financial crisis and hence in providing funds for military reform. The uneven growth in agricultural yields during the seventeenth and eighteenth centuries had tended to benefit those lords whose fiefs included more marginal land that could be brought under cultivation, especially in the fertile and thickly populated areas of the south and west, where the spread of a commercial economy increased the resources available to the ruling class; and whereas Edo proved unable effectively to control the expanding economy of the central provinces, several domains found their own less complex economies amenable to continuing feudal control by techniques the Bakufu had itself employed in an earlier phase. Some, moreover, were able to exploit particular advantages of geography and climate. Satsuma, as we have seen, had access to Japan's only sugar supply; Choshu dominated the western approaches to the Inland Sea, most important of domestic shipping routes; Tosa had rich fishing grounds and a valuable paper industry. All three attained a degree of financial stability that enabled them to engage actively in the politics of the next few decades.

This is not to imply that the Tempo reform movements made inevitable the fall of the Bakufu or determined who would overthrow it. Still less can they be described as anti-feudal, or revolutionary in the sense of being designed to implement new social patterns. A modern scholar of the period has rightly said that late Tokugawa reform was designed 'to shake off the dead hand of conservatism and lethargy ... without precipitating any cataclysmic changes'.[8] Cataclysm was to come later and, at least initially, from a different source. It was the consciousness of external threat, arising from renewed relations with the West, that was to bring a national crisis putting the whole regime in peril.

CHAPTER III

JAPAN AND THE WEST

Western attempts to open trade—the Opium War—Japanese reactions—developments in shipping and armaments

---

WHEN THE third Tokugawa ruler, Iemitsu, took the final steps in establishing Japan's policy of national seclusion in the seventeenth century, he did so for reasons that seemed to him practical and cogent. Christianity he regarded as an instrument of foreign ambitions, to be stamped out by every means at his disposal. Trade, which might provide guns and gold to a disaffected vassal, ought to be limited and controlled. Hence priests were excluded; those who brought them were punished; and the few Dutch and Chinese merchants still permitted at Nagasaki were closely watched. With the passage of time, trade itself came into disfavour, on the grounds that what the foreigners brought were luxuries and what they took were goods that Japan could hardly spare, while the suspicions on which Iemitsu had acted became inflated by constant repetition until the whole structure of his belief became hallowed as ancestral law.

The difficulty about enforcing this law, however, was that it depended on the willingness of other countries to accept the ban, as well as on Japan's ability to resist any demands they might make for its removal. In both respects the position changed gradually to Japan's disadvantage. Advances in European science and technology, unmatched elsewhere, had by the nineteenth century made it impossible for Japan to defend herself successfully in the event of war. Similarly, a new wave of European expansion, linked with the growth of industry and a search for markets, ensured that she would not be left alone for ever. In the south, after about 1775, Britain, followed by the

United States, began to establish an important trade with China. In the north, Russian settlements appeared on the Sea of Okhotsk, from which explorers eventually made contact with Japan.

Russian attention was first drawn to that country by the discovery of a Japanese castaway on Kamchatka in 1697. There followed a number of exploratory voyages to the Kuriles and Hokkaido, but it was not until 1792 that Adam Laxman, with Catherine the Great's approval, left Okhotsk in a formal attempt to communicate with Japan under the pretext of returning a group of shipwrecked seamen. He wintered in Hokkaido and had amicable discussions with officials there, but in July 1793 was told he must not continue to Edo. Nor was he allowed to open questions of trade, since this, it was said, could only be done at Nagasaki. However, he was given a permit for one Russian ship to visit that port for the purpose of making the request.

The permit was not used until after the establishment of the Russian-American Company in 1799, when Nikolai Rezanov, a shareholder in the company and an advocate of Russian commercial expansion in China and Japan, secured imperial approval for a further voyage, together with a letter from Alexander I for delivery to the Japanese government. He sailed from Kronstadt in 1803 and reached Kamchatka, via Cape Horn, in the following year, eventually arriving at Nagasaki on October 20, 1804. There his reception was far from friendly. His ship was put under close guard while a copy of the Tsar's letter was sent to Edo. Moreover, the accommodation provided for him ashore was more a prison than an ambassador's residence and he was forced to wait six months for the Bakufu's decision. When, after all this, permission to go to Edo was refused and all the Russian proposals were rejected, Rezanov was furious; and before returning home he left orders with two Russian officers in Okhotsk which led to a series of raids on Japanese settlements in the north during 1806 and 1807. This in turn embittered the Japanese, who had their revenge a few years later when they seized the captain of a Russian survey vessel, Vasilii Golovnin, who landed on one of the Kurile islands in July 1811, holding him prisoner in Hokkaido for a little over two years until his ship returned with official disclaimers of the 1806–7 raids from the governor of Irkutsk. Thereafter Russo-Japanese relations for a generation or more were reduced to scattered contact in the islands.

British relations with Japan in this period were equally sporadic. In 1791 a private trader, James Colnett, cruised up the west coast of Kyushu, trying cautiously to open trade by approaches to ships offshore, but his total failure seems to have discouraged others from repeating the experiment. Then in 1808 a British frigate, the *Phaeton*, entered Nagasaki harbour under Dutch colours and took hostages to ensure the prompt supply of stores. Such high-handed action caused a great commotion ashore, but it was in fact incidental to the *Phaeton*'s purpose: she was concerned merely to seize Dutch ships, as a part of wartime operations against Napoleon's empire. However, the incident had repercussions a few years later, when a deliberate attack on Japan's seclusion was planned by Thomas Stamford Raffles. As lieutenant-governor of Java, newly captured from the Dutch, Raffles tried twice in 1813–14 to substitute a British trade with Deshima for that of Holland. Each time the men he sent to carry out his orders were foiled by the Dutch factor at Deshima, Hendrik Doeff, who threatened to reveal their identity to Japanese officials and so involve them in the hostility incurred by the *Phaeton*'s action. The effectiveness of this threat depended partly on the fact that Raffles' policy had been coldly received in London and was actively opposed by the governor-general in Calcutta, which made it necessary for him to proceed with caution, but in any case the opportunity to act at all was not of long duration, since Java was handed back to the Dutch soon after.

In the next twenty years British interest in Japan was rare and action based upon it even rarer. An unsuccessful private voyage was made to Edo Bay in 1818 and on several occasions whaling vessels, now operating off the Japanese coast, came into contact with Japanese villagers, but this was all. A further attempt to open Japan did not come until 1837, when it took the form of a joint Anglo-American venture. The story of it began when a Japanese junk, on a coasting voyage to Edo at the end of 1832, was dismasted and driven off its course by a typhoon. Drifting for months across the Pacific, with a few of its crew managing to exist on rain-water and the ship's cargo of rice, it was wrecked on the north-west coast of America, where three survivors were rescued from the Indians in 1834 by the Hudson's Bay Company's factor at Fort Vancouver. Thinking it possible that they might be welcome as an excuse for negotiating with Japan, he sent them to London in 1835, but the British government showed little enthusiasm for this as a pretext for an official mission. They were duly transferred to Canton later in the year. Here Captain Elliott, Second Superintendent of Trade, evolved the same plan as had already occurred to the Vancouver factor. He wrote to Palmerston suggesting that the opportunity be taken to send the castaways back by warship and so open a correspondence with Japan, only to find himself firmly snubbed in a Foreign Office dispatch of September 1836. This put an end to any possibility of government action, though it still left the problem of how to get the men back to their own country, since the Foreign Office recommendation that they be sent 'quietly home' in a Chinese junk was impracticable for a variety of reasons.

A solution was found in the arrangements being made by two Americans, a merchant, C. W. King, and a missionary, Dr S. Wells Williams. They, too, had Japanese castaways—in this case, four from Manila—and hopes of gaining access to Japan. In consultation with Elliott they agreed to add his three charges to their company, the whole expedition, privately financed, to proceed to Edo Bay in the ship *Morrison* after calling at the Ryukyu capital of Naha. The plan was carried out in the summer of 1837, only to fail in both its public and its private objects. On July 30 of that year, the *Morrison* dropped anchor off Uraga and was visited by crowds of Japanese, both impassive officials and curious sightseers. Yet at dawn next day, before any formal discussions could take place, shore batteries opened fire on the anchorage, forcing the unarmed ship to sea. An attempt a few days later to establish communication with the shore at Kagoshima in the south of Kyushu met the same response. On August 27, therefore, with castaways, bibles and trade goods still intact, the *Morrison* returned to the China coast.

The *Morrison* affair, it transpired, marked the end of an era. A little over two years later war broke out between Britain and China, the so-called Opium War, which revolutionized the international politics of the region. By the treaty settlement of 1842–3 Britain acquired Hong Kong and opened additional Chinese ports to foreign trade as far north as Shanghai at the mouth of the Yangtse. This increased the possibility of visits to Japan, planned or unplanned, since Shanghai was a mere 500 miles from Nagasaki. Moreover, the resulting growth in trade soon meant that many more European merchants and far greater financial interests were involved, so that Japan was no longer to be regarded as beyond the farthest point of Europe's longest trade route, but rather as being on the fringe of an area of increasing concern to European governments. The Far East in general began to loom larger in the calculations of Western statesmen. Accordingly, they provided it with the appurtenances of modern diplomacy—consuls and gunboats —and by so doing made it easier to plan official missions to Japan. These could now be carried out with the resources of men and ships which were locally available. In other words, certain practical advantages in pursuing relations with Japan which only Russia had previously possessed were now extended to the maritime powers.

The change was reflected in the character of Japan's visitors in the next decade or so, almost all of whom were official representatives of their respective countries. For example, Japan, because its geography was so little known, acquired a certain importance as a possible danger to navigation. In 1843 a British survey ship, HMS *Samarang*, was put to work on the islands running north-east from Formosa and this brought her to Nagasaki in August 1845 with a request for stores. She carried out a surreptitious survey of the harbour before leaving. Four years later another vessel, HMS *Mariner*, arrived from Shanghai to survey the approaches to Edo; and despite Japanese objections she was able to acquire much useful information about the two ports of Uraga and Shimoda, and about Sagami Bay, which lies between them. All this was naval routine, without ulterior diplomatic motives, but it undoubtedly looked ominous to many observers.

There was, indeed, good reason for supposing that European governments would be forced by mercantile opinion at home to put an end to Japanese seclusion. There were many merchants, officials and even missionaries in the West who thought that what had been done to force trade on China was not only right in itself, but also exemplified a principle which should be applied to Japan as well. The *Edinburgh Review* put the argument as follows:

'The compulsory seclusion of the Japanese is a wrong not only to themselves, but to the civilized world . . . The Japanese undoubtedly have an exclusive right to the possession of their territory; but they must not abuse that right to the extent of debarring all other nations from a participation in its riches and virtues. The only secure title to property, whether it be a hovel or an empire, is, that the exclusive possession of one is for the benefit of all.'[9]

Ministers had henceforth to take this sort of thinking into account when framing policy.

It was in 1844 that Japanese attention was first directed officially to the situation which the Opium War had brought about. In the summer of that year a Dutch ship arrived at Nagasaki bringing a letter to the Shogun from the Dutch king, William II, setting out the changes which industrialization was causing in Europe's relations with the rest of the world and underlining their dangerous implications for Japan. The letter took the form of friendly advice, urging the Japanese govern-ment to reconsider the seclusion policy while it was still able to do so free from outside pressure. It was clear enough, how-ever, that Holland hoped for advantages for herself and that the letter was meant to be a preliminary to negotiation. Edo certainly so regarded it. Nevertheless, the Bakufu's reply to the Dutch was negative and uncompromising. Dated July 5, 1845, it reiterated the traditional view: foreign trade was limited by ancestral law to China and Holland; its extension to other countries could not be considered; correspondence on this subject must therefore cease and never be resumed.

Such an answer would almost certainly have been rejected by Britain or Russia, but it happened that action on their part was prevented, or at least delayed, by other considerations. It was in 1845, in fact, that Britain first made secret plans for a mission to Japan, proposed in May by Sir John Davis, Super-intendent of Trade at Hong Kong, and approved some months later by Aberdeen at the Foreign Office, with the expectation that they would be carried out during the summer of 1846; but in the event Davis allowed them to lapse because the navy's China squadron could not put at his disposal the amount of force which he considered necessary. And since there was not enough interest in the matter at Whitehall to make the government take action on its own, Davis's decision was accepted and the matter was allowed to drop, though subsequent Superintendents were provided with authority to go to Japan should a suitable opportunity arise. All of them proved too preoccupied with the affairs of China to try to do so.

For Russia the reasons were different but the effect the same. After the Opium War, Nicholas I had established a committee to review Russia's position in the Amur region in the light of new conditions; and a member of it, Rear-Admiral Putiatin, had put forward plans for surveying the Amur estuary and sending an expedition to Japan. They were approved by the Tsar in 1843, but were then opposed by the Foreign Minister, Nesselrode, on the grounds that Russia had no Pacific trade which was worth such effort. This proved decisive, with the result that, although the Amur survey was carried out on a small scale, nothing at all was done about Japan. The fact was that Japanese trade was never likely to be of more than subsidiary interest to Russia, important chiefly for its local value to her settlements round the Sea of Okhotsk. On the other hand, there were other motives than trade that might bring about negotiation. Russia was a territorial power in north-east Asia, with political and strategic interests there which made her inevitably concerned at any possible growth in the influence of other Western countries, such as might easily be occasioned by the opening of Japanese ports. She therefore watched closely the moves, not only of Britain, but also of the United States.

American interests in the Pacific were both commercial, like those of Britain, and strategic, like those of Russia, a combination which sufficiently explains why it was the United States that in the end successfully forced a way into Japanese waters. Her first official attempt to do so began in 1845, when a merchant, Aaron Palmer, persuaded his government that trade with Japan held out good prospects. At Palmer's urging, orders were given to Commodore James Biddle, in command of the Pacific squadron, permitting him to go to Japan and investigate the possibilities of agreement, an opportunity of which he took advantage in July 1846. Unfortunately for his chances of success, he had been instructed to avoid provocation. He therefore let pass an incident at the anchorage in Edo Bay which was widely interpreted as a gratuitous insult to his rank. This brought down on him more criticism from his fellow-countrymen and other Western residents on the China coast even than his readiness to accept a Japanese reply which was a flat refusal to grant trade or privileges and which was undated, unsigned and unaddressed. On all sides it was said that Biddle had left the situation rather worse than he had found it. His experiences certainly helped to persuade Sir John Davis to abandon the projected British mission. What is more, no greater success awaited another American venture three years later, when the USS *Preble* was sent to Nagasaki. Her commander secured the ostensible object of his voyage, the release of some seamen shipwrecked from an American whaler, but made no headway in his efforts to establish a consul in Japan and acquire a coaling station there.

On these occasions, American policy had not been pressed any more forcefully than that of Russia or of Britain. America's position with respect to the Pacific, however, was changing quickly. British recognition of US rights in the Oregon territory in 1846 and the acquisition of California after the war with Mexico in 1846–8 gave her a long Pacific coastline. A transcontinental railway was already being discussed, in terms of trade with Asia as well as of development at home, while the newly formed Pacific Mail Steamship Company was planning a route to China. Thus Japan suddenly became a factor of real importance. Her harbours—and reported coal deposits—lay directly on the route from San Francisco to Shanghai. Consequently her notorious lack of hospitality for seamen in distress or in need of supplies, displeasing enough when it affected only whalers, could not be tolerated any longer. For her coastal waters were to become a major shipping lane, used by steamers which at this early state of their development had a very limited range; and whether or not Japanese trade was likely to be of value, Japanese seclusion had therefore become an offence. The next attack on it was likely to be more determined.

This was made very clear in 1852 when it was announced

that a new American expedition would go to Japan under the command of Commodore M. C. Perry. He was to be accompanied by a sizeable force and would not be able lightly to turn away, for the whole world, including Japan, was told of the plan and its preparations. The Western press debated ends and means, confidently predicting that guns would be used if arguments failed. European governments, officially notified of America's intention, sought to clarify their attitude to it. Britain, it appeared, was prepared to let things take their course. 'Her Majesty's Government', the Foreign Secretary wrote to Hong Kong in July 1852, 'would be glad to see the trade with Japan open; but they think it better to leave it to the Government of the United States to make the experiment; and if that experiment is successful, Her Majesty's Government can take advantage of its success.'[10] Russia, by contrast, hurriedly revived the plans of 1843 and appointed Putiatin to take a squadron to Japan, with orders to watch over Russian interests and ensure that his country had a voice in any settlement. Thus Japan had become the destination, not of single ships, but of powerful and rival squadrons, one sailing from America's east coast in November 1852, the other leaving Europe two months later. To almost everyone it was apparent that the closed door must open or it would be broken down.

The development of Russian, British and American interest in the Far East, although known to Tokugawa officials, affected Japanese policy only in causing more attention to be paid to coast defence. Domains on the coast were told to keep watch for foreign ships and to have troops ready to repel them. In 1825 they were even ordered to fire on them at sight. This rule was cancelled in 1842, when Mizuno Tadakuni, influenced by events in China, issued instructions that vessels in distress were to be provided with essential stores before being ordered to depart, but he coupled this with a warning that the relaxation was not to become an excuse for carelessness over military precautions. His successor, Abe Masahiro, who became senior councillor in March 1845, was equally cautious. He showed himself willing to overlook Satsuma evasion of the strict letter of the seclusion laws in the Ryukyu islands, but not, as we have seen, to enter into negotiations with the occasional Western representatives who reached Japan. Until 1853, basic policies in this respect remained unchanged.

Yet this is not to say that basic policies were never questioned. From the end of the eighteenth century, Japanese scholars—most of whom were samurai, many of them having considerable influence as officials, teachers, or advisers to their lords—had begun seriously to debate the political and economic implications of seclusion. Among the first to do so were the Rangakusha, or 'Dutch scholars', those who studied the Dutch language in order to make use of books imported through the Deshima factory. Early representatives of the group had concentrated largely on European medicine and similar topics, but after 1790, as foreign visits to Japan increased, some of them turned to geography, world affairs and even politics. This led inevitably to a consideration of their country's foreign relations. One, for example, wrote a pamphlet in 1838 about the *Morrison* venture, under the title 'Story of a Dream'. His facts were garbled, but the point of his remarks was clear enough: Britain was a powerful adversary, well able to resent insult, and Japan had best beware how she treated British missions. In other words, seclusion might prove dangerous. For this, which officials chose to regard as an attack on the regime, the author was later imprisoned.

One of the most famous of the Rangakusha was Sakuma Shozan, a samurai of Matsushiro in Shinano, whose lord, Sanada Yukitsura, was appointed to the Council of State in Mizuno Tadakuni's time and put in charge of coast defence. A knowledge of and interest in defence policy, acquired through this connection, led Sakuma to a study of the Dutch language and Western military science, for he became convinced that only weapons of the Western type would enable Japan to defend herself successfully. It was a case which he proceeded to argue in a number of memorials to his lord. In 1842, pointing to the dangers of Russian and British attack, he urged that Japan must prepare for the struggle by purchasing modern armaments and by learning to make them, too. Within six years he had himself learnt the technique of casting cannon. Nor were his studies confined to the mechanical, though they continued to have a practical and military bent. In 1849 we find him petitioning Sanada for financial help in the preparation of a Dutch-Japanese dictionary and the publication of Dutch books, a plan he justified on the grounds that it was necessary 'to know one's enemy'.[11] In the following year he sought Bakufu help as well, arguing still more generally the superiority of Western science over· .that of China and Japan. Western countries had been able to achieve overwhelming material strength, he said, 'because foreign learning is rational and Chinese learning is not'.[12] It was China's failure to recognize this which had been responsible for her defeat; and if Japan wished to avoid the same fate she must study what the West had to teach her in a variety of fields, not merely those which were of direct application to war.

Notwithstanding his growing, if reluctant, admiration for the West's achievements, Sakuma always remained wedded to a largely traditional view of politics and society. This he expressed in the slogan, 'Eastern ethics, Western science', which was to be not far short of an official doctrine for a time after the Meiji Restoration. Sakuma, however, never lived to see this happen. He died in 1864 at the age of fifty-three, murdered by an anti-foreign extremist from Choshu—an ironic ending for a man who had spent over twenty years seeking means to preserve Japan from foreign aggression and had not long before been in prison for criticizing the Bakufu's weakness in diplomatic negotiations.

Men like Sakuma became involved in politics because foreign affairs was a political issue. Others did so because they identified themselves from the beginning with proposals for reform within Japan. Among the latter, for example, was Sato Shinen (1769–1850), advocate of radical economic and political change, of military reform and overseas expansion. Some of his lack of orthodoxy was undoubtedly due to family background, since he came of a non-samurai family in northern Japan which for several generations had produced experts in agriculture, forestry and mining. But much of it was in the man himself. He travelled extensively throughout Japan, making careful notes of all that interested him, and acquired a knowledge of Dutch which he used in the study of Western geography, history, navigation and military science. As a result he was far better equipped than most of his contemporaries to prescribe cures for the country's ills. He was initially much in favour of expanding foreign trade. However, when news of the Opium War reached Japan he began to wonder whether the economic advantages of trade were commensurate with its political risks. The same period saw him become hesitant about the possibilities of empire. He had argued in earlier days that Japan's geographical position, organizing ability and superior moral fibre made it inevitable, as well as desirable, that she should dominate China and the areas further west; but he now began to dwell anxiously on the subject of defence, as Chinese defeats began to sap his confidence.

This was a common response to the Opium War among writers of the time. More interesting in many ways was Sato's recognition that economic and military strength could not be achieved independently of political structure. In one of his books he described the sort of state—as purposeful and highly regulated a state as Sparta—which he would wish to see established in Japan. Government, he maintained, should be conducted through separate departments handling agriculture, forestry and mining, finance and commerce, manufacture, and the army and navy, with the whole population divided into hereditary classes defined by function, each under the control of one of these departments. Change of occupation would be forbidden and each group segregated from the others. This would ensure that children acquired a knowledge of their family trade in their earliest years, thus increasing specialization and efficiency. From the age of eight, moreover, children would be entitled to free education in one of the provincial schools run by a Department of Education, receiving a training designed to increase their value to the state. There would also be a national university for the privileged and able, providing, in addition to traditional subjects like philosophy and religion, instruction in law, foreign languages and Western science.

Sato's proposals foreshadow many features of Japanese life in the later nineteenth century, even—perhaps especially—in their disconcerting blend of the grim and the enlightened. Sakuma, too, provided ideas which were used by statesmen after 1868. In this respect they both, like other men of similar outlook, contributed to the process we call 'modernization'. On the other hand, it does not follow that they played a direct part in bringing about the fall of the Tokugawa, which was to be the prelude to modernization and the key to its success. In fact, the work of the early nineteenth century Mito scholars was far more relevant to this stage of the political process.

The Mito domain, held by one of the three senior Tokugawa branch houses, had long been a centre of Confucian scholarship. For generations its official scholars had engaged in writing a chronicle of early Japanese history, an undertaking which gave them a reputation for patriotism and, apparently, a lively interest in contemporary affairs. Certainly the new crisis in Japan's foreign relations which came in the eighteenth century caused them great concern. In 1797 one of them, Fujita Yukoku, warned his lord of the danger of Russian attack, criticizing the Bakufu for its failure to make adequate preparations to meet it and urging that Mito, as a coastal fief, had a special duty to do so on its own account. As means to this end he specified two things which were to be central to Mito thinking for sixty years: armaments and reform. He added that the country's leaders must show such resolution as would unite the nation, raise morale and so make victory sure.

These ideas were further developed by Aizawa Seishisai in a book called *Shinron* (New Proposals) written in 1825 and by Yukoku's son, Fujita Toko, in his *Hitachi obi* (Sash of Hitachi) twenty years later. Both argued that the urgent task was to arouse Japan to a sense of danger and to unite the country in its own defence. This done, the rest of their plans would have some meaning: the provision of new weapons, including Western-style ships; financial reform, to pay for them; and the promotion of men of ability, to secure sound administration on which all else depended. Yet a revival of traditional spirit, overcoming luxury and lethargy, could not be achieved by exhortation. Only one thing would suffice to do it, they said, an announcement that the government was resolved once and for all to reject foreign demands and fight to defend seclusion. The slogan must be 'expel the barbarian' (*jo-i*). In other words, the ports must remain closed and trade must be refused, even if this meant war.

By 1853, then, the Mito scholars had reached some very definite conclusions about foreign affairs. Japan, they believed, could only attain national strength and international equality by achieving unity at home. This, in turn, depended on war or the threat of war. Hence the Bakufu must be uncompromising in negotiation. Unfortunately, however, there was a danger that Bakufu officials, fearing defeat, might be willing to temporise in the hope of avoiding conflict, a possibility which called in question the Bakufu's capacity for leadership and shifted the discussion of reform to a new—and ominous—level. Suggestions were made that the Shogun should consult the great lords—those whose views were reliable, of course—in addition to the usual officials. There were even some who urged that success could never be complete until the emperor became once again a focus of national government, creating unity by transcending other loyalties.

This doctrine of imperial sovereignty had always been latent in Japanese thought. In the eighteenth century, however, it had emerged more widely because of attempts to revive the Shinto religion, which owed much to the studies of ancient Japanese literature and society by the scholar Motoori Norinaga (1730–1801). His work served to resurrect one particular set of Shinto beliefs that were ultimately of great political importance: briefly, that the Japanese emperor was descended directly from the sun-goddess; that his claim to temporal power rested on divine descent; that the Japanese islands and people were also of divine origin; and that Japan was by these facts made superior to other lands. The chauvinist element in this was made explicit in the nineteenth century by the publicist, Hirata Atsutane (1776–1843). 'Japanese', he wrote, 'differ completely from and are superior to the peoples of China, India, Russia, Holland, Siam, Cambodia, and all other countries of the world.'[13] It was a comforting thought to men who knew that Western countries possessed much power and an apparent willingness to use it against Japan.

Neo-Shinto ideas of this kind gained considerable influence among those who wrote on foreign affairs. This was largely, no doubt, because their anti-foreign flavour accorded well with the fears and suspicions aroused by Western encroachment, but it helped also to turn men's minds towards the emperor as a means of healing political divisions. Some of these divisions, after all, were the result of Tokugawa supremacy. Others deeply involved the samurai class, of which the Shogun was the appointed head. The Shogun, therefore, was not an entirely satisfactory focus of loyalty, whereas the emperor, being above the discord, was. Thus a second slogan, 'honour the emperor' (*son-no*), eventually came into being to reinforce that which called for expelling the barbarian.

In this way, foreign policy became linked with issues of domestic politics: first, because political and economic reform was regarded as an essential part of defence preparations; second, because men began to look to the emperor as a source of unity in the face of foreign threat. All the same, it would be quite wrong to describe this as being from the start a deliberate attack on Tokugawa authority. Even allowing for the fact that such ideas would have been dangerous to express, it is still significant that contemporary literature reveals practically nothing in the way of threats to overthrow the existing order. When the Mito scholars spoke of 'reform', they meant policies that would make the best of society as it was. When they talked of 'honouring the emperor', they meant to strengthen the Shogun's power in a time of growing unrest by using the emperor's name in the Bakufu's service. The way to unity was through a loyalty that must be duly hierarchical. As Tokugawa Nariaki, lord of Mito, wrote in 1842:

'If the Shogun takes the lead in showing respect for the throne, the whole country will naturally be united, but it is vital that in this each should preserve his proper place. The samurai shows respect for his lord, the lord shows respect for the Shogun, the Shogun shows respect for the Emperor.'[14]

One can hardly call this subversive.

It took the events of 1853–60, with which we shall deal in the next chapter, to make the ideas of the Mito school the basis for an anti-Tokugawa movement. By that time they had been disseminated widely by the writings and personal teaching of the domain's outstanding scholars, Fujita Toko and Aizawa Seishisai, the first of whom lived till 1855 and the second till 1863. Their fame was such that many came to study under them. Others met them in Edo or learnt their views at second hand, until it is fair to say that most samurai of the period knew at least their slogans.

This was to be enormously important. Nevertheless, their

only sure way of influencing policy, as distinct from opinion, was through their lord, Tokugawa Nariaki, whose actions in this period speak eloquently of their success. In 1842 he opposed Mizuno Tadakuni's plan to relax the seclusion laws, on the grounds that it was pusillanimous. In 1846 he urged Abe Masahiro, the senior Bakufu councillor, to arrange for translations of Dutch works on military subjects to be made widely available as a step towards improving Japan's defences. In 1853 and after he was a consistent opponent of diplomatic concession and an advocate of Bakufu reform. Since he was not only a senior member of the Tokugawa house, but also, through the marriage of his daughters and the adoption of his sons, closely connected with two leading families of the Imperial Court and several of the most powerful *tozama* lords, his advice was not lightly to be rejected or ignored. Nor did Nariaki confine himself to the giving of advice. Within the boundaries of his own domain he was free to do many things without interference from the Shogun and he therefore did what he could to prepare for the coming struggle. His financial and administrative reforms became a model. In addition, by encouraging the study and use of Western techniques which had military importance, he put Mito in the forefront of modernization in the 1850s, with an iron industry and western-style shipbuilding already established on a small scale by 1858. Meanwhile, however, his plans had brought him into conflict with Bakufu authority. In 1844, because he had begun casting cannon without Edo's permission—in direct contravention of the regulations governing internal security—he was ordered to retire from headship of the fief in favour of his son. This he did, but his personal standing was such that he continued to dominate Mito policies until his death in 1860.

Tokugawa Nariaki and Mito were not alone in turning to Western technology for anti-Western ends, though others did not always justify their actions by the same loyalist and chauvinistic reasoning. A number of domains, as well as the Bakufu itself, encouraged Dutch studies and established translation offices. One or two, those which had the necessary economic resources, tried to put what they learnt to use. Conspicuous among them were Hizen and Satsuma, the former under Nabeshima Kanso (1814-71), *daimyo* from 1831 to 1861, the latter under Shimazu Nariakira (1809–58), *daimyo* from 1851 to 1858.

Nabeshima, as the man responsible for the Nagasaki defences, was able to tackle the problems of cannon-founding with Bakufu support and Dutch technical advice. In 1850 his domain built Japan's first successful reverberatory furnace, thus obtaining the higher quality iron which was needed to replace copper in making modern cannon. Production of these began in 1853. Thereafter the technique was applied regularly to supply the Bakufu with weapons, while a number of other lords, including those of Satsuma and Mito, sent men to learn it. From guns Hizen turned to shipping, experimenting first with models and then ordering a complete shipbuilding plant from Holland in 1856. It proved too expensive and was handed over to the Tokugawa in 1859, but even without it Hizen was able to turn out a ship's boiler in 1861 and a small steamer in 1865. Three years later an agreement was made for joint operation of the Takashima colliery with a British firm.

Much of this development took place after the ports were opened in 1858, but it is significant that much of it had started well before. The same was true in Satsuma. Attempts to improve artillery methods there had begun under Zusho Hiromichi in 1842 and had been followed by the introduction of some Western techniques in gun-making in 1846. When Shimazu Nariakira became *daimyo*, however, the speed and scope of change increased considerably. In 1852 artillery specialists were ordered to learn Western drill, while in 1853, reverberatory and blast furnaces were built, copied from Hizen, so that Satsuma, too, was able to turn out modern weapons. In the same years Dutch infantry methods were studied, the castle-town samurai were reorganized into companies for training, and a start was made on creating a cavalry force after French models. In 1856 Satsuma began to train a Western-style navy with samurai volunteers. Docks had already been built at Kagoshima the previous year and a steamer launched, though most of the domain's modern ships were acquired by purchase from abroad: seventeen of them between 1854 and 1868. In addition, a number of non-military industries were established or improved by the use of the new technology, including the manufacture of leather goods, paper, iron tools, glass and porcelain. So rapidly were the results apparent that a Dutch visitor to Kagoshima in 1858, some months before Japan's ports were fully opened to foreign trade, estimated that over 1,200 men were employed in the domain's industrial undertakings.

In Bakufu territories it seems to have been more difficult for military reformers to make headway. Takashima Shuhan, for example, a minor official in Nagasaki, tried to persuade Edo in 1841 to adopt Western drill and use modern guns, like those he had just imported from Holland on his own responsibility. He was ordered to start a training school to teach his methods, but incurred the suspicions of jealous and conservative seniors, at whose instigation he was imprisoned the following year. A similar fate overtook many of the 'Dutch scholars', though the Bakufu had been sufficiently aware of their usefulness to establish a translation office as early as 1808. In fact, little was done in the way of modernization by the Shogun's government until Perry arrived in 1853. Even then progress was slow and depended on foreign technicians. A naval training school with Dutch instructors was founded in 1855 and shipbuilding was begun at Uraga and Shimoda in 1855–6. Work was started on constructing a Nagasaki iron foundry in 1857, again with foreign help, and this was completed in 1861, though its facilities for ship repair soon proved inadequate. Subsequently the Bakufu obtained French assistance and began to work on a larger scale, but this phase belongs to the years of the regime's fall and discussion of it is best left to a later chapter.

In all this the Bakufu acted too slowly and with too little imagination, letting the initiative in modernization fall into the hands of a few of the great domains, whose financial reforms had made such development possible and whose leaders recognized the need. As a result, the gap which had set the Tokugawa so much above their rivals a century earlier, already reduced by economic change, was narrowed further. Indeed, the effectiveness of the Bakufu's military establishment was soon brought to a level only slightly above that of its potential enemies. Its authority was diminished in proportion. Nevertheless, this alone did not ensure its fall. It was the treaty negotiations of 1853-8 and the diplomatic disputes of the years that followed, revealing an inability either to satisfy Western demands or to silence domestic critics, that were to provide the crucial, because public, evidence of Tokugawa weakness.

What is more, the same events were to convert a recognition of external threat, which, as we have seen, was already widespread in Japan, into something much closer to nationalism in the modern Western sense. The conclusion of 'unequal treaties', together with military failure, as exemplified in bombardments by foreign warships in 1863 and 1864, aroused anti-foreign sentiment, which had as one of its facets an enhanced consciousness of what it meant to be Japanese. This, in turn, had important repercussions on both domestic politics and foreign affairs. It gave an impetus to the search for national strength, and hence for unity, constituting on the one hand a move towards a new kind of patriotism, in which the country, rather than the province or domain, was to be the focus of loyalty, and on the other an emotional basis for attacks on a regime which was said to have failed in its duty of protecting the nation's honour. The Bakufu, by its inability to exploit the change—or even, perhaps, to recognize its importance—helped largely to seal its own fate.

CHAPTER IV

TREATIES AND POLITICS
1853-1860

Trading agreements—repercussions in Japan—agitation for reform

COMMODORE MATTHEW CALBRAITH PERRY, whose ships were the first modern Western squadron to reach Japan, was a senior and distinguished officer of the United States Navy. He had only accepted the Pacific command with reluctance, in the expectation that he would be provided with a force commensurate with his rank and reputation, and he had no intention of suffering the same kind of treatment in Japan as had been meted out to previous Western envoys. On July 8, 1853, therefore, when his two steamers and two sailing vessels anchored off Uraga, his orders were that no insults or slights in any form were to be tolerated. The ships were to be cleared for action at all times. Only officials were to be allowed on board. These, moreover, were to be told that only an envoy of high rank, appointed by the Japanese government, would be permitted to see the commodore, who would deliver to him in proper manner a letter from President Fillmore, together with a number of presents for the Japanese ruler. The letter was intended subsequently to form the basis of negotiations. Meanwhile, no matter what arguments and entreaties the Japanese employed, the commodore was not prepared to go to Nagasaki for discussions. Indeed, the only move he was prepared to consider was one which would take him nearer Edo.

In the Shogun's capital, Perry's arrival and the obvious strength of his squadron caused consternation, even though advance warning of it had been given by the Dutch several months before. As a stopgap, it was decided to accept the letters, since to do so would give time for proper consideration of the questions which they raised, and the officials at Uraga were ordered to make appropriate arrangements. This they did, the ceremony taking place with great solemnity at Kurihama on July 14. Five thousand Japanese troops surrounded the temporary building erected for the purpose and the two American steamers were less than a gunshot offshore, when Perry duly handed over the elaborate boxes in which the President's letter and the commodore's credentials were enclosed. He also added a letter of his own; and whereas the President's was a firm but friendly document, emphasizing America's desire for proper treatment of shipwrecked seamen, for ports of refuge where ships could obtain coal and stores, and for the opening of trade, Perry's came close to being a threat. If these 'very reasonable and pacific overtures' were not at once accepted, he wrote, he would have to return for a reply next spring, this time 'with a much larger force'.[15] The point was underlined in the following two days, when he took part of the squadron well into Edo Bay before leaving for the China coast.

It was Abe Masahiro, senior councillor since 1845, who had to work out a policy in response to this American demand; and recognizing that recent events had provoked widespread discussion of defence policy in Japan, causing considerable divergence of views among samurai concerning the course it was best to follow, he set out to establish a rather broader base for Bakufu decisions than had been customary hitherto. One of his first actions was to seek the support of Tokugawa Nariaki. This proved embarrassing, for Nariaki proceeded to expound the so-called 'expulsion policy' of the scholars from his own domain of Mito (see Chapter III), making few concessions to the practical difficulties raised by Perry's military superiority. The first need, he argued, was to unite the country by sounding a call to arms. Thereafter defence preparations could be pushed forward, including importation of Western arms and if necessary Western experts, until Japan was in a position to resist any foreign attack. Ideally this should be averted: 'war at home, peace abroad' was the slogan Nariaki favoured, meaning that the country was to be roused by an avowal of war's inevitability, while diplomacy sought to prevent hostilities breaking out. But if in the last resort foreigners would not accept delay, then it would be better to fight and suffer defeat than to submit and destroy Japan's morale. After all, America's strength was naval. He saw no chance of her successfully invading the interior of Japan.

While trying to bring Nariaki to a less rigid viewpoint, Abe also sent out a circular asking for the advice of officials and feudal lords. It was an unprecedented step, generally interpreted as a confession of Bakufu weakness and indecision. What is more, the replies, which reached him between August and October, did little to resolve his problem, since they simply documented differences which he already knew to exist. A majority repeated time-worn arguments, perhaps because they thought these were what the government wanted: seclusion was ancestral law; Christianity was subversive; and trade was merely the exchange of Japan's essential ores for useless foreign textiles. Others maintained that once the ports were opened, on whatever pretext, Japan could not long escape the fate of China. Only a few spoke in favour of accepting the American proposals, this chiefly on the grounds that Japan did not have the strength to resist them. Yet one fact did emerge, namely, that most wanted peace. Those who followed Tokugawa Nariaki in preferring war to compromise were a small minority, for nearly all the men who urged that seclusion must be maintained ended by admitting that such rigidity could easily be fatal, that some kind of 'temporary expedient' would have to be accepted. Also in a minority were the men who wanted positive action of a different kind. The most radical suggestion was that the Bakufu should attempt to build up Japan's strength by engaging in overseas trade and creating a Western-style navy, which could one day meet the West on equal terms. It emanated from Ii Naosuke, head of the senior *fudai* house, who argued that 'when opposing forces face each other across a river, victory is obtained by that which crosses the river and attacks'.[16] This was far too adventurous an outlook for late Tokugawa Japan, and Naosuke, like Nariaki, gained only a handful of supporters.

Both Ii Naosuke and Tokugawa Nariaki were men of influence, but in this matter each could gain greater backing in opposing the other's views than he could on behalf of his own. In any case the opinion of officialdom was more in accord with that of the majority. Many Edo officials of middling rank, to whose hands the execution of policy was likely to be entrusted, favoured a cautious approach which would avoid all risk of hostilities until the Bakufu had time to prepare its defences, a matter of several years. They therefore proposed devices for achieving this, some ingenious, some irrelevant, some quite ludicrous. What mattered more, however, was their ability to exert pressure on Abe, who became the target of a paper war in which the Bakufu divided for and against the Mito recommendations. Since disparities of status often made it impossible for the participants to argue their differences face to face, the upshot was not agreement, but verbal compromise, emerging in the form of a decree dated December 1, 1853. This admitted that Japan's defences were inadequate. Accordingly, the only practical policy to be followed on Perry's return, it said, was one of peace and procrastination. In other words, an attempt would be made to persuade Perry to depart without a clear answer to his requests one way or the other, though if this failed and he resorted to force Japan must fight, thus making it the duty of all meanwhile to join loyally in warlike preparations.

As a call to arms this left much to be desired. It was also a poor basis for negotiations. When Perry returned in February 1854, this time with eight ships, it soon became clear that he would accept no answer of the kind the Bakufu envisaged. Step by step the Japanese negotiators, in constant touch with their superiors in the capital, were forced to give way; and it was only on the question of trade that they were able to hold their own, chiefly because Perry was less inclined to press for trade than for other matters. By the end of March a treaty had taken shape and on the last day of the month it was signed at Kanagawa in Edo Bay. It opened Shimoda and Hakodate as ports of refuge, where stores could be obtained through Japanese officials; it assured castaways of good treatment and return to their own country; and it authorized the appointment of consuls at a later date. To the Bakufu, this was making the best of a bad job. To Perry, despite the absence of specific permission for trade, it was a foundation on which others could build.

Perry's attitude was also that of other Western representatives who were in a position to negotiate at this time, those of Britain and Russia. Both were admirals and neither was interested primarily in trade. Indeed, their immediate preoccupation was the fact that from the end of March 1854 their countries were at war over the Crimea. News of the terms Perry had accepted discouraged Sir John Bowring, Britain's diplomatic representative at Hong Kong, from going to Japan in search of a commercial treaty, but the outbreak of hostilities gave Rear-Admiral Stirling, commanding the China squadron, a reason for going of a different kind. In September 1854 he arrived at Nagasaki in an attempt to ensure that Japan would not give shelter to the Russian warships which it was his duty to destroy. He failed completely to make himself understood in this, partly because of inefficient interpreting, partly because the context of his statements was an international code of which Japanese officials were entirely ignorant; but when the latter in despair offered him the same terms as had been won by Perry, he accepted, in the expectation that the foothold so gained could later be extended. Soon afterwards Rear-Admiral Putiatin, who had originally been sent to the area by Russia to keep an eye on American activities and had for some months past been playing hide-and-seek with Stirling up and down the Pacific coast of Asia, arrived in Shimoda to continue negotiations which he had started earlier in Nagasaki. His reception was comparatively friendly, not even the destruction of his flagship by a tidal wave in January 1855 interrupting the talks for long. Thus early in the following month he secured a convention of what now seemed to be the standard pattern, with the addition of a frontier agreement dividing the Kurile islands between Japan and Russia at a point between Uruppu and Etorofu.

The treaties signed by Perry, Stirling and Putiatin were quite unacceptable to merchant opinion in Europe, in America and on the China coast. Western governments therefore came under pressure from commercial interests to secure trading rights in Japan on the lines of those already obtained in China, though this proved to be a policy to which all subscribed but few found opportunity to attempt in practice. Until 1856 Britain,

France and Russia were too occupied with the Crimean War to spare resources for much else. Then in October of that year came fresh disputes with China, leading to the so-called Arrow War, which engaged the whole energies of British and French representatives in the area for two years more, especially as the military forces at their disposal were weakened by the need to suppress revolt in India. Russia, meanwhile, was consolidating her position in the north along the Siberian frontier and the Amur River. Hence none of the three Powers was able to give full attention to Japan, with the result that except for occasional warships, whose actions were sometimes threatening but whose objects were never diplomatic, Japanese officials were little troubled by foreign visitors.

This does not mean that they were left entirely in peace. The Dutch minister at Deshima, Donker Curtius, kept Edo fully informed of international developments and did his best to exploit Japanese fears to his own advantage. In August 1856 he warned the Bakufu that Britain planned a mission to Japan and advised conclusion of a commercial treaty with Holland to forestall unpleasantness, remarking as an added inducement that customs duties would be a useful means of increasing government revenue. Early in 1857 he passed on news of the Arrow War, emphasizing that it sprang from Chinese attempts to evade treaty obligations. Japan's policy was just as dangerous, he pointed out, and might well bring a similar result. The logical way to prevent this was to negotiate with Holland.

Similar arguments were used by Townsend Harris, the newly arrived American consul at Shimoda. Brought there in August 1856 by an American warship—the last he was to see for over a year, as he later complained—he established himself ashore after some acrimonious debate with local officials, who at first denied his right to be in Shimoda at all. They then, when this argument was beaten down by reference to the English text of the Perry convention, installed him in a small Buddhist temple and hedged him about with all manner of petty restrictions. For some weeks he was employed largely in getting these removed. Thereafter he turned to discussion of matters arising from Perry's agreement, which led eventually in June 1857 to a further convention, settling such details as use of currency, rights of residence in the open ports and legal jurisdiction over

American citizens in Japan. Well before this, however, he had set in train the first moves towards obtaining a full commercial treaty. In October 1856 he informed the governor of Shimoda that he had a letter from the US President which he must deliver in person at an audience with the Shogun. The occasion, he said, would provide an opportunity for discussing 'an important matter of state'—the nature of which was fairly obvious, since Harris handed over at the same time a Dutch translation of America's treaty with Siam—and would enable him to reveal what he had learnt in Hong Kong about British plans. Harris, in fact, like Curtius, was prepared to threaten the Bakufu with Britain's wrath even before the Arrow War broke out. The news of hostilities came aptly to reinforce his warning.

The Japanese officials with whom decision rested were readier now to look at foreign affairs in realistic terms. Abe Masahiro, though he lacked the resolution needed to impose a consistent policy on Edo's divided councils, had brought a number of able men into the administration and thereby greatly raised the level of discussion. As his own power waned—he resigned as senior minister in November 1855, though he remained a member of the Council of State for two years longer—these new men rallied to his successor, Hotta Masayoshi, who in the early autumn of 1856, as a result of Dutch and American warnings, initiated fresh discussions of foreign policy in anticipation of the arrival of a British envoy.

It was soon obvious that a substantial and influential group favoured permitting trade in some form, either to avert danger or as a means of strengthening Japan. Accordingly, despite the continued opposition of Tokugawa Nariaki, it was decided to make a more thorough investigation of the steps that might be taken. A commission was appointed to do so in November, with Hotta at its head and a membership which included most of those who had had direct dealings with foreigners so far; its proceedings, which were at first desultory, being given new urgency at the beginning of 1857 by reports of the war in China.

On March 19, 1857, the Council ordered all senior officials to submit their advice as to the best course for Japan to follow in the light of renewed British aggression on the mainland. The document made it clear that haste and a new approach were both required. 'Any attempt on our part', it said, 'to cling to tradition, making difficulties over the merest trifles and so eventually provoking the foreigners to anger, would be impolitic in the extreme'.[17] This was reinforced by a memorandum from Hotta, who argued, first, that to have any chance of success a policy must be worked out in advance, not as a result of intimidation during negotiations, and second, that the real issue was no longer whether to permit trade, but how to regulate it. After such a lead it is not surprising that few voices were raised in favour of seclusion. Yet there were still great differences of opinion. One group of officials came down strongly on the side of opening the ports, urging that students and consuls be sent abroad and that Japan's participation in world affairs be generally increased. Another group, slightly more senior, only grudgingly accepted the changing times and regarded innovation as bringing more dangers than it did benefits. Trade was inevitable, they said, not desirable. The Bakufu should therefore go no farther than circumstances made necessary, for fear that the attack on established habits, once begun, might spread from foreign to domestic affairs and put the whole regime in jeopardy: 'to change the superficial structure of a house according to the tastes of the moment will do no great harm to the building, but to change the framework or replace the pillars and foundation-stones is to introduce weaknesses and cause complete collapse'.[18]

Hotta sought to reconcile these differences by sending a representative of each viewpoint, the progressive and the conservative, to discuss with Curtius at Nagasaki in the summer of 1857 the provisions that might be incorporated in a commercial treaty. The move was successful, for by late August a treaty had actually been drafted and formally recommended to the Edo government. It still promised many restrictions on Dutch freedom of action, but it was much more generous than anything previously considered, permitting trade to an unlimited amount at Nagasaki and Hakodate, to be carried on by private merchants under official supervision and on payment of a considerable duty. Curtius found it very satisfactory. For their part, the Japanese investigators, who had never been given power to negotiate, asked that it be concluded as a matter of urgency, pointing out that if a British envoy arrived, as was very likely, it would be essential to have the Dutch agreement ready signed, so that it could be offered him as a model.

For two months, however, the men in Nagasaki waited in vain for a Bakufu reply to their proposals. In the interval they were brought up against the very crisis they had feared, with the difference that it was not a British, but a Russian squadron that put in an appearance. Towards the end of September Putiatin arrived and announced his intention of seeking a new treaty. Talks were delayed for a week or two while he visited China, but when he returned on October 11 there was still no word from Edo and the Japanese officials decided to put into effect the plan they had recommended, namely, to sign the Dutch agreement as a prototype on which all others could be based. This they did on October 16. A week later Putiatin accepted similar terms, with the addition of a promise that another port would be opened instead of Shimoda.

These two treaties, accepted by the Bakufu after they were signed, became at once the basis of its policy. Unhappily they did not please Townsend Harris. As a former merchant he had firm views about conditions of trade and the treaties did not meet them. They were, he said later, 'disgraceful to all parties engaged in making them . . . not worth the paper on which they were written'.[19] They therefore did nothing to divert him from his intention of negotiating on quite different lines. In August he had already been promised that he should go to Edo; and the arrival of an American warship in September, making it possible for him to proceed by sea if all else failed, finally brought the Bakufu to the point of fixing a date. He left Shimoda two months later, travelling in state, and after a week of rehearsal and preparations in Edo had his audience with the Shogun on December 7, an event which cleared the way for diplomatic talks.

On December 12 Harris visited Hotta's residence and lectured him for two hours on world conditions. He repeated much that Curtius had already said, arguing that trade neither could nor ought to be refused, since it was for Japan a means to national wealth and for the countries of the West a right which they would not be denied. Britain, in particular, was ready to use force to secure it as soon as she was free of military commitments in China. It was therefore in Japan's own interest, he urged, to negotiate at once with America, peacefully and on equal terms. A fleet would certainly exact more than an ambassador—especially an ambassador deprived, like himself, of naval backing—and its manner of doing so would humble the Japanese government in the eyes of its people. (This was an argument well calculated to appeal to the susceptibilities of Bakufu officials.) For his own part, Harris concluded, he would be content with three changes in the terms embodied in the Dutch and Russian treaties: appointment of a resident American minister in Edo; trade without official interference; and an increase in the number of open ports.

Hotta decided to consult feudal opinion before taking a final decision on Harris's proposals. On December 16 he accordingly circulated to feudal lords and others a summary of what Harris had said, the replies he received during the following month revealing that most lords were now reconciled to the need for ending seclusion, though they had little idea of a policy to put in its place. Many, it is true, still dwelt hopefully on ways of postponing the inevitable. All the same, the number of those who were prepared to take positive action was slowly growing. The lord of Yanagawa urged the importance of promoting trade, increasing production and carrying out reform at home. So did the able Tokugawa relative, Matsudaira Keiei of Fukui, who wanted Japan to seize the initiative and 'shatter the selfish designs of the brutish foreigners' by building a fleet and annexing nearby territories, as well as encouraging commerce. At home, he wrote, 'the services of capable men must be enlisted from the entire country; peacetime extravagance must be cut down and the military system revised; the evil practices by which the *daimyo* and lesser lords have been impoverished must be discontinued; . . . the daily livelihood of the whole people must be fostered; and schools for the various arts and crafts must be established'.[20] This was innovation with a vengeance, and it is no wonder conservative officials were alarmed. Yet even that arch-conservative, Tokugawa Nariaki, had changed his ground under the pressure of events. He still objected strongly to any plan which would admit foreigners to Edo, but now proposed instead that he should himself be sent abroad as Japan's intermediary for trade—accompanied by lordless samurai, younger sons and others equally expendable!

The views expressed at this time are more important as evidence of a changing climate of opinion than they were for their impact on government decisions. Hotta had already made up his mind before hearing them that neither truculence nor a sulky acceptance of *force majeure* would any longer serve. Japan, he insisted, had to enrich herself by trade. She must rearm, conclude alliances, and generally adopt such foreign ways as would contribute to her national strength. This was much like the argument of Matsudaira Keiei, shorn of the latter's emphasis on reform at home. Moreover, it was supported by an important section of Bakufu officialdom, while those who still hesitated found that Hotta's position as senior minister was enough to tip the scales against them. On January 16, 1858, he summoned Harris to another interview, agreeing in substance to his previous stipulations, except that of opening more ports. It was on this basis that formal negotiations began.

The plenipotentiaries appointed by the Bakufu, knowing that Japanese opinion was divided, were in a difficult position. It was only with reluctance that they accepted Harris's draft, rather than the Dutch treaty, as a starting-point for the discussions, and in the weeks that followed they fought a stubborn rearguard action on its every detail. The number and choice of open ports, rights of travel in the interior, the place of residence for an American minister, all these matters were the subject of long debate. The delay exasperated Harris, who had thought after Hotta's statement that all would be plain sailing. Indeed, he prefaced his account of the proceedings with a sweeping indictment of Japanese diplomacy:

'In this *Journal* I shall confine myself to the main leading facts of actual transactions, omitting the interminable discourses of the Japanese where the same proposition may be repeated a dozen times; nor shall I note their positive refusal of points they subsequently grant, and meant to grant all the while; nor many absurd proposals made by them without the hope, and scarcely the wish, of having them accepted. . . .'[21]

The method, if irritating, was understandable: Japanese diplomats were having to feel their way in territory which was politically dangerous and quite unknown. Nor was the time taken so very great. By February 23 the last doubts were settled and the text of the treaty made ready for signature. What is more, Harris had got his way on all important questions. The American minister was to reside in Edo; trade was to be free of official intervention; and Japan was to open the ports of Nagasaki and Kanagawa in 1859, Niigata in 1860, Hyogo in 1863. This was in addition to Shimoda and Hakodate, already open, while traders were also to be admitted to the cities of Edo in 1862 and Osaka in 1863.

Before this agreement could be signed, however, there came a setback. In the middle of February, when it was clear what its terms would be, Hotta announced them to all feudal lords who were in Edo at the time, only to find that his critics far outnumbered his supporters. Many who had accepted the necessity for something like the Dutch treaty of October 1857 were horrified at the concessions made in this latest document. To others it was confirmation of their worst suspicions. So loud was the chorus of disapproval, in fact, that Hotta decided it would be unwise to take the matter further without doing something to reduce it. Accordingly he arranged with Harris to postpone signature of the treaty, proposing meanwhile to secure imperial sanction for his policy. To do this, his representatives explained, would be a matter of routine—a combination of threats and bribery—but once the emperor's approval was made public it would silence all those who dared to question the senior minister's decision.

In the event this optimism proved ill-founded. Notwithstanding Hotta's readiness to go in person to Kyoto to bring pressure on the Court, the Emperor and the majority of his courtiers continued to favour seclusion. Surprisingly, they were even prepared to insist on it against the Bakufu's advice. The emperor Komei himself objected to the provisions concerning Hyogo and Osaka on the grounds that these places were too near the imperial capital to be opened. He also enjoined the Bakufu to achieve unity in the face of crisis by giving more heed to the opinions of the great lords, a pronouncement which some of the latter had been intriguing busily to obtain for several weeks. It was with these two demands, therefore, that Hotta was faced when he arrived in Kyoto on March 19. After much discussion, during which it transpired that he could count on the support of the Kampaku and one or two other senior officials at the Court, an imperial decree was drafted which did not specifically approve the treaty, but recognized that decisions on foreign policy were the Bakufu's responsibility, a compromise which met Hotta's immediate needs. Even so the decree had to be forced through the imperial council against opposition and did not receive the emperor's sanction until April 27. At this point, Komei let it be known privately that he had been coerced into approving it against his will. The result was uproar, an uproar carefully organized by a small group of anti-foreign and anti-Bakufu nobles, which made it necessary for the draft to be revised and for Hotta to accept what was in effect a command to reconsider his policy. He had still been unable to get it modified when he left Kyoto on May 17.

The Court's treatment of Hotta reflected both a doubt about the Bakufu's capacity for leadership and a suspicion that its power was declining. It was certainly an affront which Edo took very seriously. Almost at once it was decided to appoint a Regent (*Tairo*), as could always be done when danger threatened, and on June 4, 1858, the Shogun announced the appointment of Ii Naosuke, head of the senior *fudai* house, who thereby superseded Hotta as the regime's most powerful official. One result was to give the Bakufu more decisive guidance than it had had for many years. Another, a few weeks later, was to settle the question of the treaty.

It was again events in China which raised this issue, just as Townsend Harris was beginning to despair of further progress. At the end of July he learnt that Britain and France had made a peace settlement with China and were planning to send an expedition to Japan, news which brought him at once to Kanagawa to urge the Japanese representatives to sign his treaty. They referred to Edo for instructions, where a council was hurriedly summoned. Most of its members advised the Regent to authorize signature without further reference to the Court, their argument being, as in the past, that Japan's first need was a model agreement which Britain would be likely to accept. Admitting the force of this, Ii gave the necessary orders and on July 29 the document was signed at last. It was only just in time. Curtius and Putiatin were already on their way and arrived soon after, concluding similar treaties on August 18 and 19 respectively. By then the British squadron, bearing Lord Elgin as plenipotentiary, had also put in an appearance, marking its independence by sweeping past Kanagawa to an anchorage off Edo, where in a mere two days of negotiation Harris's arrangements became the basis of a British treaty, too. It was signed on August 23, leaving only Baron Gros for France, who arrived in September and concluded a satisfactory agreement at the beginning of October.

It remained to regularize the position with the Imperial Court, a task which was eventually entrusted to Manabe Akikatsu, a loyal but not particularly able adherent of the Regent, who left for Kyoto in October. Like Hotta, he soon ran into difficulties. Despite long explanations of the reasons for Bakufu action, he failed for some weeks to change Komei's views and was told in December that the emperor firmly opposed any more extended foreign intercourse than Dutch and Chinese had been traditionally allowed. This brought a stiffer Bakufu response, implying that Edo would not reverse its decisions, whether the emperor approved of them or not. What the emperor could do, by giving his approval, was to make it easier to unite the country in the pursuit of national strength. A memorandum to this effect, accompanied by vague threats directed at the imperial advisers, proved sufficient to bring a compromise, this being embodied in a decree of February 2, 1859, by which the Court promised its 'forbearance' and the Bakufu undertook to prevent somehow the opening of Hyogo and Osaka. More important, both committed themselves publicly to revoking the treaties at some unspecified date: 'we must assuredly keep aloof from foreigners and revert to the sound rule of seclusion as formerly laid down in our national laws'.[22] In this were the seeds of future problems.

Some of these problems, as we shall see, were to arise from incidents concerning foreigners and the implementation of the treaties after 1859. Others had already begun to emerge from the political manoeuvrings within Japan in 1858. For the latter, if superficially a matter of treaty negotiation, had come to involve an implicit challenge to the Bakufu's authority as well.

This came in the first instance from a number of the more powerful feudal lords, motivated partly by rivalry with the

Tokugawa house, partly by a conviction that the quality of Bakufu leadership was inadequate to the tasks it had to perform. Thus the group included Tokugawa Nariaki, suspected by many in Edo of seeking to advance the interests of Mito to the detriment of those of the Shogun's hereditary retainers; Matsudaira Keiei of Fukui, whom we have already quoted as an advocate of new men and new measures in the administration; and two of the *tozama*, Shimazu Nariakira of Satsuma and Yamanouchi Yodo of Tosa, whose families were closely linked with the Tokugawa by marriage and tradition. None of these were revolutionaries, in the sense of men wishing to destroy the regime. None were openly anti-Tokugawa. On the other hand, all were reformers in their own domains, who believed that the Bakufu, too, must do some serious re-thinking if it were to overcome the difficulties it faced in finance and foreign affairs; and all were territorial magnates in their own right, anxious to secure some relaxation of Edo controls on their freedom of action. They accordingly coupled their advocacy of reform with proposals that the Shogun should consult the great lords on questions of policy and reduce the economic burdens he imposed on the domains, a means—ostensibly—of enabling the lords to devote their energies and resources to Japan's defence.

The issue which brought these men actively into politics was not diplomacy, on which they did not agree among themselves, but the succession. By the time Hotta set out for Kyoto in the spring of 1858 the childless Shogun, Iesada, was ailing and expected soon to die, a circumstance that made it urgent to choose his heir. Two candidates were favoured. One was Tokugawa Yoshitomi of Kii, nearest by descent but still only a boy. The other was Hitotsubashi Keiki, one of Tokugawa Nariaki's sons, adopted into the Hitotsubashi house and regarded as a young man of promise. It was urged on his behalf that in times of danger the Shogun must be both adult and able. For this reason he had the backing of his father, the reforming lords, and a number of Bakufu officials, especially among those of middle rank. Yoshitomi's claim was that of blood, which gave him the support of most senior officials and *fudai*, who chose to invoke the principle of heredity, to which they owed their power, and saw in Keiki the instrument of an attack on privilege. This alignment made the succession dispute a conflict of interests as well as a struggle of factions.

Because of its composition the Kii party was better placed to influence Bakufu policy from within. Its opponents sought to do so from without. Many of them had close family or personal connections with nobles at the Imperial Court and they realized, like Hotta, that an imperial pronouncement, though unenforceable without Bakufu consent, would carry immense prestige. They therefore began to intrigue to obtain one in their favour. In addition, Tokugawa Nariaki—though not his colleagues—was working to prevent Hotta from securing the emperor's consent for the American treaty, an end which was accomplished in early May, as we have seen. The effect, however, was to cause a crisis in Edo, which brought the appointment of Ii Naosuke as Regent and through it the failure of the Hitotsubashi faction's plans. Ii decided for Yoshitomi. He forced the Court after prolonged negotiation to give its consent and finally made the decision public at the beginning of August. Ten days later Iesada died and Yoshitomi succeeded him under the name of Iemochi.

For some weeks before this Ii had been taking steps to ensure that his authority would not be challenged. In the middle of June he had begun to remove or demote those officials who had supported Hitotsubashi. On August 2 he dismissed Hotta and another member of the Council, putting on them the blame for the Harris treaty. All were replaced by his own nominees. Then on August 13 he ordered into retirement or house arrest the feudal lords who had opposed his policies in Kyoto and Edo, including Tokugawa Nariaki of Mito and Tokugawa Yoshikatsu of the Owari branch, in addition to Shimazu and Yamanouchi. Many of their retainers were also punished.

One result was to disorganize the Hitotsubashi party while confirming its distrust of Bakufu power. A few years later, when its members again became active, they looked more than ever to the Court, urging what they called *kobu-gattai*, 'Court-Bakufu unity': in essence, a plan to use the emperor's prestige as a weapon to threaten Edo, and the imperial institution as cover for a new relationship between lords and Shogun. In the interval, however, some of the *dramatis personae* changed.

Shimazu Nariakira died in 1858, his place being taken by his brother, Hisamitsu, whose son succeeded to the Satsuma domain. Tokugawa Nariaki died two years later, causing a decline in the influence of Mito, though his son, Hitotsubashi Keiki, emerged as a major participant in events soon after. Matsudaira Keiei and Yamanouchi Yodo continued to play a leading role throughout the 'sixties. They were joined as a rule by Date Muneki of Uwajima, sometimes by Tokugawa Yoshikatsu of Owari and Matsudaira Katamori of Aizu.

A further result of Ii Naosuke's 'purge' was to make him virtually a dictator and—through the feeling of security that this engendered—to restore to Bakufu policy-makers the negative outlook of earlier years. Their prime task became that of preserving the regime. All attempts to take a fresh look at current problems, especially those of foreign affairs, vanished with the men who had negotiated the treaties. Most of them came under Ii's ban. For his own part, it is clear, Ii would have accepted plans for Japan to trade abroad as a means of securing military and financial benefit. Yet he was far from regarding the foreigners' coming as an opportunity for reform at home. Indeed, his whole attitude to admitting foreign trade and traders to Japan was one of suspicion and reserve, a fact which became apparent as soon as the ports were opened in 1859.

Despite this, Ii Naosuke was blamed at the time—and has been praised since—for opening the country. Such a reputation was important, for it brought into being certain political alliances which were to be vital in the next ten years. Because he stood so obviously for the preservation of the Shogun's power, he was opposed by all those who wished to weaken it, whether on behalf of the emperor, the great lords, or other sections of the population. Because he checked reform, he was hated by those who sought it. Finally, because he accepted responsibility for the signing of the treaties, he incurred the hostility both of patriots who objected to the manner of their negotiation and xenophobes who resented their terms. Thus 'honour the emperor', 'expel the barbarian' and 'reform' all became slogans which could be used against him. By association they were therefore anti-Tokugawa.

Increasingly these slogans were being used by samurai of middle, or even lower, rank, many of them brought into politics as agents in the intrigues of their seniors, many more infected by the atmosphere of danger and excitement occasioned by the coming of foreign warships to Japan. In Edo, the schools of gunnery and swordsmanship were agog, their students—young, ambitious, careless both of life and authority—vying with each other to achieve a name as monarchist or anti-foreign zealots. In Kyoto, now made a centre of politics by the disputes over the succession and the treaties, more active radicals found both a refuge and an opportunity. The patronage of Court nobles gave them some kind' of protection. It also held out the prospect of influencing the decisions, first of the Court, then of the Bakufu, something they could hardly have dared to hope a few years earlier. Samurai, especially from the *tozama* domains, began to flock there in considerable numbers.

These men, who abandoned fiefs and families at the risk of loss of rank and even severer punishments, were all critical of the Tokugawa government: of its 'weakness' abroad, of its 'autocracy' at home. They were therefore the material from which a revolutionary movement might be formed. Nevertheless, such a movement cannot be said to have existed in 1858. Few in Kyoto had the qualities to organize it or to carry out a successful *coup d'état*, most of the samurai there being fanatics, sincere but impractical, or mere youths, attracted by the prospects of adventure. They were soon to be joined, to be sure, by members of the rural upper class (village headmen and rich farmers, often with some claim to minor samurai rank), seeking a voice in politics on a larger stage than the local one and on matters of a more than local consequence. Their inclusion raises important questions about the social character of the anti-Bakufu movement as it developed in the next few years.[23] Yet the fact is that most of the activists *behaved* as samurai, whatever their origins; and although assassination or threats of it became common, few thought of them at this stage as the prelude to a concerted seizure of political authority, still less to a radical redistribution of power between different levels in Japanese society.

Among the few activists was Yoshida Shoin, teacher and samurai of Choshu, to whom many of the hotheads turned for inspiration. Born in 1830 and adopted into a family of minor feudal rank, Yoshida travelled widely as a youth and studied under such men as Sakuma Shozan. He also established connections with the Mito scholars. In 1854 he tried to stow away in one of Perry's ships with the intention of studying abroad, but he was caught by Bakufu officials and imprisoned for a time before being sent back to Choshu for punishment. There he was sentenced to house arrest, but allowed to continue teaching, his students including several of Japan's outstanding later leaders. To them he expounded a doctrine of revolution. It was based on the premise that Japan's existing rulers had sacrificed their right to power by the weakness and incompetence they had shown in the face of foreign threats; and that the country's only chance of salvation was therefore a rising of those close to the soil, men untainted by wealth or office, who would find leadership among a resolute minority of the samurai class and unity in their loyalty to the emperor.

In 1858 Yoshida turned from theory to practice, planning to assassinate Manabe, the Bakufu's emissary to Kyoto, as a stimulus to the anti-Tokugawa movement. He was detected, however, brought to trial and executed in the following year, a fate that served considerably to enhance his reputation. Many sought to emulate him in various ways. Some did so—in action —more successfully. Thus on March 24, 1860, a group of samurai, mostly from Mito, cut down Ii Naosuke outside Edo castle, achieving by far the most important political murder of the times and opening a new phase in Japan's political history. For Ii had no successor; and his death not only ended his dictatorship, it also removed the one man who had the ruthlessness to achieve a Bakufu revival. It thereby left the way open for a series of challenges to the Shogun's power which were to become steadily more effective with the years.

CHAPTER V

THE FALL OF THE TOKUGAWA
1860-1868

External relations—disputes with Britain—revival of Hitot-subashi party—Satsuma and Choshu—Meiji Restoration

THE ASSASSINATION of Ii Naosuke left the Tokugawa government without firm leadership at a time when its problems were growing rapidly more serious. Already by 1860 it was becoming clear that neither the treaty negotiations of 1858 nor the Court's half-hearted acceptance of them had solved the questions raised by the coming of Western diplomats and traders. The foreigners for their part soon found that privileges were of little use unless they could be enforced, enforcement being something which the Bakufu tried usually to prevent. On the other hand, their mere presence in the open ports was enough to arouse hostility in Japan. As this grew in vehemence, Edo's new leaders tried to meet the threat by playing off foreign against domestic enemies, a policy which led in the end to their own destruction.

An early move was to build facilities for trade at Yokohama, a fishing village, instead of nearby Kanagawa, as specified by treaty, isolating the foreign community from the main road between Edo and Osaka and making possible greater official control of access to it. Western diplomats accepted the change, but under protest. Yet within a year the newly-built town was handling the bulk of Japan's foreign trade and had become a focal point of the country's foreign relations. By comparison business elsewhere was negligible, though Nagasaki occasionally had a good year, since the domains of Satsuma, Tosa, Hizen and Fukui all traded there. As to commodities, the staple of exports was silk. Silkworm eggs also played a significant, if temporary, role, because French and Italian crops were hit by disease. Tea found a steady market, mostly in America, while in 1862–5 there was a cotton boom, due to world shortages arising from the American civil war. Imports, as one would expect, were mostly manufactured goods. Textiles were in regular demand, but there was a growing emphasis on the purchase of ships, weapons and machinery, which by 1867 had turned Japan's small favourable trading balance into an import surplus.

From the very first, official attitudes towards trade were those of restriction and control. Japanese currency was given an artificial value in terms of the Mexican dollar—the coin in normal use on the China coast—and the amount of it made available to foreigners was severely limited. Attempts were also made to prohibit or restrict the export of certain goods, until Western protests forced relaxation of these controls at the end of 1859. The Bakufu's main recourse, however, was to monopoly. In May 1860 a decree was issued granting monopoly rights in all export consignments of grains, rapeseed oil, wax, dry goods and raw silk to certain Edo wholesalers, through whose hands shipments destined for Yokohama were to pass. Since Yokohama was the main trading port and the monopolists were under Bakufu patronage, this seemed likely to give the government control over all principal items of export, except tea. But in practice the decree proved impossible to enforce. It was widely evaded and for some time was a dead letter, before being revived in November 1863 in support of the Bakufu's efforts to secure the closing of Yokohama, when it was directed against the silk trade, which it cut to negligible proportions for most of the season. The embargo ended only when the powers threatened serious consequences if Edo's commercial policy were not changed and it was not until October 1864, in fact, that the Bakufu bowed at last to the inevitable, abolishing the monopoly and leaving trade to develop in comparative freedom.

Throughout this period, the total value of trade fluctuated widely. Accurate figures are impossible to determine, but exports appear to have reached a total of about 10 million dollars by 1864, almost doubled in the next two years, then dropped back again to about 11 million, while imports rose more steadily to nearly 7 million dollars in 1864 and over 18 million in 1867. This was hardly enough to have any great impact on the Japanese economy, though concentration on a few commodities made the effect seem greater than it was. Thus foreign demand for silk and tea undoubtedly raised prices of those items, despite increasing production, and a short-lived export of gold coins in 1859, which was made profitable by the disparity between world gold: silver ratios and those of Japan, was also an inflationary stimulus.

Yet there were other results of relations with the West which were much more serious in their economic consequences. The Bakufu, it is true, received a revenue from customs duties and profits from monopoly trading, but it has been estimated that in the ten years 1859 to 1868 these came to less than half the increased expenditure on foreign affairs due to higher administrative costs, defence works, and indemnities paid for attacks on Western ships and citizens. The Shimonoseki indemnity alone, as we shall see, was put at 3 million dollars. Since Bakufu financial manipulations had already made the currency fragile, it is not surprising that inflation followed. Rice prices, the most reliable index, rose about 50 per cent in the four years after the opening of the ports. In 1865 and after, with the added effects of civil war, they jumped to three and four times the earlier figure, sometimes more.

Among the worst sufferers were the samurai, especially those living on stipends. To all their other arguments against the treaties, therefore, arising from considerations of policy or from xenophobia, was added that of economic distress, which could, rightly or wrongly, be attributed to the foreigners' coming. This added fuel to the existing fires. The more reckless tried to take vengeance on individual foreigners whom they encountered in or near the treaty ports. 'Often drunk and always insolent', the British minister called such bravos, '. . . the terror of all the unarmed population'.[24] In Yokohama two Russians were killed in August 1859 and a Dutch merchant captain in February 1860, this in addition to attacks on several Chinese and Japanese who were in foreign service. Western envoys began to fear the same treatment in Edo, where their public appearances were often greeted with volleys of abuse or stones; and in January 1861 their fears were realized, for Townsend Harris's secretary was murdered, while in July of the same year came a night attack on the British legation in which two members of the staff were wounded and several marauding samurai were killed. The result was to bring part of Britain's China squadron to Japanese waters. From this time on, as self-appointed champion of the Treaty Powers—and much the largest participant in Japanese trade—Britain began to put greater pressure on the Bakufu to carry out its treaty obligations.

At the same time, however, Edo was under a very different kind of pressure from the Imperial Court. In May 1860, Ii Naosuke's successors had sought to strengthen their position by proposing a marriage alliance between the Shogun and the emperor's sister, Princess Kazunomiya. This was eventually agreed, but the anti-foreign nobles and their samurai supporters managed to get the bargain made conditional. Within ten years, the Bakufu was forced to promise, 'action will certainly be taken either to cancel the treaties by negotiation or to expel the foreigners by force'.[25] This made specific the vague promise offered earlier by Manabe. It also conflicted sharply with the demands being urged by Sir Rutherford Alcock, making it necessary for the Shogun's government to find some gesture which would simultaneously demonstrate its sincerity to the Court and ease its difficulties with Britain.

The method chosen arose from a suggestion made by Townsend Harris. In January 1861, only a week after his secretary's murder, he expressed a willingness to help the Bakufu pacify its enemies at home by agreeing to postpone the dates set for the opening of Edo, Osaka, Hyogo and Niigata, all of which were due to admit foreigners by the beginning of 1863. This idea was readily taken up, it being formally announced in March that a mission would be sent to Europe to secure the consent of the other Treaty Powers. The Bakufu's stated object in this was to gain time to overcome the unrest caused by foreign trade and residence so far, so that when further ports were opened the same problems would not arise again. The British minister, Sir Rutherford Alcock, whose government held the key to the success of any talks, at first found the argument unconvincing. Nor was he made any more co-operative by the attack on his legation in July. Gradually, however, his opposition weakened and he even put a British ship at the embassy's disposal when it left in January 1862, though he was still quite clear at this time that so important a concession could not be made without 'equivalents' on the part of Japan. The last of his objections were then removed by the attempted murder of Ando Nobumasa, senior Councillor of State, in the following month. This convinced Alcock of the reality of the Bakufu's dangers and hence of its honesty in seeking the delay, which led him to support its proposals in London when he went on leave soon after. Alcock's approval, in turn, satisfied Lord Russell, who authorized negotiations. The resulting agreement, signed on June 6, 1862, postponed the opening of the two ports and two cities until January 1, 1868, requiring of Japan only a promise that the treaties would be fully implemented at the ports already open; and the example thus given by Britain was quickly followed by Russia, France and Holland, who agreed to similar concessions later in the year.

Russell and Alcock had acted in the belief that it was to Britain's advantage to support the Bakufu. They argued, first, that it was the duly constituted government, responsible for providing the law and order without which trade was impossible; second, that it was the power in Japan most firmly committed to friendly relations with foreign states. Both assumptions were reasonable in the light of their existing knowledge, but both were soon to be called in question. At the end of June 1862 there was a further attack on the legation in Edo, leading to the death of two men from the British guard. In September came another murder near Yokohama, at a village called Namamugi, when Charles Richardson, a British visitor from Shanghai, was killed by members of a Satsuma force because he failed to give way to the procession which they were guarding. This produced an explosion of anger from the foreign community at Yokohama, but demands that men be landed from the warships in harbour to attack the Satsuma troops were rejected by Lt-Col Neale, *chargé d'affaires* in Alcock's absence, who refused to take a step which might lead to war. All the same, he protested vigorously to Edo and sent home urgently for instructions. Bakufu officials, recognizing the dangers which the situation held, tried to secure the surrender of the murderers from the Satsuma commander, but without success; and when in October the domain sent a formal reply, it said in effect that the escort had acted in accordance with feudal custom and therefore would not be handed over for punishment. This left the Bakufu no choice but to explain to the British *chargé* that it did not have the authority to intervene directly in a *daimyo*'s territories, and could do no more.

These events, especially the Namamugi affair, brought a distinct hardening of British attitudes. In December Russell drew up full instructions concerning the reparations to be demanded: from the Japanese government, a full formal apology and an indemnity of £100,000; from Satsuma, execution of the murderers and an indemnity of £25,000. In case of refusal, he said, the naval squadron was to carry out such measures 'of reprisal or blockade, or both'[26] as seemed appropriate. In other words, London now authorized the use of force on a considerable scale. And by the end of March 1863, when he received these orders, Neale already had it at his disposal. Twelve British warships were assembled at Yokohama when he communicated the terms to Edo as an ultimatum.

Thus only two months after the Japanese mission to Europe arrived back from concluding the London Agreement, the country's foreign relations were again in a state of crisis. It was made more acute by the fact that the Bakufu was simultaneously facing demands at home for the complete expulsion of foreigners from Japan.

The death of Ii Naosuke and the indecision which characterized the actions of those who succeeded him made possible a gradual revival of the Hitotsubashi party in 1861 and 1862. By the summer of the latter year, under the leadership of Shimazu Hisamitsu of Satsuma, it was ready to make another bid for power. Again, as in 1858, it comprised a number of great feudal lords who looked to the Imperial Court for backing. This time, however, they had to be prepared to pay a higher price to get it. For one thing, the influx of radical samurai into Kyoto had continued steadily since 1858 and the connections they had formed with the lower-ranking nobles of the Court gave the latter much greater political pretensions than in the past. These operated especially in the field of foreign affairs, where, as we have seen, Kyoto was now willing to take the initiative in urging policies on Edo. As a further complication, the Choshu domain, long Satsuma's rival, had recently emerged from a period of relative inactivity on the national scene and was seeking, quite independently of the Hitotsubashi group, to turn the disputes between Court and Bakufu to its own advantage. In the process—partly because anti-foreign extremists were numerous among its own samurai—it soon revealed a willingness to encourage the Court in its chauvinist ideas, so that for some months, at least, Satsuma and Choshu seemed to be bidding for imperial favour by vying with each other in an apparent enthusiasm to achieve expulsion.

In June 1862, at the urging of these two domains, the Court decided to send a special envoy to the Shogun's capital. He was given two main tasks. First, he was to demand that Hitotsubashi Keiki and Matsudaira Keiei, Shimazu's allies in Edo, be admitted to high office. Second—and this was at Choshu's suggestion—he was to insist that the Shogun visit Kyoto to discuss expulsion.

At the beginning of August, the first of these objectives was achieved, though only after the Satsuma men in the envoy's bodyguard had openly threatened the lives of Bakufu councillors. Keiki became the Shogun's guardian and Keiei assumed the powers, though not the title, of Regent, while another Tokugawa relative, Matsudaira Katamori of Aizu, was appointed to control of Kyoto. All three then joined in proposing political reforms, despite continued obstruction from Bakufu officialdom. One of their aims, in accordance with the wishes of their *daimyo* colleagues, was to reduce the financial burdens on domains and bring the great lords into the Shogun's counsels. This was partly secured in October, when the system of 'alternate attendance' (*sankin-kotai*) was revised by cutting down the time which feudal lords were required to spend in Edo and dispensing with the system of hostages formerly associated with it. Domain establishments in the city were also to be made smaller and *daimyo* were to have the right of giving 'advice' when they visited Edo castle.

That the mission's results were mostly a success for Shimazu is not surprising, in view of the fact that he provided the envoy's escort, but they were not much to the taste of Choshu or the Kyoto samurai. Moreover, in the absence of the Satsuma forces, the extremists had achieved an unchallenged supremacy over the Imperial Court. So much was this so that on his return to Kyoto at the end of September Shimazu found the situation completely out of hand. Senior Court nobles were helpless before threats of assassination and general turbulence. Everywhere there were inflammatory placards, with brawls between Bakufu guards and samurai bravos a regular occurrence. Nothing short of force to clear the Kyoto streets seemed likely to restore the position; and Shimazu, doubting the loyalty of some of his own followers and anticipating a clash with Britain—it was on his way back from Edo that his men had murdered Richardson at Namamugi—was reluctant to provide it. Instead, he withdrew to Kagoshima, leaving the capital to its own devices. By so doing he enabled a few samurai from Choshu, Satsuma and Tosa, known to each other from the periods they had spent in attendance on their lords at Edo and sharing an outlook derived largely from Yoshida Shoin and the Mito scholars, to establish a temporary control over imperial policy. In November, at their insistence, one of their allies at Court, Sanjo Sanetomi, was appointed the emperor's second envoy to Edo, this time to require immediate action to 'expel the barbarian'.

These continuous demands for expulsion had the effect of bringing disagreement among the *daimyo* leaders of reform. Shimazu was against compromise. He would have preferred to tell the Court that its policy was impracticable and to have used force to eliminate the groups which were putting it forward. On the other hand, he could not give his whole attention to politics because of the Namamugi problem and preferred to remain for the time being in Kagoshima. Matsudaira Keiei, by contrast, was to some extent under the influence of radicals in his own domain. He argued that for the sake of national unity the emperor's orders must be accepted and the treaties cancelled, though he added that diplomatic negotiations should then be reopened on a more equal footing. With this Hitotsubashi Keiki could not agree. Like most Bakufu officials, he accepted the necessity for a limited opening of Japanese ports and held that the Court should be persuaded to change its views. He objected, however, to any suggestion of coercion on the lines Shimazu proposed.

The result of these differences was that Hitotsubashi and Matsudaira, when they went to Kyoto early in 1863 in response to the Court's demands, were at odds with each other and without Shimazu's backing. Once there, moreover, they faced concerted pressure from Court nobles and hostile samurai, acting in the emperor's name, so that when the Choshu domain also threw its weight against them they capitulated with hardly a struggle. Despite protests from Satsuma and Edo, they agreed to set June 25 as the date on which action would begin to 'exclude' the foreigners from Japan. The wording of the document they signed did not make it clear whether this meant expulsion by force or foreign withdrawal by arrangement, but it was formally notified to the domains, together with a warning that coast defences must be ready in case the foreigners attacked.

It soon became evident, nevertheless, that the Shogun's officials had no intention of provoking war if they could help it. At the beginning of June they promised to pay the indemnity which Britain was demanding for the Namamugi murder. Soon after, when the first instalment of the money was handed over, they tried to open negotiations for the closing of the ports. This, it seems, is what Hitotsubashi and the Bakufu had meant by their earlier promise. Even so, it was a great deal more than any foreign representative was likely to concede, as Neale very bluntly told them. It was also far less than Choshu and Kyoto wanted, less, indeed, than they meant to have. On June 25, 1863, the day appointed for Bakufu action, Choshu steamers attacked an American vessel in the Shimonoseki Straits. Early in July, ships and shore batteries also fired on French and Dutch vessels in the same area, inflicting casualties and damage. By the end of that month, in spite of local punitive raids by the French and American naval commanders, it had to be recognized that the Shimonoseki Straits were closed to foreign shipping.

It was not long before fighting spread to Satsuma, though for very different reasons. In August a British squadron entered Kagoshima Bay to complete the second half of Russell's orders about the Namamugi incident, that is, to demand justice and indemnity from the domain responsible. Dissatisfied with the reply the officials gave him, Neale eventually ordered the seizure of three Satsuma steamers to force compliance, but this led to an exchange of gunfire with the batteries ashore which resulted during the next few hours in the destruction of much of Kagoshima and the sinking of the steamers. The British squadron suffered heavy damage and withdrew. Negotiations were subsequently resumed at Yokohama, where the Satsuma envoys at last promised to punish Richardson's murderers, if they could find them, and pay an indemnity (which they then persuaded the Bakufu to provide).

The operations at Kagoshima and the Shimonoseki Straits were hailed by patriots as a victory over both the foreigners and Edo. They also intensified the rivalry between Satsuma and Choshu. Choshu continued to work through Kyoto, where plans had already been announced for forming an imperial army with levies to be provided by the 'loyal' feudal lords. During the summer, moreover, inflamed by success, the samurai radicals had begun to arrange for the emperor to take over in person the command of the expulsion campaign, a direct challenge to the Shogun in his military function. Violence and terrorism reached new heights as the time for this *coup* came nearer.

They were suddenly cut short by Satsuma and Aizu. The one freed from preoccupation with British gunboats, the other alarmed at the threat to Bakufu power, they showed themselves willing to act while Edo merely argued. On September 30, 1863, their troops seized the gates of the emperor's palace and within a few days the whole situation in the capital had changed. Sanjo Sanetomi and several other anti-Tokugawa nobles fled to Choshu for refuge. So did many of the samurai who had been shaping policy. Others escaped to the nearby countryside and raised the standard of revolt, though they were quickly killed or scattered. At Court, the emperor's assumption of military command was 'postponed', the plan for an imperial army was abandoned. Finally, to mark the rapprochement between Court and Bakufu, it was agreed that the Shogun should again visit Kyoto, though this time as a signal of victory, not in acceptance of defeat.

This achievement was in fact Shimazu's doing and he lost

no time in showing that he knew it. In November he arrived in Kyoto at the head of 15,000 men, followed shortly by Matsu-daira Keiei and Hitotsubashi Keiki. At Satsuma's urging, all three, together with Matsudaira of Aizu, Yamanouchi of Tosa and Date of Uwajima, were admitted regularly to discussions in the imperial palace. This was a privilege quite without precedent in recent times. And when Iemochi arrived in February 1864, an imperial letter enjoined him, too, to let them take part in the making of decisions. The document's language was fulsome, its policy Shimazu's, leaving little doubt about his dominance at Court. It was even rumoured that one of his samurai was drafting the emperor's correspondence.

To Bakufu officials this situation was no more welcome than that of the previous year, when the Court had been acting at the bidding of Choshu. What is more, their jealousy and sus-picions were conveyed to Hitotsubashi Keiki, with the result that the Shogun's visit to Kyoto, which had been planned as a means of consolidating a success, ended by provoking instead a quarrel between Satsuma and Edo. The occasion once again was foreign affairs. Shimazu, now more than ever, held that it was necessary to disillusion the emperor about the possibility of national seclusion. Hitotsubashi preferred a compromise, believing that for the Shogun's government to blow hot and cold at the dictates of whoever happened to dominate the Court would soon destroy what little prestige it had. He therefore proposed that Edo should continue to work for the closing of the port of Yokohama, in the hope that this would be a token of its sincerity in meeting the emperor's wishes, without being extreme enough to embroil Japan in foreign war. Shimazu was contemptuous of such shilly-shallying. Hitotsubashi, in turn, waxed indignant at Satsuma presump-tion. The culmination was an emotional scene on March 23, 1864, when the young man subjected Shimazu to a tirade of drunken abuse, which gained him his point, but broke up the *daimyo* coalition.

The various members of the group, except Keiki, withdrew to their own territories soon after, leaving the government to solve its foreign problems without their help. Nor was co-operation between them ever fully restored. Keiki became more and more a spokesman for Bakufu officialdom. Shimazu, by contrast, fell gradually under the influence of the anti-Tokugawa faction among his followers, while Yamanouchi, Date and Matsudaira Keiei shifted rather uneasily between the two. In sum, one might say that a common interest as great lords and a desire for moderation in reform had proved weaker than conflicting family and feudal loyalties, so that the Hitotsubashi party had dissolved at the very moment when it seemed to have victory won. From this point on, the chance of compromise between the opposing forces in Japan was very much less.

As it transpired, the foreign problems to which Edo now had to give attention centred not on the closing of Yokohama, which was brusquely refused, but on Choshu's closing of the Shimonoseki Straits. The Western representatives had waited throughout the winter of 1863-64 for instructions from home about this matter, only to find, when they received them, that the decision was left to themselves. Rutherford Alcock, now back at his post, was glad of it. The time had come, he said, to make an example of Choshu and put an end to anti-foreign demonstrations in Japan. In this his colleagues eventually concurred, so that at the end of May 1864 the French, Dutch, American and British ministers renewed their demands for the opening of the Straits, threatening to take action themselves if Edo failed to do so. The Bakufu, after some delay, again countered with a proposal that Yokohama be closed instead. This was unwise and not at all well received, the ministers beginning at once to make preparations for a joint naval expedition against Choshu.

They had no sooner assembled a squadron than their plans were delayed by new prospects of a settlement. In July two Choshu samurai, Ito Hirobumi and Inoue Kaoru, who had previously been smuggled out of Japan to study in London, arrived in Yokohama with an offer to mediate. Their efforts were unsuccessful, but took up a good deal of time. Then in August, just as the ships were ready to leave, a Japanese diplomatic mission returned from Paris, where it had been sent earlier in the year in the hope of repeating the London success of 1862. Since it had signed a convention in June—without authority to do so—which provided for the Bakufu to open the Straits, if necessary with naval help from France, matters were again held up while awaiting Edo's reactions. These were prompt in coming. On August 24 the convention was disavowed, the envoys dismissed and punished. A few days later the joint force sailed: seventeen ships (nine British, three French, four Dutch and one American) mounting nearly three hundred guns in all.

On September 5, 1864, after an abortive attempt by Choshu to negotiate, the ships carried out a heavy bombardment of the batteries in the Shimonoseki Straits. During the next two days they landed men to take the emplacements and dismantle their equipment, seizing a number of guns and destroying others. This brought Choshu to terms. By September 14 conditions for a truce were settled, including a promise that navigation would be uninterrupted and an agreement in principle to the payment of an indemnity. Discussions were then transferred to Yokohama and Edo. Here the Bakufu finally accepted responsibility for the costs of the expedition and a convention setting out the arrangements was signed on October 22. It provided for an indemnity of 3 million dollars, payable in six instalments. Instead of paying it, however, Japan was given the option of opening another port to trade, either Shimonoseki itself, or some other place in the Inland Sea. Thus, far from restricting trade, it was obvious that the Treaty Powers had every intention of increasing it—and the Bakufu was left with no illusions about its ability to resist.

After these experiences, indeed, it no longer sought to evade the demands of Western envoys. Convinced at last that the risk of foreign war was greater than that of civil commotion, it preferred to put pressure on the Court rather than to quarrel over treaties. This was made amply clear in the autumn of 1865, when the representatives of the Powers, led by the new British minister, Sir Harry Parkes, made fresh proposals concerning the Shimonoseki indemnity. They were willing, they said, to waive the remaining payments. In return they sought the immediate opening of Hyogo and a public acknowledgment by the emperor that the treaties had his consent, the latter being expected in any case as evidence of Japanese good faith. This was at the beginning of November. The argument was backed by a sizeable squadron anchored off Hyogo and led to a flurry of exchanges between Osaka castle, where the Shogun was in residence, and the Imperial Court. The latter at first refused all concessions and dismissed the two Bakufu ministers who had urged them. At this the Shogun threatened to resign, the ultimate gesture. So armed, Hitotsubashi Keiki and the Councillors of State were able to beat down Kyoto's objections, despite protests from Satsuma, and on November 22 they secured the emperor's formal sanction of the 1858 agreements. This ended expulsion as an official policy. Seven months later, in June 1866, the Bakufu signed a new commercial treaty, reducing import duties to 5 per cent and removing almost all the restrictions on foreign trade.

The events of 1863 and 1864 also contributed to a change of heart among samurai extremists. Some had expressed private doubts about the wisdom of expulsion long before, like Takasugi Shinsaku and Kido Koin of Choshu, for example, who had done so as early as 1862. Similarly, Okubo Toshimichi and Saigo Takamori of Satsuma, though impeccably patriotic, favoured trade relations with the outside world as a means of strengthening Japan. All these men were now becoming powerful in their own domains and capable of influencing general policy. Moreover, their realism was something which the guns of British warships helped to spread. For after the bombardments of Kagoshima and Shimonoseki, although there remained a good deal of anti-foreign sentiment, especially in Kyoto, and attacks on foreigners occasionally took place, more and more of the samurai became convinced that expelling the barbarian was not a practical ambition. 'The irrational extremists', Okubo wrote in 1865, 'have for the most part had their eyes opened; they argue the impossibility of expulsion and even recommend the opening of the country.'[27]

For all this there was no public disavowal of expulsion by the samurai leaders. This was partly because such action would have involved a personal risk—Takasugi at one time had to go into hiding to escape the vengeance of the xenophobes—and partly because anti-foreign sentiments could usefully be exploited in the struggle against the Tokugawa. The slogan 'expel the barbarian' continued to play its part in rallying opposition. So did that of 'honour the emperor', though its significance was fast becoming as amuletic as the other. The Satsuma and Aizu *coup d'état* of September 30, 1863, had demonstrated the impossibility of building a successful revolution round ·Court nobles and ill-organized samurai bands. Too many leaders, too little discipline, a lack of economic resources—despite the sympathy and hospitality of individual merchants—these nullified the advantages of courage and fanaticism when the conspirators found themselves confronting a coherent military force. The lesson was driven home in August 1864. In that month some 2,000 men from Choshu, with allies from other domains, tried to reverse the previous year's decision by seizing control of Kyoto in their turn. They were thrown back after bitter street fighting, in which many of the most famous loyalists lost their lives.

This was the last attempt by lesser samurai to bring down the regime by independent action and its failure brought a change in the nature of the anti-Tokugawa movement. Much of its original leadership had been removed: killed in the fighting, murdered in factional brawls, executed or imprisoned by authority. Those who were left, as well as many of the rank-and-file, were beginning to reconsider their ideas. For one thing, they were a little older, a little more experienced in affairs. For another, it had been made brutally obvious to them that unorganized, scattered violence, undertaken at individual initiative, was no more effective against the Bakufu than it was against the West. Even the substantial, if surreptitious, backing of Choshu, plus a campaign of political terrorism, had produced only short-lived success, which had ended as soon as Satsuma threw in its lot with Edo.

From these facts the more open-minded drew two conclusions: first, that opposition could not be successful unless it had the military and economic support of domain governments; second, that they should therefore concentrate attention on securing control, or at least influence, in those domains—like Choshu, Satsuma and Tosa—where their sympathizers seemed already strong. This led them to accept hereafter the leadership of samurai who instead of escaping to Kyoto or elsewhere had remained at work in official posts. These were usually men of rather more moderate anti-Tokugawa views, co-operation with whom was only possible on a basis of compromise. Yet what was lost because of this in terms of radical objectives was gained in terms of the new relationship which became possible with feudal lords and senior retainers. In substance, the samurai of middle rank who now took over direction of affairs were able to shape a much more formidable combination than any before it, embracing both remnants of the radical loyalist movement and members of the Hitotsubashi party disillusioned by their failure to achieve reform: *daimyo*, officials, Court nobles, renegade samurai, even commoners. The final stage in the story of the Bakufu's fall is that of the formation of this alliance and its harnessing to specific political ends.

Choshu remained for some time the most important centre. Its anti-foreign activities had made it a refuge for all those who had been driven out of Kyoto in 1863-4 or whose political movements in their own domains had been suppressed by conservative lords. In both Fukui and Tosa, for example, the loyalists had been imprisoned or expelled when their friends in Kyoto failed. Survivors made their way to Choshu, where their help in fighting the foreigner was welcome. Often they joined special military units, put under Choshu command. Working with them were units formed by Choshu men themselves, irregulars whose enlistment had been authorized by the domain government in September 1863 in anticipation of foreign attack. Most of them were raised and led by lesser samurai, often with money provided by rich landlords and entrepreneurs of the countryside, and were recruited from rural families on the fringe of the feudal class. Younger sons, lordless samurai and the impoverished comprised much of their total strength. This gave them greater mobility than the usual feudal levy, as well as making for more radical views. Moreover, discipline was strict and the quality of leadership high, since promotion went by ability, not by birth, while a preference for Western-style weapons and training made the whole into a formidable force. Its size is uncertain, but there seem to have been about 150 units, each of anything from 100 to 500 men, the most famous being the Kiheitai, organized by Takasugi Shinsaku, the man who was chiefly responsible for the military efficiency of the irregulars and eventually converted them to political use.

Defeat by the foreigners at Shimonoseki and by Satsuma in Kyoto during August 1864 had discredited the Choshu radicals and brought a temporary reaction, putting power into the hands of the traditionalist samurai of the castle-town. Their immediate task was to save the Mori house from the consequences of its followers' actions, for on August 24, at Bakufu prompting, Choshu had been declared outlaw by the Imperial Court and preparations had then been made for a punitive expedition against it under the command of Tokugawa Yoshikatsu of Owari, who assembled contingents from the Bakufu and great domains at Osaka in November. At this point the new Choshu leaders agreed to negotiate a settlement. In December they admitted their fault and accepted punishment. In January the Bakufu forces were ordered to disband. Before the agreements could be carried out, however, Takasugi Shinsaku and Kido Koin, aided by the irregular units under their command, once again overthrew the so-called pro-Bakufu party within the domain and made the *daimyo* their prisoner. By March 1865, with the help of moderates whose loyalty to Choshu was greater than their respect for Edo, they had formed an administration and were able to dictate policy. Thereafter it was aimed singlemindedly at the destruction of the Tokugawa house.

Satsuma took longer to reach the same conclusion. The first effects of bombardment there had been an intensification of naval and military reform, new educational provision for samurai on Western lines, and the sending of students and envoys to Europe. The domain was even separately represented at the Paris Exposition of 1867, much to the Bakufu's annoyance. All this, however, was no more than an extension of activities which had begun under Shimazu Nariakira before 1858. In politics, change, if slower, proved in the end more drastic. The events of 1864, which had spelt failure for Shimazu Hisamitsu's plans, led to a lessening of his influence in Kagoshima—he was, after all, the *daimyo's* father, not the feudal lord himself—and pressure was brought to bear on him to give greater heed to those samurai of his entourage, especially Saigo Takamori and Okubo Toshimichi, who were known to be sympathetic to the loyalist cause. These two soon became the domain's chief agents in Kyoto and it was not long before they were making policy, as well as carrying it out.

The major question to engage their attention was that of

the Bakufu's relations with Choshu. Saigo had already acted as mediator in the attempts to reach a compromise at the end of 1864, but after the victory of Takasugi and Kido early in the following year it was obvious that Choshu was no longer willing to keep the bargain. Nor, for that matter, were the Bakufu's officials. In May 1865 they announced a second punitive expedition, to be under the Shogun's personal command. Several of the great domains protested, urging the importance of unity in the face of foreign danger and objecting to the cost, which none of them could afford; but Edo was by this time convinced that there was more at stake than a factional quarrel. Failure to assert its authority over Choshu, the Bakufu maintained, would destroy that authority entirely. By the autumn, therefore, it was clear that a trial of strength was not to be avoided.

Meanwhile, Satsuma and Choshu had been gradually overcoming their suspicions of each other with the help of refugees from Tosa. In September, Ito and Inoue, the samurai who had tried last-minute negotiations to save Choshu from bombardment in 1864, were sent to Nagasaki to arrange imports of weapons from a British firm. They were offered the hospitality of the Satsuma agency and a Satsuma ship delivered the consignment. Thereafter Satsuma regularly acted as the channel through which the highly illegal cargoes of armaments reached Choshu, a form of co-operation which did much to counteract the generations of rivalry that had so far kept the two domains apart. It soon gave place to a formal alliance, concluded secretly by Kido and Saigo at Osaka in March 1866. Satsuma agreed to use its influence at Court to restore Choshu to favour. Both bound themselves to overthrow the Tokugawa and restore the emperor to his former dignities. As a result the anti-Tokugawa movement acquired for the first time a solid core of military strength which made it possible to meet the Bakufu on equal terms.

The first evidence of this was given by Choshu. In March 1866 the Bakufu issued an ultimatum setting out the terms on which it would accept Choshu's submission: a reduction of the fief's territory by 100,000 *koku* and the retirement of the *daimyo*, Mori Yoshichika, who was to be succeeded by his grandson. The ultimatum was ignored. Military operations, now inevitable, began in July with attacks launched down the Japan Sea coast, along the Inland Sea from Hiroshima and across the straits from northern Kyushu, but all were held, the one from the north being decisively repulsed. The Bakufu's greater numbers—this despite the refusal of Shimazu and several other lords to send contingents—were matched by Choshu's superior technique, largely the product of Takasugi's training. Within two months Bakufu forces were being driven back on every front. At this point there came news that the Shogun Iemochi had died on September 19, giving pretext for a truce which Edo thankfully accepted.

The death of Iemochi made Hitotsubashi Keiki Shogun, with the unenviable task of saving the Bakufu from the consequences of an outstanding military failure. He turned to administrative reform, this time under foreign guidance. That he could seek such guidance was something new, stemming from the changes induced in Japan's relations with the West as each side came to know more about the other. Britain, for example, brought into direct contact with Satsuma and Choshu by the negotiations which followed bombardment, had learnt something of their outlook, even to the extent of sympathizing with it. Having defeated them, as one British diplomat put it, 'we had come to like and respect them, while a feeling of dislike began to arise in our minds for the Tycoon's people on account of their weakness and double-dealing'.[28] Thus during the fighting between the Bakufu and Choshu in 1866 Britain seemed often to favour the latter. Certainly Parkes and his young interpreters were becoming frequent visitors at the establishments maintained in Edo and Osaka by the anti-Bakufu domains, sometimes to their territories as well. This made them suspect to Bakufu officials.

By contrast, the activities of the French minister, Leon Roches, were more to Edo's taste. He preferred to support the established government, hoping to use its suspicions of Britain as a means of furthering French influence and trade. During 1865 this policy brought him a number of successes: a small shipyard and iron-foundry was built at Yokohama with French help; a school was established there with French teachers; and a major contract was signed for the construction of a dockyard at Yokosuka, work on which began towards the end of the year, though it was still unfinished when Tokugawa rule ended in 1868. Plans were also drawn up for a Franco-Japanese trading company, to deal chiefly in silk under government patronage, though these did not materialize until September 1866. Finally, agreement was reached in November of that year for the dispatch of a French military mission to reform the Shogun's army.

In these circumstances it was natural that Keiki should turn to Roches for advice about reform. In March 1867 the two men had a meeting in Osaka at which Roches put forward proposals for a complete reorganization of the Bakufu on Western lines. The council, he recommended, should be re-modelled in the manner of a cabinet, controlling specialist departments of the army, navy, foreign affairs, finance and so on. Central control should be imposed on the domains and cash levies required from them instead of military service. A regular system of taxation would also be essential. More-over, the government should sponsor new industries, mines and commercial undertakings.

Some of these measures Bakufu officials were inclined to try, though not on the scale envisaged by Roches. Their dealings with the great lords in 1862-3 had left them disillusioned about the pros-pects of maintaining the Shogun's power by a process of political manipulation. Military failure against Choshu had demonstrated that Edo lacked the means for imposing its will by *force majeure*, which was the obvious alternative. In 1866-7, therefore, steps were taken to strengthen control over Tokugawa lands; to improve the quality of administration (by opening the way for promotion of lower-ranking vassals to high office and by introducing a greater degree of specialization of function into the feudal bureaucracy); and to extend the modernization of the Shogun's army (chiefly by equipping it more widely with Western weapons and recruiting peasants as infantrymen, the reforms to be paid for by levying a tax on Tokugawa vassals in place of military service). Much of this fore-shadowed elements in the programme later followed for the country as a whole by the Meiji government. As events were to prove, it came too late to save the Bakufu. Nevertheless, it was a reform that was in prospect alarming to the regime's enemies at home, against whom it was clearly directed. Their fears were confirmed by the events of June 1867, when the great lords and Keiki, now Shogun, again as-sembled in Kyoto for discussions of policy.

There were two matters to be decided: the opening of Hyogo and the 'punishment' of Choshu. About the necessity for the first of these there was no great difference of opinion, though the Court's known reluctance to sanction it would have to be overcome. About the second the lords and the Shogun were sharply divided. Technically, Choshu was still a rebel. The Bakufu, emphasizing this, clung to its demand for a reduction in Choshu territory. The lords, led by Shimazu, argued for a merely formal punishment and refused to consent to the opening of Hyogo unless that concession were agreed. Finally Keiki lost patience and forced the Court to endorse a compromise decision, announcing on June 26 that Hyogo was to be opened on the due date and that 'lenient treatment' would be accorded to Choshu.

This demonstration that the Bakufu could still get its own way at Court was a blow to the hopes of Okubo and Saigo. With the help of the Court noble, Iwakura Tomomi, they had been busy acquiring influence over the young emperor, Meiji, who had succeeded Komei in February. It now seemed that all this work might be wasted unless backed by force. However, the prospect of yet another armed intervention in Kyoto politics spelt danger to the moderates, like Tosa, who recognized that whereas a successful coup would leave power in the hands of Satsuma and Choshu, failure would cement the Bakufu's authority. In either case the uncommitted domains were likely to find themselves excluded from the making of decisions. Tosa therefore began to press for the formation of an imperial council of *daimyo*, presided over by Keiki, seeing this as a solution which would meet the wishes of the leading domains without entirely destroying the prestige of the Tokugawa. In October 1867, The Tosa *daimyo* and his chief adviser, Goto Shojiro, urged Keiki to resign in order to make such a council possible. Since this conformed well enough with his personal inclinations—and at the very least might postpone civil war until its reforms had made the Bakufu stronger—Keiki agreed. He submitted his resignation on November 9.

Implicitly, only the office of Shogun was at stake, not the Tokugawa lands and strongholds; but Satsuma and Choshu, though agreeable to the idea of a *daimyo* council, would not accept Keiki as its president nor his retention of the Shogun's vast estates. To do so, they held, would give him a decisive advantage in later disputes. Indeed, even before Keiki's offer to resign they had obtained in secret an imperial letter which pardoned Choshu and approved the use of force against the Tokugawa. They had also brought Satsuma troops into the capital in substantial numbers. Resolved now not to turn aside or compromise, Okubo and Saigo told Goto on December 28 of their determination to act within the next few days. On the 29th Iwakura gave the news to representatives of Owari, Tosa, Fukui and Hiroshima. Recognizing that there was nothing they could do to prevent an attempted *coup d'état*—and conscious that joining it was less dangerous than letting it succeed without them—the four domains promised their help, playing a minor supporting role when five days later the much-canvassed plot was carried out. On the morning of January 3, 1868, troops under the command of Saigo Takamori seized the palace gates. A council was summoned, from which known opponents were excluded, and a decree was approved stripping Keiki of his lands and office. A decision was also taken to return formally to the emperor the responsibility for administration. It was this which gave the event its name: the Meiji Restoration, the restoration of power to the emperor Meiji.

To many contemporaries it seemed no more than another palace revolution, a seizure of power by one feudal group, overcoming another. But time was to show that it was much more than this. Since the victors had openly condemned the Shogun for his failure to solve the problem of Japan's relations with the West, they were left with the task, if they were to keep their new authority, of finding a better solution of their own. Indeed, they had already formulated a slogan to express it: *fukoku-kyohei*, 'enrich the country, strengthen the army', a traditional concept, now refurbished so as to comprise the development of commerce and the adoption of Western military techniques. They had acted on it, as far as they could, in their own domains. Putting it into effect in the country as a whole—though few foresaw this in 1868—was to involve a substantial reshaping of political and economic institutions.

CHAPTER VI

NEW MEN AND NEW METHODS
1868-1873

Organization of new administrative machine—the Meiji oligarchy—abolition of feudal domains—land tax reform—centralization—the Iwakura mission

THE DECISIONS taken on January 3, 1868, after Satsuma and its allies had seized control of the imperial palace were not immediately made public. Nor did the emperor's new champions possess means of carrying them out. It was all very well to inform the Shogun that he was stripped of his lands and office, but none knew whether he would accept the decree or whether, if he rejected it, he could be made to submit by force. Accordingly, the next three weeks were a time of rumour and speculation, when only an inner circle of Court and Bakufu officials had any idea of what was going on. Choshu, pardoned by the Court, moved troops to Kyoto, which greatly strengthened the hand of the conspirators, while the Shogun, Keiki, withdrew to Osaka, where he had a substantial body of men at his command. Despite this he gave the impression of having abandoned all attempts to control the situation, though his chief supporters, the lords of Aizu and Kuwana, clearly wanted him to fight. Meanwhile Owari and Fukui, both of whom were Tokugawa relatives, were working to bring about a compromise, proposing that Keiki should surrender only his Court titles and such part of his lands as would provide the emperor with an adequate revenue. Keiki agreed. However, he reckoned without the growing hostility between Satsuma and Aizu. On January 26, apparently without the Shogun's authority, Aizu and Kuwana troops marched on Kyoto. Next day outside the city they clashed with those of Satsuma and Choshu. The latter, though heavily outnumbered, drove them back on Osaka, whence Keiki fled to Edo, and with this as pretext the Court was persuaded to proclaim him rebel. Japan again faced civil war, this time with the roles of Edo and Choshu reversed.

In practice the worst was avoided. During the weeks that followed the imperial forces moved steadily eastward, but there was little fighting. Most *daimyo* along the route submitted even before the advance-guard reached them. Eventually Keiki reasserted his authority over his own advisers to the point of forbidding resistance, with the result that Edo was occupied early in April and formal surrender terms were negotiated soon after. They were comparatively generous. Keiki himself was to go into retirement, but his successor as head of the Tokugawa house was to retain lands of 700,000 *koku*— about the same as Satsuma, nearly twice as much as Choshu— and this, together with the promise of pardon to all Tokugawa vassals who swore allegiance to the new government, prevented hostilities on a national scale. Aizu rejected the settlement, resisting stubbornly for another six months in the mountains round Wakamatsu, but when its lord yielded with his castle and its garrison at the beginning of November, the whole of the north surrendered too. Thereafter, the only Tokugawa adherents still at liberty were a few who had escaped to Hokkaido by sea. They managed to hold out till June of the following year.

The relative ease with which the Bakufu was overcome was a great relief to the Satsuma and Choshu leaders, whose position had at first been exceedingly precarious. Though they had the enormous advantage of control over the emperor's person, many senior Court nobles were against them and had to be dismissed, while most of the great lords remained watchful rather than friendly. Even the domains which belonged to the victorious coalition had different interests and different viewpoints, so that there was always a danger of disruption. Certainly they were not capable of giving unified direction. Nor was the Court, for it had prestige without power: no lands, no revenue, no military force of its own, no officials outside the immediate area of the capital. Decrees issued in the emperor's name could be enforced only where the imperial army happened to be fighting—an army which comprised contingents from several domains, each under its own commander. Over much of the country, in fact, enforcement was at the pleasure of the individual feudal lord. Since the Bakufu's administration had come to a standstill as well, it is fair to say that in the first few weeks of 1868 Japan had no central government at all.

One solution might have been to found a new line of Shogun, as many contemporaries thought would happen. Yet there were obstacles which made this course unlikely. Neither of the obvious contenders, Satsuma and Choshu, could establish a clear superiority over the other, while both were cordially disliked by a majority. Moreover, the position of the two *daimyo* within their own domains was not such as to allow a personal rule of the traditional kind, still less its extension to the country as a whole. This being so, it was necessary to find a new institutional framework to make government effective. Habit, sentiment and the fact of Bakufu resistance combined to ensure that it should centre on the Imperial Court. Beyond this, all remained to be decided: the name and nature of political institutions, the men who should control them, the policies they would carry out. Decision of these matters was to be the main strand of Japanese history for the next five years.

The process began with an attempt to maintain as wide as possible an alliance against the Tokugawa. If the civil war were to be successfully prosecuted, the government had to make room for all the elements which had contributed to the Bakufu's downfall, or at least as many of them as qualified by status: Court nobles, great lords, samurai officials of the domains, even representatives of the radical movement. This was reflected in the early stages of constitution-making and appointment. On January 3, 1868, an imperial council took the first step by appointing new Court advisers to replace those who had been dismissed. At the head of the regime was an imperial prince, a choice which resolved conflicting claims among the active participants in the *coup d'état*. He was given as deputies two Court nobles who had played a distinguished part in anti-Tokugawa politics, Sanjo Sanetomi and Iwakura Tomomi. Three other nobles were rewarded for similar services by appointment as senior councillors (*Gijo*), being joined as such by two more imperial princes and the five feudal lords whose troops were manning the palace gates, those of Satsuma, Tosa, Hiroshima, Owari and Fukui. As junior councillors (*Sanyo*) were several more Court nobles of minor rank and three samurai from each of the same five domains, Choshu being added to their number later. In February the pattern was extended by the creation of administrative departments. At their head were *Gijo*, with *Sanyo* as their deputies or assistants, the latter being responsible in each case for the actual work of the department. This change made necessary an increase in the number of councillors, as also did the accession to the alliance of domains like Uwajima, Kumamoto and Tottori, so that by the beginning of June over one hundred *Sanyo* had been appointed. Since their duties were ill-defined and there was virtually no machinery to carry them out, this was clearly a move designed to influence opinion.

Two other devices were also designed to serve this end. The first, which was announced in March, was the summoning of delegates from all the domains to act as a consultative assembly. This proved a useful means of gauging feudal opinion and rallying support. The second, known as the Charter Oath of April 6, 1868, was a public statement in the emperor's name of the government's intentions, which promised that policy would be formulated only after wide consultation and that 'base customs of former times shall be abolished'.[29] The implication was that the old exclusiveness of Bakufu rule was not to be repeated, nor a new Bakufu established. This was to reassure those who were suspicious of Satsuma and Choshu. It was also to provide a basis for reconciliation with the defeated Tokugawa and the trained officials in their service, whose help was urgently needed if the national administration were to operate smoothly.

Once Edo had surrendered there was less need to maintain an appearance of universal support for the new regime, even though fighting still continued in the north. Moreover, the prospect of acquiring the bulk of the Tokugawa lands meant that Kyoto would shortly have something to govern, making it desirable that the administration contained fewer nonentities in high office. In June 1868, therefore, came a major reorganization. It was designed ostensibly to put into effect the principles of the Charter Oath; and in its enunciation of a separation of powers—nullified in practice by an interlocking of both men and functions between legislature, executive and judiciary —it gave evidence that study was already being made of Western constitutions. Its most important feature, however, was the re-distribution of posts. This was especially marked at the level of junior councillor and vice-minister of department, where there was a sharp reduction in total numbers, effected by cutting the representation of Court nobles (to three from over forty) and excluding many of the domains. The nineteen samurai nominated in the fourteen months for which the system lasted came from only seven territories: Satsuma, Choshu, Tosa, Hizen, Hiroshima, Fukui and Kumamoto. Two-thirds of them were men of middling rank and nearly all had held office in domain governments.

This tendency towards concentration of power in fewer hands increased as the controlling group gained confidence and strength. In August 1869, when all the fighting was over, the administration was again revised, taking this time the shape which it was to retain until the introduction of a Western-style cabinet sixteen years later. The Executive Council (*Dajokan*) became clearly the strongest arm of government. At its head was Sanjo, supported by a number of advisers of varying rank who together supervised the six executive departments: Civil Affairs (reorganized as Home Affairs in November 1873), Finance, War (divided into Army and Navy separately at the beginning of 1872), Justice, Imperial Household and Foreign Affairs. The high-ranking dignitaries who were ministers of these departments were all, except in the Imperial Household department, given samurai assistants. Moreover, only samurai were appointed to the key position of councillor (*Sangi*) to the Executive Council. A few Court nobles—Sanjo, Iwakura and perhaps half a dozen more—still held offices of some consequence. Two former *daimyo*, Date Muneki of Uwajima and Nabeshima Naomasa of Hizen, retained official standing, the first for almost two years, the second for a little less. But for the most part authority now passed into the hands of a small group of samurai from Satsuma, Choshu, Tosa and Hizen, other domains being excluded from all but subordinate posts. Even the consultative assembly of samurai, though it continued in a modified form, was allowed to fall into disuse. Its discussions were adjourned in October 1870 and it never met again, sure sign that the government no longer felt the need to win friends in the country at large.

From this time on, each crisis successfully weathered meant a more open assumption of power by the inner group. In the summer of 1871, when the old domains were abolished (*see below*), samurai took over as heads of two vital departments, Finance and Foreign Affairs. In October 1873, after a dispute over priorities which split the councillors into two hostile factions, the victors took direct responsibility for the formulation, as well as the execution, of government policy. Figureheads were no longer needed. Appearance and reality were one. In other words, the men who had first learnt to manipulate their own feudal lords, then their emperor and his courtiers, had at last achieved a position in which they could dispense with camouflage and avow their power. The 'Meiji oligarchy' was taking shape, with samurai from the south and west as its leading figures.

The senior member of the group was in fact a Court noble, Iwakura Tomomi (1825-83). Shrewd and capable, exercising great personal influence over the emperor and the Court, he served first as councillor, briefly as Foreign Minister in the autumn of 1871, then as senior minister until his death in 1883. Of the samurai, Saigo Takamori (1828-77), who had commanded the Satsuma troops in the civil war and negotiated the Tokugawa surrender, was at once the most popular and most contradictory. Acclaimed as champion and exemplar of the samurai class, he tried after 1868 to hold aloof from politics, only to find himself, because of his reputation and sense of duty, involved in every crisis. A conservative become revolutionary against his will, he ended as a rebel under arms. In sharp contrast was his boyhood friend, Okubo Toshimichi (1830-78). Okubo was by nature a politician, a ruthless and clear-sighted one, with an instinct for governing. In 1871 he became Minister of Finance and from November 1873, as Home Minister, emerged as the administration's strongest personality. He was responsible more than any other for the fact that its critics, including Saigo, were unable to divert it from its chosen course, a role which eventually cost him his life at the hands of former samurai. Less incisive, but more flexible and open to new ideas, was Kido Koin (1833–77). The premature death of Takasugi Shinsaku in the spring of 1867 had left Kido almost unchallenged in his control of Choshu politics and hence the domain's chief representative in the central government. There he became an advocate of radical change, especially in political institutions, arguing persistently and often successfully against the more traditional outlook of the majority of his colleagues.

For all their differences of temperament, these four men had much in common. They were of the same generation and in origin of similar social standing. Iwakura, as a Court noble, was in theory vastly above the other three, but he came from the middle levels of his own class, just as they did from theirs. Saigo, Okubo and Kido were from families of full samurai rank, though with little pretension to wealth. They were respectable enough to qualify for office even under the old regime, but had had to win promotion in the only way open to them in a society where status and authority were closely linked, through the household or entourage of their feudal lords. Iwakura had broken through barriers at Court in much the same manner by using the emperor's personal favour. Their colleagues, too, were men very like themselves, able but relatively junior members of the feudal ruling class, who were increasingly chosen for appointment by criteria of efficiency and experience. Those whose only claim to consideration rested on radical views and a record of anti-Tokugawa violence found honours easier to come by than responsibility, while some who had served the Bakufu found even this no disability once a year or two had passed and wounds were healed. Katsu Awa (1823–99) is a good example. A samurai of modest rank, formerly serving Edo as a naval expert, he was the only councillor appointed between 1869 and 1885 who did not come from one of the four paramount domains.

Within these domains there was emerging also a slightly younger generation, already important and destined to survive into the twentieth century. From Satsuma there was Matsukata Masayoshi (1837–1924), a man of semi-samurai descent, who was to become Finance Minister in 1881 and to hold that office for over fifteen years. From Tosa came Itagaki Taisuke (1837–

1919), a loyalist, military expert and eventually political party leader. Okuma Shigenobu (1838–1922) was from Hizen, where he had studied both Dutch and English before the Restoration, as well as supervising the fief's foreign trade. In 1869 he was made deputy in the two departments of Finance and Civil Affairs, Minister of Finance from 1873 to 1880, later party politician, founder of Waseda University, Foreign Minister. Two Choshu men, both of whom were of something less than full samurai rank by birth, achieved even greater fame. Yamagata Aritomo (1838–1922) was soldier more than politician, at least until his middle years. Ito Hirobumi (1841–1909) was, like Okuma, a modernizer with more than average knowledge of the West, having studied in London during 1863–4, in America during 1870–1. The training stood him in good stead when he was Minister of Public Works from 1873 to 1881. Thereafter, with the help of Iwakura, he succeeded Okubo as the government's outstanding leader, to be succeeded in his turn by Yamagata when the century ended.

It is true that these men were younger than Kido, Saigo, Okubo and Iwakura, as were six or seven others of similar background who served with them in the cabinets of 1885 and after. Yet they were old enough to have shared in the political struggles of 1860–68, as well as to have experienced the life of Edo, Kyoto and castle-town under the Tokugawa. This created a certain community of outlook which persisted despite quarrels and factional strife. For forty years after the Restoration, Japanese policy was determined by men from only four domains, forming a group which was homogeneous in age, social origin and political experience. This fact was vital to the success of the new government, for it gave a consistency and continuity to its actions which enabled fresh habits to become deep-rooted before another generation rose to challenge them.

Before this oligarchy could be said to rule Japan there had to be an authority it could wield. In 1869 this was yet to be created. The central government still depended on the domains for its military force, on former Tokugawa lands for most of its revenue, on the emperor's prestige for what obedience it could command. In fact, before any major decision could be taken and carried out, Kido, Okubo and Iwakura had to conduct a series of difficult negotiations. They had first to secure the support of Satsuma and Choshu—and the two *daimyo*, to say nothing of their senior retainers, did not always co-operate willingly—then that of the Imperial Court. This done, a combination of exhortation and intrigue would be employed to get the concurrence of the other feudal lords. It was all very complex and unsatisfactory. To samurai who were conscious of their ability and had been brought up in an authoritarian tradition, it seemed far better that the imperial government should possess real power. Moreover, as individuals they had little to lose by transferring their allegiance to it. What they might lose by way of feudal influence and standing would be more than balanced, if they were successful, by the rewards of office in an administration which really governed on a national scale.

Several steps taken during 1868 had indicated a desire to weaken feudal separatism. For example, the Court re-issued in its own name many of the old Bakufu restrictions on the activities of *daimyo*, such as the ban on issuing coinage or forming marriage alliances. It also ordered samurai who accepted office in the central government to sever relations with their original domains. In December came direct intervention, in the form of a decree which specified the titles to be held by senior domain officials, described them as 'subject to the Imperial authority' and ordered feudal lords to choose them from 'the fittest and ablest . . . irrespective of any other considerations'.[30] The implications of this were far-reaching, though the immediate effect was small. Also significant, perhaps, was the fact that confiscated Tokugawa estates were put under imperial officers, not re-distributed by way of reward to loyalists.

To several of the new leaders this was not nearly enough. As Ito put it many years later, 'the whole fabric of the feudal system, which with its obsolete shackles and formalities hindered us at every step . . . had to be uprooted and destroyed'.[31] Kido had advanced this view early in 1868, but it was far too radical for his colleagues and his proposals had been rejected. This did not stop him. In June he returned to Choshu and tried to persuade Mori to set an example, urging him to offer his lands voluntarily to the emperor. The plan aroused much hostility within the domain, but it was eventually adopted, with the proviso that Satsuma must be willing to act in similar fashion. This left Kido to try his arguments once again in Kyoto. In November, Okubo rather guardedly agreed. By February 1869 other Satsuma samurai had been won over, as had Itagaki of Tosa and Okuma of Hizen, and together they overcame the objections of their lords. On March 2 the four domains submitted a joint memorial putting their lands and people at the emperor's disposal.

It has never been quite clear what this document was intended to imply. Superficially, it was an offer to surrender feudal rights entirely, as some obviously meant it to be. On the other hand, its wording was capable of a different interpretation. Whether intentionally or not, references to the desirability of creating a single source of authority could as easily have been a condemnation of Court-Bakufu dualism as a plea for abolishing the autonomy of the feudal lords. Equally, the request that the emperor dispose of feudal territories at will, 'giving what should be given and taking away what should be taken away',[32] has something of the air of seeking confirmation of existing privileges, as was customary when one feudal regime succeeded another. There were certainly a good many who read it in this light, to judge by later reactions. Even within the inner circles of government the enthusiasm of Kido and Ito was by no means universal. Okubo felt that it was too soon for a trial of strength, especially as the samurai assembly gave the proposal no warm welcome. He supported a compromise, the terms of which were agreed after long debate and in July 1869 were at last put into effect. The memorial was accepted and all *daimyo* who had not already done so were ordered to follow the example of Satsuma, Choshu, Tosa and Hizen; but the lands surrendered were not brought under direct imperial control. Instead, the feudal lords were appointed governors in their own domains, with the right of choosing their subordinates. In principle, they became imperial officials. In practice, their position seemed likely to be much what it had been before. Most of them, after all, had inherited titles derived from just such offices as these, which their predecessors had usurped several centuries earlier.

That the government did not mean the change to be one in

name alone was made apparent by orders which were issued shortly after. Domain revenues were re-allocated, part to the former *daimyo*, part to specific administrative expenses, while reports were called for concerning levels of taxation, military force, population and similar matters. Samurai stipends were to be reviewed—many were in fact reduced—and some simplification made of the multitudinous subdivisions in samurai rank. All this accompanied the administrative reorganization of August 1869, which narrowed the basis of recruitment for the central government. The result was widespread criticism from those sections of the feudal class which felt their position threatened. It was of greatest importance, of course, in Satsuma and Choshu, without whose support the regime might easily have collapsed. In both, the feudal lord was hostile, as also was Saigo Takamori, and attempts to win them over early in 1870 failed. It therefore became necessary to postpone any further attack on domain privileges until unity had been restored.

By this time Okubo was convinced of the need to finish what had been begun, but neither he nor Kido wished to act without Saigo, since Saigo held the loyalty of the Satsuma troops. In March 1871, convinced that further delay would be dangerous, they made another effort at reconciliation. Iwakura was appointed special imperial envoy to Satsuma and Choshu. Kido and Okubo took the opportunity of bringing moral pressure to bear on their fellow-clansmen under cover of the ceremonies that this entailed, this time with success, for Saigo returned with them and entered into their plans for the total abolition of the feudal structure. In April they reached agreement with Itagaki of Tosa and in June troops from all three domains began to move into the capital. August 1871 saw the preparations completed. Okubo took over as Minister of Finance; Kido and Saigo became councillors, the other samurai resigning to make way for them; then Itagaki and Okuma joined the council as representatives of Tosa and Hizen. On August 29, having thus ensured control of the administration, the decisive step was taken. The emperor summoned to his presence those feudal lords who were available in the city and announced the abolition of the domains. All land was to become imperial territory, he told them. Local jurisdiction was to cease at once. A month later the domain armies, except those serving under imperial command, were ordered to disband, leaving the central government as the only legal possessor of military force.

This kind of treatment was a far cry from the blandishments which had been lavished on the *daimyo* only a year or two before. All the same, it was not dependent for its success only on the use of threats. A financial inducement was involved as well. Since the summer of 1869 the feudal lords had been receiving as governors one-tenth of the revenue from their domains and this sum was now to become for each of them a private income. It was a generous price for an office which had given more worry than power. The samurai, by contrast, did not fare so well. They were promised that their stipends would continue, but it was to be at the levels introduced as part of an economy drive in the past two years, so that a man who had held 100 *koku* before the Restoration might now receive as little as 60 *koku* or even a good deal less. The exceptions were the loyalists, who had been granted additional stipends, sometimes large ones, for their part in overthrowing the Tokugawa.

In abolishing the domains Kido and Okubo had gambled for high stakes and success marked a new stage in their fortunes. It brought them jurisdiction over the whole of the country's land and population, together with control of all the former revenues of the domains, so that the central government at last possessed the basic requirements for the creation of a modern state. At the same time, it had inherited a number of financial problems. One was the enormous burden imposed by the payment of stipends. Another, the first to be tackled, was the inefficiency in revenue collection which was caused by local differences in tax level and feudal custom.

As a first step to clarifying the tax position it was necessary to settle the question of land ownership. The feudal ban on the transfer or sale of land—which had been in existence, though often evaded, since 1643—was abolished in February 1872 and a start made on issuing certificates of title. By the following year this was well advanced and Okuma Shigenobu, as Vice-Minister of Finance, had worked out the details of a new land-tax system. They were announced on July 28, 1873. All land was to be valued—at its market price if it had recently changed

THE MODERN HISTORY OF JAPAN

hands, at an estimated price if not—and the owner of it was to
pay an annual tax of 3 per cent of its value, which, it was
calculated, would yield on average the same amount as had
been paid in feudal dues. To the government, the advantages
would be considerable: the amount of revenue would be predictable, both because it would no longer vary with the harvests
and because it would be paid in cash; and there would not be
the same sharp differences between place and place. To the owner
and cultivator the system was less attractive, if only because
it left fewer loopholes for evasion. It became, as we shall see,
a major cause of rural unrest.

It was four years before the land-tax regulations of 1873 had
been applied to all arable land and another four years before
their extension to mountain and forest, but once this was done
Japan had been given a modern system of taxation. This was
true, at least, so far as concerned the land, which still provided
far and away the largest part of the country's revenue. During
the same period, moreover, the government had turned its
attention to the samurai stipends. At the end of 1871 samurai
had been given permission to enter farming, commerce and
other occupations, but many had soon found themselves in difficulties for lack of capital. For this reason—avowedly—those
whose stipends were less than 100 *koku* were informed in
December 1873 that they would be allowed to commute them
for cash. Relatively few chose to do so. Accordingly, on
August 5, 1876, what had been optional for some was made
compulsory for all. A scale was published showing the amount
in government bonds which would now be granted instead of
the annual allowance, all being required to accept the transfer.
For the very largest pensions, those of the great lords, bonds
were to be issued equal to five years' purchase, bearing interest
at 5 per cent. For the very smallest it would be fourteen years
at 7 per cent, with a series of gradations in between, stipends
which were only tenable for life being redeemed at half these
rates. The result was to provide former *daimyo* with substantial
capital sums, whereas the poorest samurai received in interest
a good deal less than they could live on; while for its own part
the government achieved the economy it desired, reducing
annual expenditure on this item to about half the cost of the
stipends of 1871. At some loss to their reputation for good

faith, the oligarchs were making their regime not only centralized but solvent.

They were also beginning to make it modern. The process of modernization will be discussed more fully in a later chapter, but it is important to note here that the Meiji leaders were from the start engaged in building a new Japan, not merely a new regime. Their motives stemmed partly from personal ambition, but even more from their views on the international situation. Again and again they had been told about European encroachments elsewhere in Asia. They had seen evidence of aggression, or so they regarded it, in bombardments of the Japanese coastline, events in which several of them had taken part. They had been given visual evidence of the West's superiority in arms and military organization, enough to convince them that Japan could only hold her own by adopting similar methods. They were, in other words, the heirs of Sakuma Shozan, Sato Shinen and Yoshida Shoin. There was the difference, however, that after 1868 such men were able to act, not merely recommend. Especially was this true after the abolition of the domains in 1871, which removed the greatest political obstacle from their path and opened the way for any number of reforms.

Even before this there had been indications that the new order was to be quite unlike the old. In 1868, for example, the government had been transferred to Edo, which was renamed Tokyo, and in November the emperor had taken up residence in the Shogun's former castle. In the following year, after the surrender of domain registers, changes had been made in class nomenclature. Court and feudal nobles were made members of a single peerage (*kazoku*), their retainers became gentry (*shizoku*), the lesser feudal ranks were combined under the label *sotsu*—abolished early in 1872—and the rest of the population became commoners (*heimin*). This did away with the functional groupings so beloved of Tokugawa scholars: the hierarchy of samurai, farmer, artisan and merchant. More important, it made a start on creating the sense of national unity for which the Mito school had pleaded. The attack, after all, was not only on class distinctions, but also on those lines of division which had split Tokugawa society between Court and Bakufu, *tozama* and *fudai*. It led logically to the abolition of the domains in August 1871, with its implied destruction of regional loyalties, or at least of their institutional focus. A month later came three measures which foreshadowed also the end of social status in its traditional forms. Commoners were given permission to intermarry with members of the peerage. Samurai lost the right of *kirisute-gomen*, that is, of using their swords on the lower orders with impunity. Last, and most ominous, they were to be permitted not to wear a sword at all. After this, it was not unduly surprising that in March 1876, when the government felt more confident of its position, a law was issued banning the wearing of swords entirely.

Samurai were also the chief sufferers from attempts to modernize the military establishment. It was obviously unsatisfactory that the imperial army should consist of units placed at the emperor's disposal by the domains, even when the domains were loyal. The arrangement became impossible once the domains had ceased to exist. The chosen substitute was conscription, a concept for which there were classical precedents both in Chinese and Japanese history, though the model now chosen was a Western one, largely worked out by Yamagata after a visit to Europe. The first regulations concerning it were published in January 1871, to come into force the following year, but the abolition of the domains soon made them out of date. In December 1872 a new system was announced, providing that all men reaching the age of twenty might be required to serve three years with the colours and establishing the peacetime force at 36,000 men. The result was to deprive the samurai of their monopoly of arms and military skill, and of the claim to privilege based on it. As the government announcement of the measure said, 'all are now equal in the empire and without distinction in their duty to serve the nation'.[33]

The conscript army was to be a means by which the government could indoctrinate a rising generation in chosen ideas. So was education. It was in September 1872 that plans were announced for a compulsory system of primary schools. Much was also done to modernize Japan's communications, most matters pertaining to this being put under the supervision of a Department of Public Works in December 1870. By that time telegraphs were already in use in the Tokyo-Yokohama region.

In 1871 Japan was linked by cable with Shanghai and Vladivostock. On British advice plans were also drawn up for a
railway to link Tokyo with Kyoto, Osaka and Kobe, the
Tokyo-Yokohama section being completed in September 1872
after a little over two years work. Meanwhile, a government
mail service had been instituted, first between Tokyo and
Osaka in the spring of 1871, then for the whole country in
1872. All these developments helped to increase the authority
and prestige, both national and international, of the central
administration.

Some members of the government entered into the reform
programme with enthusiasm, notably Okuma and Ito in the
departments of Finance and Public Works respectively. Others
accepted it as a necessary ingredient of national strength,
though the details were not always to their taste and some of
the social implications filled conservatives with horror. On
balance, however, one can say that thus far the government's
domestic policies seemed to have adequate support. By contrast, the handling of foreign affairs soon revealed differences
that led directly to a quarrel.

In 1868 Okubo and his colleagues had lost no time in dis-
avowing the expulsion policies with which the anti-Tokugawa
movement had been linked in earlier days. They continued
their association with the British minister, Parkes, who persuaded the foreign envoys to declare neutrality in the civil war;
and they took prompt steps to suppress those of their own
followers who found the change of front too sudden to com-
prehend. Various attacks on foreigners in the first few months
after the Restoration, including an attempt to assassinate
Parkes in March, brought forth all that could be desired by way
of punishment and apologies. For all this, the Meiji leaders
made it clear that in Japanese eyes the existing treaties were
anathema. As soon as political stability had been achieved, they
said, it was intended to revise them. Especially unpopular were
the provisions concerning consular jurisdiction and the limitation of customs dues, the first being detrimental to national
sovereignty, the second to government finance.

An opportunity to act on these ideas did not come until after
the abolition of the domains, but in the autumn of 1871 it was

at last decided to send a diplomatic mission to the United States and Europe to seek revision of the treaties. It was to be impressive in its size and composition, far more so than the embassies which the Bakufu had dispatched in previous years, since Iwakura was to lead it, supported by Okubo, Kido, Ito and a number of other senior officials, while the whole, with students, secretaries and interpreters, amounted to over fifty men. They left Yokohama in December 1871 and were received ceremonially both in San Francisco and in Washington. They were told, however, that talk about treaty revision was still premature. London's attitude was the same when they went there later in 1872 and the lesson was repeated by Bismarck in Berlin during March 1873, leaving no doubt that a variety of reforms, including a complete revision of Japan's legal system, would have to be carried out before the powers would accept a new relationship. Indeed, the envoys had the evidence of their own eyes to show them that Japan had far to go before she would be in a position to negotiate on equal terms. In eighteen months abroad—the first time for Iwakura, Okubo and Kido—they saw much of the West's economic and military progress; and it convinced them that their main task on returning home would be to step up the pace of modernization.

Unhappily, the caretaker government which they had left in Tokyo had meanwhile taken decisions of a very different kind, arising from Japan's relations with Korea. These had been uneasy ever since 1868, for Korea insisted on maintaining a traditional seclusion, which both Japan and China had abandoned, and rejected all overtures from Japan's new government on the grounds that they departed from established ways. Many Japanese were genuinely indignant at this, among them the Foreign Minister, Soejima Taneomi. Others, inspired by the expansionist ideas which had been taught by men like Yoshida Shoin, regarded Korea as a proper field for the growth of Japanese influence. They demanded military action, both to avenge insult and to extend their country's power. What is more, several of the government leaders were willing to back them, though it was for reasons which sprang from domestic rather than from foreign issues. War with Korea, they thought, might distract the advocates of expulsion from the dangerous subject of Japan's relations with the West. It might also serve as an outlet for samurai frustration, while a victorious campaign would provide rewards in land which could do much to relieve samurai distress. At one time such arguments were advanced by Kido. Saigo Takamori also used them, with increasing vehemence as it became obvious that the samurai class was losing its privileged position in Japanese society. He was supported, partly out of conviction, partly out of a desire to weaken the solidarity of Satsuma and Choshu, by Goto and Itagaki of Tosa, Soejima and Eto of Hizen.

Trouble came to a head with the rebuff of another Japanese envoy to Korea while the Iwakura mission was in Europe. Saigo, seeking a solution to personal as well as national problems, offered himself as next to go, in the expectation that he would be killed and so provide an excuse for war. The plan was agreed by the Executive Council in the summer of 1873, but before it could be carried out Iwakura and his colleagues were back from Europe and demanding that the decision be reversed. In October Okubo with some reluctance became their spokesman. He argued, first, that Japan's finances could not stand the strain of war; second, that all the country's energy and resources were needed for the task of reform; and third, that a Japanese–Korean struggle would make it all too easy for the powers to fish in troubled waters, to the evident disadvantage of Japan. Saigo's convictions were unshaken by this, but he could not withstand the pressures that were brought against him. Iwakura secured the emperor's support, Okubo and Kido that of most samurai officials. As a result the Korean expedition was abandoned and it was decided, instead, to concentrate on development at home.

The price was the unity of the ruling group. Saigo, Soejima, Eto, Goto and Itagaki all resigned, followed by many of their juniors, while those remaining in office closed their ranks. Ito, as Minister of Public Works, became a councillor on October 25, the day after Saigo's resignation, and Okuma took over as Minister of Finance. Okubo became the first Minister for Home Affairs in the following month. These three, with Iwakura, became the chief architects of a modernization policy which had for the first time been debated and resolved in general terms. Plans which had been piecemeal were now made coherent and purposeful. They were also based on detailed knowledge.

The Iwakura mission had been accompanied by a number of officials whose task it had been to study Western political, economic and military institutions, with a view to identifying those which could most usefully be transplanted to Japan. Accordingly, while the experience gained on the mission provided the basis for an act of political will on the part of a section of the leadership, the information acquired, which was embodied in extensive reports, furnished the material for Western-style reforms, implemented during the next twenty years.

Nevertheless, neither the policy nor the men who carried it out were to go unchallenged. The divisions which made one part of the leadership so powerful made the other into a new and effective opposition, in which Eto and Saigo turned to force, the rest, more dangerously, to political organization. As a result, the dispute over Korea in 1873 settled the pattern not only of policy, but also of politics, for the best part of a generation.

CHAPTER VII

GOVERNMENT AND POLITICS
1873-1894

The Korean crisis—movement for representative government—Press Law—repression of liberalism—the bureaucracy—the Meiji constitution

---

THE DISPUTE over policy towards Korea, which split the Meiji leadership towards the end of 1873, had far-reaching repercussions on Japanese politics. Several of those who resigned office proved irreconcilable, despite conciliatory gestures from the government, and some had recourse to armed revolt. Eto Shimpei, for example, led an uprising in Hizen early in 1874, though it was easily suppressed. His colleagues from Satsuma and Tosa proved at first more cautious, but they, too, began to organize the discontented samurai in their former feudal territories, a process made all the easier by the moves towards commutation of stipends which soon followed the Korean crisis. In Tosa this brought the formation of political parties and a demand for representative institutions. In Satsuma it led eventually to a major rebellion under the leadership of Saigo Takamori.

Saigo was a romantic figure, almost destined, one might think, to be a leader of lost causes. He was more powerfully built than most Japanese, an excellent swordsman, an enthusiastic hunter and fisherman, a man with all the samurai virtues: courage, generosity, lack of ostentation, a contempt for money. With them went an impatience with routine that made him a poor administrator, a loyalty towards his subordinates that made it easy for them to sway him. He was traditional in outlook, if not always in policy, and was pledged above all to the interests of Satsuma and the samurai class, a fact which brought him inevitably into conflict with men like Okubo and Kido, whose centralizing activities constituted an attack on Satsuma's local independence and whose search for national unity involved the destruction of samurai privilege. The clash of interests became abundantly clear in 1873 and thereafter Saigo held aloof from politics, manifestly disapproving. He devoted his energies instead to the affairs of his home province, where he founded a network of so-called 'private schools', aimed at training samurai in the military skills and providing them with a means of livelihood in what was fast becoming a discouraging environment. As the number of his 'pupils' grew—they were said to have totalled 20,000 in 1877—so did his influence. Before long Satsuma was outside the jurisdiction of the central government in all but name, for it had become an area in which no official appointment could be made without Saigo's tacit approval and no official policy could be implemented if he opposed it. It was a situation that could not be tolerated indefinitely by a government careful of its authority.

In 1876 came three actions that exacerbated the samurai sense of grievance. Early in the year the government concluded a treaty opening Korean ports to trade, a diplomatic victory achieved by methods that had been used on Japan herself only twenty years earlier, but none the less anathema to those for whom negotiation was only of value as providing a pretext for war. At home, in March the samurai lost their right to bear swords, the last surviving symbol of superior status. In August they lost their stipends, compulsorily commuted for cash or bonds at rates which represented a considerable loss of income. The result was an increasing, though local, turbulence. In October a small force of samurai attacked Kumamoto and a month later Maebara Issei led several hundred in revolt in Choshu. Saigo made no move; but Satsuma was clearly restless and the government played for safety by trying to remove stocks of arms and ammunition from Kagoshima, the provincial capital, late in January 1877. The attempt was anticipated by Saigo's followers, who seized the munitions themselves and claimed simultaneously to have uncovered a plot against Saigo's life, supposedly originating with Okubo in Tokyo, and in the ensuing uproar Saigo found his men were out of hand. He was forced to put himself at their head to seek redress by marching on the capital, a decision which on February 20 brought a proclamation declaring him a rebel.

What had been planned as a triumphal march met with unexpected resistance from the garrison at Kumamoto. This confined the rebellion to southern Kyushu and doomed it to failure, for the government was thereby given time to marshal its forces. Even so, it took over 40,000 men—the whole of the standing army and reserves—and some six months of steady campaigning before Saigo was driven back to make his last stand at Kagoshima. The end came in September 1877, when he and his chief followers died there in the face of overwhelming odds. They left behind them a legend which still haunts the city. More important, they had demonstrated that the samurai with his sword was no match for a peasant conscript army trained in Western methods and backed by a modern system of communications.

This proved to be the last of the feudal risings against the Meiji government. It was not, however, the end of samurai opposition. Members of the former feudal class in other areas had not been sufficiently at one with Saigo to rally behind him, but he had many sympathizers among them and they continued to advocate his policies for many years. Especially was this so of his plans for Japanese expansion on the mainland, which were taken up by men who formed the first patriotic societies of the period, some of whom were not averse to using force at home. Indeed, one result of the Satsuma Rebellion was to reinforce the connection which had earlier been established between foreign policy and assassination, ranging from the murder of Ii Naosuke in 1860 to an abortive attempt on Iwakura's life in January 1874. Okubo himself was a victim, killed in May 1878, and intermittent attacks on public figures continued for the following forty years: on Okuma in 1889; on Li Hung-chang in 1895, during the negotiations at Shimonoseki; on Ito in 1909; on Hara, as premier, in 1921. Not all these incidents involved ex-samurai, of course. Yet most were connected in one way or another with organizations that grew originally out of samurai discontent and continued to look back to samurai traditions of violence, both in domestic and in foreign affairs.

Violence was not entirely absent even from party politics, for these, too, owed their origin to samurai, specifically, in the first instance, to groups led by Itagaki Taisuke and Goto Shojiro of Tosa and Soejima Taneomi of Hizen. Like Saigo, they had resigned in 1873; and, like him again, it was not merely because of differences over foreign policy. For them, however, the additional motive was resentment of the monopoly of office by Satsuma and Choshu, not opposition to the process of modernization, so their subsequent actions took a different course. Soon after the Korea dispute they set out to marshal samurai opinion, especially that of Tosa and Hizen, behind demands for a constitution on Western lines. The choice was partly determined by a genuine interest in Western political institutions, which as early as 1868 had led Goto to question an English diplomat concerning the working of the parliamentary system and had prompted several other ex-samurai to write treatises on constitutional government, the role of the executive, and so on. Many Japanese in those early days saw some kind of representative assembly as the solution to the problem of replacing a Tokugawa Shogun by a coalition of domains. Thus when Itagaki, Goto and Soejima petitioned for the creation of an elected legislature early in 1874, they could legitimately claim to be speaking for a considerable segment of informed opinion: in their own words, for 'the samurai and the richer farmers and merchants . . . who produced the leaders of the revolution of 1868'.[34] There was even backing for their ideas among members of the oligarchy still in office.

Nevertheless, it was not the theoretical attractions of parliamentary government that gave the movement its political strength. Rather, it was the continued existence in Japanese society of a variety of discontents. There were many, not only among samurai, to whom change was not always pleasing, from misfits who found that they lacked the ability to achieve in the new order the status which birth had given them in the old, to the simply ignorant who regarded newfangled devices like the telegraph and the railway with a superstitious dread. There were also the disappointed, men who had given their services in the Restoration movement, only to find their interests apparently disregarded by the Meiji rulers. Especially was this so in the countryside. The abolition of feudalism had given a new class of landowners a formal title to their land and a measure of social equality with those who had been their betters, but it had not as yet given them a voice in the running of affairs. The poorer farmers fared even worse, for the change of masters had in no way relieved them of their debts, while the new tax-collector—regular, impersonal, and demanding cash— was often more difficult to deal with than a feudal lord. Land tax, in fact, was a general grievance, affecting the whole village from landlord to tenant farmer. Not only was it as heavy a burden as feudal dues had been, but it was also demonstrably heavier than the taxation levied on industry and commerce.

Many of the aggrieved came to see in the demand for representative institutions, or 'popular rights', as contemporaries called it, a solution to their various ills, so that the movement soon became something much wider than a protest by the samurai of Tosa and Hizen. In its composition and complexity it resembled rather the pre-Restoration loyalist movement, shorn of those who had achieved office in later years. There were even certain similarities of doctrine. The establishment of a constitution was urged as a means of controlling the emperor's advisers, not of limiting the emperor's power, and was justified as necessary for the attainment of unity in the face of foreign threat. There were echoes here of 'honour the emperor and expel the barbarian', betraying the authoritarian and military backgounds of those who were the movement's leaders. As a modern scholar has put it, 'a warrior spirit shone through the liberal garment'.[35]

Such ideas gave the demand for popular rights a certain colouring of respectability, but they did nothing to make it welcome to the Meiji government, at least in so far as ministers saw it as an attack on themselves. On the other hand, the demand was in some respects acceptable to the government for other reasons. Constitutions were respectable in the eyes of the Western powers, on whose attitudes depended the success of Japanese attempts at treaty revision. More, the argument about national unity was cogent and had a powerful advocate in Kido. During his travels abroad in 1872-3 he had been convinced that the creation of an elected assembly would be the best device for gaining widespread support for the government's objectives. Okubo in part agreed with him, though he differed from Kido about the powers which an assembly should be given. The matter was accordingly passed to a committee for detailed study.

Before the report of the committee came up for discussion, some major changes had taken place in the structure of government leadership. Kido had died in May 1877, Saigo and Okubo within the year thereafter, leaving Iwakura as the only survivor of the original senior group. Three younger men now joined him in the inner circle: Okuma Shigenobu of Hizen, Minister of Finance since 1873 and largely responsible for implementing the new taxation system; Ito Hirobumi of Choshu, in charge of Public Works during the same period and hence controlling much of the modernization programme; and Yamagata Aritomo, also of Choshu, chief architect of Japan's new army. It was these three, with Iwakura, who had to settle the matter of the constitution.

During the next two years, Ito, Yamagata and Iwakura reached agreement on a number of propositions. First, they recognized that there was a good deal of criticism in Japan concerning the government's actions. Second, they admitted that the creation of a popular assembly on Western lines would be the most effective means of preventing opposition from becoming dangerous. Third, they showed themselves determined that such an assembly should not be given the power to challenge their own control of policy, not, at least, until several years of training and experiment had provided it with a suitably amenable membership.

Okuma made no contribution to these decisions. He knew, as did the others, that the constitutional movement was rapidly gaining strength in the country, but it was not until March 1881 that he made his own views known. When he did so, it was as a move in his struggle for power with Ito. The two had long been rivals, with Okuma getting rather the better of the early exchanges and securing the more influential posts, but in 1878 Ito had succeeded Okubo in the key office of Home Affairs. With the help of Iwakura and the powerful Choshu faction, he showed every sign of becoming Okubo's successor in something more than name, a prospect that seems to have determined Okuma's subsequent actions. His memorandum of

March 1881 was an attempt to redress the balance by putting himself at the head of the popular rights movement and securing the type of constitution which would give the leader of the elected representatives—in anticipation, himself—real authority. This would involve, he said, party governments and a cabinet responsible to parliament in the English manner, matters far more important than a sterile analysis of forms. Moreover, he demanded early action: framing of a constitution in 1881, an announcement of it in 1882, the first elections in 1883.

Okuma's more conservative colleagues took up this challenge. His proposals were formally rejected in June; and when he responded by associating himself with public criticism of certain supposed scandals concerning the sale of government undertakings in Hokkaido, they decided to oust him from office altogether. This was done in October 1881 with the emperor's consent. Simultaneously, in an attempt to disarm opposition, especially that to be expected from Okuma, they announced that the decision to grant a constitution had been taken in principle and would be implemented in 1890. Meanwhile, the imperial edict warned, 'those who may advocate sudden and violent changes, thus disturbing the peace of Our realm, will fall under Our displeasure'.[36]

There were a good many who were prepared to run this risk. Within a few days, Itagaki and Goto had formed a political organization called the Jiyuto, or Liberal Party.[37] Before long Okuma followed suit with his Progressives, the Kaishinto. Both groups hoped to influence the drafting of the constitution and to prepare for the day when they could take advantage of its provisions. Yet in other respects they were most dissimilar. The Liberals were linked regionally with Tosa, ideologically with French radicalism, and drew most of their support from rural areas. The Progressives, by contrast, looked to the city, English liberalism, and Hizen, their nucleus being a number of disaffected bureaucrats and intelligentsia, backed by wealthy merchants and industrialists. Moderation was their watchword, though this did not save them from persecution. Both parties, in fact, soon found that the government's threats were seriously meant.

Some years before this the government had taken powers to

control or suppress expressions of opinion hostile to itself, especially those that appeared in the rapidly expanding daily press. The first Japanese newspapers, dating from the closing years of Tokugawa rule, had been noted for their lack of editorial comment, but this omission was soon repaired by their successors after 1868. Most, moreover, tended to be anti-government, like the *Mainichi* and Okuma's *Yubin Hochi*. It was partly for this reason, partly because journalistic standards were universally low, that the Press Law was enacted in 1875. It required that owner, editor and printer be registered; that all comment be signed and pen-names prohibited; and that the editor be held responsible for any subversive or slanderous articles published, including any matter that 'reviles existing laws, or confuses the sense of duty of the people to observe them'.[38] Penalties included imprisonment as well as fines and were imposed freely in the next two years. Then in July 1877 the law was revised to give the Home Minister even greater powers. Thereafter he had the right to prohibit or delay publication of any offending paper, a measure of authority that was used extensively to muzzle public discussion of the promised constitution.

In April 1880 the range of controls had been extended to include the activities of political parties and similar organizations. Political meetings were put under police supervision; members of the armed forces, police, teachers and students (whether in public or private schools) were forbidden to attend them; and associations formed for political ends were forbidden to advertise meetings, to solicit membership, and to combine or correspond with similar groups in other parts of the country. This might have seemed sufficiently comprehensive, but more was yet to come. In December 1887 the Peace Preservation Regulations were announced, again strengthening the hand of the police in suppressing secret societies and political associations. They were now authorized to 'exile' from the immediate area of the capital city any person plotting or inciting a disturbance, 'or who is judged to be scheming something detrimental to public tranquillity'[39]; while a few days later the Home Minister was given powers to suspend or prohibit the publication of books, periodicals and newspapers on pretexts that were equally flimsy.

Regulations of this kind were ostensibly of general application, but in practice they were directed against the advocates of parliamentary rule. Arrests, both of editors and politicians, became frequent. The effect was to discourage the faint-hearted and anger the extremists, thereby helping to emphasize differences within the opposition ranks; while the resulting disunity was accentuated by the ban on combination and correspondence, which prevented the political parties from becoming national organizations with centralized control, since they made it necessary for each local group of sympathizers to remain—at least legally—distinct. As a consequence, such groups tended under pressure to go their separate ways, tearing the movement to pieces as they did so.

It was the Jiyuto (Liberal Party) which suffered most severely. As leadership became local rather than national, so the conflict of interest between two of its elements, the landlords and the farmers, became more acute. For the political crisis coincided with the adoption of deflationary financial policies in 1881, which checked the rise in farm prices, especially of rice, and brought much hardship in the countryside, its impact being greatest on those with least reserves, namely, the tenants and poorer owner-cultivators. Friction between them and the relatively wealthy landlords had in any case been growing throughout the century, as the commercialization of agriculture tended more and more to thin the ranks of the middle farmers, enriching a few, impoverishing most; and the process quickened after the reforms in land tenure and land tax during the years 1871-3. In the past, the peasant's ultimate appeal in such a situation had been to force. This, however, was becoming increasingly difficult as the state, now provided with modern police and a conscript army, gained strength. Accordingly, many farmers had found an outlet for their discontent through support for the new political parties, looking to them for redress much as they had done—briefly—to the anti-Tokugawa movement fifteen years before. But this time the government proved stronger than its opponents. When this became apparent, the more desperate turned once more to violence, directed, as it had nearly always been, against the nearest enemy, the village landlord. Riots of this kind became widespread in 1884, the immediate effect being to alarm most landlords, as well as moderate samurai leaders, into with-drawing from the organization in whose name much of this activity was being carried on. This was the final blow, bringing formal dissolution of the Jiyuto in October 1884. Okuma and several of his friends left the Kaishinto soon after.

Thus the government's efforts to weaken its opponents by censorship and police action clearly paid good dividends. They were not, however, its only recourse. Apart from an unsuccessful and short-lived attempt to create a government party, the Teiseito, it also developed a more constructive policy aimed at establishing new political institutions. This was designed partly to consolidate the hold which the ruling group had already secured over the principal organs of the state. Yet it was also a continuation of the progressive centralization of authority which had begun with the abolition of feudalism, training the people, in Ito's words, 'to extend their vision beyond the pale of their village communities, to look upon the affairs of their districts and prefectures as their own, until finally they could interest themselves in the affairs of state and nation as strongly as, or even more strongly than, in the affairs of their own villages'.[40]

It is convenient to look first at the administrative aspects of this process, which had given evidence of the oligarchy's intentions even before Okuma had challenged it in 1881. When the domains were abolished in 1872 they had been re-named prefectures (*ken*), making, with those already formed from the Tokugawa lands, 302 in all, in addition to the three cities (*fu*) of Tokyo, Kyoto and Osaka, which were separate local government areas. At the beginning of 1872 the prefectural boundaries were re-drawn and their total number reduced to 72 (dropping to 45 by 1890). In them, during the next few years, a system of local officialdom was gradually built up, codified in November 1875 by the issue of regulations defining the titles, functions and authority of its members. The range of their activities was wide. It included: supervision of shrines and temples; maintaining schools and public buildings; control of patents and copyright; tax re-assessment after local calamities; reclamation of forest land; riparian and harbour works; the maintenance of roads and bridges; census returns and land registration. Most important of all was the fact that the prefectural governor had control of the police and was therefore responsible for carrying out the various laws against political association.

This system of local administration was tied to the central government through its subordination to the Home Ministry, established in November 1873. In view of the strong tradition of provincial autonomy inherited from feudalism, it was at first necessary to provide specifically for the ministry's right to intervene in local matters, but under Okubo's strong guidance this phase did not last long. By 1876 the prefectural authorities not only looked to Tokyo for appointment, but had also been made subject to a system of rewards and punishments. They thus became part of a national bureaucracy which depended for its power on central, not local, connections and drew its personnel from a variety of sources: former samurai officials of the domains, including those of the Tokugawa; Japanese who despite relatively low birth had acquired special knowledge by travel or study abroad; and some, though they were few as yet, who qualified by possession of commercial and industrial expertise. That most were ex-samurai reflected the limited educational opportunities of the old order as much as it did the prejudices of the new. What is more, despite the assertions of the government's critics, it does not appear that the men of Satsuma and Choshu had any overwhelming advantage, except at the very top. For the majority, the determining factors were ability, experience and loyalty, not geography or inherited status.

Under Ito's influence, bureaucratic practice was reduced to written rule. In December 1880 regulations were issued for the conduct of business in the chief ministries: Foreign Affairs, Home Affairs, Finance, Army, Navy, Education, Public Works, Justice, and Imperial Household. The powers and duties of the minister and his subordinates were defined and those matters listed in which the Council's authority was needed before action could be taken. Nevertheless, this did not prevent the re-appearance of administrative abuses which had been a familiar feature of the Tokugawa period. There were some new ones, too. Lack of a proper budgeting procedure and of a fixed establishment in the lower ranks enabled men to put their friends on the pay-roll, increasing the government's salary bill by 60 per cent between 1873 and 1884 without any commensurate increase in work done. Indeed, the work done seemed to grow less, as government business became submerged in a sea of paper. Insistence on centralized control involved constant appeals from juniors to seniors, bringing delays, a loss of confidence and initiative, a proliferation of memoranda. All these points were made by Ito in a circular to departmental heads in December 1885. He called on them to remedy the faults and re-impose a proper discipline. Two months later came a new set of civil service regulations, designed to close the loopholes he had noted. They created a system of examinations to decide appointments and promotion; prescribed the limits of departmental budgets; laid down with precision the number of posts to be filled; and dealt with a host of details concerning the keeping of archives and accounts, such as the issue of warrants to authorize payment, the use of entry books, the numbering of letters, the circulation and approval of drafts. One may question whether this was the best way of restoring a sense of responsibility to individual members of the government machine. Nevertheless, there is no doubt that it took Japan a step nearer to being a modern state.

So did the other institutional changes of these years, those which involved advisory and policy-making organs. In July 1884 a new peerage was established, providing for five ranks, those of prince, marquis, count, viscount and baron. The new titles were not territorial—a further departure from the feudal pattern—but of the 500 created in the first instance all but about thirty went to families of the old nobility. Sanjo and Iwakura were made princes, the latter posthumously, since he had died in 1883, while Okubo and Kido, also posthumously, were given the rank of marquis. Of more direct importance were the counts, whose numbers included fourteen members of the ruling oligarchy, mostly ex-samurai. Among them were Ito and Yamagata. Of the viscounts, twelve (out of 321) were generals and admirals of the new armed forces. Thus rewards were granted sparingly. Still that very fact made them the more impressive and helped to reconcile the former ruling class to the intrusion of powerful upstarts. It also underlined the dangers of nonconformity. Goto, Itagaki and Okuma had done as much as any to deserve recognition in the early days of the Restoration, but their names were pointedly omitted from the list of honours.

Another step was taken in December 1885, at the same time as Ito's move to reform the civil service. This was the creation of a cabinet on European lines to replace the Executive Council (Dajokan), with its unwieldy mechanism for controlling the administration. Ostensibly this was intended to increase efficiency by making it clear where the responsibility for any major decision rested. In practice it marked the open emergence of Ito to a dominant position, giving him as Premier powers of overall supervision, while the eight ministers who made up his cabinet were each responsible only for their own departments.

Both the peerage and the cabinet were important as preliminaries to the granting of a constitution, the former because it made possible an Upper House with a well-nigh handpicked membership, the latter because it established in advance the principle that ministers were responsible to the Throne, not to an elected legislature. The coping-stone was set on this edifice by the creation of a Privy Council in April 1888. It was to be the highest advisory body of the state, consulted, among other things, on all matters pertaining to the interpretation or revision of a constitution. Since appointments to it were controlled by the existing government and it was forbidden to receive petitions from the public, there was little chance of it succumbing to opposition pressure. In the circumstances it seemed a work of supererogation to provide that 'it shall not interfere with the executive'.[41]

Nothing, in fact, was to be allowed to interfere with the executive, least of all the elected representatives of the people. This had first been made clear in the local assemblies, created for prefectures in 1878 and for towns and cities two years later, in which electoral rights were limited to substantial citizens and business was restricted to debate. Officialdom, in the persons of the local governor and the Home Minister, retained the power to initiate bills, to veto recommendations, and to suspend or dissolve an assembly's sittings, a degree of authority which the government hoped to secure for itself over any national legislature created at a later date. This ambition was made manifest in the outline constitutional provisions which

Ito and Iwakura worked out in the summer of 1881. They were embodied in a memorandum by Iwakura in July and accepted by the inner council in October, thus providing an unpublished but authoritative sketch of what was meant by the promise that the emperor would grant a constitution: a cabinet responsible to the emperor; a bicameral assembly with an elected lower house, but without the right to initiate legislation or, in the last resort, to deny the government money; and an electorate based on a property qualification. Despite Iwakura's death in 1883 this plan was closely followed.

In March 1882 Ito left on a visit to Europe which was to last almost eighteen months. His avowed aim was to study European constitutions with a view to advising the emperor concerning that which was to be issued in Japan, but, as we have seen, he was already fairly sure what it was he wanted. Accordingly, he went straight to Berlin and Vienna, where he expected to find it, and only later paid visits to Paris and London, whose traditions were alien to his purpose. Most of his time was spent studying under men like Rudolph Gneist and Lorenz von Stein, whose views confirmed Ito's existing predilections and were later injected directly into the drafting of the constitution by two German participants, Alfred Mosse and Hermann Roesler. A brief excursion into the theory of parliamentary government under the guidance of Herbert Spencer did little to reduce the predominantly German tone of the expedition.

For some time after his return to Japan Ito was preoccupied with establishing the peerage, cabinet and civil service, so that it was not until 1886 that detailed work was started on the constitution itself. When it was, the discussions were held in secret and under Ito's personal supervision, mostly in the Imperial Household Ministry and at Ito's summer residence. Thus it is not surprising that the pace was leisurely, little affected by the occasional outbursts of popular agitation. Nor is it to be wondered at that the principles observed did not differ fundamentally from those laid down in 1881, since only men of Ito's own choosing had any part in the deliberations. Indeed, the document laid before the Privy Council in May 1888 and promulgated at a short private ceremony within the palace on February 11, 1889, might well be described as little more than an expansion of the points originally made by Iwakura.

Its philosophical basis was Lorenz von Stein's concept of a 'social monarchy' that would arbitrate the competing interests of different groups in society, that is, would personify the general will and remain 'transcendentally' above the class struggle, preventing the exploitation of the weak by the strong and ensuring social harmony. As expounded by Roesler and interpreted to Ito by Inoue Kowashi, some of the social purpose disappeared from this argument; but the emphasis on harmony remained, appealing greatly to men whose object was to strengthen Japan. After all, to them political dissent was seditious, because it weakened the state. Removing it was one step toward achieving national strength. To quote Ito again, 'the onslaught of extremely democratic ideas' had to be resisted because 'in such a country as ours, it was evident that it would be necessary to compensate for its smallness of size and population by a compact solidity of organization.'[42] The constitution would be a means to this end.

Hence many powers were reserved to the emperor, to be exercised in fact by his advisers, including declaration of war, conclusion of treaties and supreme command of the armed services. In addition, the emperor had extensive ordinance rights, while he could freely adjourn or prorogue the assembly, which was to be called the Diet. As regards finance, some important items of regular expenditure were excluded from the Diet's consideration altogether. More significant, it was laid down that should the assembly fail to pass the budget the government was entitled to carry out the budget of the previous year. Thus parliamentary control went no farther than the right to deny new taxes; and though this could be a potent weapon in harassing a cabinet, as the next few years were to show, it did not provide a sufficient means of exercising influence over general policy. What is more, it was by no means certain that the lower house could even control the policies of the Diet. The House of Peers, after all, had equal authority with it and a membership that tended naturally to support the regime. When one adds to this the fact that the initiative for constitutional revision could come only from the emperor, there seemed little chance that the political parties would be able to secure real power.

On the other hand, although the Meiji Constitution imposed serious disabilities on any opposition, it did not follow that these must prove enduring. Other men at other times and places had faced institutional obstacles just as great and had overcome them. It is true that there was bound to be a struggle in Japan between parties which upheld the principles of parliamentary rule and oligarchs who believed in government that was 'transcendental', that is, above sectional interests and therefore above party; but in that struggle, victory would go to the side which was stronger. It was not certain that this would be the side which the constitution favoured. Only when the Diet opened, in fact, would the time of testing begin, to see whether Ito's judgment as a politician equalled his skill as a constitutional draftsman.

As a preliminary, Yamagata Aritomo became Premier in December 1889, supported by Ito, though the latter was not a member of the cabinet. In the following July they carried out the first elections for the lower house. Only about 500,000 electors were qualified to vote (out of a population of forty million), but most of them did so and proceedings were generally orderly. Less successful, from the government's point of view, were the returns. Goto's party gained sixty seats and those of Itagaki and Okuma fifty each, while many of the 140 independents who made up the rest of the representatives were equally hostile to the administration. The result was a clash as soon as the session opened in November, with the Diet demanding heavy cuts in the budget and accepting a compromise only after Yamagata had made extensive use of threats and bribery. In the interval between sessions, Yamagata handed over to Matsukata Masayoshi, famous as Minister of Finance since 1881, but this did nothing to save the next budget. Matsukata was forced to dissolve the Lower House in December 1891 without having got it through.

The elections of February 1892 were notorious for the government's attempt to use the police to dictate the voting, an attempt which left twenty-five dead and nearly 400 injured to mark the campaign. Nor did it in any way reduce the Diet's hostility to the men in office. The session, which started in May, was as stormy as ever and brought Matsukata's resignation, Ito following him as Premier in August, with Yamagata at the Ministry of Justice. They in their turn were faced with a vote of impeachment in February 1893. Ito now tried a new technique: direct imperial intervention on the cabinet's behalf, which worked for the moment, but did not save him from having to seek a dissolution in December. The resulting election was held in March 1894; the session opened in May; and the Lower House was dissolved again at the beginning of June. It began to look as if the constitution was unworkable altogether.

Yet the frequent clashes were slowly tending to the government's advantage. Elections were expensive and their constant repetition cured many politicians of a taste for electioneering. Moreover, party leaders were becoming convinced that the deadlock could not be broken in the Diet's favour. This implied that it might be in their own interests to seek a compromise with those in power; and as ex-oligarchs they would not find it difficult to do so. Goto, indeed, had held a cabinet post for the past three years. Ito, for his part—though over Yamagata's protests—was willing to conclude an alliance with them, in the hope of securing votes for the government in the Lower House without sacrificing its ultimate control of policy. He had actually begun discussions with Itagaki on this basis in 1893 and within a year or two was to consider forming a party of his own. Thus events were moving towards a new phase, one in which the Diet was to become the scene of a struggle, not between parties and government, but between party and party, with office, though not always power, as the prize.

The key to it was to be the role of the senior oligarchs. Having created a constitution which they believed would accord with their plans for modernization, they were committed to making it work, if only for the sake of national prestige. They differed, however, about *how* it should work: Yamagata uncompromisingly 'transcendental', Ito willing to be flexible for the sake of harmony. The rift between them provided the parties with a tactical opportunity to match their new constitutional rights. Exploiting it, they were eventually able to win themselves a larger measure of influence than the drafters of the constitution had envisaged.

CHAPTER VIII

MODERNIZATION 1873-1894

*Reorganization of army and navy—law—national education
system—agricultural development—transport—state factories
—textiles—knowledge of the West*

ON JANUARY 1, 1873, a new calendar was brought into force
in Japan: the Gregorian calendar, as used in western Europe,
which replaced the lunar calendar originally derived from
China. The change affected much that was familiar. Dates
for festivals, the beginning of the four seasons, the New Year
itself, all now fell on different days. The farmer had to learn
new designations for his times of planting and harvesting, the
merchant for his debt-collecting, the priest for his ceremonials.
Even though many preferred to go on using the old system
side by side with the new, the decision had repercussions which
struck deep into Japanese life. Equally, it symbolized an important aspect of the government's policy, its determination to
turn away from the traditional and towards the modern, away
from China and towards the West, at least in those matters on
which the building of a powerful and well respected state
depended. The policy was not entirely new, either in concept
or in method. Nevertheless, the Meiji leaders gave it a breadth
and drive that were to revolutionize society. Indeed, by 1904
they had transformed a backward, largely feudal, Japan into
one which was capable of winning a modern war, an achievement that made them the envy of all Asia.

Some of the foundations for it had been laid before the
Restoration. For several generations Japanese scholars had
been studying the West, especially its military science, and

after Perry's arrival their efforts had received official support. In 1855 the Tokugawa council established a bureau for the translation of foreign books. In the 1860s it regularly sent students abroad to study, attaching them to various diplomatic missions. This was an example which was followed, whenever opportunity offered, by a few of the great domains, though for the latter it was action which had sometimes to be taken illegally and hence in secret. Moreover, natural curiosity soon extended the field of interest to include geography, politics, economics and much else, so that by 1868 Japan had already at her disposal a nucleus of men trained in Western skills. Others had acquired experience at home, running the Western-style plants which had been set up in different areas— the Saga cannon foundry, a cotton-spinning factory at Kagoshima and several more—or learning to navigate and maintain the steamers which their feudal lords had purchased. It was the existence of such men, most of them young, that made modernization possible.

Equally important were the qualities of leadership shown by the Meiji government. Its members, as we have seen, were convinced that their country was in danger of foreign attack, that it could be saved only by strong rule and an efficient military machine. To achieve these quickly was therefore the task to which all other considerations were made subordinate. Ideas of social welfare were never allowed to divert policy from the chosen ends. Opposition that threatened those ends was crushed. It is true that political and personal ambition played a part in this, but it was not a controlling part: the oligarchs, as their record shows, were patriots as well as politicians. And they were capable of a surprising degree of detachment in their patriotism, a ruthlessness in sacrificing the picturesque to the efficient which offended traditionalists at the time and has provoked critics since. It mattered little to Okubo and Iwakura and their like that a foreign observer in 1868 described their troops as 'horribly untidy soldiers'.[43] It mattered much that the soldiers were winning a civil war. A similarly pragmatic outlook was to govern their attitude towards telegraph wires, railway lines and factory chimneys, however much these might be thought to mar the beauty of a Japanese landscape.

Politics came first in the regime's calculations because it was on this that all else depended. Thus the earliest reforms were directed towards increasing the government's authority: the abolition of feudalism, new methods of taxation, even the improved communications which were developed by the Department of Public Works in 1871–3. Other aspects of modernization, too, had a political function. The conscript army, for instance, provided a loyal force capable of quelling unrest at home, as it demonstrated in 1877 with the defeat of Saigo's rebels. It was also used to end the peasant revolts to which Japan had been subject for over a century and it later became a means of indoctrinating a substantial number of young men in their duties to an authoritarian state.

All the same, the army's main role was to defend Japan against a possible enemy attack. Already in the late Tokugawa period feudal rulers had done what they could to prepare for this, with the result that the new government inherited some useful military establishments, a number of gunnery and naval specialists, and a varied knowledge of Western military techniques. There was an arsenal at Osaka and a naval dockyard at Yokosuka. There was a valuable fund of experience gained when the Bakufu, albeit belatedly, had tried to reorganize its army under the tutelage of France; more still derived from the experiments of Satsuma and Choshu, the first in the creation of a naval squadron, the second in arming and training a land force in the European manner. Against this background, it is not surprising that military reform was given high priority in the Meiji government's plans. This was so even in the early days, when preoccupations were political, and its importance increased as the danger of successful insurrection passed. More and more, attention was concentrated on Japan's ability to fight a foreign war.

In 1878 Yamagata carried out a reorganization of army administration on German lines, including the creation of a General Staff, and in the following year increased the period which a conscript had to serve in the reserves. He raised it again in 1883 to make a total of twelve years' service, three of which were with the colours. This provided a peacetime establishment of 73,000 men and a total wartime strength of 200,000 more, the whole force being equipped by 1894 with modern rifles and artillery, mostly of Japanese manufacture. The decade after 1883 also saw the opening of a Staff College;

greater specialization of function (infantry, artillery, engineers, supply); an improvement in training methods; and a sharp rise in the army budget.

The navy shared in the expansion, too, though its growth relied more on foreign help. In 1872 the newly-formed Navy Ministry had possessed seventeen ships, totalling almost 14,000 tons, of which only two were ironclads. Two Japanese-built steamers of moderate size were added in 1875-6, three much larger vessels were bought from England in 1878, and further building or buying programmes were announced in 1882, 1886 and 1892. At the outbreak of war with China in 1894 the fleet included twenty-eight modern ships, aggregating 57,000 tons, plus twenty-four torpedo-boats. Dockyard facilities were by that time sufficient for full repairs and maintenance, while training was thoroughly up-to-date. What is more, Japan was able to make her own torpedoes and quick-firing guns.

All this is evidence of a strong military emphasis in the government's policies, confirmed by the fact that at the end of the period one-third of the national budget was being spent on the army and navy. Military industry was kept under close official control, as were other installations that had a military use, like the telegraph system. Telephones were made a government monopoly when they were introduced for public use in 1890, while the railways, about 30 per cent of which were government-built, were nationalized in 1906 to ensure their proper development for strategic purposes. In other words, one is conscious of military considerations underlying many phases of the modernization process.

Yet modernization was by no means confined to things political and military. It extended also to the law, to education, to the economy and much else, affecting in the end almost every part of Japanese society. Indeed, it is the very comprehensiveness of reform that justifies the application of the label 'modernization' to it. China, after all, also adopted something of the West's military methods in the nineteenth century and learned to use the telegraph and railways, but the Chinese did not thereby achieve a revolution in their way of life. That the Japanese did so was due in large measure to the readiness of their leaders to reform radically and fundamentally in every field. For this they had to be imaginative as well as ruthless.

Some changes stemmed from a desire to achieve respectability in Western eyes, this being a step on the road to full equality. For example, the Iwakura mission had learnt in 1872–3 that neither America nor the European powers would contemplate revising the legal provisions of the existing treaties—those which put foreign residents in Japan exclusively under the jurisdiction of their own consuls—until they were convinced that Japan's judicial practice was up to Western standards; and recognition of this fact brought a complex series of law reforms, largely under foreign guidance, which lasted twenty-five years. They began at the end of 1873 with the appointment of a French lawyer, Gustave Boissonade de Fontarabie, as adviser to the Ministry of Justice. In this capacity he at once set about drafting a criminal code based on elements of Japanese feudal law and the Code Napoléon of 1810, the draft being completed in 1877, reviewed at length by the politicians, then promulgated so as to come into force at the beginning of 1882. His proposals for a civil code, however, had a rougher passage. The first version was rejected in 1878 as being too French and it took a series of committees twelve more years to produce something to the government's satisfaction. Even so, the code's promulgation in 1890 aroused a storm of protest, led by those who had been trained in English law, with the result that the Diet voted to postpone the date of its enforcement. A similar fate overtook most sections of the new commercial code, which had been devised under Hermann Roesler's supervision in the period 1881–90. Both documents were therefore reviewed again and did not receive final approval until 1898–9, when they were submitted in a form which revealed signs of increasing German influence.

Some provisions of the new legal system, such as the abolition of torture, the creation of a trained judiciary and the setting out of rules of evidence and procedure for the courts, were generally admitted to be necessary, but there were many who felt that in matters affecting property and the family the codes had departed too far from Japanese tradition. Much of the political excitement concerning this subject in and after 1890 was due to feelings of this kind. Similar hostility was also aroused from time to time by other results of government sensitivity to foreign views, especially where these were aimed at achieving a degree of social respectability in Western eyes. Often the action taken was thought to be trivial or degrading, like the holding of balls for the diplomatic corps or the use of Western dress at Court. Often it was merely alien and inexplicable. Thus the attempts which were made to prevent mixed bathing in Tokyo's public bathhouses, to establish censorship of stage jokes, to prohibit the sale of pornographic art and in other ways to provide an atmosphere which Victorians might find congenial, met with little sympathy or understanding among large sections of the Japanese public.

There is no doubt that in these social matters Japanese officials were under some pressure from foreign missionaries and other residents. Many foreigners, however, also offered help and advice in fields where it was better received and more effectively carried out. This was notable in education, where much that was new in both content and administration derived from foreign advisers, and much that was taught depended on American and European teachers. Nevertheless, it was the Japanese themselves, in the last resort, who had to make the system work. For their success in doing so, the credit must be shared: by the Meiji government, because of its energy and farsightedness; and by members of the ruling class as a whole, in whom an essentially Confucian training had bred a respect for learning that was reflected, *inter alia*, in an enthusiasm for the founding and running of schools.

The government's plans, as announced in September 1872, envisaged dividing Japan into eight educational regions, in each of which there were to be one university and thirty-two secondary schools. Each secondary school district, in turn, was to include 210 primary schools—one for every 600 of the population—where all children after reaching the age of six were to receive sixteen months of compulsory education. The scheme was ambitious, almost too ambitious for a country that had abolished feudalism only a year before, but progress under it was astonishingly rapid. By 1880 there were 28,000 primary schools with over 2 million pupils (about 40 per cent of the children of school age) and it had become possible to increase the compulsory period to three years. In 1886 attendance was 46 per cent and the period was increased again, by a further year. Thereafter, attendance continued steadily to rise. It was

60 per cent by 1895, 90 per cent by 1900, 95 per cent in 1906. In the same period secondary education was becoming specialized, with the creation of normal schools (1872), middle schools (1881), higher middle schools (1886) and girls high schools (1889). To complete the pyramid, various government institutions of higher education, which had been amalgamated in 1877, were reorganized as Tokyo Imperial University in 1886.

A key part in this development was played by Mori Arinori, a former member of the Iwakura mission, who was Minister of Education from 1885 to 1889. It was his ordinances, issued in the spring of 1886, that gave the system the shape it was to retain for twenty years: an eight-year period of primary schooling, half of it compulsory, involving attendance for five hours a day, six days a week; a middle school course of four years with similar hours; then a range of higher levels, reaching to the newly-created university. He also ensured close government control, thereby confirming a tendency that had existed since 1880. From this time on, the Ministry prescribed all textbooks, while exercising general supervision of the schools through the workings of local government, that is, by its influence with the town and village authorities to whom the details of administration were entrusted. Private foundations were made subject to official licence and inspection. Thus the whole of education was made subservient to the state's own needs, providing on the one hand a practical training, through a curriculum on Western lines, on the other a moral education based on Confucian ethics and an emperor-centred nationalism. Together the two elements were to produce good citizens: good in that they were loyal to the regime; and good in that they had acquired the basic skills which modern life demanded.

In the twentieth century this education system was to prove an essential unifying force in the Japanese body politic. It was also fundamental to the full development of an industrial society. But in the earlier stages of economic growth education was less crucial than those features of government policy that were directly designed to stimulate the increase of national wealth. It is to this aspect of Meiji history—a new and more sophisticated application of the slogan *fukoku-kyohei*, 'rich country, strong army'—that Japan owed most of her initial success.

Economic modernization began, not with the factory, but with the farm. To men who had begun life as feudal retainers, it was axiomatic that land was the chief source of government revenue and that the encouragement of production on it was the first task of an official. The difference was that they could now draw on the experience and technology of the West, as well as of Japan. They lost no time in doing so. Agricultural students were sent abroad; foreign experts were invited to advise on specific projects, such as the opening up of land in the island of Hokkaido; new strains of plants and seeds were imported; Western farming implements were bought and tried. All this was done on government initiative, sometimes with more fervour than understanding. Attempts to plant vineyards and introduce sheep-farming, for example, were among the early failures. By contrast, the innovations in irrigation and the use of fertilizers proved generally successful, while the greatest advances of all in the long term were achieved by the founding of experimental stations and agricultural colleges. The most famous of them were established in Hokkaido in 1876 and in Tokyo in 1877, but others soon appeared throughout the country. The results of their work, moreover, were made widely available by travelling instructors, appointed to advise farmers on new techniques (both Japanese and foreign).

In some ways agriculture was little changed by these developments. Plots remained small—just over an acre was a typical holding—and cultivation remained intensive, for these things were part of the fundamental pattern: Japan's villages had little land, much labour, and grew rice as their staple crop. On the other hand, the commercialization of agriculture, which had begun under the Tokugawa, increased with the removal of feudal controls, thereby bringing still greater concentration in landholding and a steady growth of tenancy. About 40 per cent of the land was held by tenants in 1890, compared with an estimated 20 per cent at the time of the Restoration; and since rents were high and paid in kind, half the crop being a not uncommon rent for rice paddy, the change brought much distress in rural areas. All the same, it cannot be claimed that the village as a whole suffered a decline in standards. Total rice yield grew over 30 per cent between 1880 and 1894, partly because the area under cultivation was enlarged, but mostly because new farming methods gave a 20 per cent increase in yield per acre. Lesser crops, like wheat and barley, showed a similar improvement. As a consequence, agricultural production not only kept pace with a considerable growth in population, but also made possible an increase in *per capita* rice consumption, which rose in the same period from four bushels a year to five. This was a national gain, not a merely rural one, but one can hardly suppose that the countryside did not share it. Indeed, since there was no substantial price move against farm products, landlords and owner-occupiers, if not tenants, can be said to have enjoyed a measure of prosperity.

Apart from cereals, economic change also affected other items to which the Japanese farmer looked for income. In coastal villages, where farming was often combined with fishing, better boats and equipment tipped the scales in favour of the latter and eventually—after 1900—made fishery a major industry. Elsewhere, greater demand for cotton textiles and the growth of a native spinning industry brought a steady increase in the quantity of cotton grown. By 1887 Japan was almost self-sufficient in it. However, imports tended to rise thereafter as competition came from India, and by the end of the century home production had dropped sharply on this account. Of the cottage industries, some, notably the spinning, reeling and weaving processes for textiles, declined at about the same time, unable to compete with the price and quality of factory-made materials. A modest call for handicrafts like fans and lanterns gave some compensation, but it was silk, above all, that now became the farmer's stand-by. An export market was first created for it in the 1860s because of silkworm disease in Europe. Subsequently the high quality of the Japanese product maintained and expanded the demand, so that more and more families entered the business, while increased scale made possible a number of technical improvements. By the nineties, even double-cropping was becoming common, giving a summer-autumn crop as well as one in spring. As a result, annual production of raw silk easily topped a million *kan* in 1900 (1 *kan* = 8·27 lbs.), as against 278,000 *kan* in 1868 and 457,000 in 1883. Exports, at an annual average of 27 million yen for the years 1889–93, accounted for a third of Japan's export trade by value.

These figures give some idea of the importance of agriculture to the country. And one could easily add more. For example, agriculture was, and long remained, Japan's commonest occupation: something like three-quarters of the population earned their living by it in 1872 and a fraction over half did so as late as 1920. Moreover, it provided about 80 per cent of total tax revenue up to 1880, still over 60 per cent in 1894. This made it as much a factor in the formulation of government policy as it was in the daily life of the Japanese people. Indeed, it is clear that industrialization itself could not have been achieved so quickly—even, perhaps, at all—had it not been for the rise in agricultural productivity and the changes associated with it.

Economists are agreed that agriculture generated much of the savings that supported private and public investment in Meiji industry. There is disagreement about whether this was the result of a rapid rise in agricultural production in the early Meiji years or of the diversion to other uses of resources built up over a long period of time; but there is little doubt that wealth in the hands of landlords, men who had a high propensity to save, was an important element in Japan's accumulation of capital.[44] Equally, former feudal policies, directed toward keeping the farm population in the village, had built up what now became a pool of cheap rural labour that could be diverted to new kinds of enterprise, while the growth of farm cash incomes (from silk and other commercial crops) helped to create a home market which, though small, was essential to capitalist development. In addition, agricultural exports, such as tea and silk, paid for much of the industrial machinery and materials that had to be bought abroad. And land tax financed most of the government's own investment programmes.

This brings us to the question of the Meiji government's part in the process, which is also a matter of some controversy.[45] It can be argued that Japan's economic modernization did not achieve take-off until late in the nineteenth century, when private entrepreneurs assumed a major role in business and industry. Nevertheless it is clear that before then the policies of government had already given stimulus and direction to the growth of the economy. The Meiji oligarchy, after all, came early to the belief, to which foreigners so obviously subscribed, that trade and industry were the foundations on which Western greatness rested. Emulation, ambition, and the fear of Western aggression all predisposed them to seek such sources of greatness for Japan herself. This meant intervening, both directly and indirectly, in the country's economy.

For example, the abolition of feudalism gave freedom of occupation to millions of peasant families, making possible the emergence of a mobile labour force; and the breaking down of local separatism, to which it also led, completed the process of creating a national market. Thereafter, by maintaining political order and financial stability, by ensuring security of property and person, the politicians provided an environment which was favourable to all forms of economic growth. The new communications network, too, had economic as well as administrative value. But in addition to all this, the government took steps to foster the particular kinds of activity of which it approved. By engaging in foreign trade on its own account it obtained funds to import goods and machinery, lending some of them to local authorities to serve as models for Japanese manufacturers, selling others on an instalment plan to those who needed capital equipment. It organized trade fairs, set up technical schools, sent students for training to Europe and America. Foreign instructors, advisers and engineers were brought in to run a number of the new concerns and train the technicians who were to run them in the future, as many as 130 being employed by the Department of Public Works alone by 1879. Official policy, however, was to replace them as soon as possible by Japanese, whose salaries were smaller, an attitude which led one British resident to observe that 'the Japanese only look upon foreigners as schoolmasters. As long as they cannot help themselves they make use of them; and then they send them about their business. . . .'[46] It was precisely this, of course, that eventually made Japan's industrial technology self-sustaining, in contrast to that of other Asian countries, which remained for the most part dependent on foreign help.

Another vital field of government action was the provision of capital in those sections of the economy where private investment was slow in coming. Much of the accumulated wealth of Tokugawa merchants had been put to use in various financial and commercial schemes of the Bakufu or domains and had therefore been lost when those institutions were destroyed. Much else was invested in usury or land, outlets that continued, because of high rents and interest rates, to attract a large proportion of the country's savings. Large-scale 'modern' ventures clearly involved greater risk and lower returns, at least initially. For this reason they were left to the adventurous, men with strong official connections—and often not of merchant origin—who shared the government's patriotic aims. Even the private capital created by the commutation of samurai stipends in 1876 found its way mostly into the more respectable and profitable field of banking, not directly into industry; and such investors as did turn to the latter were inclined to put their money into businesses that were smallscale and relatively familiar. It was not until the mid 1880s, when some of the new enterprises, like cotton textiles, were shown to be highly profitable, that private merchant capital from Osaka and other 'old' financial centres was attracted into them. Until then, plans needing heavy long-term investment had usually to depend on state finance and the co-operation of a new class of privileged entrepreneurs.

This can be seen in the history of modern transport. Coastal shipping was the easiest form to develop, both for geographical reasons and because it had become the commonest means for the bulk movement of goods in the Tokugawa period, so that some of the necessary commercial facilities and organization already existed. There were even one or two Western-style shipyards, built before the Restoration at places like Uraga and Nagasaki. Hence the main need was for better ships; and this was met partly by using those which had originally been bought from foreigners by various feudal lords, partly by government help to some outstanding entrepreneurs of the Meiji era. The former Tosa samurai, Iwasaki Yataro, whose firm became known as Mitsubishi in 1873, is a notable example. He began with a few ships acquired from his domain at its dissolution. Soon after he absorbed another concern, operating between Tokyo and Osaka; he ran (and then took over) vessels bought by the government for use as military transports; and he established a foreign service, with routes to Hong Kong (1879) and Vladivostock (1881). In 1885 his line amalgamated with some of its rivals in the coastal trade to form the Nippon Yusen Kaisha (NYK), with fifty-eight ships totalling 65,000 tons. Dividends were guaranteed by the state at 8 per cent for fifteen years. Moreover, like others in the business, the company continued to receive subsidies, mail contracts and similar forms of government help, accepting in return government supervision of its routes and operations.

In railway building, a quite new form of enterprise, the role of government was at first much greater. It controlled all construction up to 1877, by which date three short sections of the planned Tokyo-Kobe line had been completed: those between Tokyo and Yokohama (1872), Kobe and Osaka (1874), Osaka and Kyoto (1877). The slow progress was due in part to political unrest, in part to lack of experience, but after the Satsuma Rebellion work speeded up, with private companies also beginning to participate. The latter, indeed, soon owned more mileage than the government. From 130 miles in 1885 they expanded to over 1,500 miles ten years later, while government track in the same period increased only from 220 to 580 miles. At this stage, the main line ran along the Pacific coast from Aomori in the north to Kobe on the Inland Sea, with plans already made for extending it to Nagasaki. A spur had also been built across the mountains from Tokyo to Naoetsu. Since freight traffic was heavy and profits high, the investors who had followed the state's lead in putting capital into these lines, mostly former samurai and feudal lords, found themselves well rewarded.

The development of manufacturing industry followed a similar pattern: of state initiative at first and private investment later, with the year 1881 marking a watershed between the two. In the first phase government activity took the form of establishing and operating factories, some of them designed as models to encourage the introduction of new techniques, some to fill needs which, though important, were unlikely to be a source of profit. Thus silk-reeling plants of the French and Italian type were opened at Tomioka and Maebashi in 1870, in order to stimulate the export trade by standardizing quality. A cement works was established in 1872, partly to reduce expensive imports at a time of trade imbalance. The manufacture of tiles, glass and chemicals was also started. Modern cotton-spinning was introduced in the Nagoya area in 1878, this with the double object of diverting traditional skills into new channels and providing employment in a region which had been badly hit by foreign competition, while other attempts to stimulate regional development brought, for example, a brewery and a sugar factory to Hokkaido. Altogether such government-owned concerns numbered fifty-two by 1880, to say nothing of three shipyards, ten mines and five munitions works.

The cost of investment in these various undertakings was considerable, averaging more than 5 per cent of ordinary revenue for the years 1868–80. Heavy expenses were also incurred towards the end of the period for the payment of samurai stipends and suppression of the Satsuma Revolt, so that the Treasury's problems, complicated by a drain of specie arising from the persistent excess of imports over exports, began to seem alarming. By the late 'seventies recourse to further note issues had brought inflation, despite an expanding economy's greater need for cash. The value of government paper dropped sharply. Rice prices jumped from Y5·7 per *koku* in 1877 to Y9·4 in 1879, Y12·2 in 1880. Farmers found the change much to their advantage; but for the government it had serious implications, since it not only reduced the real revenue to be obtained from land tax, but also put in jeopardy the income which ex-samurai received from bonds, thereby adding to their discontent. The crisis, in fact, was political as well as financial and was grave enough on both counts to endanger the regime.

In the course of 1880 and 1881 the government sought urgently for remedies, but it was not until November of the latter year, with the appointment of Matsukata Masayoshi as Minister of Finance, that its policies can be said to have become effective. Under Matsukata's guidance, strenuous efforts were made to balance revenue and expenditure New taxes were imposed on rice-wine and tobacco; government grants and subsidies were much reduced; and stringent economy was observed in administration. The result was a gradual restoration of stability. By 1886 it proved possible to redeem government bonds bearing interest at 8 to 10 per cent by a conversion issue at 5 per cent, while by 1894 parity had been restored between yen notes and silver.

Towards the end of 1880, in the early stages of this economy drive, it had been decided to dispose of the government's factories. Those which were engaged in the manufacture of munitions were excepted, but the rest, it was announced, would be sold to the highest bidder, a decision that was to have important repercussions. It was not due to a sudden change of heart about the role of private enterprise in industry. Nor was it, as has sometimes been alleged, part of a conspiracy to transfer valuable plants at bargain prices to the oligarchy's friends among the businessmen, though this, it is true, was often the effect. Rather, it was a financial measure, aimed at reducing calls on revenue and recouping some part of the funds that had been invested. Even this was not easy to accomplish. The shortage of capital, which had been a factor in producing state initiative in the first place, still persisted. The prices offered were accordingly low; and that they came from friends of those in power was often because such men were in a better position to assess long-term advantages, not because they were given an opportunity for rapid profit. Most of the concerns, after all, were running at a loss, which is why they were for sale. They continued to do so for some time afterwards. It was not until Japan had a far more highly developed domestic market that the yields from industrial pioneering could be counted in substantial sums. When this did happen, however, it contributed largely to the dominant position which a few great firms were able to win in the Japanese economy. Outstanding among them were those who bought government plants in the early 'eighties: Iwasaki's Mitsubishi company, which acquired the Nagasaki shipyard in 1884; the house of Mitsui, one of the very few great merchant families of Tokugawa times that continued to thrive and expand in the modern era, now purchaser of the Tomioka silk-reeling mill; and others like Asano and Furukawa, investors, respectively, in cement and mining.

The sale of government undertakings marked the beginning of a new phase in economic policy, one in which subsidies and contracts awarded to private firms replaced state ownership and operation. With such encouragement heavy industry continued slowly to increase. New shipyards were opened in 1881 and 1883. The Shibaura Engineering Works was founded in 1887. In 1892, like several others, it began to produce electrical equipment and machinery, while the same year also saw the appearance of the first Japanese-built locomotive. In mining, application of modern methods maintained a steady rise in output. Annual coal production, for example, actually reached 5 million tons (metric) in 1895. At that time it was an export item, as was copper, though industry still relied on purchases abroad for most of its iron and almost all its steel.

Striking as many of these achievements were, they were still far from altering the character of the Japanese economy. Engineering, shipbuilding and similar trades were in their infancy, important because of their promise for the future, but having less effect in the short term than the many smaller innovations that contributed to economic growth: 'the ricksha and the bicycle; the rodent-proof warehouse; elementary sanitation; better seeds and more fertilizer; the kerosene and then the electric lamp; a simple power loom; the gas engine in the fishing boat; the divorce of personal from business accounts; the principle of limited liability'.[47] It was through such unspectacular changes in the first place that the national wealth increased. This in turn, by virtue of the purchasing power that it created, made possible the profitable development of large-scale manufacture.

One field in which modest improvements brought notable results was textiles. Spinning, reeling and weaving required less capital outlay and less technical knowledge than trades like heavy engineering; they could be successfully carried on in small workshops, as distinct from large factories; and they made use of a type of labour which Japan's farm households could easily provide. For these reasons the textile industry was the first to attract private entrepreneurs and to free itself from dependence on government aid. Silk textiles were least affected at this stage, probably because the bulk of the demand was for exports of raw silk, not for thread or fabric, so that few firms were using power-driven filatures or looms in 1894. Modernization in the cotton industry, by contrast, was by then much more advanced. In spinning, the number of spindles rose from 8,000 in 1877 to 77,000 ten years later, this being no more than the equipment of a fair-sized Lancashire mill, but with 382,000 spindles in 1893 the annual output of yarn increased to 88 million pounds. Significantly, this was accompanied by a sharp rise in imports of the raw material, nearly all from India. The market for the yarn was largely domestic and the piecegoods into which it was made were woven for the most part on narrow handlooms, but the rapid expansion of output that began about 1890 soon led to the increased use of power. Installation of power looms had already been undertaken here and there, but it was not until the great growth of exports after 1895 that it was to become widespread. Meanwhile, enough had been achieved in the adoption of modern machinery and techniques to enable the export opportunity, when it came, to be exploited.

This, indeed, is true of the economy as a whole, not just of textiles. Statistics of industrial activity on the eve of the war with China, though small by contemporary Western standards, are impressive when compared with those of a decade earlier— a sixfold increase in factory consumption of coal, for example, and an output of cotton yarn that had been multiplied by more than twenty—and even seem considerable in absolute terms for a country where development was so recent. Coal consumption in factories was a million tons, yarn output a hundred million pounds, in 1894. Foreign trade, too, though as yet on a modest scale, with annual averages for both imports and exports at less than 80 million yen in 1888–93, was beginning to change its character. Between 1878–82 and 1893–97, purchases of finished goods dropped from 48·6 per cent of imports as a whole to 35·1 per cent, while imports of raw materials rose from 3·5 to 22·7 per cent. Similarly, exports of finished goods increased—chiefly because of textiles—from 7·2 to 26·2 per cent. For the first time, moreover, the country had an export surplus. This was still not the pattern that one associates with a fully industrial state, such as Japan was to develop in the twentieth century. It implies, however, that this was the direction of change, that industrial growth was now great enough to have a substantial effect on foreign trade. In other words, some twenty years of effort were bearing fruit.

So far in this chapter the emphasis has been on the actions and policies of government. This is reasonable enough, for in this first stage of modernization it was the Meiji government that provided the leadership, the framework and many of the stimuli without which success could not have been achieved.

But it must not be thought because of this that the Japanese people were entirely passive. Not everything was planned and centrally directed, not all change happened where and how the government wished. Indeed, once the years of preparation were over and those of reward began—something which in most fields of activity came soon after the war of 1894–5—it transpired that expansion was often greatest in those areas where government action had been least, like textiles. Certainly modernization could never have succeeded had it not been for the many thousands of Japanese who showed themselves willing, sometimes more than willing, to try new ways of earning a living, to study (and let their children study) foreign books, to adopt habits that were alien to their own upbringing and traditions.

Many of the men who set an example in these matters were former samurai, like Iwasaki Yataro, with an outlook and interests that followed closely those of the Meiji leaders. Others were of merchant stock, like the Mitsui (though the Mitsui firm was substantially reorganized by newly recruited managers). Others again came from the richer farming families of central and west Japan, usually claiming some kind of samurai background, whose members had already shown themselves interested in various forms of non-agricultural enterprise before the Restoration. In fact, the entrepreneurs, like those other recruits to the Meiji ruling class, the bureaucrats, had usually been men of some standing in the old society, but not of enough standing to realize their larger ambitions. So recognition, as much as wealth, was the goal they now sought. For most of them, knowledge of the West was one of the keys to achieving it: a source of essential skills, through which one could acquire a measure of prestige and gain the ear of those in office.

This gave a particular importance to the translators and writers, whose books on Western customs and behaviour became for many the only reliable guide in an otherwise uncertain world. Fukuzawa Yukichi (1835–1901) is an outstanding example. As a young man, a samurai of low rank in a Kyushu domain, he was sent to study gunnery and Dutch at Nagasaki. Later, on his own initiative he added medicine and English. By 1862 he had already visited both America and Europe as interpreter to diplomatic missions, but thereafter fear of assassination in an age of frequent anti-foreign violence turned him away from politics and public office to a life of teaching, writing and translating. His first book, *Seiyo Jijo* (Conditions in Western Lands), achieved immediate success. A compendium on European countries, their governments and their economies, it was the forerunner of many more in which he dealt with subjects as apparently remote from each other as food and clothing, elementary science, parliamentary procedure. All, to him, were relevant as parts of Western life. The earnings from these publications, which were considerable, were devoted to a school that he established in 1863 to teach a Western-style curriculum. It eventually became Keio Gijuku, one of the two earliest and greatest of Japan's private universities (the other being Waseda, founded by Okuma Shigenobu in 1881).

Reading Fukuzawa's autobiography one gets the impression of a man not always likeable but of a formidable purpose. As a liberal he insisted on the importance of merit, rather than birth. As an educator he was a constant critic of things traditionally Japanese, praising the Western alternatives to them. Above all, his aims were patriotic: 'the purpose of my entire work', he wrote, 'has not only been to gather young men together and give them the benefit of foreign books, but to open this "closed" country of ours and bring it wholly into the light of Western civilization. For only thus may Japan become strong in both the arts of war and peace. . . .'[48]

In this task Fukuzawa, like others, was helped by a spate of translations from books in Western languages, which often ran as serials in newspapers and magazines. Among the most influential was Samuel Smiles' *Self-help*, published in 1871. Bulwer-Lytton's *Ernest Maltravers*, translated in 1878-9, was much imitated as a novel and much valued for its information on Western manners; Jules Verne's *Round the World in Eighty Days* (1878) had great vogue as a sort of annotated handbook on foreign travel; while translations also appeared of *Robinson Crusoe, Aesop's Fables, The Arabian Nights* and *Pilgrim's Progress*, to say nothing of Moore's *Utopia* and Rousseau's *Contrat Social*. All these were available by 1880. A decade later attention had turned to the moderns: Turgenev, Dostoievsky, Tolstoy,

Victor Hugo, Ibsen. And there was even a version of *Little Lord Fauntleroy* in 1892.

One result of the flood of information derived from these and other sources was to bring changes in Japanese literature and art. Novels became more realistic, though very dull, with themes that were thought to be attractive to the 'modern' public, such as politics, history and world affairs. Among the most popular, for example, partly because of its 'beautiful Chinese style, suitable for chant reading',[49] was one called *Kajin no kigu* (Strange Encounters of Elegant Women). In it the reader was taken through a survey of world revolutionary and independence movements, escorted by two female beauties, one from Ireland and one from Spain—an exercise that was of doubtful value as literature, but enabled the author to exploit contemporary interest in the liberal movement and international problems. Not unnaturally, the book is now more an object of curiosity than of admiration. One could be equally disparaging about the first examples of the Meiji period's drama, or the attempts to write rhyming verse; but since these, like the political novels, were no more than experiments, which eventually made way for something very much better, it is more charitable to avoid discussing them at all.

A similar discretion is appropriate in commenting on some other aesthetic imports from the West, like painting, new forms of which were stimulated by the founding of a government art school in 1876, or architecture, which was regarded as so severely practical a subject that at the imperial university it was included under engineering. In these matters, perhaps, it would have been better had Japan come under Europe's influence at a different date. Certainly the gulf that existed between the artistic criteria of traditional Japanese society and those which were now acquired proved too great to be bridged, at least for another fifty years. The country was left with two quite different standards. One, reflecting the taste of late nineteenth century Europe, applied to the architecture of government offices, banks and railway stations, to the design of goods for export, to furniture and interior decoration in the Western manner. The other, which maintained the inherited emphasis on line and texture, rather than on colour, continued to determine the appearance of such buildings as shrines and the majority of private dwellings, as well as that of articles and utensils made for everyday use. The dichotomy between the two became one of the unmistakable features of modern Japan. Behind it there was something more than fashion. Many Japanese, like Fukuzawa, studied the West not merely because it was a source of 'wealth and strength', but also because it was the home of 'civilization and enlightenment' (*bummei-kaika*). To them, industrial civilization, which the West exemplified, was a stage of development to which all societies should aspire, including that of Japan. Hence all the manifestations of change we have been discussing—constitutions, conscript armies, factories, Western-style novels and art— were related phenomena. They were parts of a whole that embodied universal, not just Western values; to excel in them was to be civilized.

Not all Japanese felt like this, however. Many opposed modernization because of its cost, or in defence of vested interests; others from simple conservatism. And there were some who found a subservience to Western values, such as seemed inherent in the doctrines of *bummei-kaika*, distasteful not only because it was a denial of tradition, but also because it contradicted the very 'Japaneseness' that the whole Meiji programme was supposed to defend. Sometimes such sentiments found an outlet in opposition to the Meiji government, causing a reassessment of policy. More often they went to swell the rising tide of nationalism that increasingly helped to decide what aims Japan's 'modern' skills should serve.

CHAPTER IX

NATISM AND FOREIGN AFFAIRS 1890-1905

Political indoctrination and traditionalist sentiment—war with China—the Triple Intervention—military build-up—Anglo-Japanese alliance—war with Russia

IN THE twenty years of social, political and economic reform that followed the Restoration, Japanese attitudes towards the outside world underwent a gradual change. On the one hand, greater knowledge of Western habits and institutions brought the Japanese people a new awareness of what was individual about their own. On the other, the frustrations which arose from a sense of inferiority in dealings with the West, an inevitable concomitant of diplomatic weakness and cultural borrowing, not only gave emotional impetus to policies aimed at increasing national strength, but also became linked with specific objectives in foreign affairs. The result was an upsurge of nationalism and a decade of military effort. At the end of it, Japan had achieved the equality of status for which she longed and had begun to lay the foundations of an empire, so marking the end of the first stage of her modern growth.

The beginnings of this process can be traced to the handful of samurai publicists of the century's middle years, whose patriotism was communicated in the 1860s to most members of their class and helped to give a constructive turn to what began as an anti-Tokugawa movement (see Chapter III). Subsequently the prevalence of samurai at all levels of early Meiji leadership ensured patriotism a continued importance in political debate. Okubo and Ito, when the Iwakura mission ended, gave it as a reason for concentrating on reform at home, rather than expansion abroad. Saigo used it to justify his plans for attacking

Korea and opposing a government that refused to carry them out. Itagaki and his followers claimed it for the political parties. Thus by 1880 'love of country' (*aikoku*) had assumed something like the place in politics that 'expulsion of the barbarians' (*joi*) held twenty years earlier: a symbol of respectability to which appeal could successfully be made because it touched emotions shared by all. What is more, its most vociferous expression came from the opponents of the men in power —as had been true also under the Tokugawa—for it was one of the few weapons that could be safely used against an authoritarian regime that had declared for a foreign policy of moderation.

A number of factors operated to spread this patriotic sentiment throughout the population and thereby establish a basis for nationalism in the modern sense. The government's efforts at political unification, its attempts to marshal support by the creation of local elected councils and assemblies, its development of an efficient system of communications, all these helped indirectly to foster a sense of national consciousness. So did compulsory education, both by reducing regional differences of speech and manners and by enlarging the reading public. Nor was any opportunity lost of bombarding the literate with political propaganda. Newspapers of the period tended to be political and scurrilous, novels political and dull, and both were written in a language much closer to the vernacular than had been fashionable hitherto, which made them accessible to a wider circle. Accordingly, more and more Japanese were encouraged to have views about their country's politics and future.

The Meiji government did not object to this, providing the views themselves were such as it approved. And it took steps to make sure they were. One means to this end was an extensive use of powers of censorship, especially of the press. Another was a programme of political indoctrination, aimed at making the emperor a focus of national unity. It owed much to official sponsorship of the Shinto faith, for it was Shinto, after all, that rationalized the emperor's authority as deriving from divine descent and gave him quasi-sacerdotal functions. It is not surprising, therefore, that Shinto was given a place of honour in the constitutional arrangements of 1868–9 and became for a time something very much like a State religion. Later the army also played its part: a conscript's training naturally laid stress on loyalty towards the man who was both ruler and commander-in-chief. The generality of Japanese, moreover, acquired the proper sentiments at school. The compulsory course in 'ethics', worked out with much debate in the 1880s, emphasized in about equal proportions the Confucian obligation of filial piety and the national one of loyalty, the two going hand in hand with military drill, also introduced into the curriculum at about this time, as determinants of the future citizen's attitude towards his civic duty.

The trend was given formal expression in the Constitution of February 1889 and the Imperial Rescript on Education of October 1890. The first defined the subject's relationship to his monarch, putting traditional concepts in modern dress. The second made it clear that education was to be subordinate to the service of the State, outlining the substance of what was to constitute 'ethics' and providing for ceremonial expressions of loyalty in the daily life of schools. Though some objected—mostly Christians—that this was to give official sanction to an essentially religious act, they were overruled. Education and patriotism remained thereafter in close alliance.

Patriotism, of course, was in this context equated with loyalty to the emperor, as was to be expected from a regime which depended largely for its authority on control of the emperor's person. But it was already acquiring other connotations, too. Many Japanese, offended by the uncritical enthusiasm for Western dress, customs and gadgets which had characterized the first decade of Meiji history, came to think it patriotic to eschew them altogether when one could. Others, less consciously or less militantly anti-Western, began to rediscover arts and pastimes which preoccupation with the West had made neglected. In 1881, for example, a society was formed to revive interest in Japan's own traditions of painting and fine art, as distinct from those more recently brought in from Europe. Iwakura, with some of his friends, sponsored performances of the classical Noh drama and helped to raise the funds to build it a new theatre in Tokyo's Shiba Park, this also in 1881, while the following decade saw a modest renewal of interest in such minor arts as flower arrangement (*ikebana*) and the tea ceremony (*cha-no-yu*), often under the patronage of newly-rich merchants and industrialists, who were in this the natural successors of feudal lords. Such men also became patrons of Japanese-style wrestling (*sumo*), which by 1900 rivalled baseball as a national sport. Other sports of Tokugawa times, like fencing (*kendo*), were kept alive by the armed forces and police, to find renewed popularity in the end in the more nationalistic atmosphere of the twentieth century.

This atmosphere, indeed, was being heralded as early as 1890. Japanese taste in Western music, which had already shown itself martial both in theme and in performance, was now being exemplified in patriotic songs, bearing titles like 'Come, foes, come' (*Kitare ya kitare*, published in 1888) or 'Though the enemy be tens of thousands strong' (*Teki wa ikuman ari totemo*, published in 1891), which were performed for schools, military units and other audiences throughout the country. The Meiji leaders, in fact, with the unconscious help of their political rivals, had created a public opinion more actively interested in Japan's international position than was entirely comfortable. Exhortations designed to increase loyalist fervour, made for the sake of political unity, and criticisms of government 'weakness' in foreign affairs, made as moves in a struggle for power, had persuaded large sections of the population to hold views on policy which did not altogether accord with what was practical. Specifically, men looked for radical revision of the old 'unequal' treaties and for some sort of military action on the Asian mainland. These were hopes that the government shared. However, it found it necessary to move more slowly towards achieving them, and to choose its methods of doing so with greater circumspection, than the press and public seemed sometimes ready to approve.

The earliest manifestations of this difference in outlook arose over treaty revision, a subject which Japanese diplomats approached with two main objects in mind: first, to abolish or modify the system of extra-territoriality, by which foreign residents in Japan came under the legal jurisdiction of their own country's consuls; second, to secure the right of adjusting Japan's tariffs on foreign goods, most of which were fixed by treaty at 5 per cent. In view of the two sides' disparity in strength, these aims were only likely to be attained by patient negotiation, as had been demonstrated in the Iwakura mission's talks in 1871-3. The lesson, moreover, was underlined by the experiences of the next few years. Thus in 1878-9, when the United States agreed to tariff autonomy for Japan, Britain refused outright. Again in 1882 Britain proved adamant over extra-territoriality. Thereafter Japanese officials recognized the need for compromise, but the first attempt at one, involving a proposal for mixed courts under Japanese and foreign judges, was wrecked by an outburst of popular criticism in 1886. In these circumstances it required some courage for Okuma, as Foreign Minister, to reopen the talks in 1888, but he chose to negotiate in the calmer atmosphere of the Western capitals and by the following autumn had won general acceptance for the abolition of extraterritoriality, subject only to the creation of mixed courts for cases of appeal. At this point the news was again made prematurely known. A storm of opposition was aroused in Tokyo, where feeling now ran very high on questions of national sovereignty, and in October Okuma himself was wounded by a bomb thrown at his carriage by a nationalist fanatic. As a result, the negotiations were dropped and the Kuroda government resigned.

With the opening of the Diet in 1890 the issue became more deeply involved than ever in domestic politics, in that the opposition parties, seeking desperately to break the grip of an entrenched oligarchy, made every use they could of popular feeling on foreign affairs. This was sometimes an embarrassment—on one occasion statements in the Diet brought a sharp protest from Great Britain—and uncertainty about their political future made it difficult for ministers to negotiate with confidence. On the other hand, it also gave them an argument they had not before possessed. When Mutsu Munemitsu, as Foreign Minister in Ito's cabinet, decided to resume talks with London in the summer of 1893, he was able to point out that Japanese public opinion would be satisfied with nothing less than the complete abolition of extra-territoriality, even to hint that if the treaties were not revised they might be renounced. Since the veiled threat was accompanied by an offer of commercial advantages, it sufficed as a basis for discussion and brought eventual success. Details were worked out during the next few months, providing that extra-territoriality should end after Japan's new civil code came into force (ultimately this was in 1899) and that foreign merchants, in exchange, should for the first time be given access to Japan outside the treaty ports. An agreement embodying these terms was signed in July 1894. Similar ones with the other powers came soon after, for in these matters Britain's example was decisive.

The event, unhappily, gained less applause than it might otherwise have done, because it came at a time when attention was concentrated on another aspect of the country's foreign affairs, its relations with the neighbouring mainland. These had long been a matter of vital interest to Japan. Writers throughout the century, as we have seen, had looked to China, Manchuria and Korea as the natural outlet for Japan's ambitions. Even in the dark days after the signing of the treaties, when realization of national weakness had induced a defensive attitude in nearly all, there were still some, like Yoshida Shoin, who had thought survival impossible without a continental foothold. A number of the Meiji leaders, several of them Yoshida's students, shared this view. They were strengthened in it by the activities of Saigo Takamori. In 1881, after Saigo's death, survivors of his rebellion and others sympathetic to them formed a patriotic society, the Genyosha, designed to promote such expansionist ideas, to which end they took every opportunity of bringing pressure to bear on government leaders and stirring up nationalist opinion. Korea became an important focus of their efforts, as it did also for pamphleteers and politicians. As a result, Korea, like the treaties, was made a subject of debate; and many Japanese in all walks of life became convinced of the need to intervene there, either from a belief that Korea should be made to follow Japan's example of reform and modernization, under Japanese tutelage, to make her a worthy ally against Western dominance, or in the conviction that Japan must create an anti-Western league, which China and Korea must somehow be made to join, as a means of saving both herself and her neighbours from continued exploitation.

Such reasoning was not in itself unwelcome to the Meiji government. It did conflict, however, with the policy of restraint laid down in 1873. For although this had not entirely precluded territorial advances—in 1874, for example, Japan won tacit Chinese acceptance of her control of the Ryukyu islands and in 1875 took over the northern Kurile chain from Russia, in return for waiving her claims to Sakhalin—it had certainly implied a resolve to follow the paths of compromise and negotiation. Yet where Korea was concerned this proved difficult to do. The formal establishment of relations between the two countries, a treaty which opened two Korean ports to trade in 1876, was only made possible by the threat of force. Once completed, moreover, it was immediately challenged by China, on the grounds that Korea was a Chinese vassal state, incapable of concluding such an agreement with another country. The claim initiated an era of intrigue in which both China and Japan entered into a struggle between factions at the Korean court, their rivalry culminating in an armed clash between Chinese and Japanese forces in Seoul at the end of 1884. It took direct negotiations between Ito and Li Hung-chang the following spring to avert hostilities.

Both sides on this occasion agreed to withdraw their troops, but this did not mean that either had yielded its position. Inevitably there came another crisis. In June 1894 a number of local revolts broke out in Korea, organized by anti-Western groups called Tong-haks, and the king, acknowledging his vassal status, called for Chinese help. This was quickly given. Japan, however, held that the action was contrary to the 1885 convention. She therefore sent forces of her own, so shifting the emphasis from the Tong-hak revolts, which were in any case soon suppressed, to the much more dangerous issue of Sino-Japanese conflict.

Several factors contributed to making the situation more serious than it had been in 1884. For China's part, French and British encroachment along the frontiers of Tongking, Tibet and Burma had induced a stiffer attitude concerning her rights in border areas, an attitude made all the more uncompromising by the greater self-confidence with which she could approach a struggle against Japan. The latter, on the other hand, was also confident, for the previous decade had seen a considerable growth in the size and efficiency of her army and navy, as well as a solution to her most pressing financial problems. Hence caution in her international dealings seemed less needed than it had been before. Indeed, too much caution would provoke the parties and public opinion, as the Diet's vociferous comments on treaty revision had already shown. This being so, the specific considerations making for action in Korea gained greater weight. These were partly economic, arising from the trade recently established between the two, but mostly strategic, in that Korea was Japan's obvious route of access to northeast Asia. Both would be threatened if Korea fell under another power's control. From Japan's viewpoint, therefore, whether one saw the danger as coming from China, seeking to make her suzerainty effective, or from Russia, who had just announced plans for building a railway to her Siberian possessions, there seemed good cause for taking action before the threat developed. Yamagata, in particular, urged that this was so.

It is impossible to tell how much of this reasoning Ito accepted in 1894. It is certain, nevertheless, that his actions had an air of purpose which had been lacking hitherto. At the end of June, far from withdrawing Japanese troops, he announced his intention of keeping them in Korea until the Korean government had carried out an extensive catalogue of reforms, one effect of which would have been to substitute Japanese for Chinese influence and end all Chinese pretensions to special rights. In July he warned China to send in no more men, while shortly after his own took over the Korean royal palace. This left China no choice but to submit or fight. Since she refused to relinquish her rights without an effort to defend them, there was from this point no hope of avoiding war.

Its formal declaration came at the beginning of August and was followed by a series of startling Japanese victories. In fact Chinese resistance was so weak, Yamagata commented later, that 'Japanese officers did not encounter any serious problems worthy of careful consideration'.[50] By the end of September the Japanese army controlled most of Korea and the navy had command of the Yellow Sea. In October, two divisions under Yamagata moved into South Manchuria. Three more under Oyama moved against Liaotung, capturing Port Arthur the following month, and then took Weihaiwei in February 1895. The road was now open for an advance against Peking. With seven Japanese divisions poised to take it, China was forced to come to terms, sending Li Hung-chang to negotiate with Ito in Japan and agreeing to virtually any conditions he chose to state. Not unnaturally the peace treaty, signed in April at Shimonoseki, was harsh. It recognized the independence of Korea, thus ending Chinese claims to suzerainty; it ceded to Japan the island of Formosa (Taiwan) and the Liaotung peninsula, including Port Arthur; it opened four additional Chinese cities to foreign trade; and it provided for the payment by China of a substantial indemnity in cash. To the Japanese, both government and people, the fruits of victory seemed very sweet.

Japan's victory over China had a number of repercussions. It demonstrated that China's weakness was more than had been thought. It also revealed that Japan's modernization had been remarkably successful. Together these pieces of knowledge were to change the international scene. Japan, moreover, gained a new sense of satisfaction and achievement, to say nothing of more practical rewards: scope for her activities in Korea; status as a 'treaty power' in China's foreign trade; the acquisition of a useful colony, Formosa.

Yet not all was to the good, as the country was quickly to discover. International prestige also brought with it responsibilities and dangers. By making herself a factor to be reckoned with in Far Eastern affairs, Japan had involved herself more closely in the rivalries of the powers, not always to her own advantage. The first proof of it came within a week of the signing of the Shimonoseki treaty. On April 23 the representatives of Russia, France and Germany informed Tokyo that their governments viewed with concern the prospect of the Liaotung peninsula being transferred to Japan. They advised its return to China. Ostensibly they did so because Japan's control of the peninsula would be a threat to China and to the peace of the area. In fact the motives were less altruistic: Russia aimed at preserving her own opportunities for expansion; France, her ally, hoped to gain Russian support for French ambitions in the south; and Germany sought to edge Russia away from European politics. None of this, strictly speaking, involved Japan; but it was Japan, because of the new relationship she had established with China, that gave the three powers their opening to act.

The information available to Ito's cabinet was that Russia,

at least, was willing to back her demands with force. Nor would she modify her terms. What is more, although feelers put out to other capitals revealed a certain amount of sympathy for Japan, they brought no definite promise of support. Since the country was exhausted by the war with China and could not hope to resist alone, the cabinet had no choice but to communicate to the governments concerned its formal decision to submit. This was on May 5, three days before ratifications of the treaty were exchanged. All that Japan could get to salve her pride was an increase in the size of the indemnity.

Pride, there is no doubt, was at the heart of the matter. The loss of Liaotung did not by any means rob the treaty of all its value, but the manner of the loss affected Japanese opinion as if it had. The war had brought a tremendous wave of enthusiasm in Japan, silencing even the government's critics in the Diet. Victory was hailed with exultation. Then, without warning, came humiliation, a savage reminder that half a century's work had still not put Japan in a position to ignore or reject the 'advice' of one of the Powers. It is no wonder that the shock was great and that it brought a mood of bitterness. For years thereafter the Japanese public remained resentful, more open than ever to the persuasions of nationalist extremists, more anxious than ever that its own government's policies should be such as would bring prestige. In this sense the Triple Intervention, as it was called, served to rally Japan for another advance, despite the further measure of hardship that this entailed.

The government's own immediate reactions were military, devised to ensure that next time indignity could be properly resented. Thus in 1896 six new divisions were added to the regular army, bringing its total to thirteen and doubling its first-line strength. In 1898 both cavalry and artillery were organized as independent brigades. Meanwhile every effort was being made to improve equipment, especially to provide better rifles for the infantry and quick-firing guns for the artillery, as well as to set up facilities for their manufacture in Japan. By 1904 this had been achieved. Similarly, the country was made self-sufficient in naval armaments and the navy was greatly increased in size. A naval building programme, starting in 1896–7, budgeted for the addition of four battleships, sixteen cruisers, twenty-three destroyers and over 600 other craft to the existing fleet, bringing the total of major war vessels (destroyers and above) to seventy-six, aggregating 258,000 tons, by the end of 1903.

The cost of these developments was heavy. Army expenditure, just under 15 million yen in 1893, rose to 53 million in 1896 and remained at about that level till the Russian war. Naval expenditure was more variable, but was still appreciably higher than before: 13 million yen in 1895, rising to over 50 million in 1898, then declining to 28 million in 1903. Most of this was met by the government from its own resources, by means of an increase in taxation on business and personal incomes, the levy of a tax on rice-wine, and the creation of official monopolies in camphor and tobacco. To these were added a number of foreign and domestic loans which doubled the national debt within a decade. Even so, government debt was only a little over 500 million yen in 1903, a figure which the rising national income, now showing the effect of industrial growth, made quite admissible.

Direct measures of rearmament were supplemented by policies designed to channel investment into heavy industry, in particular those sectors of it which had a military importance. Thus the paid-up capital of the engineering industry rose from 2·6 million yen in 1893 to 14·6 million ten years later. Shipping and shipbuilding received substantial subsidies, dating from 1896, which had it as their object to increase both the use and the construction of vessels of a modern type. This they did, bringing a sharp rise in total merchant tonnage—35 per cent of ships entering Japanese ports in 1903 flew the Japanese flag, compared with 14 per cent in 1893—and a modest but respectable development of yards able to build steel ships. The government also decided in 1896 to establish an iron and steel industry. Its great Yawata works, founded as a result of this decision, began production in 1901 and was largely responsible for raising the annual output of pig-iron to 243,000 tons and of steel to 255,000 tons (metric) by 1913. Coal output, too, rose rapidly, from 5 million tons in 1895 to 13 million tons in 1905. More significant, perhaps, was the fact that much of the coal was being used by factories.

The economic implications of these developments will be

discussed in a later chapter. Here it is sufficient to underline their importance for foreign affairs: first, as a measure of the government's determination; second, as one explanation of its growing self-confidence after 1900. Nevertheless, any examination of Japanese policy in these years must begin by emphasizing not its confidence but its caution, a quality due not only to memories of the Triple Intervention, but also to the very real difficulties with which Japan was faced.

They arose chiefly from the change that was taking place in Europe's relationships with China. The exclusive concern with trade, which had determined China's earlier relations with the West, was being supplemented in the last quarter of the century by a rising volume of investment, involving railway-building, the exploitation of mineral resources, sometimes the establishment of industrial plants. These gave the Powers new rights which they thought it their duty to protect. What is more, the distribution of investment tended to fall into regional patterns, so that each Power had greater interests in some areas of China than in others. The result was greatly to increase the dangers of partition, the more so because several of the Powers were already established on the Chinese frontier: Russia in the north, France and Britain in the south, all looking for special privileges in the regions contiguous with their existing holdings.

Matters came to a head with Japan's victory over China, partly because it raised doubts about the ability of the Chinese government to protect foreign investments and therefore tempted the Powers to take action on their own, partly because it enabled Russia, France and Germany to seek rewards for their intervention. In 1896 Russia made the first move, securing the right to construct a railway, the Chinese Eastern, across Manchuria, to link Vladivostock with Russian territory farther west. In November 1897 the murder of two Roman Catholic priests gave Germany in her turn an opportunity to present demands, these resulting in a treaty (March 1898) which gave her a naval base at Kiaochow and extensive economic rights in the province of Shantung. News of it precipitated a scramble for concessions by the other Powers. Within a few days Russia received a lease of Port Arthur and recognition of her special position in Manchuria. France, a month later, acquired a base at Kwangchow-wan, railway rights in Yunnan, and China's promise that she would not alienate Yunnan, Kwangtung or Kwangsi to any other power. This led Britain to safeguard her own strategic and economic interests. By July she had obtained a non-alienation agreement concerning the Yangtse valley, an extension of territory opposite Hong Kong, and the lease of a base at Weihaiwei.

These events caused Japan considerable concern. It was bad enough to see those who had checked her own ambitions engaged in rewarding themselves in the manner which they had described, when Japan had tried it, as a threat to peace. It was worse still to realize that she could neither prevent them from doing so nor effectively share the spoils. To be sure, she was able to secure a pledge of non-alienation for Fukien, the province opposite Formosa. But for the most part she could only watch and wait, hoping that Britain and America would serve both Japan's ends and their own by preventing the complete dismemberment of China.

The Yamagata government, which took office at the end of 1898, was able to do something more constructive. During 1899 Chinese resentment of foreign actions was manifested in widespread anti-foreign outbreaks, the most serious of which, in Shantung and the north, were led by groups called Boxers. In the spring of 1900 they seized the approaches to Peking and laid seige to the foreign legations, thus making necessary an immediate military intervention by the treaty Powers. Japan alone was in a position to send substantial reinforcements quickly. She therefore played a leading part in the operations that followed, providing nearly half the troops that relieved the legations in August and occupied Peking. Yet for all this she acted with circumspection, showing a studious care for her allies' susceptibilities—even at some risk of delaying the expedition—and observing all proper military and diplomatic etiquette. Her behaviour, in fact, much enhanced her international reputation. It also gave her a voice in the negotiations by which a settlement was reached in 1901 and a share in the huge indemnity required from China.

To set against this was a deterioration in her relations with Russia. These had improved slightly after 1895, despite the growth of direct rivalry between the two in Korea, for Russia

was too preoccupied with China and Manchuria, Japan too conscious of her recent rebuff, to push matters to extremes. In 1896
they agreed to co-operate in Korea's development and in April
1898 Russia even recognized Japan's greater claim to economic
preference in that country. This eased the tension, at least till
Manchuria brought it back, a development that occurred as a
by-product of the Boxer troubles. Russia held conspicuously
aloof from the plans to relieve the legations at Peking. By
contrast, she used the spread of the outbreaks to the north-east
provinces as an excuse to occupy Manchuria entirely. Nor
would she evacuate the area until China came to terms. Since
the terms, as stated in February 1901, would have made Manchuria a Russian protectorate, they brought urgent protests
from the powers, most vigorously from Japan, forcing Russia
to deny any territorial ambitions. At this the crisis died, becoming submerged for a time in the acrimonious exchanges
about allocation of the Boxer indemnity between its various
claimants.

One result of these manoeuvres was to bring Britain and
Japan together, since they had a common interest in opposing
Russian expansion. Britain feared for her influence in China if
the Russian occupation of Manchuria were to prove permanent.
Japan saw it as blocking her own best route to the mainland
and also as a threat to Korea. Neither could afford to let it pass
unchallenged. Yet a formal agreement to oppose it was not an
easy step to take. For Britain it would involve a break with the
diplomacy of 'splendid isolation'. For Japan it might well mean
abandoning hope of a local compromise with Russia, though
many in Tokyo, including Ito, still saw such a compromise as
the country's wisest course. On both sides, therefore, the
approach to an agreement was cautious and its outcome by no
means inevitable.

The possibility of alliance had been widely canvassed in both
countries since 1895, when Britain's refusal to join the Triple
Intervention—because she approved the commercial provisions
laid down at Shimonoseki—had done something to wipe out
the memory of her earlier opposition to treaty revision. Still,
this seemed a slender base on which to found a diplomatic and
military arrangement. More important, in fact, were the personal links established between the two countries by Britain's

role as a tutor in modernization. By the training of naval officers, the education of students, the provision of experts in many fields, she had helped to create a group in Tokyo that favoured closer ties. It was strengthened by the unobtrusive but effective co-operation between British and Japanese officials over details of the Boxer expedition and indemnity. Publicly, the case for alliance was urged by a number of propagandists. Two in particular, Captain Frank Brinkley, owner of the *Japan Mail* and Tokyo correspondent of *The Times*, and Edwin Arnold of the *Telegraph*, were able to influence opinion in London, while the approval of Okuma was enough to bring favourable comment from the *Mainichi* and *Yomiuri* in Japan.

It is probable that none of this would have done more than create a friendly atmosphere, had there not been a practical issue for cabinets to resolve, such as was provided by the Russian moves in China. Indeed, it was not until the summer of 1901 that private feelers and unofficial talks gave way to negotiation proper. In July, Hayashi, Japan's minister in London and long an advocate of alliance, had a meeting on the subject with the British Foreign Secretary, Lord Lansdowne. This resulted in Hayashi seeking formal instructions from his government and, when these proved encouraging, in an exchange of views about the terms which alliance might involve. Two difficulties rapidly became apparent. Both sides wished to guarantee the *status quo* in China and prevent Russian annexation of the Manchurian provinces. Britain, however, wanted any promise of mutual support to apply also to the defence of India. To this Japan objected on the grounds that it would weight the bargain heavily in Britain's favour. By the same token, Britain was hesitant about giving full support to Japan's position in Korea, since she had no desire to become involved in an exclusively Russo-Japanese quarrel. Discussion of these points, as well as of a difference about the distribution of naval forces, lasted into November.

There then occurred a short delay, occasioned by the activities of Ito. He had been succeeded as premier in June by Katsura Taro, a protegé of Yamagata, but he remained exceedingly influential and convinced of the need for talks with Russia. In mid November he persuaded the cabinet to hold up further discussions until he had made a private visit to St

Petersburg. This took place at the end of the month. Early in December, he had a number of meetings with Lamsdorff, Russia's Foreign Minister, and although they did not go well, Lamsdorff eventually offered some small concessions about Korea as a basis for formal exchanges. He expected in return a free hand for Russia in northern China. But the concessions, such as they were, had already been made abortive by events. Before Ito could report the result of his proceedings to Tokyo, British suspicions of possible duplicity—the visit to Russia was widely known—forced Hayashi to resume negotiations and Katsura to support his doing so.

An alliance was now inevitable, if the problem of its terms could be overcome. And after hard bargaining, this was at last achieved. The naval question was left for separate discussion by the naval staffs; Britain's demand that India be included in the scope of the agreement was dropped; and the difficulty over Japan's position in Korea was met by careful drafting. As finally signed on January 30, 1902, the treaty recognized that 'Japan, in addition to the interests which she possesses in China, is interested in a peculiar degree politically as well as commercially and industrially in Corea',[51] but it did not provide automatically for British help if Japan became on this account involved in war with Russia. Instead, each country agreed to remain neutral if the other became engaged in hostilities in the Far East area. This, at least, held good when only one enemy was concerned. If either was attacked by two Powers or more, the military provisions of the alliance were to become effective.

The agreement, despite the care taken in its wording, meant something different to each of the parties to it. From the British viewpoint it was to be a warning to Russia, but not a provocation, as the public announcement of its contents took pains to show. To Japan it was a triumph, this not merely because it gave her an alliance on a footing of equality with the greatest of the Powers, but also because it enabled her to treat with Russia on more even terms. There could be no repetition of the Triple Intervention, it was clear, while Britain held the ring. In this sense Japanese extremists saw the alliance as an invitation to aggression. Even the moderates, among whom the government must be numbered, were emboldened by it to refuse any unfavourable compromise about Korea.

The immediate results—or apparent results—were highly satisfactory to both Japan and Britain, for in April Russia agreed to withdraw her forces from Manchuria, the operation to be effected in stages at six-month intervals. The first, in October, was duly carried out, though the troops were only transferred elsewhere in the region. The second stage, however, expected in April 1903, did not take place. Instead, Russia gave every indication of preparing for another advance. In June, therefore, a Japanese imperial conference took the decision to propose a general settlement with Russia. It was to be on the basis of a joint undertaking to respect the territorial integrity of China and Korea, coupled with a recognition of Russian railway rights in Manchuria and Japanese interests, both political and economic, in Korea. To this Russia responded in October with counter-proposals as severe as if the Anglo-Japanese alliance had never been signed. She demanded a guarantee of territorial integrity for Korea only, excluding China (and hence Manchuria); a promise by Japan not to fortify the Korean coast; and recognition that Manchuria was outside the Japanese sphere of interest. Katsura, under pressure from a public opinion increasingly eager to fight, could not entertain such terms. It seemed better—and more practical, if his military advisers were to be believed—to gamble on a war which might resolve the question once and for all, rather than accept a line of containment drawn by Russia. Hence Japan's reply in January 1904 stated her minimum terms in the form of an ultimatum. When it was ignored she declared war.

This was on February 10, but diplomatic relations had been severed four days earlier and hostilities had already begun. Russian troops had crossed the frontier into Korea. Japanese naval units had attacked a Russian squadron. For Japan, indeed, the important task at this stage was to secure control of the straits across which her reinforcements had to move to enter Korea. It was accomplished on April 13 by victory over a Russian naval force outside Port Arthur. The Japanese First Army was now able to strike along the Yalu River, forcing a crossing on May 1 and moving into south Manchuria, while the Second Army landed in the Liaotung peninsula a few days later. Within a month General Nogi's Third Army had laid siege to Port Arthur itself, though the garrison's capitulation did not come until the following New Year, after some of the bitterest fighting of the war. Meanwhile in late August and early September Oyama's forces took Liaoyang and drove the Russians back on Mukden. Here a decisive battle was fought in February and March 1905, sixteen Japanese divisions, numbering some 400,000 men, being thrown in to achieve the capture of the city. As a final blow to Russia's hopes, her Baltic fleet, which had left Europe in November and sailed halfway round the world to break the blockade of Vladivostock, was met by Admiral Togo's forces in the Tsushima Straits on May 27 and practically annihilated.

These events made peace negotiations possible, especially as both sides had other reasons for wishing to end the struggle. Russia, although not admitting that her military resources were at an end, was in difficulties with political unrest at home. Japan was on the verge of financial exhaustion. Accordingly, when Japan asked for American mediation, a peace conference was arranged at Portsmouth, New Hampshire, and plenipotentiaries met there in August 1905. Japan's demands were stiff, as befitted an apparent victor. They included recognition of her supremacy in Korea; transfer to Japan of Russian interests in south Manchuria, including the railway and Liaotung; the cession of Sakhalin; and payment of a war indemnity. The last two Russia flatly rejected, giving every indication that she would break off the talks if Japan continued to press them. Even American intervention only succeeded in modifying her stand a little, to the extent of offering the southern half of Sakhalin. An indemnity she would not on any account consider. Disappointed, but unable to face the prospect of further fighting, the Japanese government gave way and on September 5 its representatives signed the Treaty of Portsmouth in its modified form.

Unsatisfactory as this was to the Japanese public, which had been led to expect a far greater return for its efforts and expressed its displeasure in riots that occasioned martial law, it was nevertheless a very great achievement. For the first time in modern history an Asian country had defeated one of the Powers in full-scale war. By doing so, it had secured both real advantages and symbols of prestige: a paramount position in Korea and valuable rights in South Manchuria, to be added to

Formosa and a share in the China trade. Indeed, if the Anglo-Japanese alliance had signified the attainment of equality, the Russo-Japanese war had set Japan on the road towards acquiring an empire of her own. It had also brought a change in the considerations on which her future foreign policy must be based. She now had rights and privileges to defend, not a position of inferiority to make good. Consequently, in government circles the debate became one between caution, manifested in a desire to hold (and to exploit) what had already been won, and ambition, couched mostly in terms of fresh advantages in China. This left the appeal to idealism and sense of mission in Japan's international role to be pre-empted by those who challenged the government's policies at home. After all, there had long been evidence of a growing rift between government intentions and public expectations, seen in the tumult about treaty revision and the rioting that followed the Portsmouth settlement. To this was now added a new ingredient: the disenchantment of men who would have preferred Japan to promote an Asian revolution against the West, beginning in China, rather than to emulate the imperialism which she had for more than a generation proclaimed it her intention to resist. And as the progress of modernization produced social discontents, such disenchantment was politically reinforced—to the point where it seemed likely to challenge the whole Meiji settlement.

CHAPTER X

THE END OF AN ERA

Annexation of Korea—political society—the economy—city life
—religion

THE MEIJI emperor died on July 30, 1912, after a reign of forty-five years which had seen astonishing changes. His own status had been raised from that of an ineffective recluse, regarded by foreign visitors as something akin to a pope, to that of a semi-divine monarch of a vigorous nation state. His country after years of international weakness had won two wars and acquired the beginnings of an empire. His subjects had learnt and put to use new ways of making wealth. They were already beginning to show the effects of it in their standard of living. They were also more efficiently governed, better educated and more conscious of participating in national life than they had ever been before. In sum, the first stage of modernization had been successfully completed.

It is useful at this point to survey the effect of these achievements and the kind of society they had brought into being, for Japanese history in the twentieth century was to be in many ways an extension of them. Nor was it always a pleasing one. Industrialization was to bring not only a higher level of national wealth, but also a clash of interests between town and country, manager and worker, reactionary and progressive, arising from the pattern of its distribution. It was to contribute to a weakening of the family and of the community in their older forms. Again, the stresses which this introduced were to be the greater because of a growing awareness of the dichotomy between what was Japanese and what was foreign, what was traditional and what was modern, in ideas, in politics, in social custom and much else. Thus Japan under her next two emperors became the scene of a new kind of quarrel, which threatened to disrupt society far more completely than it had been in the time of Meiji. It also turned, partly for the same reasons, to a career of expansion abroad, as the urge to achieve equality became chauvinism of a virulently racial type.

The revolution in Japan's international position, which made many of these later developments possible, had been one of the major objectives, as well as one of the greatest successes, of the Meiji leaders. It was certainly the most striking to contemporary observers. In a little over eleven years—from 1894 to 1905—Japanese diplomacy, backed on two occasions by military force, had secured revision of the unequal treaties, alliance with one of the great Powers, colonies in Formosa (Taiwan) and southern Sakhalin (Karafuto), a preponderant position in Korea and important rights in South Manchuria, including Liaotung. Very soon these gains were confirmed and extended. In July 1905 the United States had given its blessing to Korea's subordinate status and in August the Anglo-Japanese alliance was renewed, its scope being extended to provide for the defence of British interests in India and a more precise recognition of Japan's hegemony in Korea. In September came the Treaty of Portsmouth, ending the Russian war. In November, Ito negotiated an agreement by which Korea became a Japanese protectorate, giving Japan control of the country's foreign affairs. A month later China acquiesced in the arrangements made about her various possessions, so that by the end of the year Japan was ready to exploit her gains with little fear of international interference.

The first step was the appointment of Ito as Resident-General in Seoul in February 1906. He had extensive powers, but they were not enough to overcome Korean opposition or to prevent a Korean appeal for help to the Hague conference in June 1907. Accordingly, the king was made to abdicate in July of that year and Japan assumed responsibility for domestic as well as foreign policy, though unrest continued to frustrate many of her plans until the date of Ito's resignation two years later. Outright annexation had by then become the Japanese aim and Ito's murder by a Korean fanatic at Harbin in October 1909 gave pretext for it. In the following May, General

Terauchi Masatake, War Minister since 1902, was appointed concurrently Resident-General, with orders to assert complete control of the country by police and army. This done, on August 22, 1910, he forced the Korean government to sign the annexation treaty.

Events in Manchuria meanwhile had gone more smoothly. In June 1906 exploitation of Japan's rights there was entrusted to the newly-formed South Manchuria Railway Company, in which the government held half the capital and had the right to appoint the two chief officers. Apart from running the railways and building more, the company was empowered to engage in mining, public utilities and the sale of goods, in addition to collecting taxes and conducting administration in the railway zone. It was designed, in other words, to be as much an organ of policy as a source of profit. Under its patronage and control, which were shared in the political and diplomatic fields with the Governor-General of Kwantung (Liaotung), first appointed in August 1906, Japanese investment proceeded rapidly. This was recognized as inevitable by the Powers. A rapprochement with France and Russia in 1907, under the stimulus of Britain's example, and confirmation of the 1905 agreement with America, which came in the Root-Takahira notes of 1908, virtually insured international acquiescence in the special privileges being accorded to Japanese business in Manchuria. There were rumblings of protest from London, but not enough to prevent renewal of the Anglo-Japanese alliance in 1911.

During the same period, Japan's economic interests in China were growing rapidly. At the time of the Sino-Japanese war her total exports had totalled about 62 million US dollars, of which 8.4 per cent went to China (1892–6 averages). By the First World War (1912–16 averages) total exports were $355 million, of which 25 per cent went to China; and her share of foreign investment in China had risen to 13.6 per cent (1914) from almost nothing at the beginning of the century. These gains were clearly the fruits of military and diplomatic success, as well as of economic development.

Their maintenance and, if possible, improvement depended in some degree on social and political stability at home, something which in the first decade of the twentieth century the country seemed well on the way to achieving. The institutions created in the previous forty years had not been intended to destroy one ruling class and substitute another, with all the upheaval such a process would have entailed. Rather they had shifted the distribution of political authority within the ruling class and introduced new elements to it. Thus former Court nobles and feudal lords, though no longer holding important office, were reconciled to the regime by wealth and dignity, the first deriving from bonds which the state had given them, the second from their position in the peerage. The most able of the ex-samurai, profiting from superior training and experience, had also found a satisfying niche in the established order. Some became—or perhaps, one should say, remained—soldiers and bureaucrats. Others became leaders of industry and commerce. Both groups were eligible for appointment to the peerage, which underlines the fact that the new society, if it retained much of the respect for place that had characterized the old, had no intention of perpetuating wholly useless privilege. For men of modest birth but great achievement, power and honours now ran together. The Meiji leaders, after all, had won their way not only to the highest offices, but also to the topmost ranks—Ito and Yamagata both held the title of Prince—setting an example that was valid at every level. As a result, a soldier or bureaucrat could look forward to becoming baron or viscount, as well as general or vice-minister.

The services and the bureaucracy were in fact the most usual and most respectable route to such advancement. Both were alike in requiring discipline, professional efficiency and high standards of personal conduct from their members, while their insistence that appointment and promotion go by merit meant that a career in them was open to all who could pass the appropriate examinations. Since education was equally open, it followed that any family which could put its sons through the proper school and college training could hope to enter them in the upper grades of government service. With few exceptions, the poor were in practice excluded. But the prospect was a real one for many families that could not otherwise have expected to be part of a ruling class: modest landowners and well-to-do farmers in the countryside, the smaller merchants and industrialists of the towns.

To all who had ambition, whether for themselves or for their sons, education, especially higher education, therefore became an important preoccupation. Primary schools already catered for 97 per cent of the seven million children of school age in 1907, when the length of the compulsory course was raised from four years to six. Secondary schools in the same year had about 150,000 pupils. The numbers at university were also rising and there was still a large unsatisfied demand for places. To the three existing universities in Tokyo (the Imperial University and the private foundations of Keio and Waseda) were added others elsewhere—Kyoto in 1903, Sendai in 1907, Fukuoka in 1910—whose graduates helped to fill responsible posts in the bureaucracy and other fields. Even so, competition for entry remained fierce, extending to the better high schools as well as the more popular university departments; and it is one of the more significant, not to say commendable, features of modern Japan that the vast majority of applications were decided by ability, not by birth or wealth, except in so far as a moderate degree of wealth was necessary to enable a family to maintain its sons in full-time study.

In many ways, in fact, Meiji Japan had done much towards realizing an ideal of the late Tokugawa reformers, that is, the promotion of men of ability regardless of inherited rank. By so doing it had reduced the dangers of subversion. Nevertheless, the existence of a career genuinely open to talent, while it made revolution unlikely, did not preclude political disputes. There were many, even among those who had helped to bring the regime about, who had been neither fortunate nor successful under its rule and who accordingly sought to change its policies. It was of such men that political parties had been formed: disgruntled oligarchs, who had fallen out with their fellows; landowners and farmers disgusted at fiscal discrimination against the village for the benefit of the town; merchants and industrialists who felt their influence to be less than their wealth deserved; and numerous ex-samurai who lacked the ability or the luck which would have let them preserve an earlier way of life in a changing world. These were not revolutionaries, in the sense of men wishing to overturn society. But they were hostile to the oligarchy which governed Japan and determined, if possible, to make it share its power.

Yet on the face of it the oligarchy seemed as strongly entrenched as ever at the end of the Meiji period. Its senior members—Ito, Yamagata and Matsukata—had become Genro, men who because of long and meritorious service had been made permanent and personal counsellors to the throne, advising the emperor on his choice of a Prime Minister and consequently able to keep a large measure of control over both the composition and the policy of each new government. Through the years, moreover, they had put their nominees into most key positions outside the cabinet. Appointments to the Privy Council, the House of Peers, the high command of the armed forces and the upper ranks of the central bureaucracy were an imperial prerogative, which was exercised, of course, on the advice of the men in power. This implied an important limitation on the practice of promotion by ability. Though birth or wealth would not in themselves suffice, a man who wished to attain the very highest place, at least politically, needed to have or to establish 'connections' with the inner group, links of lineage or marriage or obligation which were a guarantee of his loyalty. One might recall Ito's description of the Japanese polity: that of an overgrown village, in which 'family and quasi-family ties permeated and formed the essence of every social organization', so that 'cold intellect and calculation of public events were always restrained and even often hindered by warm emotions between man and man'. This, as he said, was 'a healthy barrier against the threatening advance of socialistic ideas'. Equally, it produced a situation in which 'free discussion is apt to be smothered, attainment and transference of power liable to become a family question . . .'[52] The words were written of the days before the granting of a constitution, but they remained valid of the twentieth century, too.

To set against this close-knit monopoly of office, opponents of the Meiji government had two main weapons. The first was public opinion, expressed through a vigorous daily press and occasionally by riotous assembly, though the latter had the drawback that it was only effective at moments of crisis, usually after, not before, a decision was taken. The second was the elected lower house of the Diet and the political parties that were active in it. Between 1890 and 1894, as we have seen (see Chapter VII), the parties had fought, though unsuccessfully, to establish control of the budget and through it of policy as a whole, the struggle being marked by a series of dissolutions and elections and by the attempted use of force to decide them. Then came the war with China, submerging partisan feeling for a time in a wave of patriotism. After it, Japanese political life moved, if rather jerkily, towards a compromise. This depended on a realization by the oligarchs, on the one hand, that they could not make the constitutional machinery work if the Diet remained permanently obstructive, and by the politicians, on the other, that short of revolution the oligarchy's defences were impregnable. Since both sides were committed to ideas that made revolution out of the question—an emperor-centred state and a people united in pursuit of national strength—this eventually led the one to offer cabinet posts and minor concessions on matters of policy, the other to accept them.

The first sign of the change came in 1895, when Ito won the support of the Liberal Party (Jiyuto), the largest group in the lower house, and gave the Home Ministry to Itagaki. On the fall of Ito's government in 1896 his successor, Matsukata, made an alliance with Okuma's party on similar terms. However, neither arrangement worked very well, for there was much disagreement with it on both sides, notably from Yamagata, and Ito could not repeat the pattern when he became premier again in 1898. Yet without it he was unable to overcome the hostility of the lower house. He therefore took the initiative in bringing the Okuma and Itagaki groups together to form the first party cabinet in Japanese history. The two men took office on June 30, 1898, Okuma as premier and Foreign Minister, Itagaki as Home Minister, and they were backed by a newly-formed party which included the followers of both, the Constitutional Party (Kenseito), standing for loyalty to the throne, maintenance of the constitution and cabinet responsibility to the Diet. Unhappily, these were platitudes which only glossed over the differences between the party's two original components, adherents of Itagaki and Okuma respectively. They soon fell out over taxation policy, in which they represented different interests, and over the division of political spoils. Equally serious, they faced a united and uncooperative bureaucracy, for the effect of Ito's move had been to change the nature of the struggle only in the sense of making it a contest between cabinet and oligarchs, instead of between cabinet and Diet. In fact, the Diet played no part in the matter at all, since the government resigned on October 31, before the session had begun. It was replaced by that of Yamagata, who for the next two years secured parliamentary majorities for vital bills by the use of bribery.

The situation was complicated by a growing rivalry between Ito and Yamagata, partly personal, partly due to differences over foreign policy, partly reflecting a conflict between civil and military interests within the Meiji leadership. In September 1900 Ito tried to strengthen his hand by forming a party of his own, organizing what was left of the old Liberals into an Association of Political Friends (Seiyukai), but forcing them to accept as the price of patronage his own view that cabinets must be 'independent'; in other words, that party representation in the cabinet did not involve the cabinet's subordination to party. On this basis a government was formed, though it proved short-lived. Yamagata opposed it, exploiting the ascendancy he had established in the services and the House of Peers; and Ito could not entirely match this combination, even by invoking the emperor's intervention, a device he had earlier used against the Diet with striking success. In June 1901 he resigned again, after less than a year in office.

From this time on, Ito and Yamagata were represented in politics by their respective protégés, Saionji Kimmochi and Katsura Taro, who alternated as Prime Minister for the next twelve years. The later part of this period is known as that of 'the Katsura-Saionji truce', a phrase which fairly reflects the tacit understanding between the two main groups. Each possessed the power to obstruct the other, each realized that it was usually better to refrain from using it. Saionji, after he succeeded Ito as president of the Seiyukai in 1903, commanded a fairly docile majority in the lower house of the Diet and the support of Ito's friends in the bureaucracy. Katsura had the backing of Yamagata, the services and the House of Peers. Either could therefore govern as long as he had the other's consent, neither could do so without it.

It was the Seiyukai's Hara Kei, architect of 'the politics of compromise',[53] who brought a new emphasis into this situation. As we have seen, the reforms introduced in the

1870s and 1880s had opened the way for the country's more substantial citizens to play some part in public life: as recruits to the bureaucracy; as members of prefectural and municipal assemblies; as voters electing representatives to the Diet (the property qualification for suffrage was still in 1912 the payment of 15 yen a year in national taxes, giving the vote to no more than 3 per cent of the population). Thus landlords, entrepreneurs and ex-samurai had been won over to support a regime dominated by men from Satsuma, Choshu, Tosa and Hizen. Hara sought to redirect their allegiance towards the Seiyukai, that is, to change the balance of power within the existing framework by attracting the support of the well-to-do to the parties, not officialdom.

The lever he used was provided by the cabinet posts the Seiyukai gained as the price of its support for non-party governments after the Russo-Japanese war. Three times between 1905 and 1915 Hara became Home Minister. From this vantage-point he was able to use his power over promotions and dismissals to persuade or coerce many of the new university-trained bureaucrats in central and local government —men with no specific domain allegiances—to co-operate with him and join his party. This gave him a power base within officialdom similar to that of Ito and Yamagata, though at a lower level. He also turned to the wooing of local interest groups by the manipulation of government spending, especially in railway-building and other development projects. By the time the Meiji emperor died these devices had made the Seiyukai a formidable political machine, controlling the lower house of the Diet and able to strike a hard bargain with oligarchs who wanted its backing.

In effect, Hara had harnessed some of the new forces in Meiji society to the service of constitutional government, as he interpreted it. While he was doing so, however, another change was taking place in Japanese politics, this time a negative one, that had at least an equal importance for the future. As spokesmen for a 'transcendental' monarch, claiming to uphold a public interest, not a sectional one, the Meiji leaders—notably the Genro—had given themselves the co-ordinating role in an institutional system comprising parts that were separately responsible to the Throne. It was their personal, extra-constitutional, 'imperial' authority that held together bureaucracy, armed forces, Privy Council and Diet in a workable whole. But now that authority was beginning to weaken: because of age and death; but also because it was resented by the Genro's political heirs. On the other hand, none of those heirs was able to inherit the whole complex of connections that had made up the power of an Ito or a Yamagata, for these had been the product of particular circumstances. They were not transmittable. What was emerging instead was a situation in which those who represented the different parts of the complex competed with each other for power, so that decision-making in Japan in the first decades of the twentieth century came to depend on the balance between, rather than the co-ordination of, different groups within the official structure. The work of Hara Kei ensured that the parties, too, would have their place in it.

Something of this was already to be seen in the crisis that developed in 1913. Katsura Taro, succeeding Saionji once again as Prime Minister in December 1912, decided to bid for power: to make himself independent of the Seiyukai by forming a party of his own and independent of the Genro by direct use of the emperor's authority. He seems to have thought of himself as saving the oligarchy from a mounting Seiyukai threat and putting himself at its head in place of his former mentors. All he did, however, was to unite all elements against his own 'dictatorship'. In February 1913 the Seiyukai launched violent attacks on him in the Diet. Outside the building thousands rioted, storming the offices of pro-government papers. Katsura resigned.

Katsura's failure to find a new formula for oligarchic rule —he died within a few months of these events—marked the end of an era in Japanese politics. Thereafter, as the few remaining Genro disappeared one by one from the scene, so it became clear that no other group could establish an ascendancy such as they had held. The consequences were not immediately serious; but in the long run they were to prove fatally disruptive, as social change, stemming from economic growth, put the political system under critical new strains.

Agriculture was still the chief sector of the Japanese economy in the early twentieth century, despite all the efforts to foster industry in the previous generation. It employed about 14 million people, and this, as late as 1920, represented just over half the occupied population. Production of the two main crops, rice and raw silk, was steadily increasing. Rice production, the annual average of which was some 30 million *koku* in 1880–84, became 40 million *koku* in 1890–94, almost 45 million in 1900–04, and 51 million in 1910–14, most of this being due to a 50 per cent rise in yield per acre. There were proportional increases in the yields of lesser crops like wheat and barley. Output of raw silk grew even faster: 11·5 millions lbs in 1894, 16·5 million in 1904, 31 million in 1914. By the end of the period it accounted for exports valued at 144 million yen, nearly a third of the country's export total.

Over the same years, the process by which the farmer became involved in production for the market and the level of his money expenditure was raised had been completed. He now had to buy fertilizer, tools and seed as well as a variety of household goods, while taxation had also to be paid in cash, not kind. Thus subsistence farming had become impossible. Many owner-cultivators were unable to solve the problems which this situation posed and sank to the status of tenants. As a result two-fifths of the land was tenant-held by 1900. Others, the more successful, became landowners on a larger scale, marking the continued separation of the village into rich and poor. To the rich—a proportion of whom were absentees, since land remained a profitable investment for men who made their money in the towns—the new society gave opportunities of influence, education and good living rather greater than had been enjoyed by their predecessors in feudal Japan. To the poor it gave an opportunity of a different kind: that of finding employment for daughters and younger sons whom the family could no longer support.

For the most part this was in the textile trades, which were the most highly developed sector of Japanese industry. Silk reeling and weaving remained largely rural and provided a good deal of local employment, much of it in the large modern filatures that appeared after 1890. Cotton was even more important, though the location of its factories forced labour to leave the village for the town. As a crop, cotton had ceased to be of value, since the removal of duties in 1896 had made it impossible for home growers to compete with imports from India, but the spinning and weaving sections of the industry were entering a phase of rapid expansion. The number of factory spindles rose from 382,000 in 1893 to 2·4 million twenty years later, yarn output from 116 million lbs to over 650 million lbs in a similar period. At the end, between 30 and 40 per cent of the yarn was going to export. The rest went to domestic weavers, of whom a considerable proportion were still engaged in household industry, using handlooms. By 1913, however, there were 85,000 persons employed in concerns with at least five workers. Some of them were specialist weaving firms, producing mostly narrow widths for the home market and as often equipped with handlooms as with power. Others—and these usually the largest—were power-equipped weaving sheds attached to spinning mills, producing wide standardized fabrics for foreign trade. Their exports of piece-goods were valued at 33 million yen in 1913, compared with only 5·7 million in 1900.

Heavy industry, although it had received a great stimulus from government policies of subsidy and investment after the Sino-Japanese war, was as yet impressive for its rate of growth rather than its volume of output. In shipbuilding the annual average of tonnage launched reached 50,000 tons in 1909–13, when there were six yards capable of building steel ships of a thousand tons or more. Pig-iron and steel production had both reached substantial levels: about a quarter of a million tons of each in 1913, representing a half and a third of the country's needs, respectively. Progress had also been made in some types of heavy engineering, notably the manufacture of railway locomotives and rolling stock, while there were a few large firms engaged in making items like electrical equipment, cement, paper, china, glass and so on. Even so, much of the production of consumer goods, including many of Western type, like bicycle parts and other engineering components, was carried on in a host of small family workshops that were to be found in every industrial town.

The development of factories and workshops, whatever their size and type, depended a good deal on the provision of power and transport. In this much had been achieved. Coal output, 5 million metric tons in 1895, was 21 million tons in 1913, of which 40 per cent was used in industry. Electricity, both for power and lighting, had also become available since 1900, mostly from hydraulic plants. One of them gave Tokyo its first large-scale supply in 1907, another, reputedly the largest in Asia, did the same for Osaka four years later. In 1913 the total generator capacity in operation was over half a million kilowatts.

The railway network by that date served most parts of the Japanese islands. The main line, which in 1891 had stretched from Aomori to Kobe, with a spur from Tokyo to the Japan Sea coast at Naoetsu, had been extended by 1901 to Shimonoseki and Nagasaki. In 1906 the decision was taken to nationalize that part of the track which was owned by private companies— about two-thirds—on the grounds that private ownership had led to a lack of standardization and too great an emphasis on immediate returns. The result was to give the government control of all but about 10 per cent of the 5,000 miles of railway then in use. A map of it in 1907 shows, apart from the Aomori-Nagasaki route, on which sleepers and dining cars were now available, two fairly complex local networks round Tokyo and Kyoto-Osaka, with several extensions begun or completed in northern Kyushu and along the Japan Sea coast. Only Hokkaido and Shikoku were completely without a line. Over those elsewhere, 140 million passengers and 24 million tons of goods were carried in this same year.

Locally, the rail system was supplemented by roads, rough but adequate, which made possible the movement of a vastly greater number of carts and other vehicles. The registered number of horsecarts alone rose from under 1,000 to over 86,000 in the twenty years ending in 1897. At the ports the railways linked with coastal and foreign shipping services, of which an increasing proportion were run by Japanese. The merchant marine had grown to 2·4 million gross tons by 1913, 60 per cent being powered by steam or motor; and at this date it carried approximately half the cargoes entering and leaving the country, providing a daily steamer service between Yokohama and Kobe, as well as at least two a week to Nagasaki and Hakodate, and operating regular liner routes to

Korea, China, the Philippines, Australia, India, Europe and
North America. San Francisco could be reached in sixteen
days. Passengers for Europe had a choice of several lines via
Suez (P and O, Messageries Maritimes and Norddeutscher
Lloyd, in addition to the Japanese NYK), all taking about
forty days, or they could travel on the weekly service to
Vladivostock and thence by the Trans-Siberian railway.

Japan, in fact, was nothing like so remote and isolated as
it had been a generation earlier. Nor did it any longer look
quite so oriental, at least in the principal towns. Two of these
were large by any standards: Osaka with nearly a million residents at the 1903 census, Tokyo almost twice that size. They
also contained much that was familiar to a Western visitor.
Both by 1907 had a waterworks, local electric railways, the
beginnings of a street electric tramway, and numerous public
buildings, banks and offices in the Western style. Less sightly
still was the network of telegraph, telephone and electric light
wires overhead. Ironically, even the hundreds of rickshaws,
which gave the streets an aspect so unlike those of Europe and
America, were a modern addition, only a little older than the
bicycles that were just beginning to replace them.

What was true of Tokyo and Osaka also held good on a
smaller scale for Kyoto, Yokohama, Nagoya and Kobe, with
their resident populations ranging between 250,000 and 400,000
in 1903, and the other nineteen provincial cities which had
50,000 people or more. All had their quota of modern facilities
and of brick or concrete buildings to contrast with the traditional architecture of shrines and private homes. Sometimes
one could find such things in the countryside, too. Government
offices and schools, wherever situated, usually looked thoroughly un-Japanese. Moreover, although the traveller who
wished to visit mountainous regions was advised by a guide-
book of 1907[54] to take food, flea-powder, disinfectant, soap
and candles, as well as bedding, and to be prepared to walk—
'the Japanese pack-saddle is torture'—with baggage carried, in
the absence of pack-horses, by a coolie—'not improbably a
grandfather superannuated from regular work, or possibly a
buxom lass'—there were also rural areas which could be easily
reached and where a good deal of comfort could be had.
Tourist hotels at Nikko and Miyanoshita, their very existence

symbolic of change, advertised their possession of electric light, telephones and billiard-rooms; and local inns might well be found to provide chairs and tables, sheets and pillows, if not beds.

All this was symptomatic of something more than a mere desire to emulate the West. The character of the cities and the rate at which their facilities were growing indicated that the modern sector of the economy was at last becoming a significant feature of national life. The proportion of urban population was increasing: 16 per cent lived in towns of over 10,000 inhabitants in 1893, 21 per cent in 1903, 28 per cent in 1913. The number of factory workers, 420,000 in 1900, was twice as large a decade later. Foreign trade figures told a similar story. Exports of semi-manufactured goods, mostly silk, remained a fairly constant 40 to 50 per cent of the whole, but those of food and raw materials were declining, while those of finished articles grew. These last two groups reached equality in 1893–7, when each accounted for about 26 per cent of exports. After another ten years, the percentages were 21 for food and raw materials, 31 for manufactured goods. Similarly imports of raw materials, especially iron ore and cotton, were also getting larger, comprising 22 per cent of total imports in 1893–7, 44 per cent in 1908–12. The pattern is one that is appropriate to a period of steady industrialization.

Thus the first few years of the twentieth century mark a definite stage in Japan's economic history, dividing, one might say, the time of preparation from that of achievement. What is more, there were signs of what the latter might bring by way of benefits and problems. Statistics concerning wages for the period before 1914 are unreliable, but such as they are they indicate a rise in real wages in the twenty years after the China war of the order of 30 per cent. There had already been an increase in *per capita* consumption of rice in the 1880s, from 0·8 *koku* (4 bushels) a person every year to a fraction over a *koku* (5 bushels). This level was maintained, though not improved upon, for half a century. Since rice was very much the preferred diet of Japanese, this must count as better living. So must the greater consumption of textiles, for exports of these did not by any means take the whole of the increase in production.

On the other hand, the country's population had risen from 35 million in 1873 to 46 million in 1903 and the graph was still moving rapidly upward. There were therefore more people to share the available food and goods. Soon after 1890, indeed, Japan became a net importer of rice and by 1904 was buying nearly 3 million *koku* a year abroad, mostly from Korea and Formosa. Thereafter she faced the familiar problem of the densely populated industrial state, the need to import sub-stantial food supplies and to export goods in payment for them, complicated in her case by negligible home production of raw materials like iron ore, lead, tin, petroleum, cotton and wool, large quantities of which had therefore to be imported too.

These circumstances, in conjunction with the government's resolve to maintain a large military establishment, helped to hold back the rate of increase in standards of living. And such increase as did occur was not evenly apportioned. The town profited more than the village, the owner and manager more than the urban worker. It is true that this was in one sense a stimulus to economic development, in that it made possible a high level of savings and investment, for example, and en-sured ample supplies of cheap industrial labour, but it also threatened to bring political unrest. Entrepreneurs, acquiring wealth, sought influence, usually through the existing political parties. Workers, suffering from low wages and atrocious labour conditions, began to organize trade unions and parties of their own. They met with a sharp reaction from officialdom. In 1900 police regulations were issued making strikes illegal and in the following year a new Social Democratic Party was suppressed within a day of its formation. Moreover, attempts to introduce labour legislation, beginning as early as 1898, met with obstruction from vested interests represented in the Diet. In the cotton industry, especially—where young female work-ers, 'hired from the countryside by practices which bordered often on seduction'[55] and lodged in factory dormitories, were required to work a twelve-hour day or more in even the best concerns—mill owners fought stubbornly to delay the passage of a Factory Act prescribing a maximum of an eleven-hour day for women and children. It was 1911 before the bill became law and another five years to its enforcement.

Before then there had been signs of some of the extreme

forms of protest that these conditions were to generate. In 1906 the young Kita Ikki (1883–1937) published—at his family's expense—a book attacking the Meiji leaders and the 'economic daimyo class' for having perverted Japan's true national polity. To set things right, he said, required national-ization of land and capital at home, plus a vigorous struggle against the voracious Western powers abroad. His book was promptly banned. At almost the same time the slightly older Kotoku Shusui (1871–1911) was declaring for direct action in the people's struggle against 'the monied middle class', but in the name of international socialism, not traditional norms. Within a year or two this led him to involve himself in a plot to kill the emperor, for which he was arrested in 1910 and executed early the following year. The affair enabled the government, through propaganda and police action, to sup-press the socialist movement for a decade. It was, however, ominous of things to come. Socially and temperamentally Kita and Kotoku were akin both to the terrorists of the 1860s and to those of the 1930s.[56] Historically, if not ideologically, they provide a link between the two.

The influences that were changing the Japanese city were also changing the life of its inhabitants, not only in respect of where they worked and what they did there, or of the politics they argued, but also in terms of what they wore and ate and how they spent their leisure. An early sign of it was the disappear-ance of traditional hairstyles, chiefly among men, and the substitution of close cutting in the European manner. Official approval of the change was announced in September 1871. By that date Japanese were already to be seen in public wearing a fine array of international clothing—there are references to Prussian hats, French shoes and invernesses—and in 1873, it is said, Satsuma samurai appearing in Tokyo in the old costume 'were as much stared at as foreigners had formerly been'.[57] Thereafter the example of the Court (which had adopted West-ern ceremonial dress at the end of 1872), the cabinet and the diplomatic corps, to say nothing of the uniforms used by the services, police and railway officials, all helped to make the new clothing widely accepted. By the end of the century it was worn almost universally among the upper classes, at least on public and business occasions. Frock coat and top hat (or kimono with bowler) became the norm in family photographs. If one adds that the use of visiting cards was general and that the smoking of cigars and cigarettes was becoming popular, it is clear that the visitor could soon be made to feel at home. In the towns he could get beer, which was successfully produced in Tokyo and Yokohama, and most varieties of Western food, though elsewhere he might find it difficult to obtain bread, meat or milk and might have to depend on the rice and fish, supplemented by chicken and eggs, of which the more expensive versions of the Japanese diet consisted.

All Western foods, of course, were still luxuries to Japanese, as were most of the country's imported pastimes and entertainments. Western music, for example, had first been performed in the 1880s at the Rokumeikan, a hall built in Tokyo to provide a place at which Japanese official society could meet foreign diplomats and other residents. The newly-formed services bands and some of the court musicians played there in concerts and also for dancing, lessons being given by a German instructor. Before long, as a result, Western music became a polite accomplishment. It was taught at the Tokyo School of Music, founded in 1887, which in 1903 helped to put on the first opera in Japanese, a translation of Gluck's *Orpheus*, with the help of a foreign conductor and pianist. Such pleasures were for the few, however. Popular taste remained wedded to martial music—also in the Western style—like the marches and military songs that were taught in schools, which from August 1905 could be heard at the new bandstand in Tokyo's Hibiya Park, where army and navy performed alternately.

In the theatre the Japanese tradition proved better able to hold its own, for although the revival of Noh towards the end of the nineteenth century was a matter largely of aristocratic patronage, the Kabuki drama, with its melodramatic plots, coarse humour and vivid spectacle, continued to have a wide appeal. It was handicapped for a time by government insistence that its stories be useful and rewarding—and by attempts to perform translated Western plays, for which its techniques were quite unsuitable—but it nevertheless remained far more successful than performances in the Western style. These, too, relied heavily on translations at first, with Shakespeare,

Molière and Ibsen all represented. What is more, it was not until late in the Meiji period that the acting and staging of them reached competent standards.

Concerts and the theatre in their new forms were for those who lived in, or could visit, one of the major cities. The rest knew of them by hearsay or by what they read. Indeed, much of what was new in Japanese life in general found an expression in its literature, not now because books had a didactic purpose, like those just after the Restoration, which had been concerned to introduce novelties of thought and custom to the uninformed reader, but because they reflected an environment in which the writer lived and worked. For example, Nagai Kafu's *Sumida-gawa* (The Sumida River, 1909), a novel about the passing of the old Tokyo, is full of references to things like night school, tramcars, gaslight in the theatre, an isolation hospital, and so on, an apparently random selection of modern trappings which yet form an essential background to the plot. The story and its characters depend on changes in society in a much more funda-mental way. Central to them are the student, Chokichi, whose mother, a teacher of dramatic recitation, wants to put him through university in order that he may qualify for the security of a salaried job. He, however, is drawn to the theatre, a kind of disobedience which is also a turning back to a way of life his mother had rejected for him, though it was in a sense her own. The resulting conflicts, between duty, defined as respect for parental authority, and inclination, as well as between the traditional and the modern in Japanese living, are themes that were to be characteristic of many books, plays and eventually films in the twentieth century. Of a different kind, but equally contemporary in concept and setting, was Tayama Katai's *Ippeisotsu* (One Soldier, 1908), a grimly realistic story of a private serving in the Russo-Japanese war, whom illness, lone-liness and hardship drain of patriotism and courage until he can do no more than hide himself and die. The idea, the treatment, even the prose in which they were written, made novels like these a far cry from those of a generation earlier.

Yet literature had not entirely abandoned its past. There was a novel called *Takekurabe* (Growing Up, 1895) by the woman novelist Higuchi Ichiyo, about a group of boys and girls in their 'teens who lived on the outskirts of Tokyo's pleasure quarter, the Yoshiwara. Acute in observation, it had strong echoes of the better Tokugawa writing, like that of Saikaku, so much so that it makes one hardly aware of a changing world at all. Were it not for references to the new currency, the *yen*, the scene might easily be Edo. Nor is this due to mere nostalgia on the author's part. Rather, it is because she had chosen for her subject an aspect of Japanese society which had itself changed little, if at all.

This serves to emphasize something which an interest in the modern might easily lead one to overlook, the fact that there were many things in Japan which had been hardly touched by the Meiji reforms, at least in their essentials. The manners and outlook of the Yoshiwara and the Kabuki theatre, the seasonal rhythm of life on the farm, the social exchanges properly to be observed between families and persons, these remained much as they had been in 1800. So did a great part of Japanese religion. Buddhism, it is true, to some extent declined. De-prived of official support by the fall of the Tokugawa, it was sharply attacked after 1868 by the adherents of Shinto, who on a number of occasions used force against its priests and temples. Moreover, they were encouraged in their actions by the policies of the Meiji government. Dependent for their own authority on that of the emperor, the new leaders were naturally preju-diced in favour of a religion which asserted his divine descent. They therefore gave it a place of honour, not only in court ceremonies, where it had always been predominant, but also in administration, setting the Council of Shinto Religion above even the Council of State in the formal hierarchy of their first constitutional arrangements. When this plan was aban-doned in 1872, Shinto still received direct government patron-age through the appointment of official teachers to promote its spread.

Greater knowledge of Western practice, together with a limited revival of Buddhism, brought a change in 1877. There-after government policy distinguished between two different kinds of Shinto: that which had a direct bearing on questions of state and that which was concerned only with religious belief, the first being put under the supervision of a depart-ment within the Home Ministry, which became responsible for classifying and financing most national, and many local, shrines, while the second became a matter for private organizations acting on their own. After a few years several of the latter received official recognition as separate religious bodies, that is, as Shinto sects.

Thus by 1900 State Shinto and Sect Shinto were clearly separated, the one concerned largely with the emperor and official ceremonial, the other with those elements of popular belief which had for centuries been the chief part of religion as the majority of Japanese knew it. Within the average household, in fact, religious observance had been little changed. It had long been eclectic, linked to the rituals of birth, marriage and death and to the festivals of local deities, rather than to broad concepts of faith and organization. Accordingly, a relative increase in the influence of Shinto on the national scene, and a relative decline in that of Buddhism, made little difference, for to the family it meant no more than a shift of emphasis within a common tradition.

The challenge to this tradition that came from Christianity, though radical, was no more productive of widespread change. It was not until 1873 that diplomatic pressure made Christianity legal and for some years afterwards the missionaries had to struggle against the heritage of Tokugawa anti-Christian propaganda. The frenzy of enthusiasm for all things Western, which engulfed Japan at the end of the 1870s, eventually helped them to overcome it, as did recognition of, and respect for, missionary achievements in medicine and education, but the churches suffered setbacks again a decade later from the growth of nationalism and a revival of anti-foreign feeling. The result, despite a great outpouring of funds and human effort, was a total of no more than 140,000 converts by 1907. Of these, 60,000 were Roman Catholics, with an archbishop in Tokyo and bishops in Osaka, Sendai and Nagasaki; just under 50,000 were Protestants; and 29,000 were followers of the Greek Orthodox faith, which had been propagated with considerable success by a handful of priests from Russia.

Christianity was often more important in its influence on ideas than the number of its adherents would lead one to expect. Nevertheless, it was not strong enough to revolutionize the whole outlook of Japanese society. Indeed, if the Meiji era brought a challenge to the old beliefs at all, it was the threat to Confucian ethics and the patterns of behaviour based upon them that came from the temporal strand of Western thought, now embodied in the curriculum of schools throughout Japan and in much of the country's daily life. Institutionally, Confucianism had suffered severely from the Restoration, because of the abolition of the establishments for teaching it which had been maintained by the Bakufu and feudal lords. Moreover, the cosmological elements in Confucian philosophy, like those in Western religion, proved unable to survive the growth of science.[58] On the other hand, in matters of politics and ethics Confucian tenets remained the norm. They found their way habitually into government edicts and they played a vital part in shaping the education system's course in 'morals', so that Confucian virtues of loyalty, harmony and filial piety, in which schools had to provide instruction, became the basis of civic and social duty in the modern state.

This was a situation that greatly appealed to conservatives, who could console themselves with the observation that however much the mechanisms of government were of alien origin, the ideas that suffused its working were Japanese. Patriotism and a respect for the past for them went hand in hand. By contrast, radicals and reformers turned more and more to the West for inspiration, not only in science and technology—which were patriotic because they contributed to national strength—but also in questions of human behaviour and relationships. Christianity, for the most part, they rejected, just as they rejected the ancient religions and philosophy of Japan. Instead, they turned to the example of a new generation of Western thinkers for theories that were secular, pragmatic, even anti-religious, thereby initiating a conflict which, because it involved the emotions of nationalism as well as the traditions of family life, contributed largely to the turbulence of the following fifty years.

CHAPTER XI

JAPAN BECOMES A WORLD POWER
1914-1922

Japan and the mainland—declaration of war on Germany—the Twenty-one Demands—relations with the Allies—peace settlement—the Washington Conference

WHEN A MAJOR war broke out in Europe in August 1914, Japan, by virtue of the progress she had made in the previous fifty years, was for the first time in a position to intervene in European questions. By 1918, when the war ended, doing so had made her a world Power, with a military and naval establishment capable of giving substance to the rights she claimed, as well as an economy far enough developed to support her forces, population and prestige. Thus at Versailles Japan's delegates ranked next in importance to those of Britain, France and the United States. In the League of Nations she had one of the permanent seats on the Council. Finally, at Washington in 1922 her activities became the subject of international agreements which sought to restrict the Japanese advance in China and elsewhere, an event that constituted a tribute, if an unwelcome one, to the speed at which her strength and influence were growing.

This was a situation very different from that which the Tokugawa had faced, or the Meiji leaders, yet the policies that brought it about were nevertheless a development of, rather than a departure from, those of the nineteenth century. The fear of Western encroachment still lingered in Japanese thinking on foreign affairs, bringing an almost universal acceptance of the need for national strength. Behind it lay the same ambivalence of reaction, paralleling, though in a new context, what an earlier age had labelled *kaikoku* ('open the country') and *joi* ('expel the barbarian'). There were men who argued, like the supporters of *kaikoku*, that the country must observe the rules of procedure that the West laid down and seek recognition, as well as safety, within them, forming alliances, exchanging goods, borrowing ideas. There were others, the uncompromising, who wished instead to turn away from the West entirely. They did not, it is true, urge seclusion or a war of liberation, as *joi* advocates had done; but by demanding for Japan a position of supremacy in East Asia, which would make her independent of Western help and able to repel any new attempt at extending Western dominance, they were appealing to the same prejudices and emotions.

Among both groups, preoccupation with the nearby mainland was as great as ever. Since 1894 the ties of geography and tradition had been reinforced by two successful wars and the acquisition of territorial possession, giving Japan important interests to defend and a foothold on the continent from which others might rapidly be added. The result was to make China and her northern neighbours more than ever a focus of Japanese ambitions. One contemporary described these bluntly as 'a determination to be undisputed masters of Eastern Asia',[59] which war in Europe, distracting the attention of the Powers, made practical. The description gains validity from the actions of Japanese governments between 1914 and 1922. On the other hand, Japanese policy was neither so consistent nor so easily agreed upon as this might make one think, for there were differences of outlook, even as regards China, which led at times to bitter argument.

In fact, one can identify three main strands in the debate on Far East policies:

First, exemplified in the demands for reform in Korea, which had precipitated the war of 1894–5, was the desire to create a defensive league of states, modernized and under Japanese leadership, which would free its members from subjection to the West. This concept helped bring about the annexation of Korea, a step justified as the sole means of overcoming Korean lethargy and reaction. It also led to much dabbling in the politics of China, undertaken in a search for men who would co-operate if they were backed—and their reluctance occasionally overborne—by Japanese arms and money. There were, however, contradictions: supporting revolutionaries overseas might be a way to stimulate modernization, but there was always the risk that it might encourage radicals at home; while intervention designed to make China resist the West tended, paradoxically, to arouse a nationalism which had as the target of its hostility, Japan.

Second, alternative to such a league, were plans for an empire on the continent from which Japan would gain strength enough to defend the area singlehanded. This began as military strategy, involving Korea, Manchuria and perhaps Mongolia, with defence against Russia as its primary object; but in the twentieth century, when the region gained importance as a market and source of raw materials, it had an economic side as well. This was to culminate in the industrialization of North Korea and South Manchuria, chiefly after 1930.

Third, was the application of a similar plan to China, though with greater emphasis on trade and outlets for investment. There were men, undoubtedly, who hoped to find in China the kind of opportunities that Britain had found in India—just as there were men who thought in terms more grandiose still, of an empire stretching to the Indo-Chinese peninsula and beyond—but for the majority, China, if not an ally, was to be a source of Japanese wealth. As such, whether she wished it or not, she would contribute to the area's security. Yet even in this there were problems. Trade, if China proved obstinate, would have to be supported by bases, sometimes by the use of force. It might also, if Japan's rights were privileged or exclusive, evoke the hostility of Britain and America. Economic expansion, therefore, for all that it was apparently peaceful in intent, involved risks which not everyone was prepared to take.

These plans and policies were not incompatible with each other in one respect, for all could usefully contribute to the increase of Japanese strength. They might thus be regarded as different methods for the attainment of a single goal, divergent rather than contradictory, with belief in one not necessarily a barrier to acceptance of the rest. On the other hand, they were not sufficiently alike to ensure unanimity in action. When the moment came for making practical decisions—drafting a diplomatic note, for example, or moving troops—a country with limited resources had to be clear what its immediate objectives were. Was it more important at a given time to placate Western opinion or to secure a vital base? Was it better to browbeat or to woo the Chinese leaders? Was action in China or Manchuria the more appropriate, taking account of the fact that different foreign powers might be concerned, according to the choice that was made? These were the sort of questions a government would have to ask. That its members were committed in general to a policy of expansion did not guarantee that they would arrive at identical answers.

The surviving Meiji leaders, now, as Genro, the emperor's senior advisers on matters of state, were inclined to caution. Yamagata Aritomo, much the most influential since Ito's death, has always been regarded as a militarist, but his comments on foreign affairs in 1914 and 1915 show a marked reluctance to approve provocative measures. He agreed that Japan must strengthen her position in China and Manchuria. At the same time, he identified two limiting factors: first, that nothing be done to provoke the Powers; second, that China be won to an attitude of genuine co-operation. Only in this way could Japan consolidate her gains and retain them when the European war was over. For once the war ended, he thought, 'the various countries will again focus their attention on the Far East and the benefits and rights they might derive from this region', exacerbating 'the rivalry between the white and non-white races'.[60] In such a situation, Japan and China would have to co-operate to survive. This would be impossible if Japan had meanwhile acted so as to alienate China, driving her, perhaps, into America's arms.

In the army, many senior officers accepted Yamagata's views. Others preferred Japan to rely on her own efforts, as she had done against Russia in 1904, and concentrate on building up her military bases in the north. Diplomats, by contrast, were with few exceptions anxious to proceed by negotiation, not by force. Party politicians were attracted to the support of economic penetration by their links with businessmen, to a desire for quick successes by their need for votes. As a result, all variations on the theme of priority were represented in policy discussions. Moreover, the decision reached at any given time was likely to reflect the balance of political strength between these groups and individuals, not necessarily a reconciliation of ideas.

It might also be influenced by pressures from outside. Newspapers, popular and thoroughly nationalist in tone, could be counted on to demand 'strong' action whatever the issue. So might the mobs, the more easily incited on this question because of the loyalty they were taught at school or in a conscript army. Then there were the personal pressures, difficult to assess but certainly exerted, that were brought to bear on public figures. Not least were those that emanated from societies of patriots, the first of which, the Genyosha, founded by ex-samurai in Fukuoka in 1881, had a range of activities that ran all the way from espionage, agitation and murder in Korea, to the provision of strong-arm men for use in Diet elections and attempts at intimidating those whom it accused of 'weakness' in foreign affairs. The bomb attack on Okuma in 1889, for example, was by one of its members, the assassination of the Korean queen in 1895 by others. It was a Genyosha man, Uchida Ryohei, with the patronage of another, Toyama Mitsuru, who founded a still more famous organization in 1901, the Kokuryukai (the Amur River Society, more often called the Black Dragon Society). This carried on the Genyosha's work, but with emphasis on Manchuria instead of Korea. After 1905, anticipating the next stage of Japan's advance, it turned to China, establishing connections with men like Sun Yat-sen and acting as a semi-official intelligence corps for the Japanese army. Simultaneously it sought to bring Japanese leaders into conformity with its plans, sometimes by threats, sometimes by persuasion—Uchida and Toyama, as ex-samurai of manifest sincerity, had access to the very highest circles—and sometimes by public demonstrations. The plans themselves were outlined in a memorandum which Uchida sent to government officials in November 1914: Japanese agents were to incite their friends among the Chinese radicals to revolt;

the Japanese army would be sent to restore order, bringing its protégés to power; and a defensive alliance could then be concluded between the two governments. It was the pattern of Korea in 1894, repeated.

Though neither the Kokuryukai nor any other single group was able to exercise a decisive influence on Japanese policy, the effect of all these pressures, both within the government and outside it, was to create a climate of opinion in which an advance of some kind on the Asian mainland—whether military or economic, in China or Manchuria, with Chinese co-operation or without it—became axiomatic. Despite the ebb and flow, as first one faction gained the upper hand and then another, and despite some changes of direction, there resulted an overall movement towards Japanese domination of an area comprising China, Manchuria, Korea and the adjacent islands. This is the theme of the country's foreign relations between 1914 and 1922.

The European crisis of 1914 came at a time when Japan had a government willing to exploit it. The Yamamoto cabinet, which had succeeded that of Katsura in the previous year, fell in March 1914 as a result of revelations that bribery had been used to influence the placing of naval contracts. This brought to power Okuma Shigenobu as Prime Minister, with Kato Komei to handle foreign affairs. Both were party politicians. Both were also supporters of the Anglo-Japanese alliance, but they did not feel themselves committed on this account to maintaining the *status quo* in China, notwithstanding the fact that this was ostensibly a principal aim of the agreement. Indeed, they were anxious that Japan's position in China be strengthened by all possible means.

This became apparent at the beginning of August, when Russia, France and Britain in quick succession declared war on Germany. Their action raised the question whether Japan's alliance with Britain, even though it did not apply specifically to Europe, imposed on her any military obligations in such a situation, an issue raised by Britain herself a few days later when she sought Japanese help in protecting Hong Kong and Weihaiwei, as well as in naval action against German commerce raiders in the Pacific. Kato, in particular, felt that this was too limited and unprofitable a form of co-operation, arguing that full belligerent status would be more advantageous. On August 8 he persuaded the cabinet and Genro to his point of view. The news greatly alarmed London. Believing that Kato's intentions were to involve China in the war and so exploit Europe's preoccupation with its own affairs, Britain tried without success to get the decision changed, or to secure an assurance that no action would be taken against German bases on the China coast. On August 15 Japan demanded that Germany withdraw or disarm her warships in Far Eastern waters and surrender the leased territory of Kiaochow. When the ultimatum was ignored, a declaration of war followed.

Japan's military action was prompt and successful. On September 2, 1914, her troops began to land in the Shantung peninsula and advance towards Tsingtao and Kiaochow Bay. By November 7 Tsingtao had fallen, marking the completion of the campaign. Meanwhile, naval operations during October had led to the occupation of the German-held Pacific islands north of the equator. Thus in less than three months all German bases, railways and other installations in Japan's desired sphere of interest had been taken over.

This left the way clear for action regarding China. Two different considerations, both related to the revolution which had overthrown the Manchus and led to the creation of a republic in 1912, made action there seem necessary. For some time Japan had been seeking to extend the leases and railway rights in Manchuria which she had taken over from Russia in 1905. In view of the political turbulence in China, coupled as it was with anti-imperialist sentiment, this now became urgent. More widely, there was a danger that the change of regime in China might undermine the whole structure of foreign rights and privileges in that country, including those of Japan. There were two ways in which such a danger could be averted. One was to work closely with the Chinese revolutionaries and lead them towards a policy of modernization in co-operation with Japan. Various Japanese groups and companies had already established links with Sun Yat-sen with that possibility in mind, but their plans were frustrated in 1913 by the failure of Sun's attempt to overthrow the President of the new republic, Yuan Shih-k'ai. Also at that time, Chinese troops under the command of Chang Hsun, who had been sent to suppress the revolt, had killed and manhandled a number of Japanese in Nanking, an event which aroused much public indignation in Japan and brought demands for strong action against Yuan's government. Such demands accorded well enough with the personal inclinations of Prime Minister Okuma.

The alternative to co-operation with Chinese revolutionaries was some kind of political intervention in China, by which Japan could put herself in a position to defend her interests with or without Chinese consent. On two occasions since the outbreak of the revolution, Japanese army leaders had given covert support to plots aimed at re-establishing the former Chinese ruling dynasty in its Manchu homeland, in the hope that this would be a means of securing Japanese influence there. One objection to this, that it would make Chinese opinion irreconcilable, carried enough weight with the cabinet to prevent such activities from getting government approval, but there is no doubt that most army opinion continued to press for something more than diplomatic protests to Peking, however strong. Another objection, that the Powers with interests in China would react strongly to an independent Japanese *démarche*, was negated, at least temporarily, by the outbreak of the European war. It was therefore in the context of that war that Kato defined his China policy.

Late in 1914 he and his advisers worked out a list of concessions which were to be won from China as soon as opportunity offered. They provided, first, for the transfer to Japan of former German rights in the province of Shantung, including Kiaochow. Next, they specified additional railway and mining rights to be granted in Manchuria and Mongolia, as well as other economic and political privileges in that region. Finally, China was to be required to give an undertaking not to cede or lease coastal territory to any other Power—there was special mention of Fukien—while arrangements were also to be made for the appointment of Japanese political, financial and military advisers to the Chinese government, for joint Sino-Japanese police administration in key areas, and for the use by China of Japanese munitions.

Such were the Twenty-one Demands, a draft of which was handed to Japan's minister in Peking in December 1914 with instructions to use it when occasion arose. This proved to be in January 1915, when Yuan Shih-k'ai asked that foreign troops be withdrawn from the war zone in Shantung, operations having ended. The request was at once described as an unfriendly act by the Japanese, whose prepared demands were presented: secretly to

Yuan in person, with a hint that if he rejected them, Japanese help might be given to those in China who sought his fall.

Yuan could do little in face of Japan's obvious determination when those most likely to help him were already involved in war. Inspired leaks of information from Peking brought protests to Japan from various quarters, especially the United States, but none were strong enough to prevent Foreign Minister Kato from pressing his advantage home. In May, after several weeks of fruitless talks, he modified the proposals, leaving out the most objectionable of those in the final section, but making the rest an ultimatum. This brought quick compliance. Treaties signed on May 25, 1915, together with an accompanying exchange of notes, gave Japan most of what she wanted. It included Chinese approval of any agreement about German rights in Shantung that might be concluded between Japan and Germany, with the proviso that Japan would restore the Kiaochow lease to China in return for the port being opened to foreign trade; an extension of existing leases in Manchuria and a promise of Japanese priority in all development there; and a number of useful, if less sweeping, gains elsewhere.

The agreement, notwithstanding the fact that it gave Japan a preponderance she could not have dared to hope for ten years earlier, was not received without criticism in Tokyo. Some thought it had fallen short of what might have been achieved, some that the effort had been geographically too diffuse, others again that it was a betrayal of the Chinese radicals and reformers. These were the objections of minorities, however, coming chiefly from outside the ruling circle. More important were the objections raised by Yamagata Aritomo and the new leader of the Seiyukai, Hara Kei (Takashi), who, although far apart in politics, were united in condemning the methods by which the new privileges had been obtained. By his bullying, they said, Kato had aroused the hostility of both China and the Powers. Consequently, when the latter tried to resume their pre-war position in the Far East at the end of hostilities, as inevitably they would, Japan would be handicapped in resisting them by Chinese enmity. The solution, as Yamagata saw it, was to limit the government's immediate objectives to securing Yuan's acceptance of two basic propositions: first, that Japan's expansion in Manchuria was inevitable, both as an outlet for her growing population and as a means of defending China from Russian attack; second, that the two countries must co-operate against the West.

Yamagata failed to force this plan on Okuma, though his strictures had the effect of getting Kato excluded from the cabinet when it was reorganized in the following August. Moreover, a year later Yamagata was able to block an attempt by Okuma to bring Kato back as premier, securing the appointment instead for his own protégé, Terauchi Masatake, who as governor-general in Korea had already come to much the same conclusions about the mainland as his mentor. Thus when he formed his government in October 1916 it was with certain intentions clearly in his mind. Policy towards China, which he kept under his own control, was to be directed towards conciliation. This was to be attained, however, not by reducing Japan's requirements, but by working closely with such Chinese leaders as were willing to promote them, especially Tuan Ch'i-jui, most likely successor to Yuan Shih-k'ai, who had died in June. Accordingly, between February 1917, when Nishihara Kamezo visited Peking as Terauchi's personal emissary, and September 1918, when Terauchi himself resigned, Tuan and his immediate colleagues received consistent Japanese support. It helped to keep them most of the time in office, chiefly through a series of so-called 'Nishihara loans', totalling 145 million yen, which were ostensibly for the development of telegraphs, railways, mining and timber concessions, but in fact did more for Tuan's political funds than for China's economic growth.

Notwithstanding the fact that Tuan's government had little authority, since effective power in most parts of China had been seized by local warlords, former henchmen of Yuan Shih-k'ai, Terauchi found it highly convenient to have a measure of co-operation from the country's official rulers. Nevertheless, this by itself was not sufficient to guarantee Japan's position. As a corollary to the policy, therefore, he set out to gain European recognition of the benefits his predecessors had secured. A first move in this direction had been made by Okuma, who had taken steps—mostly at the urging of Yamagata Aritomo—to negotiate a secret Russo-Japanese alliance in July 1916, designed to protect the Far Eastern interests of its signatories, including those which Japan had just obtained in Manchuria and Mongolia. Terauchi determined to complete the pattern by gaining similar assurances from the other Powers, using as his bargaining point the question of Japan's participation in the war. She had several times refused requests to send troops to Europe or to provide naval forces for the Baltic, Mediterranean and Dardanelles, on the grounds that all her strength was needed for her own defence; but in January 1917, when he received another such request, this time from Britain for naval assistance against German submarines, Terauchi did not reject it. Instead, he seized the opportunity to conclude a secret agreement, dated February 16, 1917, by which he promised to provide a naval escort group for service in European waters and to support British claims to the former German islands in the Pacific south of the equator, in return for a British undertaking to back Japan's claims in Shantung, the Carolines, Marianas and Marshalls. Within a few weeks France and Italy had been induced to make similar commitments, in this case as the price for Japanese help in persuading China to declare war on Germany.

There remained the United States, sympathetic towards China and much less susceptible to blackmail over military co-operation. Here Japan tried promises, not threats. In September 1917 she sent a special ambassador to Washington, Ishii Kikujiro, who in November carried out a public exchange of notes with Lansing, the American Secretary of State. They committed Japan to respecting the independence and territorial integrity of China, as well as to promoting equal opportunity for all in China's foreign trade. On the other hand, America recognized that 'territorial propinquity' gave Japan 'special interests', which she was entitled to protect.

This was all that could immediately be done to prepare against the expected recriminations. But when the war was over the peace conference at Versailles provided an occasion for Japan to get her rights and status written into a general treaty. Hara Kei was by this time premier, having succeeded Terauchi in September 1918, and Saionji, youngest of the Genro at seventy-four, was sent as Japan's chief delegate; but the change of men did not involve a change of policy. Saionji, starting with the advantage of having known Clemenceau as a student and of being accepted on equal terms by Wilson and Lloyd George, soon showed that he was determined to hold his country's allies to their promises. He was the better able to do so, more-over, because of Japan's known reserves of military strength. Indeed, considering how little part she had played in war-time operations, it was a great tribute to her general standing that she was one of the five Powers to have representatives on the Council of Ten, which began discussion of the peace terms in January 1919.

For the most part the Japanese delegates spoke only on matters which their government regarded as its direct concern: Shantung; the Pacific islands; and racial equality. The first of them, Shantung, proved from the beginning to be a major stumbling-block. China had sent a strong delegation, which engaged vigorously in propaganda to convince both the coun-cil and the press that the 1915 treaties were invalid because they had been signed under the threat of force; and although the argument was not convincing legally—as well as suffering tactically from the disadvantage that it could be extended to all the other treaties of the Powers with China—it had American sympathy, so that considerable efforts were made to find a compromise. Japan, trusting to the promises made in 1917, remained unmoved, rejecting first an American proposal for joint action by the Powers, then a British proposal for a Shan-tung mandate; and she gained her point at last on April 30, when it was decided to include in the treaty a clause admitting her claim to Germany's former rights, subject to such arrange-ments as she might make with China. This was not the end of the story, however, for the Chinese representatives refused to sign the treaty in that form. Thus when the conference ended late in June, Japan's position, though she was in *de facto* control of Shantung and diplomatically unassailable, still lacked legal sanction.

The Pacific islands question caused little dispute and Japan was given those she claimed as a League of Nations mandate. But in the negotiations concerning the establishment of the League itself she suffered a reverse. Prompted partly by mem-ories of the unequal treaties, partly by more recent restrictions on Japanese emigration to Australia and the American west coast—by this time population pressure at home was causing a good many Japanese to seek opportunities of settlement overseas, chiefly in those parts of the world where standards of living were relatively high—public opinion in Japan had seized on the idea of embodying a racial equality clause in the League of Nations charter. This was proposed in February 1919 by Makino, the Japanese member of the drafting commission, and was supported by China, Czecho-Slovakia, France, Greece, Italy and Poland. However, bitter opposition from Hughes of Australia caused a decision to be postponed and before Makino raised the matter again in April at the commission's last meeting, Australian and Californian pressure had made certain that neither Britain nor the United States would accept the motion. This ensured its defeat, leaving Japan with a feeling of resentment that was never entirely assuaged, even by her permanent seat on the Council and full representation in the League's committees and secretariat.

Another failure, more costly both in money and reputation, had meanwhile arisen from a matter that was not on the Versailles agenda at all. This was the Siberian affair, stemming from the Russian revolution of 1917. For the revolution had not only robbed the allies of Russia's military assistance, it had also brought chaos to Russia's Far Eastern possessions, which threatened to spread to neighbouring Manchuria and undermine Russo-Japanese co-operation there, on which both countries had come to rely in preventing interference from other powers in their respective spheres of influence. Some Japanese, moreover, saw the disorder as an opportunity for pushing Japan's sphere northward into Russian territory. By December 1917, only a month after the Bolshevik coup, the army was discussing plans to send troops into Siberia, seize the railways and support whatever anti-Bolsheviks it could find. At the Foreign Ministry, Motono Ichiro also made proposals to intervene, though rather with a view to strengthening Japan's position against the expected renewal of international rivalries in the postwar era. These differences of emphasis in the objectives envisaged by different Japanese authorities were made more embarrassing by the fact that Saionji and Hara, in particular, insisted that Japan must do nothing that would jeopardize her relations with her allies, because of the dangers that diplomatic isolation would pose to her interests in China. The result was

deadlock within the cabinet and among its principal advisers, not resolved until March 1918, when Yamagata declared himself against
intervention. It would, he thought, almost certainly mean fullscale
hostilities against both Germany and the Soviets, which Japan could
only contemplate if she had the backing of France, Britain and the
United States.

This did nothing to change the views of the army, which was
much less under Yamagata's control than in the past and went
on working out the details of extensive operations. It did,
however, bring Terauchi temporarily into alliance with Hara
and force the resignation of Foreign Minister Motono, leaving
his successor to set about the task of gaining American agreement to some kind of Japanese move. For some weeks he could
make little headway, though it was known that both Britain
and France were prepared to approve the idea in general terms.
Then in June and July Czech forces, fighting their way out of
Russia in an attempt to continue the war against Germany
despite Russia's surrender, seized Vladivostock and the eastern
sections of the Trans-Siberian railway. At this the United
States proposed limited intervention to cover the Czech withdrawal, an offer which precipitated another crisis in Japanese
policy formation by resurrecting the arguments of the winter
and spring. The army by this time was thinking of a force of
seven divisions, operating throughout the area east of Irkutsk.
The American plan, by contrast, which Hara and his friends
preferred, envisaged a single division at most, based on Vladivostock. In such circumstances Terauchi had to work hard
to preserve even a semblance of government unity and the
final decision, reached on August 2, 1918, was the best
compromise he could effect: one, or perhaps two, Japanese
divisions to be sent to Siberia, with another force, rather
smaller, supporting them in Manchuria. Nothing beyond this
would be undertaken, he promised Hara, without further
consultation.

Despite this assurance, it was the army's original plans, or
something like them, that were actually carried out. By the end
of 1918 four or five Japanese divisions were operating in the
Amur basin, controlling the whole of the railway and far out-
numbering the American and other allied contingents. Hara,
now Prime Minister, found it impossible to exercise control or

to effect withdrawal, even though Japan's policy was unpopular both at home and abroad. Nor was anything of substance being achieved. White Russian and Cossack puppet leaders proved more a liability than a help. They were quite unable to govern, equally unable to check the advance of Soviet forces from the Urals which began in the following year, so that by November 1919 the Soviets were in Omsk and moving steadily east. In January 1920, therefore, the American government announced the recall of its troops, an example quickly followed by Britain, France and Canada. Only the Japanese remained, actually extending their occupation to northern Sakhalin soon after, in retaliation for a massacre of Japanese citizens at Nikolaevsk; but even to them it was clear by the middle of 1920 that the venture was doomed to failure within a very short time.

Siberia was one of several problems in the Pacific area that had yet to be settled, all of them concerning Japan in one way or another. China still refused to come to terms over Shantung, though it was obvious that Japan had built up too great a stake there to evacuate entirely. American-Japanese relations, already strained by disagreement over Siberia, were being exacerbated by continued disputes over immigration, while a naval armaments race had developed between the two countries which involved Great Britain as well. In fact, there seemed to many governments a real danger that the hostility between America and Japan might end in war, a prospect which filled British statesmen, in particular, with alarm, in view of their obligations under the Anglo-Japanese alliance. In June 1921, therefore, they decided, largely at the instigation of Canada, that the alliance could more safely be replaced by a multilateral agreement. This opened up the possibility of a general discussion of Pacific affairs, which the United States now took the initiative in arranging.

Accordingly the representatives of the Powers gathered in Washington in November 1921 to consider a whole range of Pacific and Far Eastern questions, decisions on which confirmed the new pattern of international relations that the war had shaped. The first to be announced was a Four Power Pact of December 13, 1921, by which Britain, Japan, France and the United States agreed to respect each other's rights in the area and to consult together in the event of a crisis arising. This took the place of the Anglo-Japanese alliance, which was eventually allowed to lapse in August 1923. On the subject of naval armaments, the United States proposed limiting the size and firepower of capital ships and scrapping many of them altogether, with Britain, America and Japan maintaining their respective tonnage for the future at a ratio of 5 : 5 : 3. Japan argued for a ratio of 10 : 10 : 7, but when the other two were stubborn she substituted a suggestion for a standstill in Pacific fortification, which they accepted. Thus the treaty, as signed, not only fixed a 5 : 5 : 3 ratio for total tonnage of capital ships, but also provided that battleships were not to exceed 35,000 tons or aircraft carriers 27,000 tons, that naval guns were not to be larger than 16-inch in calibre, and that no new fortifications were to be constructed at Guam, Hong Kong, Manila or any other base nearer to Japan than Hawaii and Singapore. This gave Japan naval predominance in the West Pacific and an unbreakable grip on the approaches to the China coast.

As to China itself, a Nine Power Treaty, signed by Belgium, Italy, the Netherlands, and Portugal, as well as China and the parties to the Four Power Pact, was concluded in February 1922. It gave China greater control over her own customs revenue and put into due form the platitudes reiterated for the previous twenty years: that the Powers would respect Chinese independence and integrity, would refrain from seeking special rights at each other's expense and would avoid interference with China's attempts 'to develop and maintain for herself an effective and stable government'.[61] That such promises were needed at all was itself significant. That they would be fulfilled was unlikely, especially as the treaty set up no machinery for enforcement.

In the long run, the attempt to introduce some kind of internationally acceptable order into the dealings of the Powers with China (and with each other on the subject of China) ran into difficulties that were not foreseen at Washington. The most intractable ones arose from the fact that three of the countries concerned with Far Eastern affairs were no longer willing, or became less and less willing, to accept a framework of relations that was inherited from an imperialist past: Russia, out of ideological conviction; China, because of growing nationalism; Japan, intermittently and increasingly, from a belief that her self-interest could be better served by going it alone. Imperialism itself was by no means dead, of course. Indeed, the development of an American economic expansionism in China and Japan in the 1920s suggested that it was self-renewing. But the activities of Russia, China and Japan eventually brought to an end the diplomatic system through which the operation of imperialism had been normalized and regulated, thus leaving the powers in disarray.

In fact, a temporary easing of international tensions, not leading to any new balance or permanent settlement, was the main achievement of the Washington meetings. Japan and China were able nominally to settle their differences over Shantung in a bilateral agreement on February 4, 1922, restoring Chinese sovereignty in the province and ratifying Japan's economic privileges there. In October 1922 Japan decided at last to withdraw her divisions from Siberia, though it was another three years before she evacuated northern Sakhalin and resumed diplomatic relations with Russia. And for the next few years her China policy was marked by an emphasis on economic, not military, expansion that was associated with the name of Shidehara Kijuro, Foreign Minister from June 1924 to April 1927 and again from July 1929 to December 1931.

On the other hand, the air of compromise which characterized Shidehara's actions was in some respects misleading. Japan's wartime gains were not renounced, but were on the contrary fully exploited. Nor was the political balance within Japan, which made moderation possible, as firmly established as it seemed. Ominously, there had already been signs of institutional weakness in the conduct of Japanese foreign affairs, stemming from the disappearance or declining influence of the Genro, which made the basis of Shidehara's policy unstable. Outstanding was the fact that the army had not only developed views of its own on what it wished to see done, especially in China and Manchuria, but had also found means of putting these into effect, regardless of cabinet decisions. The problems which this posed, first illustrated in the disputes over Siberia, were not solved by the army's temporary loss of popularity thereafter and were to become acute again in 1928 and 1931.

Before pursuing this topic further, however, it is necessary that we examine another aspect of Japanese history since 1914: the growth in the economy, occasioned by the war, and its effects on domestic politics. It was developments in this field, after all, that made Shidehara's methods a valid, if not a lasting, reflection of Japanese desires. Equally, they contributed to the activities of those who sought to turn foreign policy once again in the direction chosen by Okuma and Terauchi, coupling their arguments with strictures on the kind of society that evolved during the decade of 'the liberal 'twenties' and finding their support increasingly among those segments of the population that acquired grievances—or ambitions—as a result of economic change.

CHAPTER XII

THE LIBERAL 'TWENTIES

*Industrial expansion—party politics—inflation and recession
—radicalism*

THE GREAT WAR of 1914–18 was important to Japan not
only because it provided an opportunity for raising her international standing and prestige, but also because of the stimulus
it gave to her economy. By the war's end she had become in the
full sense an industrial state. As such she faced political problems of a kind new in her experience, arising both from the
pressures of industrial wealth on political and social privilege
and from the unrest that infused a growing urban proletariat.
Moreover, extension of the 'modern' element in her society
had by this time brought changes in patterns of wage-earning,
of consumption and of social custom to much of the country's
population, changes that were to be of lasting effect, notwithstanding the vociferous—indeed, hysterical—traditionalist reaction they provoked in the next two decades.

The beginnings of industrialization, fundamental to this process, date back to the Meiji period, but it was the outbreak of
war in Europe that gave it greater pace and scale. For Europe's
preoccupation with her own affairs proved to be Japan's
economic, as well as diplomatic, opportunity. Diverted to war
production, European factories could no longer supply many
of the goods they had formerly exported, enabling Japan to
increase her sales in markets she had already begun to exploit,
like China and America, and to penetrate new ones, like India
and South East Asia. With little war effort of her own to support she was also able to accept orders for munitions from her
allies, while increased demands for shipping, due to the losses
which U-boats inflicted on the maritime Powers, made it

profitable for her greatly to expand her mercantile marine. Her total of steamships and motor vessels doubled, from 1·5 million tons in 1914 to 3 million tons in 1918. In the same years her annual income from freights multiplied ten times, reaching over 400 million yen. Meanwhile the country's growing foreign trade had turned an annual average import surplus of 65 million yen into an export surplus of 350 million, raising Japan's net wartime earnings on international account to some 3,000 million yen in all. Though much of this was frittered away on political loans to China, much was still held as an overseas balance when the peace treaty was signed.

The end of hostilities brought a temporary recession, occasioned partly by the cancellation of munitions contracts, partly by the renewal of European competition; but this had the effect of eliminating the less efficient firms rather than of cutting back industrial growth in general. Many of the export markets that had been won were still retained. Much of industry continued to expand. In fact, the index of manufacturing production (1910–14 = 100) rose from an average of 160 in 1915–19 to 313 in 1925–29, while in foreign trade (1913 = 100) the index of imports by volume moved from 126 in 1919 to 199 in 1929, that of exports from 127 to 205.

Textiles accounted for a large percentage of the export trade, raw silk, sold mostly to the United States, comprising about 36 per cent of the whole by value in 1929 and cotton goods, notably piece-goods for India and China, only a little less. These two items together totalled two-thirds of Japan's exports in that year, as compared with just over half in 1913. Among imports, food and raw materials (Korean rice, Formosan sugar, Indian cotton) were an even larger proportion. In other words the country's foreign trade, though highly specialized as to both markets and commodities, now reflected chiefly the needs and achievements of Japanese manufacturers.

Similar growth had taken place in heavy industry. Despite continued dependence on imports for a good deal of engineering equipment, Japan was producing much of her own textile and electrical machinery, railway rolling stock and bicycles, as well as building a substantial quantity of the world's ships. Electric generating capacity increased from 1 million kilowatts in 1919 to 4 million in 1929, two-thirds of the power being used in manufacturing and mining. Coal production, however, after rising from 21 to 31 million tons between 1913 and 1919, had failed to keep up with demand, especially for coking coal, so that in 1929, with an output of 34 million tons, Japan was a net importer. Neither steel nor iron was yet in sufficient supply, though for the former, at least, the gap between need and output was quickly narrowing. A quarter of a million tons of steel had been produced in 1913, twice that amount in 1919 and over 2 million tons in 1929, these figures representing about 30, 45 and 70 per cent of contemporary consumption.

One feature of this industrial development, as we have mentioned earlier, was the emergence side by side of two very different types of organization: the small workshop, usually a family business, on the one hand, and the large factory on the other. In the light engineering trades, for example, and in many industries catering for the domestic rather than the export market, the spread of technical education and the availability of cheap electric power had made it possible for many individual entrepreneurs, despite a relative lack of capital, to engage in the manufacture of goods which others more widely organized would market, or parts which the large-scale factories could use. By 1930 workshops of this kind, each with less than five employees, numbered over a million. They employed 2·5 million people and were responsible for some 30 per cent of Japan's manufacturing product. In sharp contrast were the huge plants engaged in the production of iron and steel, cement, chemicals, heavy engineering equipment and similar goods, as well as some of those on the export side of the textile trades. In these both the factories and the firms that owned them were growing larger. Thus in cotton spinning, the 2·4 million spindles installed by 1913 were owned by forty-four companies controlling 152 mills, while 6·6 million spindles in 1929 were divided between only fifty-nine companies with 247 mills, an increase from 16,000 to 27,000 in the number of spindles per mill and from 55,000 to 113,000 in the number per company. Much the same trend is apparent in cotton weaving, especially where firms used the wide looms needed for export cloth.

The outstanding examples of large-scale organization were the concerns which were known as *zaibatsu*, with Mitsui,

Mitsubishi, Yasuda and Sumitomo chief among them. Their origins were diverse—the Mitsui had been a wealthy merchant house in Tokugawa times, whereas Mitsubishi was founded after the Restoration by an ex-samurai of Tosa, Iwasaki Yataro —but all had been closely linked with the Meiji government, owing much in their early days to its subsidies and contracts. In return they had supported it financially and invested in the new industrial undertakings which it sought to promote. This put them in a position to profit greatly by developments of the early twentieth century. They extended their operations into banking, heavy industry, shipping, commerce (both whole-sale and retail) and all other forms of economic activity that promised large returns, thereby creating a web of interlocking financial, industrial and commercial holdings that could survive, because of their multiple interests, the crises from which the economy intermittently suffered. In doing so they absorbed many older and smaller rivals. They also acquired enormous wealth, controlled as a rule through a family holding company and administered by an extremely able managerial group whose members often married into the founder family. Close connec-tions with leaders of government, the Diet, the bureaucracy and the Imperial Court made their position wellnigh impregnable.

Yet increasing scale, of which the *zaibatsu* firms were extreme examples, was not everywhere typical of Japanese develop-ment. One could argue that the workshops of the cities were not truly exceptions, in that they formed part of a structure which the major distributors and manufacturers were able to dominate. Even farm households raising silk cocoons—and by 1929 this was secondary employment for 40 per cent of them— were subject in some degree to external control by large-scale undertakings, exercised through financing and purchase of the crop. Nevertheless, agriculture in general, employing half the country's working population, remained a matter of individual family holdings, growing rice as a staple food by labour-intensive methods. In the 1920s almost 50 per cent of Japan's farmers held less than half a *cho* (1 *cho* = 2·45 acres). About 24 per cent held between half a *cho* and a *cho*, 18 per cent between one *cho* and three *cho*. Very few, therefore, could be described as important landowners, despite the fact that two-thirds were wholly or partly tenants.

This fragmentation undoubtedly made radical changes in the technique of cultivation difficult, if not impossible, though it is by no means certain that larger units would have helped to raise production, as distinct from making economies in man-power. In the Meiji period, as we have seen, fairly simple technical improvements, such as a more widespread use of fertilizers, had brought an increase in yield per acre of about 50 per cent. Thus with only a small area of new land coming under cultivation it had still been possible to increase the rice crop from 30 million *koku* in 1880–84 (1 *koku* = 5 bushels approximately) to 51 million in 1910–14. Thereafter, however, the rate of increase slowed, apparently because the scope for technological advance was now more limited. Certainly yield per acre rose by less than 10 per cent in the following twenty years and rice production in 1930–34 averaged only 62 million *koku*. Since population was growing more quickly—from 46 million in 1903 to 64 million in 1930—and consumption per head remained unchanged, imports of rice moved inevitably upward. Over 10 million *koku* were imported in 1930–34, com-pared with less than 3 million in 1910–14.

Rice imports amounting to nearly 15 per cent of consump-tion can be taken as symbolic of the shift of emphasis from agriculture to industry in the Japanese economy. So, too, can the increasing degree of urbanization. The fact that the num-bers engaged in farming remained constant at about five and a half million families throughout this period means that all those who in any given year comprised the population increase were finding their way to urban areas, where the new forms of economic activity were in greatest concentration and the chance of jobs was best. Townships of less than 10,000 persons accounted for 72 per cent of the population in 1913, only 59 per cent in 1930. Cities of 50,000 persons and more held 14 per cent in the first of these years, 25 per cent in the second. Agriculture, in other words, seemed to have reached some-thing like the limit of its potential in absorbing manpower, as well as producing food.

The cities that were now emerging undoubtedly brought misery and hardship to many people, for these seem every-where to be concomitants of industrial growth. To this aspect we shall have to return. But not all the change was for the worse. On average the Japanese diet became more varied and more sustaining in the early twentieth century. More fish, fruit and sugar were eaten; and the increase in *per capita* consumption of rice that had been achieved in the Meiji period was maintained, despite a sharply rising population. Moreover, Japanese were better clad as well as better fed, to judge by sales of clothing textiles in the domestic market, while those who lived in towns, at least, could enjoy amenities like electric light, improved facilities for travel, cheaper and more plentiful books and daily newspapers.

Prices, of course, had risen, as was evident on every side. The cost of living, if one takes 1914 as the base, had doubled a decade later. Yet money wages had trebled, so that real wages had risen by a half and were to hold the gain, even increase it slightly, for some time to come. It is true that the figures conceal wide variations between different groups and different occupations, farm workers being worse off than those in industry, the unskilled relatively less favoured than the skilled, a circumstance that does much to explain increasing tensions; but on balance society was more prosperous than it had been before the war. Some of its members were very much so. Successful businessmen had begun to build themselves country villas, the well-to-do to add a Western-style room or wing to their homes for entertaining. Geisha, the most expensive providers of entertainment in Japan, found their patrons more numerous and more lavish in spending. For the less affluent there were the dance-halls, whose taxi-dancers provided a cheaper, if untraditional, alternative. Restaurants flourished. And the Japanese became, as they have remained ever since, inveterate travellers: so much so, wrote a British resident, that 'it came to a pitch where, especially on Sundays and holidays, it was easier to find room in a third-class railway carriage than in the superior classes'.[62]

One result of this expansion of the economy was greatly to increase the size of the industrial and commercial middle class. This was a matter of political importance, for members of that class, men of substance and education, began to seek ways of getting their interests served. Some, like the *zaibatsu*, already had means of doing so through their connections with government. Others, if they were really wealthy, might hope to achieve their ends by bribes. Almost all found it possible, because of the country's new education system, to put sons or dependants into the bureaucracy, though the effect of this was reduced by that body's conspicuous ability to assimilate its recruits and mould their standards to its own.

Businessmen also began to organize themselves as pressure groups. Among the earliest was the Tokyo Chamber of Commerce, which under the leadership of a banker, Shibusawa Eiichi, had begun to campaign vigorously on several issues of economic policy even before the Meiji period ended. By the 'twenties, chambers of commerce, Rotary Clubs and associations of traders or manufacturers were familiar features of the urban scene. Some of them were assuming a directly political role, acting as pressure groups that sought to influence the government's outlook and specific decisions. But potentially more effective were the political parties, with which business had close links. They alone of the acknowledged components of the constitution opened a way to the control of policy by legal means. What is more, the support of business interests, which were rapidly achieving a position in society that no government could afford to ignore, promised to give the politicians a chance of the power which had so long eluded them.

The timing was apt, for the established order was facing a crisis of leadership that made it less able to resist attack. Of the Meiji statesmen, Ito had died in 1909 and Matsukata had ceased to play an active part in politics long before his death in 1924. Yamagata was a very old man, eighty in the year the war ended. Although he retained immense prestige, his hold on the Choshu faction was beginning to weaken. Itagaki, who had long been in retirement, died in 1919, Okuma, like Yamagata, in 1922. Nor were their successors men of equal calibre. Overshadowed by long-lived elders, the new generation seemed more concerned with power than with its uses, except perhaps in foreign affairs, and had little that was constructive to offer when its authority was challenged. Only Saionji was of any stature; and as a liberal, a protégé of Ito and a former party president, he was least likely to oppose the parties' claims.

The Okuma government of 1914–16 had demonstrated that even under a prime minister of great experience and the highest standing it was easier to manipulate votes in the Diet than to destroy the privileges of bureaucracy and Genro. In fact, only the patriotism of his China policy saved Okuma from early defeat. So when he attempted to name his own successor, choosing Kato Komei (Takaaki), another party man, Yamagata lost little time in bringing him down. Terauchi Masatake was installed in his place, forming an alliance with the Seiyukai and helping it to win an election in April 1917, while Kato organized a new group, the Kenseikai.

It is clear that the Seiyukai was the stronger of the two parties at this stage. During the previous decade Hara Kei, now the party's leader, had established a strong basis of support within the bureaucracy and among local men of influence in the constituencies (mostly businessmen and officials), which enabled him to strike bargains with the Genro. He had also shown himself willing to compromise with the oligarchy, however, and able to impose discipline on his followers in the Diet. He was therefore 'acceptable'. Accordingly, when popular criticism of Terauchi reached dangerous levels in 1918, chiefly because of a sharp rise in commodity prices, Yamagata and Saionji were able to agree on appointing Hara to succeed him. Japan thus acquired for the first time a 'commoner' as premier: a man who, although of upper samurai descent, had remained aloof from the Court establishment to the extent of not acquiring a title in the peerage. Significantly, he was supported by ministers who were all members of his party (except those holding the portfolios of Foreign Afairs, War, and Navy, who were a career diplomat and two senior officers of the services concerned).

To those who hailed this event as a victory for liberalism and democracy the next three years were disappointing. As a good party man Hara tried with some success to get his followers appointed to a number of posts, such as prefectural and colonial governorships, which had previously been reserved for bureaucrats, but he showed little enthusiasm for reform in general. His position depended too much on the Genro and the House of Peers to permit constitutional adventures, for which in any case he had little taste. Hence as long as he remained in office, proposals for an extension of the franchise were stead- fastly put aside. Socialist thought, stimulated by news of events in Germany and Russia, was ruthlessly suppressed. Signs of corruption were ignored. Even cabinet attempts to restrain the army's intervention in Siberia failed, though this was evidence of institutional weakness, not lack of will.

Hara's assassination on November 4, 1921, an act carried out by a young fanatic for no very obvious reason, robbed the party movement of an able politician rather than an inspiring statesman. Nonetheless, Hara had held his men together and led them to new positions of responsibility. His immediate successors could not do the same. His place was taken by the Finance Minister, Takahashi Korekiyo, who soon found the task too much for him and resigned the following June. For eighteen months thereafter the Seiyukai majority was used to back non-party governments, rather than give the Kenseikai a chance of power.

However, in the climate of opinion that was now forming in Japan such an arrangement could not last. Kato's demands for responsible party cabinets received increasing popular support and he eventually succeeded in splitting the Seiyukai on this issue, forcing a dissolution early in 1924 and winning the ensuing election. His coalition, which included groups led by Takahashi and Inukai Ki (Tsuyoshi), now made the government's position hopeless in the lower house. It resigned in June. This left the way clear for Kato himself to form an administration, first on the basis of coalition, then, after August 1925, from the Kenseikai alone.

His cabinet contained some notable members. Both the Home Minister, Wakatsuki Reijiro, and the Finance Minister, Hamaguchi Yuko, were to serve as premier in the next few years. The Foreign Minister, Shidehara Kijuro, a non-party man, was to become a symbol of moderation in respect of Sino-Japanese relations and a staunch, though unsuccessful, defender of such policies against army attacks. Yet it was Kato who dominated the scene. Wealthy, married to an Iwasaki (Mitsubishi), he had been ambassador to London and Foreign Minister to Okuma at the time of the Twenty-one Demands. With this background he could meet oligarchs, bureaucrats and Privy Councillors on equal terms, an advantage which in a Japanese context far outweighed the stiffness and reserve that kept him from being really popular. He was also a man of principle, a sincere advocate of parliamentary rule. In May 1925 he passed the Universal Manhood Suffrage Act, giving the vote to males over 25, which increased the size of the electo rate from three million to thirteen. He made economies in the bureaucracy, reducing its membership by 20,000, and cut the service budgets to under 30 per cent of the national total, compared with 40 per cent in 1919–22. The army lost four divisions in the process, though it was partly compensated by a measure of re-equipment. On the other hand, Kato was no more able than Hara had been to reform the House of Peers or reduce the authority of the senior bureaucrats, while only a week after Manhood Suffrage conservative pressure brought the Peace Preservation Law, providing penalties of up to ten years' imprisonment for participation in the more extreme forms of left-wing politics.

Kato died in January 1926. Both the party and the government were taken over by Wakatsuki, who continued along the same lines, despite growing army opposition on foreign affairs, until the Privy Council's refusal to confirm a proposed emergency ordinance in the financial crisis of early 1927. This brought his resignation and—an important step—an invitation to the Seiyukai to provide the next cabinet. Equally important, the Seiyukai, as a minority party, dissolved the lower house and sought to better its position through elections. It began to look as if two principles might become established: first, that the defeat of one party must bring the other to power; second, that the government must have a Diet majority. Such, at least, was the pattern for the next few years.

The Seiyukai, led by a general, Tanaka Giichi, who took office in April 1927, won the 1928 election, but did so only by the narrowest of margins. Notwithstanding police intervention against its opponents—now renamed the Minseito—and extensive use of private strong-arm squads under government patronage, victory was by a mere two seats, a fact which made for turbulent debates in the months that followed. Yet it was the army, not the Diet, that caused the government's fall. Though Tanaka was an advocate of sterner policies in China, the murder of the Chinese war-lord Chang Tso-lin in June 1928, apparently engineered by Japanese officers in Manchuria, brought him into conflict with the high command. His demands for disciplinary action were ignored and he finally resigned, being replaced in July 1929 by Hamaguchi. In 1930 Hamaguchi's Minseito won an election in its turn, doing so by methods that were rather less reprehensible than those of its rivals, but the world slump of that year and the signing of the London Naval Treaty soon brought it trouble. Its attempts to cut civil service salaries as part of an economy drive were fiercely resisted, while its acceptance of limitations on naval armament brought a head-on clash with the military and the Privy Council. At this juncture, in November 1930, Hamaguchi was shot and wounded at Tokyo railway station. He died a few months later and Wakatsuki again stepped in, as he had done at the death of Kato, only to face another dispute with the army in September 1931 over the invasion of Manchuria, which most members of his cabinet opposed, as well as a bitter struggle for power within the party. This led to his resignation in the following December. His successor was Inukai, now the Seiyukai's president, but Inukai had an even shorter tenure. In May 1932 he was assassinated at his official residence by a group of young army and navy officers who hoped to bring about a military *coup d'état*.

As this summary indicates, after 1930 the parties were coming under increasing attacks from right-wing fanatics, attacks that quickly weakened their grip on power. Some of the reasons for this were external to the party movement and will be considered in a later chapter. Others, however, were inherent in the way party politics had developed.

The parties had their origin in sectional protests against Meiji centralization and the Satsuma-Choshu monopoly of power. They had therefore tended to be coalitions of groups, each with its own leader, having strong local or regional connections and bound together more by the fact of opposition to the Meiji oligarchy than by commitment to programmes of their own. The introduction of the Meiji Constitution did not at once change this situation. In its early years the Diet's ability to obstruct official business certainly gave the parties an additional weapon, but it was a negative one, which enabled them to blackmail the government into concessions without being able to gain control. Hence, although a number of party leaders found it possible to secure office and even share its fruits with their followers, they did so only at the cost of bargains with the oligarchy that amounted to a denial of party rule.

The work of Hara Kei altered this pattern: directly for the Seiyukai, but indirectly for its rivals as well. By shifting his party's basis of support from young idealists and the disgruntled to men of substance among landlords, businessmen and officials, he made it representative of those who were profiting from, rather than offended by, Japan's new society; and this so strengthened his bargaining position that by the time of his death in 1921 he had not only formed and led a party government, but also given the parties an opportunity of competing with the Court, the Privy Council, the armed forces and the bureaucracy—competing on something like equal terms—for the privilege of inheriting the mantle of authority that was then falling from the shoulders of the surviving Genro. For a time during the next decade it seemed that they might do so.

Yet 'seemed' is a proper description. In order to secure a share of power the parties had had to become 'respectable', to accept the norms of political life as the Genro shaped them. This meant accepting an institutional framework in which party politics had little place: accepting it in the sense that they could not change institutions to their own advantage, least of all substitute some new organizing principle for the emperor-centred one on which the Meiji leaders had relied. Consequently, they were unable to bid for the allegiance of the increasingly powerful elements in Japanese society that wanted 'reform', that is, a substantial adjustment of institutional and power patterns in the light of changes effected by Meiji modernization. More, the parties were left with an outdated set of habits and attitudes, developed in the process of winning recognition for themselves, that were often disadvantageous in the Japan they now sought to rule. These made them targets of widespread criticism and disgust just as power was almost within their grasp.

Factionalism, turbulence and the politics of intrigue were especially criticized. Policy differences remained comparatively unimportant in parliamentary life, and decision-taking often depended on striking bargains with interest groups outside the

Diet, not on public debate. In these circumstances government commonly took place behind closed doors; party loyalty became a rare virtue (rarer than factional loyalty); and office was put before principle. Rank-and-file members showed no more scruple than their leaders and a good deal less decorum. Knowing that major issues did not really depend on a Diet vote, they reduced debates to the level of the trivial. Minority parties, seeing little point in a rational exposition of their views, tried to hoot their opponents down. They even had recourse to violence. 'Flushed gentlemen,' writes Morgan Young, 'clad without in frockcoats but warmed within by too copious draughts of saké, roared and bellowed, and arguments frequently culminated in a rush for the rostrum, whence the speaker of the moment would be dragged in the midst of a free fight.'[63]

Corruption was another element in political life by which the parties were discredited. In 1914 the Yamamoto cabinet had had to resign after revelations of bribery connected with naval armament contracts. Under Hara in 1921 the South Manchuria Railway was accused of contributing illegally to Seiyukai funds. Tanaka Giichi came under particularly heavy fire in matters of this kind. As a soldier he was said to have appropriated large sums from the secret service vote during the Siberian expedition. As Seiyukai leader after 1925 he was accused of taking bribes to decide the placing of army contracts, of selling peerages, even of being subject to improper influence in the making of a cabinet appointment.

Many such charges were exaggerated and some invented altogether, for this was the way of Japanese politics; but there is no doubt that bribery existed on a considerable scale. Indeed, the relationship between parties and business made it almost inevitable. The *zaibatsu* concerns had less need of it than most, for they had many channels of influence open to them: links of long standing, reinforced by marriage and adoption. Thus Saionji and the head of the Sumitomo combine were actually brothers. Iwasaki Hisaya of Mitsubishi had a sister married to Shidehara, another to Kato, and a nephew married to the daughter of an official in the Imperial Household Ministry. In 1930 some 12 per cent of the members of the lower house of the Diet (evenly distributed between the two parties—a form of political diversification) and no less than 28 per cent of the Peers either held posts in one of the *zaibatsu* firms, or had close relatives who did. This did not necessarily enable the *zaibatsu* to control party cabinets. But it certainly provided them (in the words of Ikeda Seihin of Mitsui) with friends who 'would probably sympathize and speak up for us behind the scene'.[64]

Firms of lesser standing, especially those which had sprung up during the 1914–18 war, lacked these connections in high places and had to rely more on the political parties to serve their ends. One recourse open to them, as to the *zaibatsu*, was to get themselves or their friends elected to the Diet: about a third of the members of both houses described themselves as 'businessmen' in 1930. Another, extensively employed, was bribery, directed above all to politicians.

Because of all this, business backing, though for a time it strengthened the political parties *vis-à-vis* other interests in the state, was ultimately an element in their weakness. The giving and taking of bribes was not the most stable basis for an alliance; and while it is true that businessmen and politicians had certain aims in common, in pursuit of which they could frequently co-operate, the fact remains that their ambitions were different enough to be separately attained. Accordingly, each was willing in the last resort to dispense with the other's help. Big business, in particular, behaved more as the politician's patron than his ally, never convinced that attacks on the parliamentary system were attacks upon itself. Indeed, in the 1930s big business soon came to terms with the parties' opponents.

The parties, if they could not rely on business, failed equally to build up any popular support. This was partly because their factionalism, unruliness and corruption offended against the 'samurai' virtues that modern education was trying to implant. Partly it was because their leaders made little attempt to cultivate the appropriate skills, rightly believing that oratory and mass meetings were irrelevant to the way they conducted their trade. Party leaders, in fact, were in outlook and background much like the men they wished to drive from power, the oligarchs and bureaucrats. Kato, Tanaka, Inukai and Takahashi were all of samurai descent. If one includes Tanaka, a regular soldier, three of the four had started their careers in the bureaucracy. The exception, Inukai, had been a newspaperman and a follower of Okuma. Hamaguchi, the non-samurai, was from Tosa, entering government service by what was becoming the classic route: from Tokyo University's law faculty to the Ministry of Finance.

These were not the men to lead a social revolution, but liberals of a very conservative kind. They stood for economy, good neighbourliness, the authority of the Diet and civilian control, a programme that was modest to a degree. Yet as we shall see, it was both liberal enough and conservative enough to face a challenge from both sides: from those who objected, in the name of tradition, to parliamentary power; and from those who urged the abolition or reform of parliament in the name of the people's rights.

Wartime industrial progress contributed on average to a rise in Japanese living standards, albeit unevenly. It also produced hardship and discontent. Some nine million people were living in towns of over 50,000 population in 1920, three million more than a decade earlier. This meant a major dislocation in the lives of many Japanese, forced to earn their living in urban areas whose facilities did not always expand as quickly as their citizens' numbers. It also subjected a growing proportion to the strain of work in factories, where hours were long and conditions were under the minimum of regulation. The 1911 Factory Act, for example, which was not enforced till 1916, had done no more than prescribe an eleven-hour working day for women and children, and a minimum age of twelve. An amendment of 1923, effective in 1926, was to make the hours ten and the age fourteen, with some exceptions.

In 1918 the position was made worse by serious inflation. Overseas demand for Japanese goods and the mushroom growth of firms to meet it had made possible a rise in money incomes and profits, an expansion of note issues and bank credit, a fever of speculation. In the last months of the war this brought a sharp upward trend in prices. Rice that cost 16 yen a *koku* in January 1917 was 39 yen in August of the following year. The wholesale price index in Tokyo (1900 = 100) averaged 195 for 1917, 255 for 1918, 312 for 1919. Wages rose more slowly, as one would expect, causing thereby a wave of agitation and industrial unrest. Rice riots, starting with a house-wives' protest meeting at Toyama on August 4, 1918, spread rapidly to Kyoto, Osaka, Kobe and other centres, where the mobs attacked and sometimes burned the establishments of rice-dealers, moneylenders and unpopular profiteers. Troops had to be called out to disperse them on several occasions during the next two weeks. Meanwhile, the country was experiencing its first important series of strikes for higher pay and better conditions. Disputes affecting 66,000 workers were recorded during the year, despite the existence of police regulations that made them illegal, and in 1919 the scale of such activity increased still more. There were stoppages by railway workers, teachers, postmen, printers—who deprived Tokyo of its newspapers for over a week—and in September 1919 by 15,000 men at Kobe's Kawasaki dockyard.

Soon after this Japan began to feel the effects of the post-war trade recession, which had its severest impact on those industries, like coal-mining and ship-building, that had expanded most in the previous years. Workers in them were forced on the defensive, fighting hard to maintain their levels of employment..In Kobe the men of the Kawasaki yard were again the leaders, joined on this occasion by those from Mitsubishi, with the result that over 25,000 were involved in the strike, lock-out and demonstrations that lasted from early July 1921 into the second week of August.

Unrest spread also to the countryside, though for different reasons. The earlier inflation had not been nearly so serious for the farmer as for the city worker, because of increases in the price of rice. The trade recession, however, broke and reversed the inflationary trend. The cost of a *koku* of rice fell from 55 yen in 1920 to 25·5 yen in 1921, while the wholesale price index dropped from 343 to 265 in the same two years. This meant real poverty for farmers, now fully involved in producing for the market, especially as their most important subsidiary crop, silk, suffered a similar decline in value. Price support programmes did something to restore the position in the next few years, but competition from colonial rice growers—which governments were bound to encourage for the sake of the urban poor—set a strict upper limit to domestic prices. Villages suffered, too, from the fact that they acted as a shock absorber for urban unemployment. Although population increase forced many to the towns, there to find jobs in shops or factories, each setback to the industrial economy drove them back to seek refuge on the farm. The resulting gain in social stability for the country as a whole was offset in part by the loss to rural standards of living.

It was the poorest farmers, especially the tenant farmers, who experienced the worst conditions. By the 1920s this meant something like half the agricultural population, for 49 per cent held plots of under one-and-a-quarter acres and over two-thirds were tenants for all or part of their land. In area, more than 45 per cent of the total was under tenancy agreements, their terms invariably favourable to the owner, since pressure of population, not all the surplus of which was absorbed by the towns, ensured that competition for the land was keen. Thus rents were payable in kind, which deprived the tenant of most of the benefits of inflation. They were also high, amounting to as much as half the crop on rice-paddy, a third for dry fields. The severity of such conditions had been mitigated before the war by the rapid expansion of agrarian production, but as this slowed down, so the agreements became a focus of rising tension. Tenancy disputes, which had usually been occasioned in the past by floods, typhoons and similar catastrophes, became more frequent, more extensive and more highly organized, especially round the periphery of urban areas. Tenant unions came into existence, claiming 132,000 members by 1922, with more everywhere being formed.

Conditions therefore existed in both the countryside and the towns that encouraged the growth of left-wing political activity: real grievances, made the harder to bear by envy, as those who reaped profits from industrial growth indulged in an extravagance and display that were supposedly foreign to the Japanese tradition. News of the German and Russian revolutions, distributed by an efficient daily press, suggested the possibility of successful protest. Knowledge of Western literature contributed plans and programmes. From all this a new element in politics emerged, a left-wing movement stimulated partly by the intellectuals, partly by trade unions.

Among the earliest of the radicals was Oi Kentaro, who combined an extreme nationalism with support for Sun Yat-sen in China and demands that the state should exercise economic controls for the protection of the poor. His Oriental Liberal Party (Toyo Jiyuto), founded in 1892, in some ways foreshadowed the kind of link between nationalism and the left that was to characterize the 1930s. More moderate was the Social Democratic Party (Shakai Minshuto) of 1901, with its appeal for free education, an eight-hour day and the abolition of child labour, though its moderation did not stop the police from suppressing it as soon as it was formed. An attempt to create a Socialist Party in 1906 was equally unsuccessful. It was not until 1920, in fact, in the atmosphere of turbulence after the war, that such groups stood any real chance of survival; and even then they often broke up within a matter of weeks or months because of their own disunity. Such, at least, was the fate of the Socialist League, formed in December 1920 as a means of bringing together all shades of left-wing thought. The first Communist Party, too, founded in 1921 after contacts with the Far Eastern Comintern at Shanghai, failed to overcome the combination of police action and doctrinal disputes. It went into voluntary dissolution in March 1924 after a brief but colourful career of argument and propaganda.

The members of these organizations included both those who believed in violence and those who did not. Of the radical leaders, several were Christians: a lawyer, Suzuki Bunji, founder of a national labour organization, the Yuaikai, in 1912; a minister, Kagawa Toyohiko, who was imprisoned briefly for his part in the Kobe strikes of 1921; and the American-trained Abe Isoo, a teacher at Waseda University. A good many other moderates were university professors, like Yoshino Sakuzo, an outstanding political scientist, and Kawai Eijiro. Kawai, when on trial in 1939, probably best expressed their creed. 'Although I talk about socialism,' he said, '. . . I reject illegal and espouse legal methods, abhor violent revolution, and prefer parliamentary means. Consequently, I do not address myself to the lowly plebs. I have never discussed socialism at a meeting of workers.'[65] Making due allowance for the circumstances in which this statement was made, there is still a quality of the intellectual about it that was characteristic. It was to be found also among the advocates of force. For example, Kawakami Hajime—journalist, poet, professor and Communist—

was in many ways typical of the radical idealist, deeply influenced by Christianity and Zen Buddhism in his youth, later a Communist from emotion rather than experience. His outlook was religious in its passion for humility and charity, his belief in Marxism that of a pacifist, who saw in the destruction of capitalism the only way of removing the social and economic evils that bred war.

The trade unions were a very different proposition, despite the fact that their leaders were not necessarily drawn from the ranks of labour. The earliest unions—like those formed among ironworkers in 1897 and railwaymen in 1898—had found their activities severely handicapped by police regulations after 1900, so that numbers remained small until the end of the war. From 1918, however, the movement began to increase in both militancy and size. By 1920 there were over 200 unions, most of them newly formed, and they had begun to organize in larger groups. Suzuki's Yuaikai, which had been hitherto a kind of friendly society, became the Federation of Labour (Sodomei) in 1919 and soon comprised seventy constituent organizations claiming 30,000 members in all. It continued to grow steadily in the next few years.

Nevertheless, the labour movement from the beginning had major disadvantages to overcome. One was the existence of a huge pool of cheap rural labour, flooding into the towns and destroying union bargaining strength (as well as making the workforce harder to organize). Another was factionalism. In the Sodomei, for example, 1922 saw the defeat of anarchist and of syndicalist supporters, leaving Communists and social democrats still to resolve their disagreements. Then a year later, on September 1, 1923, a terrible earthquake shook the Tokyo-Yokohama region, bringing in its train an outbreak of panic-stricken attacks on radicals and others, especially Koreans, for alleged looting, plotting and similar crimes. The offences existed largely in the imaginations of police and public, but the arrests and interrogations to which they gave rise had the effect of revealing that Communist penetration of the Sodomei had gone farther than anyone suspected. This led to fresh recriminations at its general meeting in 1924. Thereafter the moderates gradually gained the upper hand, until in May 1925 the Communist unions, in membership a little more than a third, broke away to form an organization of their own.

These events took place against a background of strikes and pamphleteering, for the hostility of the police, together with the restriction of the electorate by a property qualification, seemed to make any attempt to win seats in the Diet a waste of time. This remained so until 1925, but in that year the introduction of universal manhood suffrage rendered the objection largely void. A proletarian party to fight elections now became in theory possible, providing it could skirt the laws about subversion which the Peace Preservation Act had simultaneously reinforced. There was still, however, some difficulty in getting the politicians to reach agreement among themselves. Indeed, the first attempt at action foundered on this problem, since the Sodomei leaders withdrew from the discussions and the proposed party's extremist rump became an inevitable target for official intervention. Called the Farmer-Labour Party (Nomin Rodoto), it was banned thirty minutes after it came formally into existence on December 1, 1925. The moderates were next to try, forming a Labour-Farmer Party (Rodo Nominto) which was pledged to follow constitutional means, but within a few months of its foundation (March 1926) it had split on the question of establishing a popular front. By the end of the year its centre and right had broken off to form no less than three separate parties. Adding to the confusion, the Communist Party was reconstituted in December, but it became so deeply involved in ideological controversy and so violently at loggerheads with every other left-wing group that one can only feel surprise at the reluctance of the police to leave it alone.

On this sort of record the left was no more likely to win popular support than were the Seiyukai and Minseito. Moreover, the latter were very much better organized for rallying votes. This became evident in the 1928 elections, when the four left-wing parties—excluding the Communists, who did not compete—polled less than half a million votes between them, about one-eighth of the number that went to each of their rivals. From eighty-eight candidates they elected only eight, of whom four were social democrats. The failure underlined the need for more co-operation and led to new proposals for alliance, but these were again rejected by both the extreme left and the moderate right. Thus the Japan Mass Party (Nihon

Taishuto), founded in December 1928, proved to be no more than a variation on familiar themes. It certainly did nothing to bring greater unity, and results in the 1930 and 1932 elections were therefore no better than those of 1928.

Throughout this phase of their history the left-wing parties were being hampered by the activities of the police, who used censorship, arrest and even violence against them. Police regulations dating from 1900 already conferred extensive powers, but these had been increased in 1925 by the addition of penalties of up to ten years' hard labour for certain offences, notably that of joining any society which was designed to overthrow the Japanese form of government or abolish private ownership. Directed ostensibly against communists and anarchists, the law was passed enthusiastically by the lower house. Yet it soon transpired that the lack of precision in its wording opened the way for many kinds of interference with personal liberties and did not by any means confine their application to extremists. In March 1928, soon after the elections, police raids on a large scale rounded up about a thousand communists and communist sympathizers. A year later the technique was tried again, this time bringing in many non-communist radicals as well. Thereafter men and women of known left-wing proclivities were always liable to arrest, imprisonment and often torture without apparent cause or warning.

One result of this, both because the extreme left suffered more than any other group and because there was a tendency for factions to unite when under attack, was that most remaining members of the labour movement, that is, those of the right and centre, were at last brought together to form the Social Mass Party (Shakai Taishuto) in July 1932. This managed to maintain a semblance of unity right down to 1940, when all political parties were dissolved, and even to build up a substantial representation in the Diet, adopting for this purpose the nationalist slogans of the age and exploiting the popular resentment caused by army intervention in national politics.

Nevertheless, before 1945 the parties of the left failed to make any great mark on Japanese society. One reason was their failure to win a substantial following in the conservative strongholds of a landlord-dominated countryside (notwithstanding tenancy disputes). Another was disunity, enhanced by government persecution. In addition, their disputes with the 'liberal' parties had reduced the effectiveness of both in seeking power, in that the struggle for control of the Diet played its part in hampering the Diet's bid for control of national policy. Disunity, in other words, operated not only within parties, but also between them, and this when unity was their greatest need. The Seiyukai and Minseito, while they tried to make cabinets responsible to the lower house, encouraged the police to suppress the left. The left, in turn, was at least as hostile to the bourgeois politicians as it was to oligarchs and Genro.

Fundamentally, however, it was the failure to secure popular support that condemned both kinds of parties to defeat. The reasons for it are not to be found in any single factor, not even wholly in the politicians' defects. They lie rather in those ideas and institutions which had turned the Japanese people away from the pursuit of individual freedoms and towards the attainment of collective goals: the formative pressures of the education system; an emperor-centred state religion; conscription, with its accompanying indoctrination; and the persistence of traditional authoritarian attitudes in important areas of bureaucratic and family behaviour. In sum, these enabled the discontents arising from economic change to be marshalled in the service of ambitions quite distinct from those of either the liberal or the labour movements, ambitions which brought Japan close to another 'Restoration' and plunged her into a major war.

CHAPTER XIII

PATRIOTS AND SOLDIERS
1930-1941

Ultranationalism—army plots—Manchuria—military factions—
insurrection of February 1936—preparations for war

To describe the 1920s as 'liberal' is to focus on an aspect of Japanese political society. It is in many ways more informative to use the label 'bourgeois', because it has wider application. This is especially true when seeking to analyse the nature of the opposition to what was taking place. Politically, the emphasis on parliamentary politics offended many Japanese for a variety of reasons: because it reflected a power balance in which business interests figured more largely than in the past; because it relied on an imported ideology, weakening the traditional concepts of an emperor-centred polity, strengthening those of popular rights and individualism; because it contributed to types of public behaviour that were alien and distasteful. Yet there was a good deal more to it than that. The greater importance of industry and commerce detracted from that of agriculture, reducing the role of landlords in the parties and sacrificing the farmer's income to the needs of urban consumers through the import of cheap rice from Korea and Taiwan. Attempts to minimize the taxation of business involved retrenchment in the military budget. Thus two strongholds of traditionalist values, the village and the army, suffered while the cities prospered.

The profits from industry tempted those who shared them into new forms of extravagance, nearly all imported and Western. Their unequal distribution prompted 'dangerous thoughts'—equally Western—like socialism and communism, the very existence of which implied that something was seriously wrong with the body politic. In fact, dance-halls, luxury, corruption, big business, trade unions, strikes, agrarian unrest and debased standards of every kind could all in a sense be lumped together as products of an over-indulgence in foreign ways. Accordingly, their presence raised in a new form the old questions about Japan's 'proper' response to Western civilization. In the Meiji period, much that was culturally shocking or distasteful had been accepted as the price that had to be paid for 'wealth and strength'. Moreover, some fundamentals had been successfully defended: the emperor system; the Confucian ethic; the samurai tradition of public service. But by the 1920s it began to seem that these, too, might be in jeopardy, that Japanese-ness itself was to be a victim of modernization.

What made this particularly disturbing to some was a belief that strength, if not wealth, was to be part of the sacrifice. In East Asia, the gains Japan had made as a result of Meiji policies had been of two kinds. On the adjacent mainland and immediately to the north she had acquired territory (Korea and Karafuto), plus a network of special rights (the Liaotung lease, the South Manchuria Railway), which made a good part of China's Manchurian provinces into a Japanese sphere of influence. Further south, the whole of 'China proper' had been opened to Japanese economic penetration within the framework of the treaty port system, in which Japan had been able since about 1900 to claim full equality with Britain, France, Germany and the United States. In fact, the strength of Japan's economic challenge to the other Powers in China had brought attempts on their part to restrain her ambitions. This had been impli-cit in the arrangements made at the Washington Conference. Such efforts had not been wholly successful, but they contributed to a shift in the direction of Japanese policy. Reflecting the relative weakness of Russia in East Asia after the 1917 revolution, which reduced Japan's strategic preoccupations, plus the rapid growth of Japanese industry during the period 1914-19, which increased the country's export capacity, the main thrust in the 1920s—associated chiefly with the name of Foreign Minister Shidehara Kijuro—had been towards exploiting economic opportunities in China. This did not imply a willingness to abandon special privileges in Manchuria and elsewhere, but it did limit the 'political' content in Japanese ac-tivities in China compared with, say, the Twenty-one Demands.

The principal restraint on the development of this policy proved to be not the rivalry of the powers, but Chinese politics. After 1919 there was a great upsurge of nationalism in China, channelling res-entment against imperialism and its economic concomitants into

demands for treaty revision, as well as anti-foreign strikes and boy-
cotts. Nationalist grievances also became a stimulus towards restoring Chinese unity, on which the ability to resist the foreigner
depended; and in the first stage these sentiments were most effectively organized in support of the Kuomintang, under the leadership of Chiang Kai-shek, who in 1926, starting from bases in the
south, launched a military expedition to assert control over central
and northern China. By so doing he challenged Japanese interests in
two ways. First, he put himself in a position to demand a review of all
foreign rights, including those of Japan, threatening to end the
treaty port system. Second, he put in question the continuation of
Japan's dominant role in south Manchuria, which had for some time
been maintained through close association with the semi-
independent Manchurian warlord, Chang Tso-lin, whom Chiang
seemed likely to overcome.

The rise of the Kuomintang therefore brought the two facets of
Japanese China policy into sharp focus. To many Japanese the issues
were highly emotive, for the threat was not only to valuable
interests, but also to the symbols of international status, painfully
acquired since the days of Japan's own unequal treaties. Defending
that status was generally held to justify the use of force, just as
acquiring it had done. Certainly the appeal to international co-
operation, which Shidehara urged, seemed in this context wholly
inadequate. Belonging to a Western-devised international order, it
appeared, imperilled Japan's position on the Asian mainland. This
made it no more acceptable than those aspects of Western civilization, like parliament and individualism, that bade fair to destroy
traditional values at home.

Before about 1930 the attitudes we have been describing were
mostly to be encountered among a substantial and influential minority of Japanese, putative heirs of the 'men of spirit' of late Tokugawa days. Such men found an outlet for their aspirations in the
so-called 'patriotic societies'. Among the older societies, the
Kokuryukai, founded in 1901, had always envisaged a connection
between political action at home and Japan's relations with the
outside world. Its stated aims were to 'renovate the present system,
foster a foreign policy aiming at expansion overseas, revolutionize
domestic politics to increase the happiness of the people, and establish a social policy that will settle problems between labor and
capital . . .'.[65] Some of the newer societies, like the Dai Nihon

Kokusuikai (Japan National Essence Society), dating from 1919, and the Kokuhonsha (National Foundation Society) of 1924, were more specifically designed to save Japan from the perils of socialism. The Kokuhonsha was particularly respectable and influential: its members included three future prime ministers (Saito Makoto, Hiranuma Kiiichiro, Koiso Kuniaki), several famous generals (Ugaki Kazushige, Araki Sadao, Mazaki Jinzaburo), and a number of party politicians, representatives of *zaibatsu* firms, officials of the higher bureaucracy.

In sharp contrast were the smaller, extremist organizations which existed on the fringes of politics, dependent for funds on the contributions of non-members—obtained by methods ranging from cajolery to threats or even fraud—and for cohesion on the influence of individual 'bosses'. Often they were little more than strong-arm squads, capitalizing on the fashion for patriotism instead of crime. Sometimes, however, they were the personal following of much more dangerous men, fanatics whose views were as violent as the means by which they tried to spread them. Such was Kita Ikki, author and revolutionary, who was executed in 1937 for his part in an attempted *coup d'état*. With Okawa Shumei he founded the Yuzonsha (Society for Preservation of the National Essence) in 1921 and became the inspiration of many others like it.

Kita's chief contribution was to the ideology of the movement. In 1919 at the age of thirty-five he wrote a book entitled *An Outline Plan for the Reconstruction of Japan*, which set out his ideas at length and soon won him fame despite a police ban on its circulation. It advocated a radical revision of society in order to fit Japan for leadership in the revolutionary Asia which Kita thought bound to come: the confiscation of personal fortunes greater than one million yen, the nationalization of major industries, the establishment of an eight-hour day, the seizure and redistribution of surplus private landholdings above 100,000 yen in value, and renunciation by the emperor of his family estates. All this was to be achieved through a military *coup d'état*, which would make possible a clean sweep of the country's existing leadership—political, economic and bureaucratic—and the substitution for it of a regime based on direct relationships between the emperor and his people. When completed, it would enable Japan to act more vigorously in foreign affairs. As a member of the proletariat of nations, Kita argued, it was her task to secure justice from the wealthy, like Britain (the millionaire) and Russia (the great landowner). This could be done by launching an expansionist policy on the Asian mainland and supporting the interests of Asians everywhere against the West.

Very different were the views of Gondo Seikyo, apostle of an agrarian-centred nationalism that looked to the village as the nucleus of both political and economic life. Like Kita, he emphasized the role of the emperor in the national polity and accepted the doctrine of Japan's racial mission overseas. Unlike him, however, he wished not to socialize industry, but to destroy it, because it was a symbol of capitalism's exploitation of the countryside for the benefit of the town. His concern was for the simple ways of the farmer, who would look to the emperor as a kind of family head, and for village autonomy. Centralization, bureaucracy and things Western were to him anathema.

Gondo's ideas, too, were first published in 1919 and were propagated through an institute which he established in 1920. Another man of similar outlook, Tachibana Kosaburo, founded a communal village near Mito at this time, later conducting a school there at which he taught farming and patriotism to a handful of students. Eventually he formed links with another group in the same area, Inoue Nissho's Ketsumeidan, a blood brotherhood dedicated to a rather directer method of bringing about the agrarian millenium, namely, the assassination of leading financiers and industrialists.

The attitudes and interests represented in such societies were too varied to make it likely that they could co-operate in putting forward a political programme. Moreover, small numbers and lack of regular finances made them ineffective by themselves. On the other hand, the anti-capitalist, anti-Western prejudices which were common to the thinking of most of their members were shared by men whose ability to influence policy proved in the end to be much greater: the younger officers of the forces, especially the army. Many of these, after reforms carried out in 1924-5, were drawn from new social strata—the families of shopkeepers, small landowners and minor officials—which had not the same loyalty to the established order as had characterized the narrower oligarchy of the past, but were nevertheless unwilling to espouse the cause of communism or the urban poor. Officers with this background were more likely than their predecessors to join the radical right and to be influenced by complaints arising from the stress of economic change. Equally, they had grievances of their own. Civilian control, as advocated by the political parties, had contributed to a decline in the services' prestige. Good neighbourliness and retrenchment threatened their careers. Finally, the wealth and luxury of the privileged, notably in the cities, compared strangely in their eyes with the low pay and spartan ways which society apparently expected its soldiers to accept.

As a result, a number of officers began to form connections with the nationalist movement at a level quite distinct from the recognized channels between the high command, senior bureaucrats and politicians. Some got into touch with Kita Ikki, Okawa Shumei and their like, founding joint military-civilian organizations to discuss the possibilities of reform by force. Some established societies with a membership drawn entirely from the army and navy. Most famous—or notorious —was Lt-Col Hashimoto Kingoro's Sakurakai (Cherry Society), originating in September 1930, which at its peak comprised a hundred members, all army men of the rank of lieutenant-colonel or below. About two-fifths were from the War Ministry and General Staff, as many again from the military training schools, and the rest from units stationed in the Tokyo area.

Two phrases constantly recurred in the speeches and writings of these patriots, both military and civilian. One was *Kodo*, 'the Imperial Way', the other *Showa Ishin*, 'the Showa Restoration'. Both implied that the emperor had a special role in the country's political structure, but neither stood for a precise policy or plan. The Imperial Way had connotations of high moral purpose and of action in the emperor's name to restore the traditional values of Japanese society. Showa Restoration suggested links with what had happened in the nineteenth century—Showa being the era-name for the reign of the present emperor, just as Meiji had been that for the reign of his grandfather—a period when Japan had been beset by enemies without, by disunity within, as it was again. The label 'Restoration' made it plain that what was needed in 1930 was action as radical and decisive as that which had saved the country in 1868. It had to be directed against those who symbolized the corrupt Japan of the twentieth century: big business, especially the *zaibatsu*; party politicians; bureaucrats who worked with them. And it could only be undertaken by the modern 'men of spirit': patriots who were willing to use force against individuals or governments, and were ready to die for their ideals.

The revolutionary aspects of this 'ultranationalism' were given greater significance by economic crisis. In 1929–30 the collapse of American prosperity brought a worldwide slump, quickly reflected in a sharp decline in the demand for Japanese silk. By 1931 the index of raw silk prices (1914 = 100) had fallen to 67, compared with 151 in 1929 and 222 in 1925. The farmer had already been suffering from lower prices for his rice. In the second half of 1930 these fell still more: from 31 yen a koku to 18. Simultaneously there was a drop in overseas demand for Japanese cotton goods, causing widespread unemployment in the textile industry and driving girl factory workers to seek refuge in their native villages. The result of all this was widespread poverty in rural areas. Conditions were worst in the north and northeast, which, with Kyushu, were the army's favourite recruiting grounds; and since many junior officers also came from hard-hit families, unrest was quickly communicated to servicemen of every rank.

At the highest levels the army was deeply divided about how to act in this situation. Leaving aside those senior officers—probably still a majority—who regarded the country's politics as none of their business, there were two principal groups. One was the Imperial Way (*Kodo*) faction, centering on Generals Araki Sadao and Mazaki Jinzaburo, who showed some sympathy for Kita Ikki's ideas, but put their emphasis on loyalty and morale, rather than structural change. The other, dubbed by its opponents the *Tosei* (Control) faction, was in some ways much more revolutionary, though not in the manner of Kita or Okawa. Its members were mostly the new type of field grade officers of the General Staff, like Nagata Tetsuzan and Ishiwara Kanji, whose concern with political and economic institutions led them not so much towards an attack on capitalism and the parliamentary system as such (what Maruyama has called 'fascism from below')[66] as towards the creation of a set of state controls designed primarily to organize Japan for total war ('fascism from above'). The *Tosei* men were willing to co-operate with capitalists and bureaucrats within the existing structure, provided priority was given to their own notions about the pursuit of national strength. What is more, in a world that looked increasingly threatening they found many who were willing to work with them on these terms: *zaibatsu* leaders like Ikeda Seihin of Mitsui, turning their expertise to the problems of devising controls over industry and finance, in the hope of minimizing the damage to their business interests; senior bureaucrats, working out new administrative organs and procedures, in the belief that only thus could they preserve their country's strength and stability; scholars and publicists, formulating an appropriate ideology for the planned New Order.

Saving Japan, whether by reconstruction at home, or expansion abroad, or both, was an aim nearly all groups had in common. Where they differed was over means. Major disagreements existed over foreign policy, which we will consider more directly in the next chapter. In domestic affairs the crucial difference was about the extent to which Japan's existing leadership and institutions should be replaced. Resolving it was the main thread of politics between 1930 and 1936.

The first significant dispute concerned the Minseito government's readiness to negotiate a limitation on naval armaments. The London Naval Treaty of 1930, which confirmed, and in some respects extended, the arrangements made at Washington in 1922 (see Chapter XI), was supported by the Navy Minister but opposed by the naval Chief of Staff. Signed on April 21, despite the latter's protests, it again faced opposition when it came before the Privy Council for ratification in July, though the cabinet stood firm behind its premier, Hamaguchi Yuko, and won the day. However, it did so only by violating two principles which officers of the services had very much at heart. The first was that Japan should not accept any international agreement which limited her freedom of action in the Far East and the Pacific, even one which similarly restrained her potential rivals. Acceptance of the 5 : 5 : 3 ratio for capital ships, which it was now proposed should be applied to other major war vessels as well, was held to undermine the navy's ability to fight a defensive war against the United States, which had long been seen by naval staff as its main strategic role. Secondly, the way in which the decision had been made raised an important constitutional issue. The service ministers and chiefs of staff, both in theory and in practice, had separate functions. These might be broadly distinguished as administration, on the one hand, and planning, on the other, while it was also the duty of the minister, as a member of the cabinet, to secure government approval for the recommendations they both made and to obtain the funds by which these could be carried out. It was *not* within his powers—nor, in the view of most military men, those of the cabinet—to overrule the chief of staff on essentially operational matters, which included questions concerning the level of armament needed for defence. On this occasion, the navy's chief of staff had not only been overruled, he had even been forced to resign.

One result of the turbulence which these events produced was the shooting of Hamaguchi in November. He died of his wounds in the following year. The attack, which was made by a youth connected with one of the lesser-known patriotic societies, does not seem to have been part of any wider plot. Nor did it have any great effect on the political situation, since Hamaguchi was succeeded as Prime Minister and leader of his party in April 1931 by Wakatsuki Reijiro, a man of similar background and ideas. All the same, it was symptomatic of a state of affairs which a number of army officers hoped to use to their own, or their service's, advantage.

The first move came at the beginning of 1931. It was made by members of Lt-Col Hashimoto's Sakurakai, in conjunction with civilian extremists led by Okawa Shumei, whose plans envisaged, first, a series of riots and bomb attacks, organized by the civilians and carried out with weapons provided by the army, and, second, a declaration of martial law and the installation of a military government under General Ugaki. It is not at all certain how far Ugaki and other senior officers had advance knowledge of these proposals, though their co-operation would undoubtedly have been necessary for success. The fact that they gave orders calling off the plot in March 1931, just before the date for action, suggests that they only learnt the details at the last moment and promptly withdrew their support. Yet their complicity, no matter how slight, made it difficult to take action against the rest. Moreover, their lack of resolution convinced the conspirators that next time they would have to force the hand of the army leadership, in addition to bringing down the government, a decision that became the basis of a further plot later in the year. Again Hashimoto and Okawa were its architects, though this time they looked to General Araki Sadao as their nominee for office. This time, too, soldiers were to be more directly engaged in the preliminary stages. The cabinet, for example, was to be eliminated by air attack during one of its meetings; a Guards division was to be called out in the resulting confusion; and the War Ministry was to be isolated until martial law had been declared. This plan was betrayed and its authors arrested in October. However, the mild character of the punishments meted out showed that the high command was still reluctant to act strongly in maintaining discipline.

One reason for this was that some of its senior members had themselves been planning to bring about operations on the mainland by methods just as 'rebellious' in their way as those of Hashimoto. There had long been a feeling in military circles, especially in the Kwantung Army, which controlled Japanese troops guarding the railway zone in South Manchuria, that the threat to Japan's position there, represented by the growing authority of the Kuomintang in China, would have to be resisted forcibly. In 1928 some members of the Kwantung army staff had tried to create an opportunity for intervention by organizing the murder of the Manchurian warlord, Chang Tso-lin. Tokyo on that occasion had refused to act, but segments of the army still cherished the same ambitions. They were given greater intellectual respectability by Ishiwara Kanji's ideas about total war. As a Lt Col. on the Kwantung army staff in 1929-30 he expounded the view that it was Japan's destiny to be Asia's champion in a 'final' struggle with the United States, champion of the capitalist West. In preparation for that struggle, Japan must establish her power in Asia, a process which would probably first entail war with Soviet Russia. This in turn necessitated Japanese control of Manchuria, strategically for its territory, economically for its resources. Seizing Manchuria, in other words, was not just imperialist expansion. It was the first step towards Armageddon. In 1931 the time seemed ripe for taking it, since China was distracted by major floods in the Yangtse valley, while Britain and America were preoccupied with economic difficulties at home.

By the late summer of 1931 Ishiwara and his fellow staff officers had completed their contingency plans for troop movements in the event of an 'incident'. On September 15 the Kwantung Army was ordered to assume a state of readiness. On September 18 its plans were at last put into effect. Late that night a Japanese patrol near Mukden heard explosions. Investigating, it found slight damage to the railway line just outside the city and promptly fired on a number of Chinese soldiers who were seen in the vicinity. On this flimsy pretext the occupation of the area began, troops taking over the Mukden arsenal, airfield and radio station before dawn, the city itself, together with Changchun, in the course of the following day, and Kirin two days later. On September 21 reinforcements began to arrive from Korea, making it possible to extend operations in the next three months to the whole of the Manchurian provinces.

In Tokyo the army's Vice Chief of Staff, apparently with the sympathy, if not the active co-operation, of the War Minister, General Minami, took the necessary steps to support the forces in the field. The government, accordingly, faced a *fait accompli*. It had heard rumours of the proposed moves a few days earlier and had tried to stop them by sending a messenger to the Kwantung commander-in-chief; but the officer chosen for this duty, being a party to the conspiracy, took care not to deliver his message until it was too late. Thereafter, with its troops already committed, the cabinet tried vainly to halt the advance. Its instructions were ignored by the field commanders, on the grounds of operational necessity, and they in turn were backed by the War Minister and General Staff. In fact, the end of January 1932 saw hostilities spread to China proper, when a clash between Chinese and Japanese troops at Shanghai led to heavy fighting and at one point to a naval bombardment of Nanking. For some weeks this was the only fighting that was going on, for the occupation of Manchuria had by this time been completed and the army had given evidence of its determination not to withdraw by sponsoring a puppet government there, which declared its 'independence'—of China—on February 18, 1932. Pu Yi, the last of China's former Manchu emperors, was made head of the new state of Manchukuo in March.

The international repercussions of these events, which we shall consider in the next chapter, were serious, but no less so was the effect on developments within Japan. The Wakatsuki government, helpless in the face of the army's action, was brought down by its own disunity in December 1931. Its successor, under Inukai, leader of the Seiyukai, was handicapped in its conduct of foreign affairs by its own past record. Ministers found that the enthusiasm with which they had advocated 'positive' policies while in opposition made it difficult for them to criticize the army for carrying such policies out, however unconstitutional the manner in which it did so. What is more, members of the cabinet now had every reason to fear for their personal safety, especially if they were unwise enough to give any hint of seeking a settlement with China. The patriotic societies were delighted with what had been done. They were anxious, too, that the army be given the fullest support, preferably by establishing a new regime. Thus Inoue Nissho's blood brotherhood, dedicated to the removal of the ruling clique, made out of a list of intended victims and drew lots for the privilege of executing sentence. On February 9, 1932, one of them murdered Inoue Junnosuke, a former Finance Minister, known to oppose the Manchurian venture. Less than a month later another killed Baron Dan, head of Mitsui, though at this point the remainder were arrested and the series came to an end.

Their task was taken over, albeit with some differences of technique, by a group which had been influenced by Gondo Seikyo's agrarian doctrines. Tachibana Kosaburo was involved, as was Okawa Shumei and a son of Toyama Mitsuru, but the active leaders were some young officers from a naval air base not far from Mito and a handful of army cadets. They were supported by Tachibana's Aikyojuku, youths from the countryside, having little organization and less experience, whom a contemporary journalist described as 'adolescents straying in a pink mist'.[67] With such executants it is not surprising that much went wrong, when on May 15, 1932, they made attacks on Tokyo power stations, a bank, the headquarters of the Seiyukai party and other buildings, in an attempt to create a crisis which would lead to martial law. For the most part their efforts failed. In one thing, however, they were successful: in assassinating Prime Minister Inukai at his official residence. This, if it did not provoke an army *coup d'état*, at least proved to be a death blow to party government.

The atmosphere in which politics were to be carried on here-after was made very plain by the trials which began in the summer of 1933: separate civil trials for Inoue Nissho and Tachibana Kosaburo, each with his followers, and two court martials, one army and one navy, for the servicemen. All were public, long drawn out and wordy, the defendants being allowed to engage in fierce diatribes, sometimes lasting two or three days, against everything and everybody they thought they had reason to hate. This was their defence, an argument of patriotic motive. What is more, they were encouraged in it by judge and prosecuting counsel. Tachibana at one stage was permitted to announce each day the subject of his next day's discourse. Inoue actually complained of the judge's manners, accusing him of not paying proper attention to the speeches, and forced the appointment of a new one by refusing to go on with the trial.

The sentences, when one considers the nature of the crimes, were light, ranging from four years' imprisonment for the army cadets to life for Tachibana; and this fact did not escape the notice of other patriots or their potential victims. One result was to demoralize the political parties, the Minseito and Seiyukai presenting a spectacle of growing impotence and division in the next few years. Some factions broke away to seek power through an alliance with the ultranationalists. Others remained within the parties, but gave increasing sup-port to army policies. The only important exception was a new left-wing organization, the Shakai Taishuto (Social Mass Party), formed in July 1932, which, despite some internal dissension caused by the attractions of different brands of Japanese national socialism, managed to pursue an anti-capitalist, anti-communist and anti-fascist line until the war with China began in 1937. It was helped, undoubtedly, by the police purge of the extreme left-wing—another 2,000 arrests were made in October 1932—since this, by leaving only the moderates, gave it greater cohesion than earlier parties of its kind. It also profited to some extent from popular dissatisfaction with much that the army was trying to do. Thus in the election of 1936 it polled half a million votes and won eighteen Diet seats, a record for the left. Nevertheless, this was nothing like enough to influence the direction of events.

The defence of the constitution was therefore left more and more to the statesmen surrounding the emperor: Saionji, last of the Genro; the ex-premiers; and those who held such offices as Lord Privy Seal or President of the Privy Council. Many were liberals, who wished to see discipline restored in the services and would have preferred party cabinets to continue. On the other hand, they recognized that this was not acceptable to the army extremists and feared that any attempt to impose their ideas might lead to revolt, by which all established institutions, including the Throne itself, would be put in jeopardy. They were thus left no alternative, as they saw it, but to compromise.

For the time being this meant going back to an earlier device, in proposing governments which included members of both the principal parties, but were led by non-party men. On this basis Admiral Saito Makoto succeeded Inukai as Prime Minister in May 1932 and was followed by another admiral, Okada Keisuke, in July 1934, the choice of navy men being dictated by the belief that they were acceptable to, but more manageable than, Japan's generals. A more lasting solution, however, proved hard to find. The problem was to restore discipline over the radical elements in the army. The logical people to do this, it seemed, were that service's senior officers, for which reason it was necessary to secure the help of the high command. This, in turn, meant making concessions: in foreign affairs, by accepting expansion in Manchuria; and at home, by postponing disciplinary action until the senior officers felt able to enforce it. The upshot was a policy of 'control by concession' which ended by sacrificing all it had been devised to save.

Factional differences within the army precipitated the next phase of the power struggle in Japan. From late 1931, with Araki as War Minister and Mazaki as Vice Chief of Staff, the *Kodo* men were in a strong position, though their rivals were influential in Manchuria. Then in January 1934 Araki resigned, because of strain and ill-health, and his successor, Hayashi Senjuro, began to fall under the influence of Nagata Tetsuzan. Mazaki was by this time Director General of Military Education, one of the army's three top posts, which carried with it control of officer training; but in July 1935 Nagata at last succeeded in securing his dismissal, thereby causing serious trouble. On August 12 Nagata himself was murdered by Lt-Col Aizawa Saburo, one of Mazaki's supporters. In response, the *Tosei* leaders brought Aizawa to trial and took steps to move other troublemakers to Manchuria, a plan which persuaded the *Kodo* adherents to resort once again to force.

Their attempt to seize power was made on February 26, 1936. Early that morning, over a thousand men of the First Division, led by junior *Kodo* officers, took over the centre of the capital. Some attacked the Prime Minister's residence and only failed to kill Okada because they did not recognize him. Others murdered the Finance Minister, the new Inspector General of Military Education and the Lord Privy Seal, in addition to making more or less unsuccessful attacks on several other public figures. Pamphlets were distributed calling for the establishment of a new order, which it was hoped would be led by Mazaki. Yet neither Mazaki nor Araki made any move. Nor did society crumble at their blow, as a reading of ultra-nationalist literature might well have led them to expect. Instead, the high command, at the emperor's prompting, called out the navy and the Imperial Guards, surrounded the rebels and invited them to surrender. They did so, after a period of uneasy waiting, on the afternoon of the 29th.

This time surrender did not bring publicity or nominal sentences. Thirteen of the rebels were tried and executed in secrecy and haste, as was Aizawa, and four of their civilian allies, including Kita Ikki, met a similar fate in the following year. Araki and Mazaki were placed on the reserve; and an old rule was revived, providing that the War Minister must be an officer on the active list, by which it was hoped to keep them out of politics. The earlier arrangements to scatter the radical young officers in posts in the provinces or abroad were completed. Discipline, it was claimed, had been restored.

By virtue of these events the *Tosei* faction was able after 1936 to exercise a dominant influence on army affairs. By doing so, it could in certain respects determine national policies. Having regained its unity and saved the country from its own extremists, the army was able to insist on independence in military matters—which came to include even the choice between peace and war—and exploit its constitutional advantages to decide the composition of successive cabinets. No government could be formed without War and Navy Ministers. Since the latter had to be serving officers, no government could be formed without the co-operation of the high command. Thus when Hirota Koki became premier in March 1936, his first choice as Foreign Minister was vetoed by the army as unreliable. Hirota himself was brought down in January 1937 by army opposition, which also stopped General Ugaki from succeeding him—Ugaki was invited to form a government, but could find no one to serve as War Minister—and then foisted General Hayashi on a reluctant Court. When Hayashi resigned in May, the palace advisers turned in despair to a descendant of the old nobility, Konoe Fumimaro, in the hope that he would be able to satisfy service demands without giving way to them altogether, only to find that he became little more than a figurehead doing the army's bidding. By the time he left in January 1939, to be followed by the nationalist Hiranuma, the high command was in a position to choose, as well as to veto, nominees for cabinet appointment.

Japan's civilian statesmen, therefore, found that they had exchanged one kind of danger for another. Establishing control over *Kodo* and other radical extremists had perhaps saved the constitution and averted a threat to the basis of society. But the price they had had to pay was high. It involved an increase in the army's power to intervene in politics and the acceptance of a course which proved in the end no less destructive than revolution: expansion abroad and the building of a country organized for war.

War—though the word itself was carefully avoided—was not long in coming. In July 1937 one more in the long series of clashes between Chinese and Japanese troops in China took place near Peking. Hostilities spread and became general, so that by the end of the year, by decision of her field commanders and the military staff in Tokyo, Japan was fully committed. The resulting struggle will be discussed in the next chapter, but it can be said here that it was to be long and difficult beyond all expectations. It also had considerable impact on affairs at home. On the one hand it diverted the attention of many army hotheads from political to military matters. On the other it created an atmosphere in which their seniors could press for measures to prepare the country for a sterner test to come: re-armament, the further development of heavy industry, close government control of the economy, the destruction of liberalism, a reform of education.

An outline of these policies had been blocked out by army planners and adopted by the Hirota cabinet in August 1936, but it was not until Konoe became premier in June 1937 that their implementation really began. Within a few days of Konoe taking office, steps had been taken to bring civil aviation and the distribution of fuel under stricter government supervision. In October and November of the same year a Cabinet Planning Board was established, chiefly to co-ordinate economic policy, and an Imperial Headquarters was set up to provide for co-operation between army and navy. Other regulations had the effect of giving the services formally much of the power they already possessed in fact. All key decisions, it was agreed, were to be made at liaison conferences between the Prime Minister, Foreign Minister, War and Navy Ministers, and service Chiefs of Staff. They would then be confirmed at a meeting in the emperor's presence. This excluded other ministers, except by invitation, so that when the plan was put regularly into operation—which was in 1940—cabinet responsibility became no more than a pretence. Meanwhile the Asia Development Board, created at the end of 1938, had taken over the conduct of Japan's relations with China, a Greater East Asia Ministry being formed in November 1942 to absorb this and to handle matters pertaining to the other countries of the region. In the secretariat of all these bodies service officers held vital posts.

The extension of army influence on policy formation, which these innovations revealed, was accompanied by an increase in the government's powers of economic control. The National Mobilization Law, especially, which was passed by the Diet in March 1938, gave it a vast reserve of emergency authority, providing among other things for the direction of labour and materials, the regulation of wages and prices, government operation of certain industries, even a compulsory savings scheme and a system of national registration. Not all these measures were brought immediately into effect by any means. But their existence made it possible to establish clear priorities in economic growth.

There had already been some recovery from the trade slump of 1929-31, partly as a result of devaluation of the yen, so that both exports and imports by 1936 were about 25 per cent above the pre-slump value. Raw silk sales had fallen, but a rise in exports of textile fabrics compensated for this and stimulated a modest improvement, as well as some diversification, in the textile industry. Markets were also more varied. Less went to the United States, more to the countries of Asia and the south, where cheap manufactured goods were appropriate to local needs. The outstanding feature, however, was the growth in heavy industry. Between 1930 and 1936 the output of producer goods rose much more quickly than that of consumer goods, while the figures for both pig-iron and raw steel doubled. Coal production increased from about 30 million to 40 million metric tons, providing over half the country's fuel and power. In fact, Japan at this time accounted for a third of Asia's total coal consumption, about 90 per cent of what she needed being home produced. Shipbuilding had also recovered, the annual launch reaching nearly 300,000 tons in 1936 and the merchant marine over 4 million tons by 1937.

Government policy played an important part in these developments. At first this was because of attempts to overcome the economic crisis, but it came later to depend very largely on military needs. Military spending, for example, rose sharply, from under 500 million yen and 30 per cent of the budget in 1931 to 4,000 million yen and 70 per cent of the budget in 1937-8. After 1938, moreover, the use of controls authorized by the Mobilization Law, particularly those on raw materials, gave a more selective stimulus to chosen industries and firms. This brought significant gains in the production of motor vehicles, aircraft and warships, and helped to raise heavy industry's share of total industrial output to 73 per cent by 1942.

Manchukuo, too, conformed to the general trend. Indeed, it served in some ways as a pilot scheme for Japan itself, since military influence was paramount there from the very beginning. Its early investment pattern, directed by the South Manchuria Railway, proved too limited to meet the Kwantung Army's wishes; and in March 1938, the Manchuria Industrial Development Corporation was formed, with capital from the

Manchukuo government and a new generation of Japanese industrialists (the 'new *zaibatsu*'), with whom the army had close relations. Money was channelled into the coal, iron and steel industries and into automobile and aircraft plants. Similar steps were taken in north China, through the North China Development Corporation, and by 1940 the two areas were producing on an important scale. Together they furnished most of the country's high quality coal, about 30 per cent of its pig-iron needs, and substantial quantities of cement, chemicals and machinery.

As a different kind of contribution to national strength, economic controls were accompanied by political ones, exercised through censorship—radio, as well as press—and through supervision of 'dangerous thoughts'. Liberals were a principal target. They faced the danger of arrest whenever they criticized the government's policies and were subject to a number of public pressures which officialdom did nothing to abate. Professor Minobe, for example, a leading authority on constitutional law and a member of the House of Peers, was attacked strongly in 1934–5 on the grounds that some of his writings described the emperor as an 'organ' of the state. This, it was said, was *lèse majesté*; and in face of such a charge few had the courage to defend him. Eventually he was forced to resign from the Peers and relinquish all his honours, his books were banned, and early in 1936 he narrowly escaped assassination.

Much of this chauvinistic atmosphere was injected into the schools and universities. Many foreign books used in them were proscribed by the police—often without a very clear idea of their contents—and textbooks were rewritten in nationalist terms. Even works of serious scholarship might well begin with a precautionary reference to Japan's mission overseas. Military training was made a compulsory part of education in 1938 and the time devoted to it, including that spent on indoctrination, increased steadily thereafter, always at the expense of 'unnecessary' subjects, that is, those which contributed little to patriotism or practical knowledge. Army officers were attached to the schools to supervise this process. Moreover, in 1937 the Ministry of Education issued a new book, *Kokutai no Hongi* (Principles of the National Polity), as the main text for the course in 'ethics'. Over two million copies were sold and special commentaries on it were issued to teachers, with the result that its doctrines became the basis of an intensive propaganda directed at the young, rejecting the revolutionary, anti-capitalist elements in the thinking of the radical right, but remaining anti-liberal in the extreme. Individualism was anathema, service to the state was service in its highest form. Moreover, patriotism taught that what was bad was foreign:

'The various ideological and social evils of present-day Japan are the fruits of ignoring the fundamentals and of running into the trivial, of lack in sound judgment, and of failure to digest things thoroughly; and this is due to the fact that since the days of Meiji so many aspects of European and American culture, systems, and learning have been imported, and that, too rapidly.'[68]

It did not take long for the combined resources of press and radio, of schools and universities, of patriotic societies and army publicists, to drive such a lesson home.

It is not surprising that in this kind of atmosphere the older political parties, widely accused of being representatives of a corrupting West, found themselves unable to exercise much influence. It is true that they retained control over the lower house of the Diet. This made their support well worth having, if only as evidence of the nation's consent to what was being done in its name, so that it is still possible to talk of the Japanese constitution as parliamentary, even though the parties could not form cabinets or contribute significantly to them. Yet they could not any longer obstruct government in matters of real substance: once hostilities broke out in China in July 1937, most politicians raised the cry of national unity and showed themselves ready to pass every government bill. Before long there was talk of the need for a united front—united, not against militarism, but behind it—and in 1940 plans to form one reached fruition. The Imperial Rule Assistance Association (Taisei Yokusan Kai) was organized in October of that year. It replaced the parties, absorbed their members and pledged itself to rally opinion behind national policies.

The creation of a one-party system, in which the elected representatives of the people clearly played a very minor role in policy-making, has sometimes been taken as evidence of the 'fascist' character of Japan's political regime in the period 1937-45.[69] Since the matter is controversial, it might be useful here to recapitulate some of the regime's leading characteristics, bearing this question in mind.

The first point to be made is a negative one: that there was no charismatic individual leader in Japan. Tojo, who came closest, was no Hitler or Mussolini. His position rested solidly on the backing of the army and on his own acceptance as its representative in government circles, not on mass popular support. Indeed, it could be argued that what happened in Japan was that the army, notably its *Tosei* faction, eventually found a formula (couched in terms of a national mission overseas) that was able to reintegrate the discordant elements of the polity in a manner unknown since the Meiji leadership's pursuit of 'wealth and strength'. It thereby attracted enough backing from conservative interests in the Court, the bureaucracy, the Diet and the business world to cause most of the rest to fall into line. Indeed, censorship and police repression were hardly needed against the liberals (though much used against the left): once the new pattern emerged their response was that of conformity, or at least acquiescence.

One reason for this is that individualism had not rooted itself as firmly in Japan as the superficially Western appearance of many modern Japanese institutions would suggest. Partly this was because the premodern collectivist ethic, setting duty to the group above the rights of the individual, was perpetuated in the village, where it met the needs of both rice-farming and landlord power; thence it constantly reinforced traditionalism in the towns, through voting patterns, family links and urban influxes of rural labour. Partly it was because the ethical content of education and army training had been determined in the late Meiji period, when one object was to maintain social cohesion in the face of massive imports of ideas and habits from the West. Informal teaching within the family, also traditionalist in tone, gave support to all this. Finally, there was the fact that premodern group loyalties—to domain, village, family or guild—instead of being destroyed by modernization, had been transferred to new objects, that is, to bureaucracy (or ministry), to party (or faction), to army (or regiment), to firm or association or school. This gave a traditionalist cast to many 'modern' institutions.

In other words, Japanese 'fascism' (if such it was) had a

stronger traditionalist ingredient than that of Europe. Liberalism, socialism and communism were not only treated as threats to the established order in the context of political power. They were also attacks on the collectivist ethic and associated patterns of behaviour. And since individualism was alien, and collectivism was Japanese, the tension between them was part of Japan's cultural and political response to the West, contributing in the end to the creation of a 'New Order' in East Asia.

CHAPTER XIV

AN EMPIRE WON AND LOST
1937-1945

*Invasion of Manchuria—war with China—Anti-Comintern Pact
—Pearl Harbour—victory and defeat*

Japanese advocates of expansion after 1931 had behind them a
people easily persuaded that aggressive policies were just. History,
as taught in their schools, depicted their country as starting its international career in the nineteenth century under a number of legal
handicaps, embodied in treaties imposed by a predatory West. A
generation later it had become subject to a different kind of discrimination, when the United States and Australia, in particular, introduced controls on Japanese immigration. Public consciousness of
these disabilities was turned to good account by the apostles of
empire. During the first thirty years of the twentieth century Japanese opinion gave solid support to governments in pursuit of gain in
neighbouring territories: colonies in Korea and Taiwan; a network
of political and military privileges in Manchuria, opening the way to
exploitation of valuable mining rights; trade and financial concessions in the rest of China, where Japan joined the West in making
that country, as Sun Yat-sen once put it, 'the colony of every nation
with which it has concluded treaties.'[70]

These policies were not adopted without controversy, however.
Specifically, they gave rise to two different kinds of disagreement
within Japan. One, which might be described as tactical, was
between those who urged a concentration of Japanese effort on
securing effective control over a relatively limited sphere of
influence—commonly they had Manchuria and Inner Mongolia in
mind—and those who looked for more diffuse advantages, mostly
economic ones, in the whole of East Asia. Advocates of the former
policy, who included many army leaders, tended to emphasize

Japan's strategic needs and to argue that the country lacked the degree of economic strength to undertake competition with the West on equal terms. Advocates of the latter, typically to be found in the Foreign Ministry, criticized expansionist activities, like those pursued by the army in Manchuria, on the grounds that they offended both Chinese nationalism and the Powers, thereby handicapping Japanese trade.

Both sides of the argument in this debate were essentially pragmatic. The second source of disagreement arose from political and historical assumptions that put pragmatism itself in question. Some Japanese, usually men who had no direct responsibility for formulating national policy, started from the proposition that the fundamental conflict to be taken into consideration was that between Asia and the West. Japan, they held, must inevitably take Asia's side. There were various ways of doing so, however. One was for Japan to set herself at the head of an Asian confederation—in which China's membership was crucial—in order to destroy Western imperialism. A corollary was that Japanese actions, whether in Manchuria or elsewhere, must not be of a kind to make co-operation on China's part impossible. An alternative—based on a belief that China and the other countries of East Asia had been so reduced to weakness and disunity by the combined effects of Western dominance and their own social failings that they could not usefully be accepted as full partners—emphasized that in such a confederation Japan would provide not only leadership, but also most of the effective force. It followed that Japan should have at her disposal for this purpose the greater part of the region's resources; and if they were not freely offered, it was for the good of all that they be seized.

Such differences over policy continued into the 1930s. However, they tended then to take on new forms, partly because of developments in Japanese politics, which we have already discussed (chapter XIII), partly because the international context for Japanese action was perceived to have changed. Slump induced a worldwide trend towards protectionism and the creation of autarchic economic blocs. Belief that this was so prompted Japanese leaders to consider creating such a bloc for Japan. One could, of course, define it variously—a bloc centring on Korea and Manchuria; one including all China; one extending even into South East Asia—so the result was in one sense simply to put old arguments about objectives into new dress. Yet the military implications of what was done would clearly now be of a different order. In the existing state of international rivalries, any world war was bound eventually to affect Asia, hence Japanese interests. Prudence suggested preparation for it. Ishiwara Kanji's proposals for strengthening Japan, industrially by exploiting the resources of Manchuria and north China, politically through some kind of Asian confederation, in anticipation of war *à l'outrance* with Russia, Britain and finally America, was an extreme version of what might be done, not even fully acceptable within the army; but they did serve to indicate that Japan's relations with the countries of East Asia were likely soon to be transformed by military considerations.

None of this resolved the problem of priorities, which was to bedevil Japanese policy-making throughout the 1930s. Ishiwara himself, architect of the Japanese seizure of Manchuria at the beginning of the decade, was later to object to the application of his own methods to north China, on the grounds that military involvement there would invite a Russian counter-thrust. More generally, army field commanders, pursuing their own chosen strategies, used the argument of 'command prerogative' to justify departure from plans approved by the General Staff; the General Staff itself was frequently divided about what was needed, or at loggerheads with the War Ministry about the matching of means to ends; the War Ministry, which found it difficult to speak convincingly on behalf of the army as a whole in these circumstances, met with opposition to its proposals within the cabinet from the navy (espousing a different strategic view), from the Foreign Ministry (insisting on the importance of world opinion), or from the Finance Ministry (objecting to the economic consequences of military plans). Despite the development of additional co-ordinating machinery in government, such as the Cabinet Planning Office and the Liaison Conference (involving senior cabinet ministers and the chiefs of staff), the pluralism of Japanese decision-making organs often led to pluralism in policy: an agreement to pursue all 'desirable' lines of policy simultaneously, in preference to assigning priorities. This remained the case, notwithstanding the growing influence of the army in politics. In other words, Japanese dealings with the outside world cannot really be said to have been 'planned' in this period, even though they were consistently directed to expansion of one kind or another. This fact underlies many of the confusions in the narrative which follows.

The invasion of Manchuria in 1931 set an ominous pattern, for the Japanese troops who occupied Mukden on the night of September 18-19 were following the plans of the Kwantung Army staff, not the policies of Tokyo. The cabinet, indeed, was first consulted when it came to sending reinforcements. In the next few months, moreover, the high command as a whole gave full support to the officers in the field, repeatedly accepting orders to limit the advance, then allowing them to be ignored on a plea of operational necessity. It was by this technique that the occupied area was constantly enlarged and the diplomats faced with a series of *faits accomplis*. As a final step came the creation of the puppet state of Manchukuo in February 1932, which gave the Kwantung Army something not far short of a private empire. Its commander-in-chief, as Japanese ambassador, acquired so large a measure of independence, by exercising civil, as well as military, control, that Admiral Okada, Prime Minister in 1934-6, later stated that the government 'had no way of learning what the plans and activities of the Kwantung Army were'.[71]

Diplomacy, meanwhile, had been doing what it could to repair the damage to the country's reputation. On September 21, two days after the outbreak, China had appealed to the League of Nations and Japan had promptly denied that she was pursuing territorial ambitions. She also promised to withdraw her troops, only to find, as time passed, that Tokyo lacked the authority to do so. For several weeks, explanations and recriminations prevented further progress. Then in November, with Japanese consent, the League appointed a commission of inquiry, its members, under the chairmanship of Lord Lytton, being nominated in January 1932 and reaching Yokohama in the following month. By then their investigations had already been made abortive by the announcement of the 'independent' state of Manchukuo. Nor did anything they saw or heard thereafter give much credence to the Japanese army's case, as the report which they submitted in September 1932 made clear. This made it inevitable that recognition would be withheld from the regime which the Kwantung Army had established, so Japan, making public her own recognition of it, withdrew altogether from the League as soon as the matter came to debate at Geneva in February 1933.

China gained nothing from these moves and found Western sympathy of little help when the Japanese army resumed operations in her northern provinces at the beginning of 1933. In the first few weeks of that year a pretext was found for adding Jehol to Manchukuo. In May a truce at Tangku, negotiated without reference to the diplomats, created a demilitarized zone which insulated Japan's gains from the areas further south and gave military commanders a basis for fresh demands at a later date. In June 1935, for example, they called for the withdrawal of Chinese troops from Hopei and Chahar, on the grounds that their presence threatened the maintenance of peace. Simultaneously they encouraged such Chinese political movements in the north as might be willing to accept 'autonomy' under the patronage of Japan.

For the most part the advances Japan made in China in these years were local, intermittent and small-scale, rarely causing the sort of scandal that would have brought international intervention. They were also the army's work, with which the Foreign Ministry had more and more to conform. In April 1934 it announced the doctrine that the relationships between Japan and China—which it described in terms more appropriate to suzerainty or protectorate than to diplomacy between independent states—were in no sense the concern of the League of Nations or the Powers. Eighteen months later it proposed a basis for a general settlement: Chinese recognition of Manchukuo; suppression of anti-Japanese activities in China; and an anti-communist Sino-Japanese alliance.

Even this, however, fell short of an attempt at total domination, such as was to come before very long. Chinese stubbornness and hostility in the resulting negotiations soon began to convince Japanese leaders that their piecemeal methods were of no avail, an attitude that became more widespread when Chiang Kai-shek reached agreement with the communists at the end of 1936 on making common cause against Japan. Similarly, the Japanese high command was finding its hotheads harder to restrain, or rather, had found fresh grounds for not trying to restrain them. The failure of the military revolt in Tokyo in February 1936 had left behind it a sense of frustration and discouragement among younger officers. This might have been explosive had there been any attempt to exercise moderation

AN EMPIRE WON AND LOST 1937-1945

overseas, whereas an adventurous foreign policy had the advantage, if successful, that it might ease the political tensions building up at home and possibly show a profit economically as well. Since most of those now dominant in the army were men dedicated to pursuing Japan's 'mission' on the mainland— and most members of the public had been led to expect some outstanding achievement from them—by 1937 the prospects of a major clash with China had much increased.

It began with an incident at Marco Polo Bridge, near Peking, on the night of July 7, 1937, when firing broke out between Chinese and Japanese troops while the latter were on manoeuvres. The fighting quickly spread, becoming general in the next few weeks. One reason was that Chinese resistance proved unusually stubborn. Another was the absence of any authority on the Japanese side that seemed willing to effect a local settlement. The cabinet wanted one, as did several members of the high command, for many senior officers were reluctant to get the army deeply committed in China at the cost of leaving Manchuria and Mongolia open to Russian attack; but the field commanders and their allies, the section chiefs of the General Staff, were able to prevent any such restrictive proposals from being carried out. In this sense, the 'China Affair', as it was called, was the result of another military conspiracy.

Once the campaign was properly begun, of course, Tokyo could hardly refuse reinforcements, and this made it possible, as had happened in Manchuria six years earlier, for the scale of operations to be continually increased. By early August Tientsin and Peking had both been occupied. By September over 150,000 Japanese troops had been deployed. Hostilities had also spread to the south, beginning, once again, at Shanghai, where there was heavy fighting, and continuing with a thrust up the Yangtse river to Nanking, Chiang's capital. The city was captured in mid-December and became the scene of what were probably the worst atrocities of the war, as Japanese troops were turned loose to murder, rape, loot and burn at will. Their behaviour gained them a reputation for lust and cruelty that endured until final surrender in 1945.

Their victories, moreover, ensured that hostilities would continue. The Chinese government withdrew to the interior, eventually to Chungking, and showed some signs of a willingness to bargain, but in Tokyo the conviction grew that the only way out of hostilities that were strategically, as well as diplomatically, embarrassing was to seek a *Blitzkrieg* victory and the total overthrow of the Kuomintang. By the end of 1937 all talk of localizing the conflict had been abandoned. Accordingly, the terms offered earlier were withdrawn and the country prepared itself for waging a full-scale war. A naval blockade was extended to the whole of China's coastline. In addition, Chinese cities were heavily bombed and campaigns were launched to consolidate the territorial gains which had been made so far. During 1938, for example, the forces in north China and the Yangtse valley linked up to establish land communications with each other. In October of that year, troops moving up the Yangtse reached Hankow, others in south China reached Canton. By November, in fact, when Konoe announced his plans for a 'New Order', Japan controlled all the wealthiest and most highly populated parts of China, except Szechwan.

Since none of this brought a Kuomintang capitulation—nationalism seemed to thrive on defeats, as well as victories—the year 1939 saw a pause for reconsideration. Japan was still not fully extended by her efforts. She resembled, it has been said, 'a country engaged in a wearisome colonial war, rather than one exerting all its strength . . . against an adversary of equal power'.[72] Nevertheless, she was experiencing an economic strain and a measure of war weariness, while her military leaders were anticipating a clash with Russia in the next few years for which they needed every possible preparation. They therefore changed their strategy, seeking to exploit political rather than military advantages. As a first step they tried cutting China off from the outside world by exerting pressure on the countries that befriended her, a decision leading in February 1939 to the occupation of Hainan, a French sphere of interest, and in June to a blockade of the French and British concessions in Tientsin. The process was completed by the outbreak of the European war soon after, for in their preoccupation with it the Powers could offer little resistance to Japanese demands. Within a year France had granted Japan access to the south through Indo-China and Britain had—temporarily—closed the route from Burma to Yunnan.

Supplementing these successes was an attempt at subversion from within. Japanese army commanders had tried frequently in the past to acquire the help of Chinese local leaders, but it was not until Wang Ching-wei seceded from the Kuomintang regime that they won over a statesman of any consequence. In March 1940 Wang was established as head of a puppet government in Nanking, which it was hoped would attract support for a peace treaty on Japanese terms. In this it failed, partly because Tokyo gave it too little backing, having still in mind the possibility of a deal with Chiang Kai-shek, partly because army commanders were not willing entirely to abandon their own local Chinese puppets. Thus China remained disunited, though fragmented now by Japanese-sponsored regimes, rather than by Chinese warlords. What is more, the ideal of a China wholeheartedly co-operating with Japan, which men like Ishiwara Kanji cherished, was sacrificed to military necessity. Plans for the development of the Chinese economy under Japanese supervision rapidly deteriorated into the exploitation of economic resources vital to the Japanese war machine. Even the industrialization of Manchukuo, to which much capital was devoted after 1937, had similar motives. The pattern did nothing to reconcile Chinese to the New Order, for all its ostentatiously Confucian trimmings. In fact, one reason for the growing emphasis on military needs was the continuation of Chinese resistance. In the south-west, Chiang Kai-shek's forces still kept the field, though their military effectiveness was limited. In the north, communist guerillas controlled much of the area outside the towns, constituting a drain on Japanese strength that was to prove of substantial importance when the China struggle merged into a wider conflict.

Events in China had important repercussions on Japan's relations with the Powers. Since the spread of Japanese authority gave benefits to Japanese trade, it was in some degree an attack on the interests of Britain and America. Similarly, the means by which it was carried out provoked a number of incidents, involving, for example, British and American ships on the Yangtse, which furnished both countries with specific grievances. All this helped to encourage them in showing sympathy for China. On the other hand, neither—the one because of crises in Europe, the other because of isolationism at home

—was willing at first to take any positive steps against Japan. Nor did they, until a change in Japanese policies began to threaten them more directly after 1939.

In the interval Japan was much more concerned at the danger of being attacked by Russia. Her acquisition of the Manchurian provinces had put a check on Russia's traditional aspirations in the area, forcing her among other things to sell to Japan in 1935 the Chinese Eastern Railway (the spur from the Trans-Siberian which ran to Vladivostock via Harbin). It also gave the two a much longer common frontier, on which friction might develop. Thus a clash occurred at the junction of the Manchurian, Korean and Siberian borders in July 1938, which lasted for nearly a fortnight, and another in May 1939 at Nomonhan, between Manchuria and Outer Mongolia, which was not settled till September. Large forces were used in both, including armour; and Japan's relative lack of success on these occasions made her still more wary of Russian strength.

Her fears, plus a consciousness of the diplomatic isolation in which withdrawal from the League of Nations had left her, prompted a search for friends. This had already led to Hitler's Germany some years earlier—since Germany's enemies, anti-communist convictions and need for allies seemed very like her own—and had resulted in the signature of an Anti-Comintern Pact in November 1936, providing publicly for Japanese-German co-operation against international communism, secretly for a defensive alliance against Russia. Knowledge of it helped to convince the army in 1937 that action in China was a legitimate risk. Indeed, an influential group of officers soon began to urge something more positive and open. Closer Japanese-German ties, they thought, might serve as an insurance against Russian moves and increase the pressure on China to surrender, so in June 1938 their representative, General Oshima Hiroshi, first as military attaché, then as ambassador, began negotiations in Berlin. These failed because Germany did not want to commit herself to an exclusively anti-Russian treaty, nor Japan to an alliance of more general scope, but it was not until a Russo-German non-aggression pact was announced in August 1939 that they came formally to an end.

The second Konoe government, on taking office in July

1940, faced renewed demands from the army for a German agreement. They were enthusiastically sponsored by the Foreign Minister, Matsuoka Yosuke, who was completely confident of his ability to exploit such an arrangement to Japan's, rather than Germany's, advantage. He was also sure of German victory in Europe, from which he drew the conclusion that Japan must lose no time in negotiating a division of the spoils, since the defeat of Britain, France and Holland would leave their colonies in Asia without defence. So enticing a prospect overcame the cabinet's doubts and a Tripartite Pact with Germany and Italy was signed on September 27 of that year. It was reinforced in April 1941 by a neutrality agreement with Russia, designed to free Japan from uncertainty about her northern frontiers. Unfortunately for Matsuoka's reputation, however, the whole policy proved to be based on erroneous calculations. Britain did not succumb to German attack. What is more, Hitler, without warning to Japan, launched an invasion of Russia in June 1941. One of its by-products was Matsuoka's fall, brought about by a cabinet re-shuffle in July.

In his year of office Matsuoka had given a new dimension to Japan's ambitions by formulating plans for expansion in South East Asia. These had been discussed by military staffs as early as 1936, with a view to Japan gaining control of the region's oil, tin, rubber, bauxite and other strategic raw materials, but little had been done to put them into effect, largely because of preoccupations in China. Lack of success in China, however, gave the economic resources of South East Asia a new importance to men who were still thinking in terms of eventual total war. Hence Matsuoka raised the question afresh at a liaison conference between ministers and service chiefs on July 27, 1940. Its decision, confirmed by the inner cabinet in September, was that Japan must seize the opportunity which the European war had given her to establish herself in Indo-China, Siam (Thailand), Burma, Malaya and the Netherlands Indies. Diplomacy was to be tried in the first place to attain these ends. In particular, every effort was to be made to avoid a conflict with America. But in the last resort force would be used and the risk of war accepted.

Within a few weeks a beginning had been made in Indo-China, the French government, in return for a guarantee of

French sovereignty there, being persuaded in September 1940 to authorize the establishment of Japanese air bases in the north and to grant right of passage for Japanese troops. This was in the context of Japan's strategy in China, rather than South East Asia, but in July 1941 substantial Japanese forces entered the rest of the territory, obviously in preparation for moves further south. On the other hand, attempts to get special economic and political privileges in the Netherlands Indies in this period failed. Demands for co-operation, including the allocation to Japan of most of the colony's production of oil, were made by Japanese missions during the autumn and winter of 1940–41, only to meet with interminable difficulties and evasions. It seemed reasonable to conclude that nothing short of force would overcome them.

Germany's attack on Russia raised a different problem, since it opened the way for Japan to strike north, instead of south, if she wished to do so. Equally, of course, it made it possible to launch a campaign in South East Asia with greater confidence. Both points were strongly urged when the matter was debated in Tokyo at the beginning of July 1941, even the army being divided between their rival attractions, and the decisions that were finally taken left the issue open for a time. In effect, Japan was to concentrate on her 'New Order', acting independently of her Axis allies, and continue preparations for a major struggle without getting involved in the Russian war.

The key to a southward move, as most Japanese leaders saw it, was likely to be the reaction of the United States. The risks, in other words, would depend a good deal on whether or not America was prepared to fight, a question they found it difficult to answer. Recent omens had not been favourable. American hostility to Japanese policies in China had led Washington in July 1939 to refuse to renew its commercial treaty with Japan, which expired in the following year. 1940 saw an increase in such economic pressure, with licences introduced for exports of various kinds of oil and scrap-iron in July, an embargo on all scrap for Japan in September, its extension to iron and steel exports after the presidential elections in November. The regulations seriously handicapped Japanese stockpiling of vital materials, even though a total ban on oil supplies was not imposed. A still graver blow came in 1941, when in immediate response to the occupation of southern Indo-China in July the American government froze all Japanese assets in the United States, bringing trade almost to a standstill.

By this time the two countries had for some months been engaged in negotiations, though the effect of exchanges in April, May and June 1941 had been only to clarify the nature of their disagreement. The United States sought an undertaking that Japan would respect the independence and territorial integrity of her neighbours, including China and the Philippines; that she would pursue her policies by peaceful means; and that she would guarantee equality of economic opportunity in the areas under her control. In reply, Japan asserted that her intentions were peaceful and in no way a threat to other states. Conflict could more easily be avoided, she said, if Washington would help her to secure the oil and rubber she needed and persuade China to accept her terms. Implicit in this was an American demand that Japan withdraw from China and halt her advance in South East Asia, and a Japanese refusal to do any such thing. This brought deadlock, which the following weeks did nothing to resolve. Prime Minister Konoe tried to break it in August by proposing a personal meeting between himself and President Roosevelt. The latter, however, would not undertake it unless a measure of success were first achieved in preliminary talks, of which there was little sign. Later in the year Japan sent a special envoy, Kurusu Saburo, to assist her ambassador in Washington; but since neither side was willing to give way on matters of substance the gesture was no more effective than those that had gone before.

In Tokyo, meanwhile, staff officers had been considering the plans they would follow in the event of war. Two factors—the state of stockpiles and anticipated weather conditions—convinced them that operations would have to be begun, if at all, not later than December 1941, which meant, in turn, that a final decision on war or peace must be made by the beginning of October. This conclusion was reported to the inner circle of policy-makers in early September and accepted as setting a timetable within which they should work. Yet accepting a timetable, it proved, was easier than carrying it out. When October came, the services announced that they were agreed on giving priority to South East Asia and adamant against retreat from China, thereby ensuring that the American talks must fail. Civilian members of the government, on the other hand, were equally unwilling to admit that hostilities must be the unavoidable result. Unable to bring about a reconciliation, Konoe felt he had no choice but to resign.

He did so on October 16, 1941, and was succeeded two days later by General Tojo Hideki, promoted from the office of War Minister in the belief that he would have the army's confidence. This he undoubtedly had. A former staff officer and the army's spokesman in the cabinet disputes of the previous weeks, he was an authoritarian of rigidly military outlook who made an exemplary representative of the high command. Even his nickname, 'Razor', implied an uncompromising directness which was more appropriate to a war leader than a saviour of the peace. To make him premier, therefore, was not merely the latest step in a series of civilian attempts to control the army by concession; it was also a fatal one, leading to military dictatorship—a dictatorship of the General Staff—and war.

This rapidly became apparent in the reappraisal of policy which followed his appointment. Operational necessity was argued more strongly than ever, until it was agreed at last, much as it had been in September, that time for only one more diplomatic effort remained. There was the difference, however, that on this occasion the alternative was more clearly war, if the diplomats could not secure at least American abandonment of China and extensive economic concessions, in return for the halting of Japan's advance elsewhere. On November 5, 1941, they were given until the end of the month to secure a settlement on these terms. Inevitably they failed, despite the Kurusu mission. On November 26 Washington rejected the proposals and five days later, on December 1, an imperial conference of civilian and service leaders in Tokyo took the decision to attack. A formal statement breaking off relations was then prepared for transmission to the American government, only to be delayed, first by an excess of security consciousness at home, then by secretarial inefficiency in the Washington embassy, so that it was not delivered until hostilities had actually begun. In fact American intelligence agencies, who had already broken Japan's most important code, were able to pass a copy of the statement to the Secretary of State some hours before he received it from the Japanese ambassador.

Once Japanese strategists were convinced that the United States would not stand idly by while the countries of South East Asia were invaded, it became axiomatic that the American Pacific fleet, the only force capable of threatening Japan's communications with the south, must become the first object of attack. Accordingly, a major air strike was directed at its Hawaiian base, Pearl Harbour, on the morning of Sunday, December 7, 1941, by planes from a naval squadron which had left the Kuriles ten days earlier. Surprise was complete and success phenomenal. Eight battleships were sunk or damaged, as were seven other vessels. 90 per cent of America's air and surface strength in the area was immobilized or destroyed. Simultaneously, attacks were launched against targets in Wake, Guam, Midway, the Philippines and Hong Kong, all of them successful, while soon after a British battleship and battle-cruiser from Singapore were attacked and sunk at sea.

These operations, carefully planned and brilliantly executed, opened the way for a series of rapid campaigns in South East Asia. Hong Kong was forced to surrender on Christmas Day. Landings on Luzon brought the capture of Manila on January 2, 1942, followed quickly by the occupation of the whole of the Philippines, though an American force in Bataan held out until the beginning of May. Other Japanese troops landed on the east coast of Malaya, crossed the Kra isthmus, and advanced down both sides of the peninsula, taking Kuala Lumpur on January 11 and Singapore—supposedly impregnable—on February 15. This freed men for an assault on the Netherlands Indies, where Dutch troops capitulated on March 9, and on Burma, which was largely overrun by the end of April. At this point, therefore, Japan controlled everything from Rangoon to the mid-Pacific, from Timor to the Mongolian steppe.

Her war plans, drawn up in November 1941, had envisaged turning the whole of this area into a Greater East Asia Co-prosperity Sphere, with Japan, north China and Manchukuo as its industrial base. The other countries were to provide raw materials and form part of a vast consumer market, building a degree of economic strength that would enable Japan, first, to meet and contain any counter-attack from outside, then, if all went well, to incorporate India, Australia and Russia's Siberian provinces by further wars at a later date.

To achieve these ends it was necessary that Japanese domination be substituted for domination by the West, at least initially, a decision that led to a cultural crusade—widespread teaching of the Japanese language, reforms of education to eliminate 'undesirable' influences, the organization of literary and scientific conferences, even attempts to abolish the siesta and jazz—as well as the creation of a network of new political alignments. Some countries were from the beginning left a large measure of independence. Indo-China, for example, was left in the hands of the French, and Siam (Thailand), after signing a treaty of alliance, retained its own monarchy and administration, though both had to grant a number of special favours to Japan. Occupied China, as represented by Wang Ching-wei's regime, had already signed a peace agreement in November 1940 and was eventually persuaded to declare war on America and Britain in January 1943. This heralded an era of greater formal equality with Japan, marked by the abolition of Japanese concessions in the old treaty ports later in the year. Manchukuo, of course, had always been nominally an independent state, despite the authority of the Kwantung Army there. This situation, like the colonial status of Korea, remained unchanged.

Of the territories that had been newly conquered, Burma produced a puppet leader, Ba Maw, who was made head of a Japanese-sponsored administration on August 1, 1942. However, real power was in the hands of his military advisers and they retained it after the country was given independence in the following year, when it declared war and concluded an alliance in its turn. The Philippines, with the help of pro-Japanese collaborators, achieved independence on October 14, 1943, though its government was able to avoid declaring war on the allies until September 1944. In Malaya and the Netherlands Indies, on the other hand, because they were economically vital, Japan was more reluctant to relinquish direct control. Each was put under military administration, centralized and bureaucratic in its methods, which replaced the officialdom of the former colonial powers. Nor were freedom movements of any kind encouraged in the first two years. Even thereafter no very extensive promises were made, though regional councils were established and local residents were allowed to play some part in government. In Malaya, in fact, this was as much as was done for the rest of the war, though in the Indies a nationalist movement developed and was at last recognized by the Japanese when their defeat was obvious in 1945.

From the beginning there were important contradictions in Japan's policy towards the countries of South East Asia. The political objective of winning the support of local populations was logically contrary to the desire to extract the maximum amount of oil, tin and rubber for the Japanese war effort. A liaison conference decision of November 1941 had recognized as much: 'Economic hardship imposed upon native livelihood as a result of the acquisition of resources vital to the national defence ... must be endured....'[73] Resistance, endangering this policy, evoked a harsh response from the military. Executions and torture, in turn, made it less and less likely that Japan would succeed in her official long-term aim of creating 'an autonomous zone of peaceful living and common prosperity', comprising 'independent countries existing within the New Order of East Asia'.[74] The war itself made the Co-prosperity Sphere in its ideal form unattainable, in much the same way as it had distorted Japan's relations with China.

Nor, it transpired, was the limited military objective attainable. Lack of trained manpower, especially technicians, proved a major obstacle to restoring the trade and industry of South East Asia, above all oil production, to their former efficiency. Inadequate communications, made worse by enemy action, prevented the raw materials, once extracted, from reaching Japan. Submarine attacks interfered seriously with Japanese shipping in the islands as early as 1942. As these attacks were increasingly supplemented by air offensives later in the war, Japan found herself almost completely cut off from her more distant territories. Three-quarters of her merchant marine had been lost by the summer of 1945 in an attempt to keep the sea lanes open. Industrial production at home suffered substantially as a result.

Defending a military perimeter in the hope of forcing a stalemate peace proved no less difficult than developing the economy of the Co-prosperity Sphere. The bulk of the army was expensively pinned down on the Asian mainland: by the Chinese; from fear of Russian invasion in the north; to guard against counter-attack from India into Burma. It was, however, in the Pacific, where the size of land forces was less significant, that the decisive engagements were to be fought. The naval battles of the Coral Sea at the beginning of May 1942 and of Midway a month later foiled Japanese thrusts towards Australia and Hawaii, respectively. Australian forces fought successfully to defend southern New Guinea in the rest of the year. Then, as Japan's first major repulse on land, came the American recapture of Guadalcanal in the Solomon islands, ending six months' bitter fighting in February 1943. These operations marked a strategic turning-point.

During them, moreover, a new pattern of warfare was evolving: in naval engagements, action at long range, using aircraft from carriers as the main offensive weapons—a development which largely offset Japan's initial advantage in capital ships—and in island campaigns, close co-operation between land, sea and air forces, preferably under unified command. These became the main ingredients in an American 'island-hopping' technique designed, not to regain territory in any general sense, but to win bases from which ships and aircraft could dominate wide areas of the west Pacific.

In January 1943 allied leaders met at Casablanca and agreed to divert more resources to the war against Japan. In August they followed this up at Quebec by naming their commanders and outlining the strategy to be used. Within a few months forces under Admiral Chester Nimitz, acting in accordance with these decisions, had attacked the Marshall islands in the central Pacific, demonstrating for the first of many times the overwhelming weight of metal that could be brought against an island target and the speed with which it could be reduced if enemy reinforcement were made impossible. The key base of Kwajalein was captured in ten days' fighting in February 1944. Saipan in the Marianas took a little longer (mid-June to early July 1944) and involved a full fleet action, the battle of the Philippine Sea, to cover the landings. This broke the back of Japanese naval resistance, however, and made even more rapid progress possible elsewhere. Guam fell in August, the Palau group in September, completing an 'advance' of over two thousand miles in less than a year.

The emphasis now swung to the South West Pacific, where General Douglas MacArthur was in command. In September 1944, simultaneously with the attack on Palau, his forces landed on Morotai, midway between New Guinea and Mindanao. A month later they reached the Philippines, completing the occupation of Leyte by the end of December and invading Luzon in January 1945. Manila was captured on February 5. From this point the two commands were able to act together, their first target being Okinawa in the Ryukyu islands, which was secured by late June, their next an invasion of Japan itself. The Japanese fleet was no longer a serious threat, having been virtually destroyed in a further naval battle in the Leyte Gulf in October 1944. This left the offshore defence of the homeland to the suicide pilots (*kamikaze*), whose attacks during the Okinawa fighting, though damaging, had not been wholly effective. Meanwhile, a land campaign had been launched in Burma by forces under the command of Lord Mountbatten, marking a major diversion of allied resources to the war against Japan following the surrender of Germany in May 1945.

The first stage of preparation for invasion was the bombing of Japanese cities. The use of land-based aircraft for this purpose had begun from Saipan the previous autumn and was made easier by the capture of Iwojima in March 1945. Then operations began from Okinawa, growing rapidly in frequency and extending to the whole of Japan, so that by the summer the country was in a state of siege. Shipping to and from the mainland almost ceased. Most industrial centres, despite attempts at dispersal, suffered heavy damage, while incendiary raids on urban areas, made as an attack on Japanese morale, brought casualties which included over 200,000 killed. Rail transport, suffering not only from bombing but from lack of maintenance, began to deteriorate rapidly, contributing to a situation in which production, even of munitions, dropped sharply from its wartime peaks. Consumer goods became wellnigh unobtainable. Food was scarce, prices rising, black markets everywhere. With it all, the population was required to work harder, and for less reward, than ever before. Education had been curtailed to get more students into the army and the factories. Restrictions on the use of child and female labour had been abolished. Even the regulations which limited working hours, modest though they were, had been swept away.

Despite the evidence around them, press and radio constantly assured the Japanese that they could win the war, if only they would make a supreme effort—sometimes it was called a supreme sacrifice—in their own defence. The enemy had over-extended his communications; he had underestimated Japanese strength; he would never accept the casualties which a determined people could make him suffer. All these arguments and many more were used to justify—and make possible —a last-ditch stand.

Nevertheless, most of Japan's leaders had by this time few illusions about the fact of military defeat. Some of them, like Yoshida Shigeru, Shigemitsu Mamoru and others with a diplomatic background, had begun to think of a compromise peace as early as 1943; and their influence, together with a secret war study prepared by a member of the Naval General Staff, which clearly indicated that victory was unattainable, won over men close to the emperor, including the former Prime Minister, Konoe Fumimaro. When Saipan was captured in 1944 they moved to bring about Tojo's fall, helping to force the resignation of his cabinet on July 18. His successor, General Koiso Kuniaki, another member of the Kwantung Army group, proved no more amenable, but he, too, could not survive for long in the face of a deteriorating military situation. Air raids on Tokyo and news of the landings on Okinawa brought his resignation on April 5, 1945. This made way for an aged and much respected admiral, Suzuki Kantaro, who was known privately to favour ending the war, if it could be done with honour.

The War Minister, Anami Korechika, backed by Tojo and the high command, was still resolutely opposed to any peace moves. Accordingly, the talks now undertaken with the Russian ambassador in Japan, which superseded earlier approaches made in Konoe's name to the Swedish minister, were officially to seek a basis for improving Russo-Japanese relations, though many senior statesmen were clearly hoping to get Russian mediation in the Pacific war. Towards the end of June they succeeded, albeit with difficulty, in getting this second purpose formally avowed, only to find Russia unresponsive. Despite a proposal that Konoe should go to Moscow as an imperial envoy to negotiate a peace, no progress had been made in the discussions when the allied Powers, with Russia's concurrence, issued the Potsdam Declaration on July 26.

The declaration, made in the names of Britain, America and China, called for the unconditional surrender of Japan, to be followed by military occupation, demilitarization and loss of territory. This left little prospect of the kind of settlement which the uncommitted in Japan, especially in the services, might have been persuaded to accept. Indeed, it brought a temporary closing of the ranks behind those who were willing to go down fighting. This, however, lasted only for about a week. On August 6, 1945, the first atom bomb was dropped on Hiroshima and three days later another destroyed most of Nagasaki, the second coming less than twenty-four hours after a Russian declaration of war upon Japan. To the great majority, these events made surrender imperative—and at once.

Even so, the War Minister and the two Chiefs of Staff refused to give way, arguing throughout meetings of the Supreme War Council and the cabinet on August 9 that conditions must be attached to any acceptance of the allied ultimatum. The result was deadlock, broken at last by the emperor at an imperial conference after midnight, when he gave a ruling in favour of those who urged that surrender be subject only to a reservation of his own prerogatives as sovereign ruler. In this form the message was handed to Swiss representatives on August 10 for transmission to the allies. The latter's reply, making no mention of the imperial prerogative, precipitated another series of disputes in the next few days, which were resolved, like the previous ones, by the emperor's intervention. The decision to surrender on the allies' terms was therefore made public on August 15, 1945.

This was not quite the end of the story, for Japan's career of conquest was to end, as it had begun, with attempted mutiny and disorder. Officers of the War Ministry and General Staff, determined to prevent the emperor from broadcasting the announcement of defeat, broke into the palace on the night of August 14 to search for the recording of his speech, though they did not find it. Others set fire to the homes of the Prime Minister and President of the Privy Council. When all this failed to reverse the decision, many, including War Minister Anami himself, committed suicide, several doing so on the plaza opposite the palace gates. It was in this turbulent atmosphere that orders were given for a ceasefire on August 16 and a new government, headed by an imperial prince to give it greater prestige, formed the following day to see that they were carried out. By September 2, when members of it signed the instrument of surrender aboard the American flagship in Tokyo Bay, American troops had already begun to arrive for the occupation of Japan.

CHAPTER XV

REFORM AND REHABILITATION
1945-1972

American occupation—demilitarization—political and constitutional reform—judiciary—reform of labour laws, land tenure and education—peace treaty—foreign relations—politics after 1952

THE LANGUAGE in which the Japanese emperor told his people of the decision to surrender was elliptical in the extreme. 'Despite the best that has been done by everyone,' he said, '...the war situation has developed not necessarily to Japan's advantage.'[75] Accordingly, in order to avoid further bloodshed, perhaps even 'the total extinction of human civilization', Japan would have to 'endure the unendurable and suffer what is insufferable'. For these reasons it had been decided to accept the allied terms.

What this meant in practice was very soon made clear. The appearance of American airborne forces in Tokyo and of an allied fleet at anchor off Yokosuka, the orders given to Japanese troops overseas to lay down their arms and to those in Japan to disperse quietly to their towns and villages, all this brought home vividly the reality of defeat. In the Tokyo-Yokohama area the population stayed as much as possible indoors, fearing atrocities and reprisals. Everywhere, as they looked to their leaders for instructions, or at least for news of what was going on, they found their country's administration, like its economy, in chaos. To a nation that had for weeks been exhorted to work harder and prepare itself for a last-ditch stand, the change was bewildering, notwithstanding the bombing, the shortages and the other signs of disaster which had been multiplying on every side for the previous year. The war's ending brought a sense of relief, therefore, but also a shock of disillusion. In its train came a numbness and a dull apathy, evident in the way people walked, in the silence of the crowds, in the conscientious provision of entertainment for the conqueror.

So sharp was the break with what had gone before that one is tempted to regard it as the end, not of a chapter, but of a story, to treat all that followed as something new. Indeed, in many ways it was. For defeat seems to have been a catharsis, exhausting the emotions which Japanese had hitherto brought to their relations with the outside world, as well as opening the way for experiments in social and political institutions. In both respects it has had a profound effect. On the other hand, the change of direction can easily be overstated. Once the shock wore off and Japanese again began to take the initiative in directing their country's affairs, they gave to the new something of the flavour of the old: in society and politics, a little less of America of the 1940s, a little more of Japan of the 1920s; in attitudes and ideas, a resumption of trends and controversies which had been diverted or suppressed by ultra-nationalism; in economic development, the exploitation of wartime experience to establish a fresh industrial pattern and promote an astonishing growth. The result is that in many contexts one can trace today a far greater continuity with the past—the recent past—than would at one time have seemed possible. Hence an account of this period is not a mere post-script to what has gone before, but the continuation, if at a tangent, of the story of Japan's attempts to come to terms with the modern world.

The occupation of Japan was in all vital respects an American undertaking. It is true that a small British Commonwealth force, mostly Australian, shared the military tasks. It is also true that there was an elaborate machinery of international control, headed by a Far Eastern Commission in Washington, on which were represented all the countries that had fought against Japan. In practice, however, the execution of policy was in the hands of General Douglas MacArthur, the Supreme Commander for the Allied Powers (SCAP). As American commander-in-chief in the area he took orders only from the

United States government, through which the decisions of the Far Eastern Commission were also transmitted to him; and a natural tendency for the distinction between his two functions to become blurred meant that before long he and his immediate superiors were exercising a good deal of discretion in carrying policy out, the more so as the international committees were often deadlocked.

To assist him in Tokyo, the Supreme Commander had an enormous staff, both military and civil, forming a bureaucracy very nearly as complex, if not so large, as that of Japan itself. Few of its members had much knowledge or experience of the country they had to govern, a circumstance which led them at times to transplant American institutions to Japan, not because they were necessarily appropriate, but because they were familiar. Moreover, they lacked the means of ensuring that SCAP directives were put fully into effect, since acceptance of the need to work through a Japanese government, together with the difficulty of checking on its operations because of the shortage of trained allied personnel, made possible a considerable divergence between intention and result. If one adds the problems posed by the attempt to instil democracy through military conquest, it is surprising, one might conclude, not that mistakes were made, but that the occupation achieved so much that was of real significance.

The basic lines on which it was to work were first set out by the American government and later approved by the Far Eastern Commission. Most straightforward was the plan to demilitarize Japan, in accordance with which military supplies and installations were destroyed, over two million men demobilized at home, over three million (and as many civilians) repatriated from overseas. There was talk as well of stripping factories of their equipment to provide reparations for the countries which Japan had attacked, though little was actually done. Punishment, indeed, took a different form. Partly it was accomplished by depriving Japan of all the territorial gains she had made since 1868, including, that is, both the Ryukyu and Kurile islands. Partly it involved the trial of 'war criminals': the leaders who had brought about the war, twenty-five of whom were tried in Tokyo by an international tribunal between May 1946 and November 1948 (seven, including Tojo, being condemned to hang, the rest to prison sentences); senior officers of the services, commanding in areas where atrocities had occurred (all but two of whom successfully denied responsibility); and thousands more, accused of individual acts of cruelty and murder. Of the latter, many were brought before courts abroad, but in Yokohama alone 700 were sentenced to death and 3,000 to various terms in prison.

Nevertheless, punishment was not the only, nor, after the first few months, the primary object of the occupation. The Potsdam declaration had announced the allies' intention of removing 'all obstacles to the revival and strengthening of democratic tendencies among the Japanese people'. One measure immediately taken in this direction was a political amnesty, by which all those who had tried unsuccessfully to oppose the wartime and prewar governments in Japan were released from gaol: communists, socialists, and liberals of every kind, many of whom had been in prison for several years. Another step was the logical corollary to this, namely, the removal from public life—from key posts in administration, politics, education, the press and radio, even certain businesses—of all those whose close connection with the old order would lead them, it was thought, to sabotage the new. A few were identified personally, on the basis of their records. Many more were identified simply by the jobs they held, a method which caused much injustice, but made the procedure quick and thorough in its operation. In fact, the 'purge', as it was called, affected over 200,000 persons, so that the inroads made into Japanese leadership were heavy enough not only to weaken the hold of tradition on society, but also to reduce efficiency for a time as well.

Meanwhile, with American encouragement parties had been formed to replace the Imperial Rule Assistance Association, the most powerful of them, the Liberals and Progressives, being composed of those prewar conservative politicians who survived the purge. In the centre there appeared an uneasy combination of moderates and socialists, the Social Democratic Party, while a fringe of radical organizations came into existence on the left. Of these, the Communists, free to work openly for the first time in many years, received a great stimulus from the return to Japan in January 1946 of Nosaka Sanzo, the most able of their exiled leaders, who had been working for the Comintern in Moscow and then in China with Mao Tse-tung. By 1949 his slogans of 'peaceful revolution' and 'a lovable Communist Party' had won the support of three million voters, nearly 10 per cent of the electorate.

In addition there were all sorts of small, local parties, their numbers estimated at over 300 by the spring of 1946, which represented everything from the lunatic fringe to ambitious individuals. A good many of their members, like most of the independents—at least those who were successful at the polls —turned out to be conservatives, so that the latter, putting all parties together, were able to command nearly two-thirds of the country's votes. In the elections of April 1946, 24 per cent went to the Liberals and 19 per cent to the Progressives, giving them, respectively, 140 and 94 seats. So in May the Liberal leader, Yoshida Shigeru, an ex-diplomat with a record of opposition to the army, formed a government which included members from both parties. During the next year, however, the Progressives disappeared and the moderate right was reorganized as the Democratic Party, led by Ashida Hitoshi. This gained something like parity with the Liberals in the election of 1947, both winning about 25 per cent of the votes, as did the Social Democrats; but it was the latter, holding 143 seats, who emerged as just the largest Diet party. Ashida threw in his lot with them, first in a coalition government under the Socialist, Katayama Tetsu, in May 1947, then under his own leadership from March 1948, but the inability of the cabinet to be either socialist or liberal, partly because of its own disunity, partly because of conservative strength, forced his resignation six months later. This brought back Yoshida and his party, who remained in power for the next six years. In the elections of January 1949 they secured a clear majority—the first since the war—by returning 264 members to the lower house. The Democrats were relegated to second place with sixty-nine seats; the Social Democrats, badly split between a parliamentary right and a Marxist left, got only forty-eight; and the Communists, winning thirty-five, made their first significant gains.

By this time the parties were operating within an entirely new political and social framework. For during its first three years the occupation had brought changes in the constitution, local government, the judiciary, law, labour relations, land tenure and education which seemed likely to revolutionize Japanese life.

A summary of them begins logically with the constitution, which was drafted in MacArthur's headquarters early in 1946, when it began to appear that Japanese officials were responding too slowly to the hints that they should act themselves. Announced on March 6, 1947, its text, both in language and content, betrayed its origin. For this it has been criticized, even mocked, both in Japan and abroad. Yet by putting power firmly into the hands of the Diet it did something that the Japanese might have found it difficult to do on their own. Both houses of the new assembly were to be elective: a House of Councillors of 250 members, half of them standing for election every three years, of whom 60 per cent were to represent prefectures and 40 per cent to be chosen on a single national vote; and a House of Representatives of 467 members, drawn from 118 electoral districts, which would each choose three to five. The lower house, like the British House of Commons, could be dissolved if the government wished to hold a general election; the upper house, like the American Senate, could not. However, the right of decision on almost all matters rested in the last resort with the lower house. In the event of disagreement a finance bill would become law thirty days after the Representatives passed it and any other bill, after rejection by the Councillors, become law if the lower house passed it again by a majority of two-thirds. Similarly, the lower house was to elect the Prime Minister, whose cabinet was responsible, if to the Diet in name, to the Representatives in fact. The only important limitation on the power of the Representatives was that revision of the constitution required a two-thirds vote of *each* house, ratified by a simple majority in a national referendum.

One object achieved by these constitutional arrangements was to create a system in which there was a single centre of authority, controlled by popular vote, instead of one in which the emperor's supposedly supreme prerogatives were exercised piecemeal by different civil and military groups. Inevitably this involved a restatement of the position of the Throne. The emperor became 'the symbol of the State . . . deriving his position from the will of the people with whom resides sovereign power'.[76] His actions were made subject to cabinet approval and their scope was specified, a change which aroused profound misgivings among conservatives, but which the Court's advisers accepted, even welcomed. They began to shape the monarchy in a new image, doing so with such success that within a few years, by carefully planning the emperor's public appearances and speeches, they had made him the focus of a loyalty based rather on affection than on awe. By this means they did much for the Throne's stability and prestige at a time when defeat had left both seriously threatened.

Other changes, outlined in the constitution and worked out in detail during the next few months, were those in local government. The Home Ministry was abolished and most of its functions were dispersed, being entrusted to prefectural and city administrations which were to be headed by elected governors and mayors. Local assemblies were also to be elected, as in the past, but they were now to be given extensive powers. Education became largely a local matter, while each area acquired its own police force and civil service, paid for out of local taxes, the intention being to foster 'grass-roots democracy' by giving communities a chance to run their own affairs. Unfortunately, as it transpired, the units were often made too small, so that many of them found finance an intractable problem. The smaller the unit, moreover, the more parochial its outlook—to the detriment of social services, in particular—and the easier it was for political 'bosses' to control it. For these reasons, notwithstanding the degree of popular participation that was achieved, this aspect of reform was among the least successful.

American example, which inspired decentralization, was also followed in separating the judiciary from the executive. Administrative supervision of the courts was transferred from the Ministry of Justice to a newly-established Supreme Court, to which was deputed also the task of appointing judges (except its own members, which were to be nominated by the cabinet) and of pronouncing on the constitutionality of laws. This meant that it became the guardian of a wide range of provisions concerning human rights which had been written into the constitution, not least those giving women full legal and political equality with men. And votes for women meant the addition of several million voters to the electoral register, all, presumably, with reason to support the new regime.

Equally important was the revision of the labour laws, for this, too, had the effect of creating powerful interests committed to maintaining the reforms. A Trade Union Act in 1945 and a Labour Relations Act in 1946 gave Japanese workers the right to organize and strike, while a Labour Standards Act in 1947 gave them a guarantee of better working conditions, a health insurance scheme and accident compensation. They were quick to seize the opportunities this offered. By the end of 1948 some 34,000 unions had been formed, having a total of nearly seven million members. This represented over 40 per cent of the industrial labour force; and although there was a drop to 5·5 million members in 1949–51, because of government action against the left-wing movement generally, numbers rose again thereafter. By 1971, 34 per cent of the labour force was unionized, that is, unions had 11.7 million members. Just over a third of these were affiliated to the leftist Sohyo (General Council of Trade Unions), formed in 1950, which has been the strongest of the postwar national federations.

The encouragement of trade unions had the result, not entirely premeditated, of increasing the turbulence of Japanese politics, especially in the towns. Land reform, by contrast, which was planned in the belief that agrarian unrest had contributed to Japanese aggression, reduced tensions in the countryside to a point lower than they had ever been in modern times. The first proposals for it were prepared by Japanese officials and submitted to the government in November 1945. They were emasculated by the Diet, which would have thrown them out entirely had it not feared American intervention, and in their revised form were promptly vetoed by MacArthur, who substituted a draft proposed by the Australian representative in Japan, MacMahon Ball. This was sent privately to the Japanese cabinet in June 1946 and forced through a reluctant lower house, becoming law on October 21. It provided for the compulsory purchase of all land held by absentee landlords. Owner-farmers and resident landlords were to be allowed to retain an area ranging from 12 *cho* (just under 30 acres) in

Hokkaido to an average, varying with local conditions, of 3 *cho* elsewhere, not more than a third of which was to be let to tenants. Everything above these limits was to be sold to the government—at rates fixed in relation to the artificially low *controlled* prices for agricultural products ruling in 1945, which had long since been overtaken by inflation—and offered to the existing tenants on easy terms. The terms were made all the easier in the event by a fall in the value of money and the farmer's ability to charge black market prices for food, which wiped out farm debts and left even the poorest families with a modest cash reserve.

Some idea of the scope of what was done can be gained from the overall statistics: more than a million *cho* of rice-paddy and a little less than 800,000 *cho* of upland (1 *cho* = 2·45 acres) bought from 2·3 million landlords by August 1950 and sold to 4·7 million tenants. To put it differently, land under tenancy agreements, over 40 per cent of the whole before 1946, dropped to a mere 10 per cent, while the share of owner-cultivators rose to 90 per cent. There were still inequalities, of course. Since the least affluent landowners, who were the great majority, had had to get rid of only a small proportion of their land, their tenants had less chance of buying it than did those of former absentees. Similarly, there was room for much manoeuvring in the choice of plots to be sold, a topic which greatly exercised the land committees, each consisting of five tenants, three landlords and two owner-farmers, which were set up in every village to settle details and prevent evasion. Nevertheless, the reform made Japan substantially a country of peasant proprietors. Even such tenancy as remained was of a very different kind from that which had existed before the war. In place of high rents, which on rice-paddy had been almost invariably paid in kind and represented approximately half the crop, were substituted moderate rents in cash, with written contracts providing security of tenure. Although one must set against this a measurable decline in paternalism, which in backward areas, at least, had to some extent mitigated the harshness of the previous system, it would be difficult to deny that the changes brought 'a considerable increase in the sum of human happiness in Japanese villages'.[77]

One is tempted to say that education reforms performed a

similar service for Japanese children, since they affected the manner, as well as the matter, of teaching and introduced a far freer atmosphere into schools. Wartime chauvinism had caused a re-writing of textbooks in nationalist terms, together with an increase in military training and indoctrination. The first correctives, therefore, were negative: the abolition of suspect courses, the withdrawal of offending books. Early in 1946, however, an educational mission arrived from the United States, and its recommendations, quickly carried out, led to a complete reorganization on American lines. Administration, as we have already said, was decentralized, being put under elected boards at the prefectural and municipal level. Compulsory education was extended to a full nine years. The first six of these were to be in elementary school, the rest in a new kind of co-educational middle school, which would offer pupils a wide choice in the courses they wished to take. Beyond this came an optional three-year high school course, leading to university entrance.

At first there were many problems. A desperate shortage of buildings for a school population so suddenly enlarged was only partly solved by a recourse to shift-work. Teachers, struggling with huge classes, had to do so without books—it was several years before new ones were written and available—and under a barrage of advice about educational method. 'Subjects' were to disappear, in favour of a 'core' curriculum and 'integrated projects'; 'ethics' was to give way to 'civics'; and the day's work was no longer to begin with an obeisance to the emperor's portrait. It is not surprising that there was confusion and many mistakes, provoking the criticism that postwar children knew less and behaved worse than their fathers had ever done. Yet as the teachers gained experience and were joined by a generation that had itself been trained in the newer ways, something appeared on the credit side as well: a liveliness of outlook, more flexibility, less formality and restraint.

There were parallel changes in university education. A decision, taken by the occupation authorities in 1946, that there should be at least one university in every prefecture, precipitated a scramble among special high schools, technical colleges and similar bodies, either singly or in combination, to win university status. As a result Japan's universities, already seventy in number before the war, soon increased to over 200. By 1972, after another generation of educational development and economic growth, there were 397 four-year universities and colleges and 491 two-year junior colleges, the former providing for 1·5 million students, 19 per cent of whom were women, the latter for 288,000 of whom 84 per cent were women. This meant that over 21 per cent of the student age group was studying at a college of some kind. Moreover, some 80 per cent of children were continuing beyond the compulsory period of education into high school.

It must be said, however, that such reforms were no longer the chief preoccupation of MacArthur's headquarters after the enthusiasm of the first two years died down. For by 1948 considerations of international politics were beginning to shape matters in a different way: first, because of a sharp deterioration in Russo-American relations; secondly, because of the growing strength of the communists in China, which threatened to leave America without a Far East ally. Together these developments shifted the emphasis to the strategic aspects of America's position in Japan, giving greater importance to the country's role as a base, less to its interest as a subject of political experiment. The trend became stronger after the communist victory in the Chinese civil war in 1949 and the outbreak of hostilities in Korea in June 1950, when Japan became vital to the United Nations forces, mostly American, which were defending Syngman Rhee's republic against Korean and Chinese incursions from the north.

One early sign of the change in atmosphere was the pressure put on left-wing movements in Japan. The right of Japanese trade unions to strike had always been subject to the veto of occupation officials, as had been demonstrated in February 1947, when a proposed general stoppage of work was banned on economic grounds. But strike action was now to be limited for other than strictly economic reasons. In July 1948 at SCAP insistence civil servants were prohibited from resorting to it, the rule being extended to local government employees shortly after. Then came revision of the Trade Union Act in 1949, putting restrictions on the political activity of many workers, and revival of the 'purge' regulations, in order that they might be applied to communists. Over 20,000 were said to have been dismissed from jobs in government, education and industry during 1949 and 1950, some even from the unions themselves.

It was also in 1949 that MacArthur authorized the Japanese

government to review the application of the purges of 1946 and 1947. Progress in this was slow at first, but the pace quickened after June 1950, so that almost all those originally affected had regained their political rights by the end of 1951. Not many of them were restored to positions of influence, for their successors were by this time well established and showed little desire to make room for an older generation at the top; but a number won election to the Diet or even places in the cabinet, their presence there helping to intensify the growing conservatism of Japanese public life.

Further evidence that American policy-makers were reconsidering the past came from their handling of the question of rearmament. The 1946 constitution, supposedly at the insistence of the Supreme Commander, had included a clause to the effect that 'the Japanese people forever renounce war as a sovereign right of the nation'. It also bound them never again to maintain an army, navy or air force. In the situation immediately after the war, in which Japan appeared as a defeated enemy, whose military revival was to be prevented, this provision had seemed good sense; but there was much less to be said for it in 1950, when she was a potential ally. Accordingly, in July of that year permission was given for the creation of a National Police Reserve, a para-military force 75,000 strong, which was to take over from American troops the responsibility for security within the country. Thereafter, American urging plus Japanese right-wing support got the force's size and functions gradually extended—despite fierce opposition from those Japanese who objected to the cost or the flagrant evasion of the constitution which this entailed—until by 1960, renamed the National Defence Force, it had emerged as a fully military organization, having land, sea and air arms of substantial size, all equipped with the most modern weapons. In 1972, following a decade of further steady growth, the ground forces contained 155,000 men, whose equipment included 500 tanks and 360 aircraft; the air force had 42,000 men and 930 aircraft; the naval arm, with 37,000 men, was operating 200 combat vessels and 266 aircraft. The defence budget expanded comparably, reaching 677,000 million yen in 1971, though the rapid growth of the Japanese economy as a whole meant that it remained small in relation to gross national product.

Soon after her rearmament began, Japan had also regained her formal independence. Logic suggested that a free Japan under a friendly and conservative government would make America a better ally than one condemned to continuing foreign rule. Equally, most of what could be done by an occupying Power to promote democracy had been completed in the first few years, the rest depending on Japanese acceptance of the changes and a willingness to make them work. General MacArthur—whose reports consistently overstated the success of 'democratizing' policies in any case—had been considering the possibility of concluding a peace treaty on these grounds as early as 1947; and although he was not at that time able to carry Washington with him, the international developments of the next three years, especially the Korean war, gave his arguments much greater weight. They also ruled out any possibility of joint action by the Far Eastern Commission, leaving America to conduct the negotiations very largely on her own.

The resulting treaty was signed at San Francisco in September 1951 by most of the countries which had fought in the Pacific War. Russia refused to accept it, as did India and mainland China. But since these three played no direct part in governing Japan the military occupation came to an end when the treaty was ratified in April 1952. This did not mean a withdrawal of the occupation forces, however, since Japan, having little choice in the matter, had also signed a defence agreement by which she undertook to continue providing bases for American troops, ships and aircraft, thereby committing herself to an American alliance which was to cause considerable difficulties in her relations with Russia and the Asian neutrals.

Russia was in a position to drive a hard bargain. In the first place, having occupied the Kurile islands and southern Sakhalin at the end of the war, she controlled all routes of access to Japan's former fishing grounds in the Sea of Okhotsk. These she could threaten to close or limit, at the same time holding out the hope that Japan might, if amenable, recover one or two of the islands nearest Hokkaido. Moreover, possession of a veto in the United Nations Organization enabled her to block all Japanese attempts to seek election to that body. Yet while Russia was willing to use these weapons to strengthen her diplomacy, Japan's economic, as well as military, dependence on the United States ensured for her part a resistance to both threats and temptation, so that there was little improvement in the relations between the two for several years. It was not until June 1955, in fact, that an easing of international tension made it possible for them to open peace talks through their ambassadors in London. These ended in deadlock in March 1956 because of disagreement on the territorial issue—Japan demanded, and Russia refused, a return to the 1855 division of the Kurile islands, that is, with Japan holding Kunashiri and Etorofu—and the Japanese Foreign Minister, Shigemitsu Mamoru, was unable to make any progress on this point when he visited Moscow in August. But in October 1956 a settlement was reached on other matters: normal diplomatic relations were to be restored and a trade pact signed, the territorial question being temporarily shelved. As a result Japan became a member of the United Nations in December, as soon as ratifications of this agreement had been exchanged, and was elected to the Security Council in the following October.

Fisheries and the dispute over the Kuriles continued to bedevil Russo-Japanese relations, though during the 1960s their tone became a little warmer, especially as the two countries began to discuss the possibility of Japanese participation in the economic development of Russia's Far East territories. Japan again raised the Kuriles question in 1969, without success; and although the easing of international tensions in 1972 brought a visit to Tokyo of the Soviet Foreign Minister, Andrei Gromyko, and led to further talks, these seemed to have ended in deadlock again by the end of the year.

One apparent reason for this was the Sino-Soviet dispute. From the time of the peace treaty and defence agreement of 1951-2, Japan was closely bound by United States policies towards mainland China, including those that restricted trade in strategic goods. Japanese businessmen often showed resentment of them, in view of the immense importance which the China market had earlier had for Japan (though this did not stop them from developing very profitable links with Taiwan, which themselves depended on accepting the American view). As a result of business pressure, Japanese rules about the China trade were relaxed from July 1957, making possible 'unofficial' dealings with Communist China. However, these never amounted to a very significant total. In fact, it was not until the Sino-American *détente* of 1972 that a real breakthrough was made. In September of that year the Japanese premier, Tanaka Kakuei, followed President Nixon's example in going to Peking, where he negotiated a resumption of diplomatic relations—it was to be confirmed in a formal treaty in August 1978—which Tokyo greeted as opening the way for a great increase in trade. Yet its immediate result was a hardening of Russia's attitude concerning the Kuriles, demonstrating once again that for Japan to follow the American line about China, whether hostile or friendly, involved her inevitably in great power rivalries.

Yet the American alliance also brought certain gains. One was the return of some of the former Japanese island territories: an agreement concerning the Bonin islands in April 1968; another concerning Okinawa in November 1969. Also part of the pattern was a treaty normalizing relations with the Republic of Korea in June 1965. These arrangements were not without their difficulties—there were problems about United States bases in Okinawa and continuing disputes about fishery rights with Korea and about Korean residents in Japan—but they provided a fairly stable framework for Japan's post-treaty relations with her immediate neighbours.

Her relations with the rest of the world were determined largely by questions of trade. Attempts to revive it were at first hampered by resentments due to the war and wartime policies, especially on the part of countries like Australia and South Korea, while in South East Asia there were difficulties about reparations to be solved. Again, many people retained suspicions, dating from the 1930s, about Japanese commercial practices, such as led Britain among others to refuse to extend to Japan the full benefits of the General Agreement on Tariffs and Trade, to which she became a party in 1955. Nor did the Japanese themselves always act in a manner best calculated to overcome foreign prejudice. On one occasion, for example, when on a goodwill tour to India and her neighbours, the premier, Kishi Nobusuke, let slip the word 'Co-prosperity'. Fortunately, such incidents were rare and had only a temporary effect, so that the growth of trade was steady, if initially slow. This, however, is a topic that is best left to be considered in a further chapter, when we discuss economic development in general.

The peace treaty and its repercussions in foreign affairs were not the only results of the events of 1949-51, for in domestic politics they confirmed the domination of the conservatives and gave them an opportunity to effect a change of policy which they had long desired. The anti-left-wing proclivities of occupation headquarters in its last two years greatly helped them in this, of course. More important, however, was a change that occurred in Japanese opinion. Time, perhaps inevitably, brought a revulsion against the spate of 'Western' innovations in Japan, such as had occurred at the end of the nineteenth century and again in the 1930s; and it led to a turning back a little towards tradition, albeit a tradition expressed in terms of a very Westernized modern growth. The upshot was the 'reverse course', a re-examination, sometimes a revision, of a number of the occupation reforms.

The constitution was one target, for to many it seemed that the country's military establishment, now that independence had been regained, ought to be made more obviously legal than it had been so far. Decentralization was another, partly because it was said to be inefficient, partly because it had been applied most vigorously to conservative institutions like the bureaucracy and the police. Education also came under fire, chiefly for its failure to provide a training in ethics. Advocates of such training were careful to deny that they wished to restore prewar nationalism under another guise, but they were loud in their condemnation of a system which failed to substitute for it standards of any kind at all. Politics apart, they even found a certain sympathy for this view among the teachers, some of whom were finding it difficult to discover what kind of citizen the course in civics—at anything more than a very elementary level—was intended to produce.

Since the 'reverse course' was a policy of the right-wing parties, usually coupled with strictures on the 'excessive' liberties which had been granted to trade unions and the individual citizen in the postwar years, it is not surprising that the socialists and the labour movement opposed it bitterly. On the other hand, they had less power to do so in the Diet than they would have liked. Yoshida's Liberals, profiting from the peace treaty's popularity, won an absolute majority in the elections of October 1952. The Reform Party, formerly the Democrats, also held a substantial number of seats, thus ensuring the conservatives a firm hold on the lower house. They maintained it in the elections of April 1953 and February 1955, despite factional struggles which led to shifts in party labels and allegiances. Yoshida, for example, was challenged within his own party in 1953 by its former leader, Hatoyama Ichiro, who had been purged in 1947 and apparently expected to take over the reins again when he returned to politics in 1951; and the split, together with a steady decline in the government's popular appeal, forced the Prime Minister's resignation in December 1954. Only two weeks earlier Hatoyama had formed a new Democratic Party, composed of forty-two Liberal renegades and eighty-two members of the other right-wing Diet groups, whose votes helped to make him premier in Yoshida's stead. He then won a general election at the beginning of 1955, relegating the Liberals to second place. Since he commanded no more than a plurality, however, he was unable to remain in office without their help, a fact which led to a merger in November, creating the Liberal-Democrats. Hatoyama, though not without difficulty, became their leader. Indeed, it was soon apparent that the reorganization had not so much achieved unity as turned separate parties into factions of a larger whole. When Hatoyama resigned because of ill-health in December 1956, he was succeeded, again after much debate, by Ishibashi Tanzan, but within two months Ishibashi's health had given way in turn and Kishi Nobusuke had taken over. This was at the end of February 1957, the Kishi cabinet surviving until July 1960, when it was replaced by that of Ikeda Hayato.

All the cabinets after Yoshida's—Kishi's was reshuffled in the summer of every year—had the look of conservative coalitions. Despite this, the Liberal-Democrats were able to secure about 58 per cent of the votes and 290 seats in the elections of May 1958 and November 1960. Against this the Socialists had little more than half as many, the disparity revealing how slowly they had recovered from the setbacks of 1949. The peace treaty had in fact brought into the open the basic ideological divisions in the Socialist Party, so that it went to the polls in 1952 as two independent units, the right supporting the treaty, the left rejecting it. Each secured something over fifty seats, a little more than they had won between them in 1949. In the 1953 elections the right increased its total to sixty-six seats, the left to seventy-two, and in 1955 the figures were sixty-seven and eighty-nine respectively. But this was not enough to give either a chance of power. In October 1955, therefore, they re-united, setting an example, as we have seen, which their opponents were quick to follow. Nevertheless, the Social Democrats, as they were now to be called, continued to make only modest progress: 166 seats in 1958, 172 in 1960, the latter including seventeen held by a splinter group of moderates, the Democratic Socialists, who had broken away at the end of 1959.

Nor could the opposition expect much help from Communists, whose parliamentary representation had been wiped out by the Korean war. Russian, or rather Cominform, criticism of Nosaka's peaceful line in 1950, together with suspicions that the party had had foreknowledge of the North Korean attack, had cost it most of its public support. Government action, the so-called 'Red Purge', had then completed its discomfiture. As a result, Communist leaders and much of the party machinery went underground, preparing to pursue 'militant' policies instead of wooing votes. They lost every single seat in the elections of 1952, regained one in April 1953, two in February 1955; and although there were signs of a return to the Nosaka policies soon after, confirmed by his emergence from hiding and assumption of leadership later in the year, the long interval of militancy had done damage which it proved impossible to repair. The left-wing Socialists, chief beneficiaries of Communist failure at the polls, held what they gained, so that no more than three Communist members were elected to the lower house in 1960.

One might summarize what has been said above as follows: the conservative membership of the House of Representatives had fallen slightly, from over 70 per cent in 1952 to just under 65 per cent in 1960; that of the socialists had risen from 25 per cent to 35 per cent in the same period; and the Communists had ceased to be a major factor in Diet proceedings. It follows that governments and their policies in these years, whatever their labels, were consistently conservative. Surprisingly, how-ever, the 'reverse course' met with less success than these facts would have led one to expect.

One of its elements, constitutional reform, without which rearmament could not be made official, was blocked by the left continuing to hold more than a third of the seats in the upper house, even when it was at its weakest in the lower. Other proposals, like those for education, suffered a similar fate for different reasons, being defeated not by votes but by extra-parliamentary pressures. Thus a draft for an ethics course in schools, prepared by the Education Minister in 1951, was so widely criticized by press and public for its reactionary content that it was withdrawn. A bill to give the ministry power to license textbooks met the same response and was defeated in the Diet in 1956. Local education boards, in fact, were the only part of the educational structure to be effectively attacked, being revised in April of that year. The pattern held good for efforts to revise the police administration, too: in 1954 the Diet abolished all the smaller forces, consolidating them into pre-fectural units, with a national police to carry out co-ordination; but a bill to give the police more powers, including rights of arbitrary arrest, aroused such an outcry in October and November 1958 that the Kishi government found it best to drop it.

The methods adopted by the Socialist Party in these disputes were in some respects as retrogressive as the measures they were designed to oppose. Attempts to obstruct Diet business, some-times by a refusal to conduct debates, sometimes even by the use of force, were reminiscent of the 1920s. So, indeed, was the situation in which they were applied, since the Socialists were an opposition with little immediate hope of coming to power and an extremist wing, never fully committed to parlia-mentary means, which was willing to sacrifice long-term in-terests to short-term gains. Certainly the extremists, becoming steadily stronger as the prospects of office grew more remote, took the lead in exploiting the party's links with trade unions, student organizations and similar bodies. At their instigation, strikes, demonstrations and petitions were constantly used to influence the Diet vote, so that in 1958, for example, during the struggle over the Police Duties Bill, the General Council of Trade Unions (Sohyo) brought out over four million workers in protest rallies against the government's proposals.

This kind of politics was effective because there was a measure of public sympathy for the aims it tried to achieve—itself a tribute to the success of what America had set out to do—and because the nature of Japanese society made it easier to organize such sympathy behind specific protests than to rally it against the government in elections. Many Japanese, who for one reason or another were committed to supporting a conservative candidate, were not entirely at one with the policies his party pursued. Accordingly, they welcomed the opportunity to criticize some of its actions without taking the more drastic, and perhaps more embarrassing, step of recording their sentiment at the polls.

The tendency was greater still in discussions of foreign affairs. The American alliance was accepted as necessary, even beneficial, by a majority, their arguments reinforced by gratitude for the humanitarian and constructive purposes of the occupation. On the other hand, there was a certain uneasiness at Japan becoming involved in the 'cold war'. There was also a lingering Pan-Asianism, which led to the feeling that Japan 'ought' to belong to a neutralist Afro-Asian bloc; a revulsion against the atomic bomb, more often evident in hostility to American nuclear tests, which got more publicity, than to Russian; and a stirring of nationalism, bringing resentment of Japan's apparently 'dependent' status *vis-à-vis* the United States. All these were emotions which the Socialists, backed by Communists and the surviving ultranationalists, could use. And incidents inevitably arose on which they could be focused. In October 1956 hundreds were injured when residents of the village of Sunakawa, helped by students and trade unionists, demonstrated against a plan to extend a neighbouring American airbase at the expense of agricultural land. Legal wrangles over the arrests that were made dragged on for nearly three years, including at one point a surprise ruling from the Tokyo District Court—quickly overruled on appeal—that the presence of American bases in Japan was contrary to the constitution. In 1957 came another *cause célèbre*, concerning an American sentry who shot a Japanese woman collecting metal for scrap on a firing range. The issue this time was whether the trial was to be in a civil (Japanese) court or a military (American) one, raising questions of legality which involved the constitutions of both countries; and it was not until after much publicity that the Japanese court was adjudged to have priority. It promptly released the man on a suspended sentence.

The most famous of all these affairs, which arose in 1960, brought down a government. Recognizing that no administration could afford to ignore entirely the objections to the American connection—many of which were traditionalist and hence conservative—Prime Minister Kishi sought new arrangements which would provide sops to Japanese pride. For example, he said, Japan ought to have some kind of say in deciding the use to which American bases on her soil were put. He therefore went ahead with negotiating an agreement on these terms. By so doing, however, he focused attention on the question of whether such an arrangement should exist at all, provoking widespread nationalist opposition. This was vigorously exploited by the political left, to whom Kishi was anathema: as a prewar bureaucratic ally of the army—he was not de-purged until 1952—and as a principal architect of the 'reverse course', he had only to make a proposal for it to be automatically suspect. By the time the treaty was signed in Washington in January 1960, socialists, communists, the unions (especially Sohyo) and the student association (Zengakuren) had worked up a tumultuous popular movement against it, through which they sought to prevent its ratification.

When the treaty came before the Diet in April there were violent student demonstrations outside the building, as well as a more orderly one by politicians and unions. By May the Socialists had boycotted the Diet debates and picketed the House, having to be forcibly removed by the police. Then in their absence the government party voted ratification. This made the dispute one of parliamentary rights and raised the protests to the level of hysteria: mass demonstrations throughout Japan on May 26; student riots in Tokyo causing several hundred casualities (including the death of one girl student); enormous public petitions; a railway strike at the beginning of June.

President Eisenhower was expected on a visit to Japan within two weeks of these events, it having been assumed that he would arrive in time to celebrate the exchange of ratifications. The turbulence, openly anti-American in tone, for all that it was directed chiefly at the Kishi government, made this impossible. On June 16 an emergency cabinet meeting decided to ask Eisenhower not to come. Two days later the Diet vote for ratification of the defence agreement took effect and on June 23 America ratified in turn. Kishi at once resigned.

Yet the tumult effected remarkably little change in Japanese politics. It stimulated the use of violence: by students, who turned it more and more against their own universities in the next few years; and by right-wing fanatics, one of whom killed the Socialist leader, Asanuma Inejiro, in the following October. Violence led the government to organize special riot police, who soon totalled almost 10,000 men, half of them in Tokyo. But within the political party structure things went on much as before. The co-operation between communists, socialists and unions proved shortlived. The Communist Party remained isolated and electorally weak until 1966, when Nosaka broke with Peking and began once more to seek a parliamentary following. Much of its energies were directed against the challenge from radicals on the left, especially among students. The Socialists remained divided in both ideology and organization, slowly losing ground in elections to other opposition groups until the end of the 1960s. In fact, the biggest change had nothing to do with the crisis of 1960: the emergence of a new party, the Komeito, associated with a militant Buddhist organization called Sokagakkai. It was largely a protest movement among the urban lower middle class and quickly made inroads into the socialist strength at the poll. Formed in 1964, Komeito became the second largest opposition party after the elections of December 1969, returning 47 members to the House of Representatives. At the same time the Communists increased their representation to 14 (from 5 in 1967), while the Socialists dropped from 140 (1967) to a mere 90. From this evidence it could be argued that the Japanese opposition was becoming more fragmented and weak, not more united and powerful.

Throughout this period the Liberal Democrats stayed firmly in control, apparently unmoved by Kishi's defeat. Despite a good deal of factional rivalry, Kishi (with some co-operation from the followers of ex-premier Yoshida Shigeru) was able to hand over smoothly enough (July 1960) to another member of the party, Ikeda Hayato, who announced that he proposed to devote himself to developing the economy. This set the keynote for the decade. Four years later (November 1964) Ikeda handed over in turn—apparently in accordance with an agreement made in 1960—to Kishi's brother, Sato Eisaku, who was able to remain in office for a record-breaking eight years. And even then it was the ossification of his government, not parliamentary opposition, that forced his resignation in the summer of 1972. The fact no doubt contributed to the success of a younger man, Tanaka Kakuei, who rather unexpectedly gained the nomination as party leader, and thereafter as premier, in the factional struggle that developed in late June and early July. He promptly negotiated the normalization of Japan's relations with Peking, as we have seen. Then, like his predecessors, he appealed for public confirmation of his position through a general election.

The 1960s had seen a small decline in the Liberal Democrats' Diet strength—296 members of the lower house out of 467 in the election of November 1960, falling to 277 out of 486 in January 1967—and a similar marginal drop in its popular support. Tanaka's experience confirmed the pattern. In the election of December 1972 his party won 271 seats out of a total of 491; hardly an overwhelming endorsement, but certainly enough to show that the conservatives still had little to fear. The main difference between the new Diet and the old, in fact, was in the decline of the centre. The moderate Democratic Socialists and the Komeito both lost ground. The left-wing Socialists (118 seats, against 90 in 1969) and the Communists (38 seats, against their former 14) both gained. There was little in this to suggest an immediate shift in the locus of power. Even the degree of polarization was not very marked.

In some respects this might be described as political stability. Certainly it was an attribute of economic growth, which had the effect of persuading men to leave things much as they were. Yet by the end of the 1960s, affluence was also beginning to bring about social changes that had major implications for the nature of Japanese politics in the longer term. It is therefore to an examination of Japan's 'economic miracle' that we must turn by way of continuing this discussion.

CHAPTER XVI

PROBLEMS OF AFFLUENCE

*Economic growth—foreign trade—contemporary politics—
attitudes towards the West*

LOOKING BACK over the past century of Japanese history, two things stand out. The first is that the Meiji decision to 'strengthen the army', that is, to acquire such military strength as would enable Japan to meet the West on equal terms, was the beginning of disaster: empire and defeat were a natural extension of the drive to secure national strength that Japan initiated in the last quarter of the nineteenth century. The second is that 'enriching the country', though it, too, contributed to the tensions that led to the debacle of 1941–5, proved the more durable of the Meiji achievements. Today, if the Japan of militarism and aggression is not altogether forgotten, it is the Japan of the 'economic miracle' that engages the attention of the world.

The Japanese economy, like the Japanese polity, faced very considerable difficulties after 1945. Quite apart from the damage and dislocation which bombing had left behind, there were shortages of fuel, power and raw materials, inadequate transport, the apathy of defeat, and fears that equipment might be seized for reparations, all combining with the loss of colonies and foreign markets to hamper recovery. Even when the future became a little less uncertain, as it did within a year or two, there were still unfavourable factors. A multilateral trade, on which Japan had depended prewar, proved harder, if not impossible to maintain in a world divided into sterling and dollar blocs. Division between ideologically hostile camps had the same effect, as was exemplified in the political problems of trade with China. At home there were handicaps stemming from reform: a loss of trained leadership because of the purge; the disorganization arising from an American decision to break up the giant *zaibatsu* firms, which led to the abolition of their central holding companies and the dissolution of the combines into their component parts. If more democratic, the result was certainly less efficient than what had existed before, at least initially.

Yet balancing these drawbacks were a number of advantages. Creation of a war economy had appreciably raised the level of Japanese technical skills in several industries. The destruction of plant which bombing had entailed ensured that rebuilding, if achieved at all, would be undertaken with the most up-to-date methods and machinery. And widespread destruction and distress—paradoxically—introduced a valuable measure of flexibility into industry: in the desperate conditions they now faced, neither management nor labour was inclined to behave restrictively in such matters as work practices, technological innovation or industrial location (an advantage Japan shared with Germany).

To this one must add the assistance given by the United States. In the early days this took the form of vital shipments of food and raw materials. Later, when intensification of the cold war caused a fresh approach, there was a relaxation of the anti-*zaibatsu* policy and help towards the ending of inflation, which the Japanese government might have found it politically difficult to carry through on its own. In other respects, American aid provided a substitute for a stagnant foreign commerce; and the outbreak of the Korean war in 1950 greatly increased it, since it brought large orders for equipment for the United Nations forces, which gave Japanese production its first considerable stimulus of the postwar years. Even after 1952 aid was continued in the form of procurement orders for American troops and bases in Japan. It has been estimated that from 1952 to 1956 these paid for about a quarter of Japan's commodity imports every year.

Given this stimulus, Japanese industry quite quickly recovered, then started a period of rapid growth. In 1948 production stood at only 55 per cent of the 1934–6 figure, but by 1950 the industrial production index was 84 (1934–6=100) and in 1955 it was 181. At this point one might say that recovery had ended and expansion had begun. Despite a check in 1957, due to balance of payments problems, the index had jumped to 410 in 1960, a year in which the economy achieved a real growth rate of 13.2 per cent. Something like the same rate of advance was maintained for the following decade. Shifting to a new index (1960=100), industrial production stood at 174 in 1965 and 373 in 1970.

Much the largest share in this advance was due to manufacturing industry, especially in high-technology fields like chemicals and engineering, which had been relatively undeveloped before the war.

A few selected figures will serve to illustrate its extent and nature:

Industrial Production 1955–70

	1955	1960	1965	1970
Crude steel (million metric tons)	9.41	22.14	41.16	93.32
Steel ships (million g.r. tons launched)	0.50	1.76	5.53	12.65
Passenger cars (thousands)	20	165	696	3,178
Gasoline (million kl.)	2.46	6.12	10.9	20.89
Television sets (thousands)	137	3,580	4,190	13,780

Source Japanese Ministry of Foreign Affairs, *Statistical Survey of Japan's Economy*, 1972.

Significantly, metals, chemicals and engineering represented about 60 per cent by value of the country's gross factory production in 1960, compared with only 30 per cent in 1930, demonstrating how greatly the war, and preparation for it, had changed the direction of development. Ships, motorcycles and television equipment were already by that time important export items, soon to be joined in that category by passenger cars. But textiles, which had long held pride of place in both domestic production and foreign trade, were perhaps half as important in 1960 as in 1936. What is more, the balance within the industry had changed. Raw silk, facing severe competition from man-made fibres, totalled less than a third of the prewar figure in 1950–54 and increased only slowly thereafter. Cotton yarn output was smaller in 1960 than in 1935–7, as was the number of spindles in use. Exports of cotton piece-goods, unable to match the price of those from areas like South East Asia, had dropped by over 40 per cent in the same period. By contrast, rayons and other artificial fabrics, relying on an expanding chemical industry, had become more important. And these trends continued through the boom years of the 1960s. Whereas the index of industrial production as a whole rose from a base of 100 in 1960 to 373 in 1970, that for iron and steel rose to 410, that for machinery to 579, that for chemicals to 424. By contrast, the textile index rose only from 100 to 226.

There were a number of reasons for this sustained industrial growth, apart from those we have already mentioned. One was a high level of investment based on savings, due partly to the rapid rise of wages from the poverty levels of 1945–50, partly to a low level of tax (especially on firms), made possible by minimal government expenditure on armaments and social services. Another was a general expansion of world trade, coupled with a shortage of ships (especially of tankers after the Suez crisis). Then there was the continuing American connection, which made available to Japan the most advanced forms of industrial technology. Last, perhaps crucially, was the existence in Japan of a substantial pool of cheap labour, much of it skilled or semi-skilled, which was successfully diverted to high-productivity occupations. In the early days this derived from postwar unemployment and demobilization. In the longer term it derived from the village (and the effectiveness of the national education system).

Agriculture has also had its place in the boom, if less strikingly so than manufacturing industry. There was a rapid rise in farm production immediately after 1945, achieved by an increase in manpower (as men returned from the armed forces and the war-torn cities) and a resumption of fertiliser supplies (as industrial capacity was re-converted from wartime use). Helped by high prices, especially government support for the price of rice, production as a whole was approximately back to the 1933–5 level by 1950. It then increased by about a third in the next decade, by rather less than that in the following one.

However, these comparatively modest figures conceal some important changes. One is in the degree of diversification. Rising urban incomes created a demand in the 1960s, in particular, for more expensive varieties of food, most of which had to be imported. As a result the cost of food imports, fairly stable since 1945, rose sharply after 1960. This in turn encouraged the production of substitutes at home. Between 1960 and 1970, while annual rice production was almost unchanged and production of wheat dropped by over two-thirds, that of cows' milk more than doubled, that of pigs' meat more than quadrupled and that of chickens for eating increased more than six times. There were also substantial increases in the production of fruit and vegetables, all contributing to a greater variety in the average household diet.

During the same period, the high wages available in manufacturing and service industries began to affect the pattern of farm employment. Between 1960 and 1970 the number of farm households dropped from just over 6 million to a little over 5.3 million; while farm labour, 39 per cent of the total labour force in 1955, fell to 29 per cent in 1962 and 19 per cent in 1970. Predictably, the place of men was taken by machines, mostly small ones, appropriate to the small size of the average holding (still only about 107 ares, or 2.6 acres, per household in the years 1965–70). Power cultivators and tractors in use, a mere 38,000 in 1955, numbered half a million in 1960 and nearly 3.5 million in 1970. This still left Japanese agriculture with more men and less machinery than is common in advanced industrial countries; but the appearance of largescale co-operatives in some areas hinted that the problem of small plots, which was the main obstacle to further modernization, might eventually be overcome.

Some of the consequences of all this were readily visible: a huge, urban industrial sprawl extending almost continuously from Tokyo to Osaka, with major conurbations round Tokyo-Yokohama, Nagoya, and Osaka-Kobe; another similar but smaller industrial complex in northern Kyushu; tentacles of industrialization spreading everywhere along the coastline;

high-rise buildings in the towns, a rash of housing developments in the suburbs; crowded transport; high-density leisure facilities, constantly in use (golf ranges, pin-ball halls and bowling alleys); a polluted environment. This is the price that has been paid for better diet, more clothing, more possessions.

In 1971 there were 23 million television sets in use in Japan, over 8 million of them colour sets, which meant that there was television in 90 per cent of households. By the same year over two-thirds of the Japanese population officially lived in cities. Eleven per cent of it lived in the Tokyo metropolitan area, another fifteen per cent in Osaka-Kyoto-Kobe. Yet against that one has to set the fact that despite a steady rise in population (from 73 million in 1940 to 93 million in 1960 and 103 million in 1970) Japan has nevertheless achieved a substantial improvement in levels of income and diet. The index of real wages for workers in firms with 30 or more employees rose from 82.6 in 1960 to 146.1 in 1970. By that date, *per capita* national income in Japan was U.S. $1,658 (as against $791 in 1966). That put it below Germany, France and Britain, but a little higher than Italy; while the figure for Greece was $891, for Turkey $362, for India $88.

A success of these proportions has many ramifications, not all of them favourable. In foreign trade, for example, one could argue that Japan has succeeded too well. Here growth was slow at first: because of diversion of resources to domestic recovery; because of the loss of former privileged markets, like that of China; because of new Asian competition in textile goods. However, the 1960s showed a rapid move forward. The quantum index of foreign trade (1965=100) shows imports as having grown from 56.6 in 1960 to 224 in 1970 and exports from 43.9 to 200.8 in the same years. The composition of the trade manifested the changes taking place in industry. The value of textile exports was less than doubled during the decade, whereas the index for exports of chemicals moved from 29 (1960) to 280.4 (1970) and that for machinery from 25.9 to 263.3. This reflected the fact that Japan was rapidly becoming one of the world's largest suppliers of ships, cameras, automobiles and man-made fibres. The corollary was heavy imports of ore, especially from Australia, and oil, largely from the Middle East. Imports of petroleum and petroleum products more than doubled between 1967 and 1971.

Geographically, Japan's markets came to be those that needed advanced industrial goods, not the cheap manufactures of prewar days. In 1970, just over 30 per cent of exports went to the United States; about 15 per cent to Western Europe; fractionally over 15 per cent to South East Asia (where the largest customers were Hong Kong, the Philippines, Thailand and Singapore). Imports were drawn more evenly from a wider area, though here, too, the United States provided almost 30 per cent. For the rest, 13 per cent came from the Middle East (mostly oil), 12 per cent from South East Asia, 10 per cent from Western Europe, just under 8 per cent from Australia (mostly ores, but also wool).

One feature of this that had important international repercussions was that in 1965—for the first time since the Second World War—Japan had an export surplus. This favourable balance was then maintained, increasing sharply at the end of the decade. The result was a currency crisis, especially in relation to the American dollar. United States countermeasures brought a revaluation of the yen by 16 per cent in 1971, but this did not check the trend and by the end of 1972 Japan was having to take serious measures to prevent revaluation being forced on her again. Meanwhile she had come under heavy criticism from other countries for her restrictions on imports and movements of capital. More ominous in Japanese eyes was that there were beginning to be signs of organized resistance to Japanese exports: a planned boycott of Japanese goods in Thailand in November 1972, followed by government restrictions on foreign business activities there which hit Japanese firms hard, was so reminiscent of the 1930s in China that it brought forth a flurry of good resolutions from Japanese exporters and trade associations. Voices were also raised within Japan to criticize Japanese diplomacy, which had concentrated on economic relations throughout the decade, but—on this evidence—with only limited success. One outcome was a series of government moves to improve relations with the South East Asian countries, including an official tour by the prime minister, Tanaka Kakuei, early in 1974, an increase in Japanese credit to the area, and arrangements for closer co-operation in economic projects.

A much more serious threat to Japan's position, affecting not only foreign trade, arose from the international crisis over oil prices and supplies which began in 1973. Dependent on oil for 70 per cent of her energy needs, and on imports for over 99 per cent of her oil, Japan was more vulnerable than any other major industrial country to the rise in price and restrictions on supply which were imposed by oil producers. One effect was to stimulate rapid inflation at home. Wholesale prices rose by 29 per cent in 1973, consumer prices by 17 per cent, the rise continuing, though more slowly, for the next five years. As world trade declined and imports of oil increased in cost, Japan's balance of payments moved into deficit, sharply reducing the value of the yen. It was not until 1976 that foreign trade was to show a surplus again. In 1974 the country's gross national product failed to increase in real terms for the first time in over a decade.

Despite many obvious difficulties—unemployment, high prices, shortages, restrictions on energy consumption—Japan's economy weathered this crisis remarkably well. Adjustments in foreign policy, such as a harder line towards Israel and special investment credit for Iran, helped to maintain oil supplies from the Arab states. Determined cultivation of foreign markets, reflected in Tanaka's visit to South East Asia, preserved exports at tolerable levels, certainly at levels higher than those of many competitors. By 1976 it seemed that the worst was over: GNP was rising again (up 5.7 per cent in the fiscal year); exports were growing rapidly; the yen was strengthening. In 1977 and 1978 foreign trade showed substantial surpluses. The resilience of the new industrial Japan had been demonstrated beyond question.

There remained two substantial problems, however. One was in foreign affairs. Japan's success in preserving or even increasing the outlets for her industrial products, such as automobiles, brought conflict with countries whose markets she penetrated, notably in Western Europe and America. Agreements by Japanese firms to restrict their shipments proved no more than a palliative. Thus resentments in developed countries, which found Japan too keen a competitor, were added to those in underdeveloped countries, where Japanese economic activity sometimes seemed too much like the beginning of Japanese dominance. Such issues proved difficult to resolve, since they were inherent in Japan's rise to a position of industrial power.

The second kind of problem arose from the impact of affluence on Japanese society itself. Japan after 1970 was very different from that in which the reforms of the American occupation had been undertaken, partly because of those reforms themselves. It remains to consider, therefore, how far the political framework for democracy remained appropriate in the new era.

In 1850 Japan had an emperor in seclusion, whose authority, in so far as feudal particularism allowed, was wielded by an hereditary *de facto* monarch, the Shogun. By 1900 the Shogun had vanished, the emperor had become quasi-divine, and there was a Westernized bureaucracy ruling in his name. Now, after eighty years more, power rests openly in the hands of an elected Diet. It is exercised on the Diet's behalf by a prime minister and a cabinet responsible to the lower house, with the emperor a mere 'symbol of the state'. Moreover, the mechanisms of politics have also changed. Influence is no longer a matter of hereditary status and feudal affiliation, backed by force. Nor does it depend primarily on possessing land, or friends in office, though both remain important. Instead, it is attained—publicly, at least—by the manipulation of votes in the lower house, so that it involves parties and pressure groups; local 'machines' and professional representatives of the people; businessmen and trade unions; newspapers, radio and television; elections and electioneering.

At the higher levels, faction is still a significant element in Japanese politics, since neither conservatives nor socialists have fully outgrown the days when the activities of the Diet were chiefly concerned with spoils. Indeed, they still are, if in a new sense. Thus a prime minister has more need for the skills appropriate to maintaining a balance of factional power within his cabinet than for the qualities of forceful leadership, especially as the position of the ruling party has not been seriously challenged for over twenty years. All the same, the pattern is not in other respects that of the 1920s, because of the power the parties collectively wield. The sharp reduction in the privileges of extraparliamentary bodies, such as the Privy Council, the bureaucracy and the armed forces, has removed one obstacle to the growth of a sense of responsibility among party politicians by eliminating rivals who made their efforts ineffective. The end of military occupation removed another, in that it terminated the veto exercised by the Supreme Commander for the Allied Powers, which was hardly compatible with parliamentary sovereignty. What is more, there has been a measure of progress towards a two-party system in the postwar years, with alliances shaped by outlook rather than tactical convenience. On the right the conservative Liberal Democrats, on the left the Socialists, have for the most part maintained workable coalitions, despite occasional secessions. In opposition, to be sure, the Socialists have enjoyed no simple monopoly, substantial blocks of Lower House seats having gone to the Communists and others from time to time. Nevertheless, the Socialists have held pride of place, other groups offering themselves as potential members of an anti-government coalition rather than as serious candidates for forming a government of their own. On the whole, this fragmentation of their opponents has played a part in keeping the Liberal Democrats in power. It has also sometimes put at risk the stability of the constitution, in that the frustrations it provokes have on several occasions—notably during the security treaty crisis of 1960—led the Socialists to adopt extraparliamentary and even violent methods.

The Liberal Democrats rely heavily on their links with the bureaucracy, still an able and self-conscious elite, and big business. Bureaucrats have an important role in drafting legislation and carrying out decisions, which gives them many opportunities of modifying policy in points of detail. It also makes them an institutional link between politicians and businessmen (since much of policy-making deals with the latter's affairs). Largely for this reason, many bureaucrats after retirement join large firms or one of the parties: there is always a strong ex-bureaucrat group in the Liberal Democrat leadership. By the same token, businessmen sometimes enter the Diet. For instance, Tanaka Kakuei, who became Prime Minister in the summer of 1972, first made a fortune as a public works contractor.

More pervasively, business provides most of the funds for running conservative politics. In the 1950s this was often in the form of contributions from individual firms to parties, factions, or Diet members. But since then such unplanned contributions have more and more been replaced by those from business associations, which channel huge sums from their constituent companies into party funds. For example, the largest of them, Keidanren (the Federation of Economic Organizations) provided the Liberal Democrats with no less than 6,000 million yen for use in the 1971 elections to the upper house of the Diet and local assemblies.

The return that a body like Keidanren expects for this investment is not unlike that which the *zaibatsu* sought in the years between the wars, namely, a government broadly favourable to business interests (though it cannot be denied that some of its members also press for specific advantages). In fact, given that the *zaibatsu* concerns were not fully pieced together again after the occupation, so that Japan has rather more firms than in the past that warrant the description 'big business', and that the parties now have access to real power, making them the logical object of pressure, this kind of relationship between the two groups is a natural development from the prewar stituation.

It does, however, make Japanese politics 'capitalist' in a rather special sense. This is because electoral support depends much more on the manipulation of votes than on popular participation. Membership of political parties is small, since they consist mostly of those who can expect to be election candidates at one level or another: fulltime politicians, both national and local; bureaucrats and ex-bureaucrats; politically active businessmen and trade unionists; a sprinkling of intellectuals. And success at the polls depends on the extent to which a man can cultivate local leaders, acquire a local reputation and raise money for posters, loudspeaker vans, broadcasts and other kinds of publicity, not on activating the political loyalties of an informed electorate. In other words, it depends on spending. In the 1972 elections it was taken for granted that success would go to candidates who spent fifty million yen or more (against a theoretical limit, set under the electoral law, of five million yen or so). Rather less than half the sum would be devoted to electioneering in the usual sense, the rest to providing large numbers of small gifts and entertainment for potential backers. It is in this kind of situation that the availability of business funds has proved of enormous advantage to conservatives. It has also, of course, increased their willingness to co-operate with business when in power.

For instance, in the factional contests for the Liberal Democrat leadership during the 1960s—carrying automatic appointment as prime minister for the successful candidate—victory seems regularly to have gone to the man most favoured in the business world.

Yet one cannot simply call the Liberal Democrats the party of the businessman, because of the importance of rural constituencies. These are more numerous than the distribution of population fully justifies—increasingly so as the number of farm households declines—and hence exert a disproportionate influence on the composition of the lower house. In social and political attitudes, of course, the rural areas are something less than 'modern'. Local election issues are of greater interest there than national ones and a recommendation from village dignitaries has far more effect than a noisy campaign. Village cohesion, which makes voting a community obligation, ensures a voting rate higher than the towns; and the farmer's respect for tradition, combined with the fact that the party in power has means of wooing rural councils by promises about subsidies from central government funds or the allocation of money to particular public works, ensures that much of the vote goes to the conservatives. The latter, therefore, although no longer a party of landlords, as they were at the beginning of the century, dare not appear to be too openly the champions of commercial and industrial enterprise. Government action to maintain rice prices at well above world market levels is one of the results.

The Socialists are more sectional in the support they receive, a fact which is reflected in their electoral record. The solid footing that business and the farm give to the conservatives is for them provided by trade unions, whose resources furnish candidates, funds and organization on a substantial scale. This strengthens the socialist position, especially in the industrial towns, but is not without its disadvantages. For one thing, too close an association with organized labour tends to alienate voters of the centre and the middle class, without whose help the party is unlikely ever to come to power. For another, since the trade union movement is no less divided ideologically than the left-wing politicians, the relationship between the two does little to bring about the theoretical aim of workers' solidarity.

This is particularly so because of the nature of the trade union movement. With nearly 12 million members in 1971, that is, about 34 per cent of the labour force (against 29 per cent for the United States) this was already on the face of it a powerful one. Yet there were over 60,000 unions, giving an average membership for each of under 200 (against a 95,000 average for the United States). What is more, four-fifths were enterprise unions, comprising workers (and sometimes management) of a single firm or plant. Only coalminers and seamen (and in a slightly different sense, teachers) have achieved a national craft union of the kind that is normal in the West. All this makes it difficult to harness the strength of the movement for political ends, or even for economic ones. Sohyo (General Council of Trade Unions), having over 4 million members, has fairly consistently supported the Socialist Party, notably its left wing, whereas the next largest association, Domei (Japan Federation of Labour), only about half Sohyo's size, supports the middle-of-the-road Democratic Socialists. They can co-operate on issues like the American alliance and the Vietnam war, but not on many domestic matters, since these provoke doctrinal differences. Much the same is true of the smaller number of unions or union branches that support the Communists.

From one point of view, neither Socialists and Communists, nor the unions that back them, seriously challenge the government's preoccupation with industry: they demand a different distribution of its benefits (chiefly in the interests of skilled labour) and an improvement in welfare services, but do not reject industrial growth as an aim. Hence they do not provide an outlet for the kind of criticism that comes, for example, from right-wing agrarian traditionalists or from students of the radical left. They also fail—as do the Liberal Democrats—to give political expression to some of the aspirations and discontents that affluence has recently created.

One result has been the growth of the Komeito party, an off-shoot of the Sokagakkai Buddhist brotherhood. Its appeal is to the urban misfit: economically, to those left behind in the move to affluence, like the shopkeeper; socially, to the disoriented, whose customary group environment (the family, the neighbourhood community) seems to be breaking up without being replaced by something new (the firm, the trade union). Hence Komeito members have typically been middle-aged, lower or lower-middle class, not highly educated, including a high proportion of housewives and non-union labour (their leaders are usually younger and rather better educated—often minor intellectuals, like primary schoolteachers). Sokagakkai itself, a product mostly of the 1950s, though of prewar origin, offers its members a community framework and some promise of material betterment. Komeito, formed in 1964, is its political arm and a vehicle of protest. It is *against* any close American alliance or revision of the constitution (especially the 'peace' clause). It is *for* better relations with Peking and a kind of humanistic socialism, the latter involving a modest redistribution of wealth in a mixed economy and support for small and medium businesses. Hence it finds it relatively easy to co-operate with the Democratic Socialists, but maintains a rather non-committal relationship with the Socialist Party and the Liberal Democrats.

Komeito has not, however, been able to establish itself as an effective third force in Japanese politics, as it once seemed likely to do. After some early successes in elections for local assemblies and the upper house, it first put up candidates for the House of Representatives in 1967, when it polled 2.4 million votes and returned 25 members. In the general election of December 1969 it approximately doubled these totals (5.1 million votes and 47 members), replacing the Democratic Socialists (31 members) as the second largest opposition party. But in December 1972 this growth was not maintained. Retaining only 29 seats, it lost ground, as also did the Democratic Socialists, to both the Socialists and the Communists, a circumstance that implies a greater polarization of Japanese politics on familiar lines. Partly, no doubt, this reflects the gradual spread of affluence downward through society, so that it is now beginning to affect groups from which Komeito votes were drawn.

As problematical as the political allegiances of the misfits—potentially the source of a radical right, such as existed in the 1930s—are those of the 'salary man'; but the latter are more immediately important, because more central to the kind of society that is emerging in Japan. Large corporations have a key place in Japan's booming economy. So therefore do the men who comprise their managerial staff. Recruited chiefly on criteria of educational attainment, they are given adequate (though not generous) scales of pay, a large measure of job security, quite a lot of leisure, a predictable career pattern and a regular working week. This makes them the most credit-worthy of Japanese consumers: good customers for department stores and banks, owners of the growing mass of private automobiles ('my-cars') that clog the roads, a main target of advertising. It also makes them the envy of the better-paid skilled workers and well-to-do shopkeepers and farmers, whose ambition it increasingly is—stimulated by television—to adopt the salary man's life style. One might argue, in fact, that the salary man is becoming the twentieth-century successor to the Tokugawa merchant, setting the norms of culture for an urban middle class.

In return for all this, he owes an over-riding loyalty to his firm, which more than family or community is the focus of his way of living. Politically, this implies commitment to the capitalist system. Certainly the young executive or management trainee does not belong to the radical left (though for him to have done so as a student is apparently acceptable, whereas membership of the Communist Party is not). On the other hand, it does not necessarily imply support for the Liberal Democrats or any other conservative group. Well-educated, well-informed, a reader of the serious weekly journals, the salary man tends to find the ways of politics remote and distasteful, the affair of a series of in-groups to which he does not belong (but which he can expect to influence easily enough from outside, once he becomes senior). Accordingly, no political party has yet won his collective allegiance, so that there is something of a vacuum in Japanese politics where he ought to be. It is a situation that may in the long run, if it persists, prove to be a greater threat to parliamentary demo-cracy in Japan than big business money or the recurrent violence of the left.

One consequence of all this is that Japanese parliamentary debates rarely focus concretely on major issues of policy, which become instead the subject of polemic and philosophizing: the ideological gulf between the conservatives and their socialist opponents has not been argued in practical terms, because there has been little prospect of the latter gaining power. Hence the substance of day-to-day politics is commonly foreign policy—Vietnam, the American alliance—or scandal. The contribution of huge sums of business money to parties and factions inevitably makes corruption the most familiar form of scandal. Tanaka resigned in November 1974 in face of repeated accusations that he had exploited his office for his own financial advantage. In December he was succeeded by Miki Takeo, who pledged himself to promote 'clean government' and fight inflation. He soon had an opportunity to demonstrate his sincerity, for in February 1976 US Senate investigations revealed massive Lockheed payments to Japanese politicians and officials to influence the placing of contracts for civil and military aircraft. In the following July, Tanaka Kakuei was arrested on charges relating to this, then released on bail. The Miki government gave every indication of a readiness to pursue the matter.

Because the investigation endangered not only the Tanaka faction, but also the reputation of the Liberal Democrat Party and its fund-raising methods—the money had apparently gone into political funds, not private purses—it generated powerful opposition within the government. An anti-Miki movement emerged, led by Fukuda Takeo, Deputy Prime Minister, and Ohira Masayoshi, Finance Minister; and when Miki resigned in December 1976, following an election in which the party lost several seats, it was Fukuda who succeeded him. Two years later, he in turn was replaced by Ohira.

Although the Lockheed investigations continued, they were succeeded as a focus of attention in the Fukuda–Ohira period by the struggle in the Diet. The elections of December 1976 (for the Lower House) and July 1977 (for the Upper House) left the Liberal Democrats with the narrowest of parliamentary majorities. As a consequence, it was generally believed that if the trend continued, as seemed likely, it might be only a matter of months before their continuation in office came to depend on an alliance with one of the opposition groups. It was even possible that the latter, if they could forge a wide enough coalition, might overthrow them. Political behaviour began to change. The government showed itself readier to listen to objections to its policies. Its opponents manifested less preoccupation with ideological purity, more concern with projecting an image of 'responsibility'. Everywhere it was assumed that the next general election would mark a major turning-point in postwar political history.

In the event, it did not. Nor did the one after it. In December 1979 Ohira, having dissolved the Diet in face of a threatened no-confidence vote, emerged from an election leading a party that had lost its overall majority—having 253 seats out of a total of 511—but still able to maintain itself by virtue of the continued disunity of the opposition. Its own disunity, however, was nearly as great, the prospect of loss of power having sharpened the factional infighting. Ohira had moved closer to Tanaka (again elected to the Diet, though still on bail), while Miki and Fukuda joined to bring him down. In May 1980 they succeeded in doing so, their supporters abstaining at the last moment on a confidence vote. Once again Ohira dissolved the Diet and appealed to the country. Again the Liberal Democrats called for unity, the opposition sought—unsuccessfully—to create a coalition of the centre and the left. This time, however, one thing was to be different. In the middle of the election campaign, Ohira died; and his party was brought back to power with 284 seats on what was held to have been a sympathy vote, largely at the expense of Komeito and the Communists.

The narrative of recent politics suggests that the continued power of the Liberal Democrats can no longer be taken for granted. The party was in important respects the architect of the economic miracle and politically its main beneficiary. Nevertheless, as the spurt of economic growth came to an end and the problems associated with the 'oil shock' multiplied, it came under criticism from those—including some business interests—who felt they had not benefited, or not benefited enough, from the changes that had taken place. Had there been an alternative, operating effectively on the same broad political and economic principles, there is little doubt that the Liberal Democrats would have been rejected by the voters. In this fact lies an element of danger. For the electorate to abandon the Liberal Democrats would be to abandon in some degree the capitalist structure which has given Japan stability and affluence. In fact, there seem to be only two ways forward that might preserve these advantages. One, the less likely, would be for the opposition parties to come together in an agreed programme which implied a substantial commitment to things as they are. The other would be for the Liberal Democrats to split, in such a way as to provide voters with a choice of conservatives. Failing either, there is a real risk of political disorder. This in turn would endanger affluence.

Troubles have also beset Japanese higher education. Since graduation from a 'good' university is far and away the commonest means
of achieving the coveted status of salary man, entry to such a university becomes more than ever the object of the young (and of their
parents on their behalf). One consequence is the 'examination hell':
an intense preoccupation with marks and competitive entrance that
characterizes the whole of pre-university education. Another is the
reaction—whether of lethargy or turbulence—among university
students themselves, aware that entry to the university was their
major hurdle, more or less guaranteeing eventual graduation and a
job. A third is the vast growth of private institutions of higher education, a few of them good, but the majority understaffed and
underequipped, providing a poor education at high cost for about
three-quarters of Japan's total student body.

Given the stresses that such circumstances produce, it is not
surprising that students are turbulent, expressing dissatisfaction
not only with the specific faults of education, but also with
those of the whole social structure to which it belongs. Only a
minority are politically active, as a rule, but those that are are
very active indeed, and figure largely in the reports of television
and the press. However, like left-wing politicians generally,
disunity makes them often ineffective. On some issues they
can work together, especially Vietnam and the American
connection. Zengakuren, the association in which all students
are automatically enrolled, played a major part in the security
treaty crisis of 1960, acting on an equal footing with parties and
trade unions. On the other questions, however, a hostility to
capitalism in general and to Japanese capitalism in particular
has not proved a strong enough bond to enable students to
unite. Since 1960, despite an ability to disrupt university life by
strikes, sit-ins and violent demonstrations—at the peak of the
unrest in October 1969 no less than 77 universities were
engaged in disputes—the student movement has fragmented
and turned in upon itself, achieving little more than a much-
publicized expression of discontent. The physical restraints
imposed by the riot police provide one explanation. The pursuit
of doctrinal quarrels is another. Possibly one should add the effects
of recession, for in the 1970s students seem to have been more

concerned with finding jobs than with taking part in demonstrations (though by no means exclusively). If one can believe the opinion polls, they are also showing a greater interest in traditional values, like filial piety, and less interest, at least publicly, in political democracy and individual liberties.

There are hints, in fact, that the country is moving towards another of those periods of 'Japanese-ness' which have intermittently punctuated the process of absorbing Western ideas and institutions. This is not to suggest that there is likely to be a recurrence of the bitter chauvinism which before 1945 was fed by feelings of resentment and inferiority. Postwar nationalism has on the whole taken a different course. Sometimes it manifests itself as a simple nostalgia for a social order and way of life that economic change has substantially destroyed. Thus the call to revive ethics in schools, so that children may be taught to show a proper attitude towards parents and authority, is partly an appeal to nationalist sentiment in its traditionalist guise. Equally, there is nationalism, as well as anti-imperialism, in the student condemnation of American policies. In external affairs, however, nationalism has mostly taken the form of a search for the world's respect: through membership of the United Nations and co-operation in international economic aid; and through an emphasis on economic prowess that has made industrial performance tables into an instrument of Japanese diplomacy.

In a wider sense, Japan's relationship with the West has involved almost every aspect of her modern life. Many of its physical and institutional components, like buses, electricity, factories, joint-stock companies and water taps, to name but a random few, have become far too familiar to be thought of now as 'foreign' (and too efficient to be called 'quaint' by the visiting foreigner). Similarly, although tastes in music and sport are overwhelmingly for those of Europe and America—whether for Beethoven or jazz, for golf or baseball—the awareness that these were originally imported does not seem to mark them in the public consciousness as part of an alien culture. They have been fully acclimatized, even to their terminology. An exception, however, would seem to be Western food, which is everywhere available but not always understood. 'They have done to our food', one British resident observed, 'what they have done to our language: assimilated odds and ends and adapted them to their own needs.'[78]

By contrast, in literature the Western-style novel continues to be one of the most successful of Japan's cultural imports. Between 1918 and 1945 it often suffered from too great a preoccupation with the social and political movements of the time, as authors became proletarian or ultranationalist in outlook. There was a similar danger after 1945, when democracy threatened to become the only theme and 'the people' the universal hero. But fortunately the best of the novelists, though far from ignoring the world in which they live, have managed to resist the temptation to write books that are no more than thinly-disguised pamphlets. Of the older generation, Tanizaki Junichiro and Nagai Kafu survived into the post-1945 period from the great days after the Russo-Japanese War. More characteristic of the twentieth century, however, were writers like Kawabata Yasunari (who won a Nobel Prize), Dazai Osamu and Mishima Yukio (right-wing activist as well as novelist), all three of whom eventually committed suicide. In one respect they were as much the heirs of European as of Japanese literature, for their manner of writing and concepts of what they wished to do owed more to French and Russian novelists than to anything in Japan before the Meiji Restoration. It may be for this reason that their work has been accorded great acclaim when translated into European languages. At the same time, they were Japanese in the subjects they chose and the society they so vividly described, demonstrating, as most Japanese artists have failed to do, that Western technique and Japanese material can be brought together. Perhaps the tensions that led to suicide were the price they paid for this success.

The intellectuals of modern Japan—whose numbers are great enough to maintain the circulation of an astonishing range of serious periodicals—have all received an education in Western literature and thought that enables them to compare these eminent writers with those of similar eminence in the Western world. Gide, Sartre and Malraux are names often heard in Tokyo's cafes, where the youth of the *avant-garde* meet and talk, while a walk through the Kanda district will reveal in almost every secondhand bookshop window Japanese editions of de Maupassant, Tolstoy (who ranks among the country's ten most popular authors), Chekhov, T. S. Eliot and others like them. What is more, many of the young men and women who buy these books are better able to understand them than, say, the eleventh-century Japanese classic, *The tale of Genji*, which they will read, if at all, in a modernized version. From this point of view, at least, education has produced a generation that can face the West on equal terms, albeit at the cost of abandoning tradition.

Indeed, for most of the members of that generation Japan's own past is something romantic or entertaining, rather than real. It is *sumo* wrestling, for example, which rivals baseball as a television spectacle, or a feudal castle, carefully restored (totally reconstituted, sometimes), where one may picnic. Alternatively, it is a popular rendering of the life of the samurai, whether at the *Kabuki* theatre, where businessmen take guests on expense accounts, or at one of the few surviving cinemas not showing erotica. It is certainly not an inherited complex of ideas from which one's art draws its inspiration and one's life its standards.

This is partly because change has been so rapid in the last hundred years that 1850 and 1950 seem to belong to different worlds. Partly it is because the present is divided from the immediate past by the gulf of defeat, by which Japan's carefully fostered modern image of herself was shattered. The very inclusiveness of the ideology that was thus destroyed made all the greater the sense of vacuum its disappearance left behind; and although this made it easier for America to win support for the introduction of democracy, for instance, it also made it necessary for democracy to compete for the nation's loyalty with other creeds. Many, especially the young, soon demonstrated that they found the American ideal disappointing, because materialistic (or imperialist) and in any case tainted with military occupation. Disillusion turned some to hedonism and irresponsibility, manifested among intellectuals in a vogue for existentialism and the bohemian way of life. It turned others to the more radical forms of left-wing thought. Marxism, having all the charm of a fruit that had long been forbidden, became for a time so common in some circles as to be an emblem of intellectual respectability. Even after the novelty wore off, its satisfying dogmatism, providing a 'positive' approach to every kind of problem, continued to ensure it a wide appeal, especially among teachers and in the serious journals.

All the same, if nationalism, generating ultranationalism, was Japan's response to the nineteenth-century preponderance of the West, one cannot say that Marxism has established itself as a twentieth-century successor. Though its influence is pervasive, its direct adherents are limited to a relatively small segment of the population, which has more stridency than power. It is being weakened, moreover, by prosperity, as well as by the conservatism that often comes to even radical students with increasing age. This makes Marxism an important, but not truly a dominant, strand in Japanese thought.

It is not easy, in fact, to identify a dominant strand at all. Confucianism, which provided the ethical content of the pre-war structure, has not only lost its foothold in the schools, but is also under attack within the family, where the growing equality between man and wife, plus the ability of children to earn their living independently and even to choose marriage partners for themselves, makes nonsense of the hierarchy of relationships Confucianism once enjoined. Hence precepts based upon such relationships, though still taught in the majority of households, have ceased to form an organized and generally accepted body of belief.

Nor have the religions of Japan fared any better, though defeat produced an atmosphere which in some ways favoured religious revival. State Shinto was abolished in 1945, along with the emperor's divinity, and the great shrines have never fully regained their following (except as tourist attractions). Local shrines receive support—a community duty—and Shinto ceremonies, many of which concern the crop, are observed in rural areas. Festivals everywhere draw crowds, though this, perhaps, depends less on piety than prosperity, since one needs money to spend at sideshows and stalls. Yet there is little evidence of Shinto practices in the home, except as a matter of inherited routine; and such growth of religious sentiment as can be readily observed has been among the new Shinto (and other similar) sects, whose appeal is emotional and often traditionalist. Their numbers are quite large, but most are small in size and vague in doctrine.

Buddhism was less affected by defeat than Shinto, because it was less involved in the nationalist myth. As a result, some of its rites still seem to be observed in a majority of families and it continues to profit by conducting funerals and rituals for the dead (just as Shinto does from weddings). Buddhism has not, however, made any great impact since the war, with the possible exception of Sokagakkai, which we mentioned earlier, and a modest vogue for Zen. Both, interestingly, share a quality of 'Japanese-ness', though they offer very different solutions to the problem of relating religion to modern life.

Christianity, by contrast, is 'un-Japanese', despite the efforts made before and during the war to assimilate it more thoroughly. It profits from its association in the popular mind with Western civilization, but remains nevertheless alien; so the fact that its numbers have increased since 1945 to about half a million, restoring the losses sustained in the 1930s, is probably a significant index of Westernization. Nevertheless, a half per cent of the population is not very much, even allowing for the fact that many individual Christians are persons of influence.

One might sum this up by saying that there is no immediate indication of Japan ceasing to be a predominantly secular society. This is what Tokugawa Confucianism made it and what the Social Darwinist pursuit of national strength there-after—for all its Shinto trappings—has confirmed. Where it essentially differs now is not that the country is becoming less religious than it used to be, as many Western countries are, but that it no longer has a single pattern of belief, even a secular one, to which most of its citizens subscribe. Marxism, not-withstanding its influence, is a minority view. Democracy is not really a creed, something to fire men's imaginations or give them drive. Nor is the pursuit of wealth, despite the fact that it is the objective on which Japanese most readily agree. Japan, in other words, has not come fully to terms with the spiritual problems to which her modern development has given rise, any more than she has with the cultural ones. But then, what country has? Perhaps the present malaise, like the present affluence, is no more than evidence that Japan has at last achieved the distinction of being 'modern'.

SOME JAPANESE TERMS

BAKUFU: The central administration of Japan under a Shogun.

DAIMYO: A feudal lord of the Tokugawa period whose domain was estimated to yield an annual crop equivalent to 10,000 *koku* of rice or more. FUDAI DAIMYO were hereditary vassals of the Tokugawa. TOZAMA DAIMYO were those who were subject to the Shogun's control only by virtue of the authority which the Shogun derived from the Emperor.

KAMPAKU: The senior minister at the Imperial Court before 1868.

KAN (KWAN): Measure of weight. 1 *kan* = 8·27 lbs.

KOKU: Measure of capacity. 1 *koku* = 4.96 bushels.

ROJU: A feudal lord (specifically, a *fudai daimyo*) who was a member of the Shogun's Council of State in the Tokugawa period.

RYO: Gold coin of the Tokugawa period. Before 1850, approximately equivalent in value to 1 *koku* of rice.

SAMURAI: A member of Japan's feudal ruling class before 1871. Technically the term included the Shogun and the *daimyo*, but it was more often used of those below this rank.

SHOGUN: The Emperor's military deputy. Before 1868 the office was in effect that of an hereditary *de facto* monarch.

YEN (Y): Monetary unit of modern Japan. Until 1934 it exchanged at about 10 to the pound sterling; from 1934 to 1939 at about 17; since 1950 at about 1,000.

ZAIBATSU: 'Financial clique', or plutocracy. Term used to describe a handful of great family holding companies in modern Japan, distinguished by their enormous size and the wide spread of their economic interests.

PROVINCES AND DOMAINS
(boundaries shown by dotted lines)

A. KAI.
B. OWARI
C. ECHIZEN
D. OMI
E. KII
F. TOSA
G. CHOSHU
H. HIZEN
J. SATSUMA

IMPORTANT CASTLE TOWNS
(province or domain in brackets)

1. SENDAI
2. WAKAMATSU (AIZU)
3. MITO
4. KANAZAWA (KAGA)
5. FUKUI (ECHIZEN)
6. HIKONE
7. NAGOYA (OWARI)
8. KUWANA
9. WAKAYAMA (KII)
10. TOTTORI
11. OKAYAMA
12. HIROSHIMA
13. YAMAGUCHI (CHOSHU)
14. KOCHI (TOSA)
15. UWAJIMA
16. FUKUOKA
17. KARATSU
18. SAGA (HIZEN)
19. KUMAMOTO
20. KAGOSHIMA (SATSUMA)

HOKKAIDO
(EZO)

Hakodate

SCALE OF MILES
0   50   100   200

Niigata

HONSHU

Japan Sea

Edo
Yokohama (Kanagawa)
Uraga (Kurihama)
Shimoda

Kyoto

Hyogo   Osaka

Shimonoseki   Mitajiri

SHIKOKU

Pacific Ocean

Nagasaki

KYUSHU

Kagoshima

MAP NO. 1
TOKUGAWA JAPAN

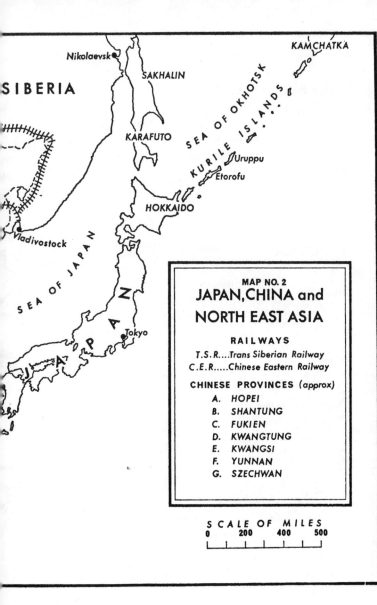

MAP NO. 2
JAPAN, CHINA and
NORTH EAST ASIA

RAILWAYS

T.S.R....Trans Siberian Railway
C.E.R.....Chinese Eastern Railway

CHINESE PROVINCES (approx)

A. HOPEI
B. SHANTUNG
C. FUKIEN
D. KWANGTUNG
E. KWANGSI
F. YUNNAN
G. SZECHWAN

SCALE OF MILES
0   200   400   500

MAP NO. 3
The FAR EAST and
The PACIFIC

ALEUTIAN ISLANDS

KURILE ISLANDS

P A C I F I C

Midway Is.

HAWAIIAN ISLANDS
Pearl Harbour

O C E A N

Wake Is.

Marshall Is.

Kwajalein

Ine Is.

SCALE OF MILES
0   500   1000

Solomon Is.

Guadalcanal

CORAL SEA

PREFECTURES

A. Miyagi
B. Yamanashi

SCALE OF MILES
0   50   100   200

Kunashiri

HOKKAIDO

Hakodate

Aomori

A
Sendai

HONSHU

Naoetsu
Nikko
Maebashi
Tomioka
B
Mito
Tokyo
Yokohama
Yokosuka

Japan Sea

Nagoya

Kyoto

Kobe   Osaka

Hiroshima

Shimonoseki
Yawata
Fukuoka

SHIKOKU

Pacific Ocean

Nagasaki

Kumamoto

KYUSHU

Kagoshima

MAP NO.4
MODERN JAPAN

A SELECT BIBLIOGRAPHY OF WORKS
IN ENGLISH

Since this book first appeared it has come to be widely used
by students, and much new work has been published concerning its subject-matter. For both reasons I have thought it
desirable to re-cast, rather than merely revise, this bibliography,
which in its new form is directed more to the needs of the
student than those of the general reader.

General Works

The standard textbook on modern Japanese history is Hugh
Borton, *Japan's Modern Century* (New York, 1955; rev. ed.,
1970). In a wider context, see the relevant chapters of J. K.
Fairbank, E. O. Reischauer and A. M. Craig, *East Asia.
The Modern Transformation* (Boston, 1965). Among the books
on more limited themes, G. B. Sansom, *The Western World and
Japan* (New York, 1950) is a brilliant·and readable study of
cultural relations between Japan and the West from the
sixteenth to the nineteenth centuries. A pioneer work on the
nineteenth century from a partly Marxist viewpoint is E. H.
Norman, *Japan's Emergence as a Modern State* (New York, 1940).
It is still useful and stimulating, though many of its conclusions
have been invalidated by later research. A more recent book,
similar in outlook, but emphasizing the importance of rural
society in the process of modernization, is Barrington Moore,
Social Origins of Dictatorship and Democracy (London, 1967).
In some respects, however, the chapters on Japan suffer from
the author's inability to make use of materials in Japanese.
Two sound political histories for the period 1868–1945, one
emphasizing parties and institutions, the other nationalism,
are R. A. Scalapino, *Democracy and the Party Movement in
Prewar Japan* (Berkeley, 1953) and D. M. Brown, *Nationalism
in Japan* (Berkeley, 1955). Neither has been effectively replaced
but both have in part been rendered out of date by some of
the recent monographs mentioned below. There is now a good
study of local government since 1868: Kurt Steiner, *Local
Government in Japan* (Stanford, 1965). Economic history is

treated more or less chronologically in G. C. Allen, *A Short Economic History of Modern Japan* (2nd. rev. ed., London, 1962) and by topics in W. W. Lockwood, *The Economic Development of Japan. Growth and Structural Change 1868–1938* (rev. ed., Princeton, 1969).

During the last ten years there has been something of a vogue for compendium volumes, comprising articles from a number of contributors. Of these, much the most generally valuable and consistently high in standard are those arising from a series of conferences on Japanese modernization, published by Princeton U.P. They are: M. B. Jansen, ed., *Changing Japanese Attitudes Toward Modernization* (1965); W. W. Lockwood, ed., *The State and Economic Enterprise in Modern Japan* (1965); R. P. Dore, ed., *Aspects of Social Change in Modern Japan* (1967); R. E. Ward, ed., *Political Development in Modern Japan* (1968); D. H. Shively, ed., *Tradition and Modernization in Japanese Culture* (1971); and J. W. Morley, ed., *Dilemmas of Growth in Prewar Japan* (1972). Together these volumes comprise the most authoritative survey of one of the two or three main themes of modern Japanese history.

Apart from these, one ought certainly to mention R. Tsunoda et al., *Sources of Japanese Tradition* (New York, 1958), which consists of translated extracts from Japanese writings of all periods, including the nineteenth and twentieth centuries, together with introductory comment. It provides an excellent basis for studying the history of ideas. On Shinto there is D. C. Holtom, *The National Faith of Japan* (London, 1938).

A valuable survey of Japanese foreign policy is Ian Nish, *Japanese Foreign Policy 1869–1942* (London, 1977). Those wanting greater detail on this subject should consult James W. Moreley, ed., *Japan's Foreign Policy 1868–1941: a research guide* (New York and London, 1974), which includes extensive discussion of the relevant literature. Marius B. Jansen, *Japan and China: from War to Peace, 1894–1972* (Chicago, 1975), is a first-rate study of a major theme in Japan's modern foreign relations. Jon Halliday, *A Political History of Japanese Capitalism* (New York, 1975), devotes much attention to Japan's external relationships, including imperialism, though it is mostly focused on twentieth-century politics, examined from a predominantly Marxist viewpoint.

A new work, covering all aspects of Japanese history, is now in preparation: the *Cambridge History of Japan*, of which volumes 5 and 6, dealing with the 19th and 20th centuries, may be available during 1981.

Tokugawa Society and the Meiji Restoration

When one turns to more detailed studies, the choice of what to suggest becomes more difficult to make. In the sections that follow I mention mostly the recent works, which should be available in large university libraries (and contain fuller bibliographies than I can give here). Several deal with aspects of Tokugawa political institutions: C. Totman, *Politics in the Tokugawa Bakufu 1600-1853* (Cambridge, Mass., 1967); T. G. Tsukahira, *Feudal Control in Tokugawa Japan: the sankin-kōtai system* (Cambridge, Mass., 1966); and H. Webb, *The Japanese Imperial Institution in the Tokugawa Period* (New York, 1968). Then there are a number of studies of pre-modern economic and social history: T. C. Smith, *The Agrarian Origins of Modern Japan* (Stanford, 1959); C. D. Sheldon, *The Rise of the Merchant Class in Tokugawa Japan 1600-1868* (Locust Valley, N.Y., 1958); and R. P. Dore, *Education in Tokugawa Japan* (London, 1965). A number of valuable articles are brought together in J. W. Hall and M. B. Jansen, eds., *Studies in the Institutional History of Early Modern Japan* (Princeton, 1968). An important recent contribution to the study of Tokugawa economic history is Susan B. Hanley and Kozo Yamamura, *Economic and Demographic Change in Preindustrial Japan 1600-1868* (Princeton, 1977).

Foreign relations in the Tokugawa period are usually quite fully covered in the general works, but the following are useful for more detailed study: G. A. Lensen, *The Russian Push toward Japan. Russo-Japanese relations 1697-1875* (Princeton, 1959); Grace Fox, *Britain and Japan 1858-1883* (Oxford, 1969); and J. R. Black, *Young Japan. Yokohama and Yedo . . . 1858 to . . . 1879* (2 vols., London, 1880-1; reprint, 1968). The part played by foreign policy in late Tokugawa politics is examined in W. G. Beasley, *Select Documents on Japanese Foreign Policy 1853-1868* (London, 1955). In addition, several authors have discussed at length the Japanese reaction to the West in the period before the Meiji Restoration, in the context of cultural assimilation and political consciousness: G. K. Goodman, *The Dutch Impact on Japan 1640-1853* (Leiden, 1967); D. Keene, *The Japanese*

Discovery of Europe (London, 1952; rev. ed., Stanford, 1969); and H. D. Harootunian, *Toward Restoration. The growth of political consciousness in Tokugawa Japan* (Berkeley, 1970). Harootunian's book is much more than a study of reactions to the West, since it treats other important aspects of the Restoration movement. Also related to this topic is D. M. Earl, *Emperor and Nation in Japan. Political thinkers of the Tokugawa period* (Seattle, 1964).

As to the Restoration generally, I have recently published a lengthy study, *The Meiji Restoration* (Stanford, 1972), covering the period down to 1873. Other works in this field deal chiefly with events to 1868. They include Paul Akamatsu, *Meiji 1868. Revolution and counterrevolution in Japan* (London, 1972; originally in French, Paris, 1968); M. B. Jansen, *Sakamoto Ryoma and the Meiji Restoration* (Princeton, 1961), which is particluarly valuable as a study of one of the activists of the Restoration movement; and A. M. Craig, *Chōshū in the Meiji Restoration* (Cambridge, Mass., 1961). Conrad Totman, *The Collapse of the Tokugawa Bakufu, 1862–1868* (Honolulu, 1980), has much new material on Bakufu politics.

From the Restoration to World War I

This was the first period of modernization and hence is treated at some length in several of the Princeton volumes, noted above. A late-Meiji Japanese view of it is given in S. Okuma, ed., *Fifty Years of New Japan* (2 vols., London, 1910). Among the more important recent studies of economic modernization there are: T. C. Smith, *Political Change and Industrial Development in Japan: government enterprise 1868–1880* (Stanford, 1955); James Nakamura, *Agricultural Production and the Economic Development of Japan 1873–1922* (Princeton, 1966; see note 44 to chapter VIII above); and J. Hirschmeier, *The Origins of Enterpreneurship in Meiji Japan* (Cambridge, Mass., 1964).

In the field of Meiji politics, R. F. Hackett has written an important study of one of the Meiji oligarchs, *Yamagata Aritomo in the Rise of Modern Japan 1838–1922* (Cambridge, Mass., 1971), while B. S. Silberman, *Ministers of Modernization. Elite mobility in the Meiji Restoration, 1868–1873* (Tucson, 1964) analyses a section of the Meiji leadership in its early years. On the establishment of the 1889 constitution, the older work

by G. M. Beckmann, *The Making of the Meiji Constitution*
(Lawrence, 1957), setting out the views of the oligarchs, now
needs to be read—as does Scalapino—in the light of the
findings of George Akita, *Foundations of Constitutional Government
in Modern Japan 1868–1900* (Cambridge, Mass., 1967), especially
on the point of motivation. A supporting study, dealing with
constitutional ideas of the period, is J. Pittau, *Political thought
in early Meiji Japan 1868–1889* (Cambridge, Mass., 1967).
N. Ike, *The Beginnings of Political Democracy in Japan* (Baltimore,
1950) is still useful on the nature of opposition to the Meiji
government, as is F. G. Notehelfer, *Kōtoku Shūsui. Portrait of a
Japanese radical* (Cambridge, 1971) for the later years. T. R. H.
Havens, *Nishi Amane and modern Japanese thought* (Princeton,
1970) gives a good picture of a man who was both bureaucrat
and advocate of *bummei-kaika*. The main thinker of the latter
school, however, was Fukuzawa Yukichi, who is the subject of
a perceptive study by Carmen Blacker, *The Japanese Enlightenment*
(Cambridge, 1964). In addition, the student of Meiji thought
should see K. B. Pyle, *The New Generation in Meiji Japan.
Problems of cultural identity 1885–1895* (Stanford, 1969) and B. K.
Marshall, *Capitalism and Nationalism in Prewar Japan. The
ideology of the business elite 1868–1941* (Stanford, 1967) on the
various manifestations of nationalism. Ivan P. Hall, *Mori Arinori*
(Cambridge, Mass., 1973), is a useful study of a Meiji modernizer.
Ishii Ryosuke, *Japanese Legislation in the Meiji Era* (Tokyo, 1969),
has valuable sections on political institutions, as well as law.

On the related subject of foreign policy there are several
well-documented works, especially for the later part of the
period. They include: H. Conroy, *The Japanese Seizure of Korea
1868–1910* (Philadephia, 1960); M. B. Jansen, *The Japanese and
Sun Yat-sen* (Cambridge, Mass., 1954), which is particularly
useful on unofficial Japanese attitudes towards China; S.
Okamoto, *The Japanese Oligarchy and the Russo-Japanese War* (New
York, 1970); I. H. Nish, *The Anglo-Japanese Alliance: the
diplomacy of two island empires 1894–1907* (London, 1966); and
the same author's *Alliance in Decline: a study in Anglo-
Japanese relations 1908–23* (London, 1972).

From World War I to World War II
During this period the two main strands of Japanese history

are the shifting locus of power in domestic politics and the growth of Japanese imperialism abroad, the two coming together in the discussion of fascism in the 1930s. Some recent work has greatly changed our view of the nature of Japanese politics in the first decades of the twentieth century, the starting point of any such discussion, especially the books by Najita and Duus on the parties: T. Najita, *Hara Kei in the Politics of Compromise 1905–1915* (Cambridge, Mass., 1967); and P. Duus, *Party Rivalry and Political Change in Taishō Japan* (Cambridge, Mass., 1968). There is also G. O. Totten, *The Social Democratic Movement in Prewar Japan* (New Haven, 1966). On the subject of fascism and ultranationalism, some penetrating essays by Maruyama Masao have been published in English under the title *Thought and Behaviour in Modern Japanese Politics* (London, 1963), while there is also a useful biography of Kita Ikki: G. M. Wilson, *Radical Nationalist in Japan* (Cambridge, Mass., 1969). G. R. Storry, *The Double Patriots* (London, 1957) remains the most useful work on the patriotic societies. Finally, it is worth consulting the translation of the standard ethics text, dating from 1937: *Kokutai no Hongi. Cardinal Principles of the National Entity of Japan*, ed. R. K. Hall (Cambridge, Mass., 1949).

Recent work on politics in this period includes a study of the agrarian strand in Japanese nationalism, Thomas R. H. Havens, *Farm and Nation in Modern Japan* (Princeton, 1974). There is also one of the political role of the imperial household: David A. Titus, *Palace and Politics in Prewar Japan* (New York and London, 1974). Gordon M. Berger, *Parties out of Power in Japan, 1931–41* (Princeton, 1977), examines primarily the working of the Diet in the prewar period, while Ben-ami Shillony, *Revolt in Japan* (Princeton, 1973), treats in some detail the Young Officers and the attempted *coup* of 1936.

On foreign policy, useful works on the years before 1930 are James W. Morley, *The Japanese Thrust into Siberia, 1918* (New York, 1957); Akira Iriye, *After Imperialism. The search for a new order in the Far East 1921–1931* (Cambridge, Mass., 1965); and William F. Morton, *Tanaka Giichi and Japan's China Policy* (Folkestone, 1980). On the period after 1930, Robert J. C. Butow, *Tojo and the Coming of the War* (Princeton, 1961), remains the most useful general account, not limited to foreign affairs. James B.

Crowley, *Japan's Quest for Autonomy. National security and foreign policy 1930–1938* (Princeton, 1966), emphasizes the military factors in policy, as does Mark R. Peattie, *Ishiwara Kanji and Japan's Confrontation with the West* (Princeton, 1975). John Hunter Boyle, *China and Japan at War 1937–1945* (Stanford, 1972), throws much new light on Japanese policies in and concerning China. A valuable and detailed study is Dorothy Borg and Shumpei Okamoto, eds., *Pearl Harbor as History. Japanese-American Relations 1931–1941* (New York and London, 1973). Publication of a major Japanese work in this field (in translation, *Japan's Road to the Pacific War*) is being undertaken in 5 volumes under the direction of James W. Morley; the first volume to appear was entitled *Deterrent Diplomacy* (New York, 1976). At a different level, David Bergamini, *Japan's Imperial Conspiracy* (London, 1971), argues a case—unconvincingly, on the whole—for asserting the emperor's personal involvement in and responsibility for the moves towards war.

On the war years, F. C. Jones, *Japan's New Order in East Asia: its rise and fall 1937–1945* (London, 1954), gives a sober account, based mostly on Western materials. Joyce C. Lebra, *Japan's Greater East Asia Co-prosperity Sphere in World War II* (Kuala Lumpur, 1975), includes valuable translated documents. For a recent Japanese view of internal and external developments, see Saburo Ienaga, *Japan's Last War* (Oxford, 1979).

Postwar Japan

There is no satisfactory single volume on Japanese history since 1945. Indeed, the student of history has to rely heavily on monographs by political scientists, sociologists and economists, many of which are very detailed and technical. Exceptions are two works of fairly wide scope, historical in approach: K. Kawai, *Japan's American Interlude* (Chicago, 1960), dealing with the military occupation and its reforms; and G. C. Allen, *Japan's Economic Expansion* (London, 1965), covering the whole postwar period. Of the many books on politics, probably the most useful are: N. Ike, *Japanese Politics* (London, 1958); R. A. Scalapino and J. Masumi, *Parties and Politics in Contemporary Japan* (Berkeley, 1962); I. Morris, *Nationalism and the Right Wing in Japan* (London, 1960); G. R. Packard, *Protest in Tokyo. The Security Treaty crisis of 1960* (Princeton, 1966), a case study relevant to several important themes; H. Fukui, *Party in Power. The Japanese Liberal-Democrats and Policy-making* (Berkeley, 1970); and C. Yanaga, *Big Business in Japanese Politics* (New Haven, 1968). A recent study of Yoshida Shigeru is J. W. Dower, *Empire and Aftermath* (Cambridge, Mass., 1979). There are several social studies of historical interest by Ronald Dore, including *City Life in Japan* (London, 1958), *Land Reform in Japan* (London, 1959), and *British Factory–Japanese Factory* (London, 1973). Ezra Vogel has written a stimulating account of the 'salary man', *Japan's New Middle Class* (Berkeley, 1967). Finally, of the studies of Soka-gakkai and its socio-political implications, perhaps the most useful in this context is James W. White, *The Sōkagakkai and Mass Society* (Stanford, 1970).

NOTES

CHAPTER I: JAPAN IN THE EARLY NINETEENTH CENTURY

1. In Tokugawa Japan it was usual to indicate the extent of landholding not by area, but by the estimated annual crop which the land would yield. This was expressed in *koku* of rice: 1 *koku* equals approximately 5 bushels.

2. Wherever possible I refer to a domain by the name of its castle-town, which is relatively easy to identify on a map. However, the greatest of them were often known by the names of the provinces which they comprised, and these names have been used extensively in books written in Western languages. Where this is so, I give the name of the province in brackets and often use it alone. The most important examples are those of domains which played a major part in nineteenth-century politics: Kagoshima (Satsuma); Yamaguchi (Choshu); Kochi (Tosa); and Saga (Hizen).

3. Translated in W. T. de Bary (ed.), *Sources of the Japanese Tradition* (New York, 1958), pp. 409-10.

   It might be relevant here to comment briefly on the subject of samurai literacy. All samurai were encouraged to study the Confucian classics; and although many achieved only the sketchiest knowledge of them, most had an education of sorts and some became scholars of great repute. Certainly the society in which they lived set a great value on books and learning, so that their opportunites for reading were considerable. The libraries of feudal lords, usually open to samurai of their domains, were numerous and often large, while the poorer samurai and merchants were in a position as a rule to borrow books from their more affluent friends and neighbours. Even the residents of the countryside were able to read the more popular works, by borrowing them from itinerant pedlars for a fee. In fact, literacy was not by any means confined to the samurai class: at modest levels it was shared by a good many commoners, who might be educated in private schools, if their families were well-to-do, or perhaps in local shrine and temple schools, if they were poor. This whole question of literacy, both of samurai and commoners, is admirably treated in R. P. Dore, *Education in Tokugawa Japan* (London, 1965).

4. Donald Keene, *Anthology of Japanese Literature* (London, 1956), p. 358.

5. Population figures for the period are unreliable in detail, but are a reasonable enough guide to relative size. They were drawn up for tax purposes and therefore exclude figures for samurai families; and this makes the real size of towns a matter of some conjecture, since most samurai were town-dwellers and they accounted in all for about 2,000,000 persons of a national total of some 30,000,000 in the nineteenth century.

6. G. B. Sansom, *Japan. A Short Cultural History* (rev. ed., London, 1952), p. 477.

CHAPTER II: ECONOMIC PROBLEMS AND REFORMS

7. The *ryo* was a gold coin which in the money markets of Edo and Osaka exchanged on average for about 60 *momme* (225 gm.) of silver in the period 1750–1800, about 64 *momme* (240 gm.) in 1800–50. Since this, despite fluctuations, was also approximately the price of 1 *koku* of rice, one can roughly

equate the *ryo* and *koku* in considering financial statements of these years. The same does not hold good after 1850, however, because of rapid inflation.

8. E. H. Norman, *Japan's emergence as a modern state* (New York, 1940), pp. 61-2.

CHAPTER III: JAPAN AND THE WEST

9. *Edinburgh Review*, xcvi, 196 (October, 1852), p. 383.
10. Quoted in W. G. Beasley, *Great Britain and the Opening of Japan 1834-1858* (London, 1951), p. 93.
11. The old Chinese tag, 'to know one's enemy and know oneself brings constant victory', was often used in the mid-nineteenth century to avert conservative criticism of the study of things Western.
12. Quoted in G. B. Sansom, *The Western World and Japan* (New York and London, 1950), p. 258.
13. de Bary, *Sources of the Japanese tradition*, p. 544.
14. Quoted in S. Toyama, *Meiji ishin* [The Meiji Restoration] (Tokyo, 1951), p. 78. [The translation is mine. W.G.B.]

CHAPTER IV: TREATIES AND POLITICS, 1853-1860

15. The texts of the President's letter and that of Perry are to be found in F. L. Hawks, *Narrative of the Expedition of an American Squadron to the China Seas and Japan* (3 vols., Washington, 1856), I, pp. 256-9.
16. W. G. Beasley, *Select Documents on Japanese Foreign Policy 1853-1868* (London, 1955), p. 117.
17. Beasley, *Select documents*, pp. 130-1.
18. Memorandum translated in Beasley, *Select documents*, p. 138.
19. Townsend Harris, *The complete journal of Townsend Harris*, ed. M. E. Cosenza (New York, 1930), p. 507.
20. Memorandum translated in Beasley, *Select documents*, p. 180.
21. Harris, *Complete Journal*, p. 505.
22. Text of imperial decree, translated in Beasley, *Select documents*, p. 194.
23. There are two main lines of controversy: first, whether the movement was prompted more by 'patriotic' motives (a response to the Western threat) or by domestic political unrest; and second, whether the latter can be characterized as 'bourgeois' (because of the participation of a class of incipient landlord-entrepreneurs), 'proletarian' (because of peasant revolt and urban rice riots), or 'reactionary' (because of samurai attempts to defend a position in society that was threatened by bourgeois and peasants). I have examined these questions at some length in my book, *The Meiji Restoration* (Stanford, 1972). On the closely related question of the development of political consciousness in late Tokugawa Japan, see the first-rate analysis by Harry D. Harootunian, *Toward Restoration* (Berkeley and London, 1970).

CHAPTER V: THE FALL OF THE TOKUGAWA, 1860-1868

24. R. Alcock, *The Capital of the Tycoon* (2 vols., London, 1863), p. 126.
25. Memorial by Bakufu Council, translated in Beasley, *Select documents*, p. 203.
26. Russell to Neale, December 24, 1862, *Parliamentary Papers 1864*, vol. LXVI, pp. 179-80.
27. Letter of Okubo Toshimichi, September 23, 1865; translated from *Okubo Toschimichi Monjo* (10 vols., Tokyo, 1927-9), I, p. 298.
28. E. Satow, *A Diplomat in Japan* (London, 1921), p. 129. Most Western visitors at this time knew the Shogun as 'the Tycoon'.

NOTES

CHAPTER VI: NEW MEN AND NEW METHODS, 1868–1873

29. Ishii Ryosuke, *Japanese Legislation in the Meiji era* (Tokyo, 1958), pp. 141–5, gives details of various drafts of the document.
30. W. W. McLaren, *Japanese Government Documents* (*Trans. Asiatic Soc. Japan*, vol. XLII, part 1; Tokyo, 1914), pp. 26–7.
31. Ito Hirobumi, writing in S. Okuma, ed., *Fifty Years of New Japan* (2 vols., London, 1910), I, p. 122.
32. The text is given in McLaren, *Japanese government documents*, pp. 29–32, where it is wrongly dated March 5, 1869, instead of March 2.
33. Quoted in Roger F. Hackett, *Yamagata Aritomo in the Rise of Modern Japan 1838–1922* (Cambridge, Mass., 1971), p. 66.

CHAPTER VII: GOVERNMENT AND POLITICS, 1873–1894

34. Memorial of February 20, 1874, in McLaren, *Japanese government documents*, p. 445.
35. R. A. Scalapino, *Democracy and the Party Movement in Prewar Japan* (Berkeley & Los Angeles, 1953), p. 63.
36. Translated in G. M. Beckmann, *The Making of the Meiji Constitution* (Univ. of Kansas, 1957), p. 149. The memorials by Ito, Yamagata and Okuma are also translated, *ibid.*, pp. 126–42.
37. This, like other standard translations of Japanese party names, is open to serious objections. However, the usage is hallowed by time and it would only cause confusion to propose alternatives here.
38. Press Law of June 28, 1875, in McLaren, *Japanese government documents*, p. 542,
39. McLaren, *Japanese government documents*, p. 503.
40. Ito Hirobumi, 'Some reminiscences of the grant of the new constitution', in Okuma (ed.), *Fifty Years of New Japan*, I, p. 125.
41. Decree of April 28, 1888, in McLaren, *Japanese government documents*, p. 128.
42. Ito, 'Some reminiscences', in Okuma, *Fifty Years of New Japan*, I, p. 127. On the ideas of Stein and Roesler, see Joseph Pittau, *Political Thought in Early Meiji Japan 1868–1889* (Cambridge, Mass., 1967), pp. 131–57.

CHAPTER VIII: MODERNIZATION, 1873–1894

43. Satow, *A diplomat in Japan*, p. 391.
44. The different viewpoints are succinctly put in two contributions to William W. Lockwood, ed., *The State and Economic Enterprise in Japan* (Princeton, 1965): the paper by Kazushi Ohkawa and Henry Rosovsky, which restates the argument that a major spurt in agricultural production came after 1868; and that by James Nakamura, which reconsiders the statistical analysis in an attempt to show that production was higher at the beginning of the period than Ohkawa and Rosovsky believe (and hence that the rate of growth was slower). Nakamura's argument is stated more fully in his book, *Agricultural Production and the Economic Development of Japan 1873–1922* (Princeton, 1966).
45. For a stimulating review of some of the arguments, see the paper by David S. Landes, 'Japan and Europe: Contrasts in Industrialization', in Lockwood, *The State and Economic Enterprise in Japan*, pp. 93–182.
46. J. R. Black, *Young Japan* (2 vols., London, 1880–1), II, p. 455.
47. W. W. Lockwood, *The Economic Development of Japan* (Princeton, 1955), p. 584.
48. *The Autobiography of Fukuzawa Yukichi* (Tokyo, 1934), p. 264.
49. Fujii Jintaro, *Outline of Japanese History in the Meiji Era* (Tokyo, 1958), p. 166. The novel is summarized at some length in G. B. Sansom, *The Western World and Japan* (New York, 1950), pp. 412–15.

CHAPTER IX: NATIONALISM AND FOREIGN AFFAIRS, 1890–1904

50. In Okuma, *Fifty years of new Japan*, I, p. 211.
51. The relevant article is quoted in Langer, *The Diplomacy of Imperialism* (rev. ed., New York, 1951), p. 777.

CHAPTER X: THE END OF AN ERA

52. In Okuma, *Fifty years of new Japan*, I, 128–9.
53. Hara's political activities are examined in Tetsuo Najita, *Hara Kei in the Politics of Compromise 1905–1915* (Cambridge, Mass., 1967).
54. Murray's *Handbook for Travellers in Japan* (1907), ed. B. H. Chamberlain and W. B. Mason. The quotations used here are taken from p. 10, but the whole book is invaluable as a source of information on Japan in the early 20th century.
55. Lockwood, *The economic development of Japan*, p. 556.
56. Kita was the son of a Sado saké-brewer, who had village headman origins and a remote claim to samurai descent. Kotoku was of similar background, but from a small town in Tosa. Both men had links with the popular rights movement of the middle Meiji period. See two recent studies: F. G. Notehelfer, *Kotoku Shusui. Portrait of a Japanese Radical* (Cambridge, 1971); and G. M. Wilson, *Radical Nationalist in Japan: Kita Ikki, 1883–1937* (Cambridge, Mass., 1969).
57. Black, *Young Japan* II, p. 407.
58. Scientific education was firmly enough established by the end of the Meiji period for Japan already to be producing research of some distinction, even though the country's first-class scientists remained very few. Thus Nagaoka Hantaro's work on atomic structure resulted in his name being linked with those of Rutherford and Bohr (and established a tradition of work in nuclear physics which was maintained later by Yukawa Hideki, whose meson theory gained him a Nobel Prize in 1949); Suzuki Umetaro independently discovered vitamins in 1910; and others made important contributions in the fields of astronomy, seismology and botany, in particular.

CHAPTER XI: JAPAN BECOMES A WORLD POWER, 1914–1922

59. A. M. Young, *Japan under Taisho Tenno* (London, 1928), p. 88.
60. Yamagata to Okuma, August 1914; in de Bary, *Sources of the Japanese tradition*, p. 714. Yamagata's views on foreign policy in this period are discussed at length in Hackett, *Yamagata*, especially pp. 272–5, 281–300.
61. From Article I. The best discussion of the significance of the Washington Conference in the Far East and Pacific is in Akira Itiye, *After Imperialism* (Cambridge, Mass., 1965), especially pp. 13–22.

CHAPTER XII: THE LIBERAL 'TWENTIES

62. Young, *Japan under Taisho Tenno*, pp. 112–13. It might be added that the rich also travelled a good deal abroad and often sent their sons to foreign universities—though the high standards maintained by the best Japanese universities ensured that a foreign education was usually regarded as a desirable addition to, rather than a necessary substitute for, that which could be obtained at home.
63. Young, *Japan under Taisho Tenno*, p. 280.
64. Quoted by Tiedemann in James Morley, ed., *Dilemmas of Growth in Prewar Japan* (Princeton, 1971), p. 285.

CHAPTER XIII: PATRIOTS AND SOLDIERS, 1930–1941

65. Translated in D. M. Brown, *Nationalism in Japan: an Introductory Historical Analysis* (Berkeley and Los Angeles, 1955), p. 139.
66. Maruyama Masao, *Thought and Behaviour in Modern Japanese Politics* (London, 1963), pp. 25–83.
67. Hugh Byas, *Government by Assassination* (London, 1943), p. 47.
68. *Kokutai no Hongi*, trans. J. O. Gauntlett (Cambridge, Mass., 1949), p. 52.
69. A recent discussion of the parliamentary aspects is Gordon Mark Berger, *Parties Out of Power in Japan, 1931–41* (Princeton, 1977), especially chaps. vi and vii. More widely, see James W. Morley, ed., *Dilemmas of Growth in Prewar Japan* (Princeton, 1971), especially chaps. 2, 6, 8, 9.

CHAPTER XIV: AN EMPIRE WON AND LOST, 1937–1945

70. Quoted in W. T. de Bary, ed., *Sources of Chinese Tradition* (New York, 1960), p.769.
71. Quoted in Y. C. Maxon, *Control of Japanese Foreign Policy ... 1930–1945* (Berkeley, 1957), p. 94.
72. F. C. Jones, *Japan's New Order in East Asia* (London, 1954), p. 83.
73. Quoted in Joyce C. Lebra, ed., *Japan's Greater East Asia Co-prosperity Sphere in World War II* (Kuala Lumpur, 1975), p. 115.
74. Draft Plan for the Greater East Asia Co-prosperity Sphere, in de Bary, *Sources of Japanese Tradition*, pp. 801–5.

CHAPTER XV: REFORM AND REHABILITATION, 1945–1972

75. The translated text can be found in R. J. C. Butow, *Japan's Decision to Surrender* (Stanford, 1954), p. 248.
76. Article I. The text of the 1946 Constitution is given in Borton, *Japan's Modern Century*, pp. 490–507, where the provisions of the Constitution of 1889 are also tabulated for comparison.
77. R. P. Dore, *Land Reform in Japan* (London, 1959), p. xvii.

CHAPTER XVI: PROBLEMS OF AFFLUENCE

78. John Morris, *Traveller from Tokyo* (London, 1943), p. 29.

INDEX

(*Note*. Where words are listed in the glossary, the glossary page reference is given first.)